MEISTER ECKHART AND C.G. JUNG

MEISTER ECKHART AND C.G. JUNG

On the Vocation of the Self

STEVEN HERRMANN

MEISTER ECKHART AND C.G. JUNG
ON THE VOCATION OF THE SELF

iUniverse books may be ordered through booksellers or by contacting:

iUniverse
1663 Liberty Drive
Bloomington, IN 47403
www.iuniverse.com
844-349-9409

Scripture quotations marked KJV are from the Holy Bible, King James Version (Authorized Version). First published in 1611. Quoted from the KJV Classic Reference Bible, Copyright © 1983 by The Zondervan Corporation.

ISBN: 978-1-6632-6352-0 (sc)
ISBN: 978-1-6632-6351-3 (e)

Library of Congress Control Number: 2024910957

Print information available on the last page.

iUniverse rev. date: 06/10/2024

To my parents, Madeleine and Fred Herrmann,
my grandmother Mutti, and my French and German
ancestors, this book is lovingly dedicated.

CONTENTS

Foreword by William Everson ix

Acknowledgments xi

Note xiii

Part I: Running into Peace with Eckhart and Jung

Chapter 1   Introduction 1

Chapter 2   A Few Biographical Notes on Eckhart 7

Chapter 3   Eckhart's Upbringing in the Thuringian Forest 14

Chapter 4   My Biographical Connections to Eckhart and Jung 20

Chapter 5   Running in Peace: Eckhart's Theology 26

Chapter 6   Pantheism and Panentheism 34

Chapter 7   Trans-Dual: Seeing God Irrationally 45

Chapter 8   Four Stages of Anima and Animus Development
in Jung's Works 61

Chapter 9   Four Levels of the Soul in Eckhart's Theology 64

Part II: Eckhart's Calling as a Dominican Preacher and Teacher

Chapter 10   The Mary-Martha Story 83

Chapter 11   Spiritual Motherhood and the Birth of the Paraclete ... 87

Chapter 12   The Influence of St. Albert on Eckhart's Theology ... 118

Chapter 13   Eckhart's Unitary Theology 129

Chapter 14   Further Thoughts on Evil 139

Chapter 15   Eckhart's Awakening to God-consciousness 157

Chapter 16 On the Meaning of the Cross 174

Chapter 17 Eckhart's Trial and Defense................................... 184

Part III: Eckhart's Influence on Jung

Chapter 18 Eckhart as a Transference Figure in Jung 201

Chapter 19 Eckhart's Influence on Jung 204

Chapter 20 The Crusader and the Red Book 215

Chapter 21 Spiritual Motherhood and the Paraclete in Jung 224

Chapter 22 Jung's Post-Eckhartian Teachings........................... 231

Chapter 23 On the Union of Christ with the Self...................... 240

Chapter 24 The Imprinter in the World Soul 250

Chapter 25 Jung's Researches into the Self and no-Self............. 253

Chapter 26 Eckhart's Self-Notion 257

Chapter 27 Incarnation in the Works of Eckhart and Jung.......... 260

Part IV: Meister Eckhart as a Dispenser of Sacred Medicine

Chapter 28 The Transference of Creativity............................... 269

Chapter 29 Eckhart as a Peacemaker....................................... 272

Chapter 30 Meister Eckhart: Dispenser of Sacred Medicine....... 282

Chapter 31 Eckhart as a Shaman for Our Times 292

Chapter 32 Imageless Meditation on the Infinite Ground 304

Chapter 33 Eight Deams about My Thesis on Eckhart.............. 316

Appendix I: Seven Sermons to the Paraclete 357

Appendix II: List of Abbreviations Used in Bibliography
               and Endnotes 363

Bibliography.. 365

Endnotes 373

Meister Eckhart and CG Jung Index...................................... 417

FOREWORD BY WILLIAM EVERSON

Evaluation of Comprehensive Examination of Steven Herrmann's Senior Thesis

Steven Herrmann has written a most impressive thesis on the relationship between spirituality and psychology as exemplified in the writings of Meister Eckhart, the fourteenth-century mystical theologian, whose work was condemned after his death, but survived underground to reemerge in this century as the link between East and West.

What Eastern sages point to in Eckhart is his positing of a metaphysical *Ground*, an unspecific totality of Divinity, existent beyond and above the Trinity. Though this tenet was not the reason for Eckhart's condemnation (now widely regarded as mistaken), nevertheless a pall still lingers, beclouding his name. Any clarification is welcome, therefore, and Steven's bringing to bear the empirical psychology and C.G. Jung paves the way for one approach to the Eckhart hypothesis. Not that psychological empiricism can confirm theological attribution, since they belong to different categories of being, nevertheless a demonstratable affinity suggests parallel correspondences that are intriguing. Thus, the trinitarian model familiar everywhere in terrestrial consciousness—thesis, antithesis and synthesis—while not confirming the Trinity, in any absolute sense, does enhance the doctrine in our eyes and affirms its fitness. And thus, Jung's positing of the *psychoid*, a broad psychic dimension suggested by Eckhart's *Ground*, is rendered persuasive by correspondence to its model.

For both Jung and Eckhart agree that the unfolding of the Self is the prime agency in the quest for the meaning of existence, and both agree that this process begins with a summons from beyond the quotidian consciousness. The roots are religious, but Jung's empirical psychology asserts the same transcendental dimension in the hearing of the call and the response to its summons. These are the implications that govern the approach of Jung to Eckhart, and Steven to them both.

Steven's distinction, then, his insight that takes his contribution beyond the mere tracing of the correlation of Jung to Eckhart, important as that is, lies in his emphasis on the crucial factor of vocation as the essential ingredient in the answer to the summons, the element that brings both masters into focus. But in the fulfillment of his project, it is not surprising that he should be more conversant with the nomenclature and methodology of Jung's system, of which he has made a profound study over the course of several years under expert direction, than the theology of Meister Eckhart which he undertook as an adjunct of that study... And yet, Steven's thesis is so challenging in its own right, directed as it is to the healing of our divergence between psychology and religion; and the healing in our global culture between Western and Eastern perspectives, that his contribution, tentative as it appears before such awesome issues, provides a significant clue. He is to be commended for his courage and psychological perspicacity. Clearly this work deserves honors.

William Everson ("Brother Antoninus"),
February 5, 1983, University of California Santa Cruz.

ACKNOWLEDGMENTS

I am very grateful to those who assisted me during the writing of this book. First, many thanks to my former teacher and mentor Brother Antoninus, or William Everson as I knew him at the University of California at Santa Cruz (UCSC). I counted him as a personal friend for fourteen years before his death in 1994. Bill was my Dominican reader on my thesis on Eckhart and Jung at UCSC, and we had wonderful talks about Eckhart and Jung over our many fond times together. Matthew Fox, the Anglican priest and prolific author, has been a friend and inspiration for many years, and I'm deeply indebted to him for his interest and enthusiasm in this project over the past fourteen years. I have known Matt now for the same length of time as I knew Bill, and he has been an invaluable support, particularly in my studies on Eckhart. I extend my warm and heartfelt gratitude to LeeAnn Pickrell who edited this book. I also would like to thank Katherine Whiteside Taylor, Clark McKowen, Allan Campo, Steve Myers, Katherine Zeigler, and Ann Lammers for their support and interest in this project. Jungian analysts John Beebe, Murray Stein, Jean Kirsch, Fred Gustafson, Charles Asher, John Ensign, and John Dourley were also very supportive over the years I was thinking about this project during my analytic training and when writing the book's chapters during and after my certification, between 2013–2023. Many thanks to everyone who assisted me at iUniverse Publishing. Finally, I thank my wife, Jungian analyst Lori Goldrich, PhD, who read the manuscript and offered her invaluable editorial suggestions, criticism, and love.

NOTE

It may take readers time to adjust to my unusual use of theological terminology in this book. In the text I discuss the Paraclete, the Third Person of the Trinity, and, as such, an archetype that is unique and distinct from the Father and the Son and at the same time One with them. The Trinity forms a unity of the Father and the Son, and the Third Person emanates from the empirical and metaphysical Ground in the human psyche, which extends to the world of matter and the Cosmos. Yet if the reader will keep in mind that I never read the Old or New Testaments before I read Eckhart, then it will become clear *why* I am preferencing the birth of the Paraclete over the birth of Christ in the human soul as the new way in postmodern times.

As a post-Jungian, Christ is to us an image of the Self, not the All. The All in Eckhart's theology is the Ground, which is always finally unrepresentable by any word, idea, or image. My exposure to Christianity was first through a Jungian lens, having read much of Jung's collected writings and many books by classical Jungians before I ever set foot on the University of California, Santa Cruz, campus where I wrote my thesis. I see and understand Christianity through Eckhart's eyes, as a post-Christian teacher and preacher, and also through Jung's eyes. Therefore, when I say *post-Christian*, I mean that Eckhart and Jung both saw themselves as incarnating two imprints that came after Christ, not the Imprinter, but an imprint.

Most Christian readers have been taught by Church theologians of many different creeds that one must have faith in Christ above everything. Eckhart and Jung taught us to have trust in *ourselves*, in our own inner images of God, or the Self first. My take on theology will therefore appear as unusual and even unorthodox in this sense, because Eckhart was for me the Church and a man of the earth who came *after Christ*. Therefore, by birth of the Paraclete, I mean the birth of the Self in Eckhart and Jung and also in me and in you, the reader. We all are *after Christs* and are therefore incarnating the Holy Spirit through our callings to individuate from the Imprinter, which is beyond God, not the traditional God of theology.

If I am charged with heresy, so be it. This is part of the projections that still adhere to the Eckhart-image in the human psyche, something this work intends to liquidate as a toxin that was unfairly projected onto his image by an infected inquisition of Church figures who knew nothing about the *living God* and wanted to kill the Word in Eckhart. One of the good things that comes with being a postmodern, post-Jungian analyst and not a member of the Catholic Church as an institution is the freedom and liberty granted to spiritually democratic people who can speak their own truths from conscience. I do not have to abide by any conventions that were corrupted by the Church, which was unfortunately the case, as you shall see with Eckhart's commissioners, the Holy See, and the French pope in Avignon who sadly sealed his fate.

I also want to add something here about the gendered language in this book. God is beyond gender. I remain true to what Eckhart said, but as everyone knows today who has made a deep reading of his works, he was in essence talking about men and women, about all people. So, I will be using the traditional "he" in reference to God, but he could be a she or an it. I am doing this because God is both God and the Goddess, or Wisdom. In fact, for Eckhart, the origin of God is *die Gottheit*, the feminine Godhead, or primal Ground of all metaphysical and empirical being. In a certain sense both theologically and psychologically speaking, the Self or Paraclete is essentially trans-dual, above all duality of male or female, God and the Supreme

Goddess, the named and nameless One. The Paraclete is an emanation from the primal Mother of the Universe itself. For Eckhart and Jung, the Paraclete includes the archetypal feminine, the soul or anima and animus in us that dreams us toward our ultimate destinies, above all categories of thought and transcendent of time and above gender.

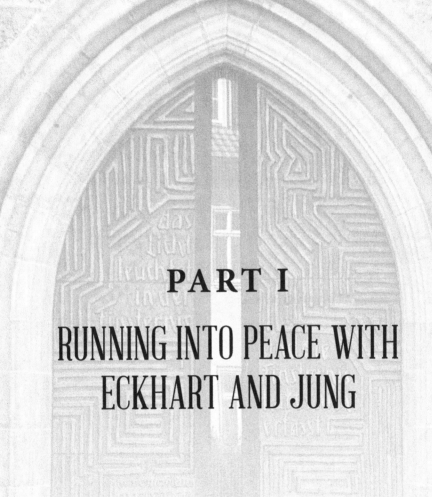

PART I

RUNNING INTO PEACE WITH ECKHART AND JUNG

CHAPTER 1

INTRODUCTION

I was born in Carmel-by-the-Sea, California, in 1956. My mother was raised Catholic in Lyon, France, about 120 miles from where Johannes (Meister) Eckhart (1260–1328) traveled on foot with a small group of supporters to defend himself against accusations of heresy in Avignon, and where he died on January 28, 1328, at the age of sixty-seven. My father was born and raised Lutheran in Plauen, Germany, which is approximately sixty miles northeast from the old medieval town of Tambach in Thuringia, where Eckhart was born in 1260. My ancestral roots go back to the very regions of Europe where Eckhart studied, taught, and preached. This makes my work *autochthonous*, which means, literally, "rooted in one's own ground."[1] By this I mean that although I am a native Californian my personal and cultural psyche is ancestrally Protestant-Catholic.

I was influenced early on by my first Jungian psychotherapist in 1975 to say the Prayer of St. Francis every day. I began saying the prayer the same year I discovered Eckhart on a bookshelf in her office. As an undergraduate at U.C. Santa Cruz, I read and reread many of the best and worst translations and commentaries on Eckhart I could find in the library. Nothing I read seemed to coincide with my own experience of him, although I learned quite a lot about what others thought. I also reviewed everything Jung said in print about him.

I was also blessed by a decade-long collegial conversation with Brother Antoninus. I worked as Everson's teaching assistant for his course "Birth of a Poet" between 1980 and 1981, a decade after he left the order (St. Albert's Dominican Priory in Oakland) to pursue his callings to marriage and fatherhood. It was during this time that I had a number of dreams about Eckhart. These dreams and my reading of Eckhart's works transformed my life and healed a split in my Catholic-Protestant psyche. It was a *spiritual healing* that was later followed by a lengthy Jungian analysis.

I had a number of dreams about Eckhart after I started reading him in 1979. These dreams contained ancestral memories that were religious and archetypal in nature. They gave me a clue that I had a calling to write about him at the University of California Santa Cruz (UCSC), where I completed my bachelor of art's thesis in 1982 titled: "Meister Eckhart: On the Recollection of the Self, A Jungian Perspective." I've been working on this book for forty-four years. Much has changed in my thinking about Eckhart and Jung since then. Nevertheless, much of what I wrote back then is still valid, and I will rely upon still-valid parts of it in what lies ahead.

Regional influences can play a significant role in shaping a young person's destiny-pattern and sometimes a series of dreams can portray a vision of a future course in life that is not altogether clear at the time, yet they somehow *feel* mysteriously fortuitous when we have them and follow the call. These are what I call *vocational dreams*. Therefore, this book will be partly autobiographical because I cannot write about Eckhart and Jung without making this book subjective as well as objective, both psychologically and theologically grounded in *facts* of my lived experience and academic studies.

This book is essentially a three-way conversation between Eckhart, Jung, and me. What I've learned over the years of reading Eckhart and Jung, side by side, is that Eckhart always aimed to lead listeners to ultimate *spiritual freedom* through the highest possible feelings of bliss and the sense of inner peace: freedom of thought, freedom of speech, freedom of individual self-expression, and freedom to be ourselves. Jung did the same.

Jung distinguished, like William James had before him, between the relative and absolute. Analytical psychology focused on a relativistic view of God. Yet Eckhart's theology of the Word focused on both the relative and the absolute, and understanding the differences freed me from one-sidedness once I began to understand him better theologically. Since I did not attend theology school, I had to read him for decades to arrive at my own understanding. Later, after 2009, I began to have monthly conversations with Matthew Fox and listened to what he thought about Eckhart. This was deeply informative. Nevertheless, I had to stay true to my own vision to write this book.

I felt so free when I first read Eckhart's sermons. Reading Eckhart *elevated me. I felt uplifted.* I later wrote some inspired post-Christian poetry before I became a candidate in analytic training at the C. G. Jung Institute in San Francisco, lines that were clearly influenced by Eckhart (Appendix I). I realized that during my pursuit of a career as a Jungian, Eckhart had been my constant inner guide and companion. He had become a transformative figure in my psyche at an early age and formed an *imprint* of an inner wise teacher who was alive in my psyche. Here are a few verses from my poems that express my general idea in this book, of letting Eckhart's spirit speak in *our* souls through free-verse: "Enter the courtyard and you will see Christ there in the flowers, the grape, and the vine; / Enter the Church and the green Christ dies; / He becomes a mere icon, / Crucified on the cross, / A dead effigy of the past, / A graven image of the Messiah."

To be sure, this poem came to me as an inspiration from the unconscious and it felt like a revelation because it was written down after I had a number of numinous dreams involving Eckhart. Such lines are not in any way meant to invalidate the image of Christ, for he is still a valid symbol for the deity in the West. As Jung wrote to Victor White on November 24, 1953: "Christ is still the valid symbol. Only God himself can 'invalidate' him through the Paraclete."[2] Thus, the seven prose poems I wrote to the Paraclete, or Holy Spirit, and which appear in Appendix I are a correction for the false teachings of the Church concerning Christ's message about the Messenger, not an invalidation of Christ. They are all Eckhart-inspired. There are more than 2.4 billion Christians today for whom Christ is alive and valid and well in the world and whose spirit will probably never be invalidated by God or human, nor should they be, for he is a central figure in our worldwide vocation of awakening in a Spiritual Democracy.

Part I, Running into Peace with Eckhart and Jung

This book is divided into four parts. In this part I offer some psychobiographical notes on Eckhart, Jung, and myself as well introducing Eckhart's theology and touching on ideas I explore in-depth later in the book.

Part II, Eckhart's Calling as a Dominican Teacher and Preacher

In Part II, I delve into Eckhart's calling as a Dominican teacher and preacher and examine the relationship between religion and psychotherapy as systems of healing. I'll also look at Eckhart as a transference figure in Jung's personal development and psychological ideas, consider the four stages of anima development in Jung's psychology of individuation, the four levels of the soul in Eckhart's typology as well as spiritual motherhood, the birth of the Paraclete, and St. Albert's influence on Eckhart's theology. I conclude with my views on Eckhart's trial and defense, and what it connotes for each of us as we pursue our own vocations in life, inspired by the inner voice or God within.

Part III, Eckhart's Influence on Jung

Jung's life and works were profoundly influenced by Eckhart, much more than most readers may realize. For instance, Eckhart was the *only* Christian figure Jung said he most strongly *identified* with. There is a winning argument for this in my analysis of a few sections from Jung's *Liber Novus*, or the *Red Book*. Jung always taught his followers not to identify with the archetypes of the collective psyche, yet with Eckhart there was a secret identity that patterned some of his most profound thoughts about the God in the human soul.

Part IV, Eckhart as a Dispenser of Sacred Medicine

For Eckhart the birth of Christ is a continuing incarnation of the Spirit within and a worship of God without—in all of the miraculous incarnations of the Spirit in Nature. Here I explore Eckhart's thoughts on the meaning of the birth of Christ and what it means to carry our own Cross, as a responsibility toward the Self for increasing spiritualization and God-consciousness in humans.

As an autochthonous writer in California, with an autochthonic Christian ancestry in Europe, I like to look into regional influences that shape the natural landscape and culture around me. Regional influences have played a pivotal part in my vocation since my early days on the UCSC campus, situated among towering redwood trees or *sequoia sempervirins*. I visit Antoninus's gravesite in Saint Dominic's Cemetery in Benicia, California, several times a year and I always feel peaceful there. Moreover, as I was writing this book, I traveled to the Preacher's Church in Erfurt in 2019 to lead an art as meditation group in the very place where Eckhart had lived, prayed, and counseled. I felt my Dominican roots there, in the ground and soil of that special church as well as in all of the rooms, prayer stalls, nave, and attic. I led a dream seminar there where I shared some of my dreams about

Eckhart. I'll provide some of my memories from my experiences there as well as my eight dreams of Eckhart.

To truly *know* Eckhart, one needs to have *affective knowledge*, which can only come by awakening his archetype,[3] his sense of presence, his thoughts, words, and deeds. Book knowledge is not enough. Dreaming with Eckhart means approximating his image within. For he is now an imprint in the World Soul or *Anima Mundi*, an inner teacher and guide, a brother, friend, and speaker of God's Word.

This was one of his greatest gifts, as I see it: to awaken us to our destiny-pattern in the Christian tradition through the *voice* of our vocations, summoning us to follow our own unique *way to God*. He lives in all of us at an imaginal level and can assist us in our work, if we pay attention and listen to him teach inside of us after he is internalized. Eckhart was a powerful teacher and a preacher. He was alive in Jung's soul, and he can awaken Christ in our souls as well. All of his works were aimed at the primary goal of leading us inward into the highest levels of the soul where Wisdom dwells. I *know* this is true because he transmitted his Spirit to me in a number of numinous dreams and through journaling meditations when I was in Erfurt in 2019.

CHAPTER 2

A FEW BIOGRAPHICAL NOTES ON ECKHART

Eckhart's spiritual ancestor was Saint Dominic, the founder of the Order of Preachers (OP). Who was Saint Dominic? A story was told that before his birth his barren mother made a pilgrimage to a French Abby in hope of receiving a blessing there. She *dreamt along the way that a dog leapt from her womb with a flaming torch in its mouth and set portions of the earth on fire.* This story probably emerged as the Dominican Order was becoming known. Saint Dominic's name in Latin, *Dominicanus,* is a play on the words *Domini canis,* or "Dog of the Lord." This story is meaningful in narrating Eckhart's psychobiography because he was part of an order that was famously known for sniffing out heresy! A leaping dog with a flaming torch in its mouth setting portions of the world on fire is hardly an image of a human God. This is a very different image than Saint Francis taming the wolf of Gubbio.

Santo Domingo (Dominic's Spanish name) was born on August 8, 1170. He was also known as Dominic de Guzmán. Dominic was a Castilian Catholic priest and the head of the Dominicans. He is a patron saint of astronomers and natural scientists and he died on August 6, 1221. Moreover, according to Dominican tradition in 1206, Dominic had been in Prouille, France, attempting to convert

Albigensian dualists back to the Catholic faith with little success, until one day he received a vision of the Blessed Virgin Mother who gave him the *rosary* as an amulet against the heretics. Mary's giving the rosary to Dominic is generally acknowledged as a Dominican legend, and this universal form of Catholic prayer was used by his followers, including Eckhart.

I will begin with a few facts of Eckhart's psychobiography that I will be covering in this book to place him in the historical context in which his theology bloomed:

- Eckhart was born in the German province of Thuringia in 1260, probably in the town of Gotha.
- Eckhart entered the Dominican Order in Erfurt, Germany, at the age of fifteen.
- In 1280 he left Erfurt for education at the Dominican *studium generale* in Cologne. It's probable that he studied there under the scientist, theologian, and student of alchemy St. Albert the Great.
- In 1293, Eckhart studied theology at the University of Paris.
- Between 1294 to 1301, he served as prior of the Dominican House of Erfurt and vicar-provincial of Thuringia.
- Eckhart received his master of theology from the University of Paris in 1302 and he taught there in 1303. During this time, he announced that he was going to write a monumental three-part work, or *Opus Tripartitium* in Latin, a publication that was projected to surpass Thomas Aquinas's *Summa Theologica*.
- From 1304 to 1311 he worked as preacher, administrator, and vicar-provincial of Saxony and continued work on and off on his three-part masterpiece.
- He returned to Paris again as a professor of theology between 1311 to 1313.
- Eckhart was then called as a delegate in 1314, by the Dominican General in Strasbourg, to deliverer pastoral sermons, teach, and

counsel nuns. It was there that his reputation began to spread throughout Europe for his preaching in Middle High German.

- In 1324 Eckhart left Strasbourg and traveled again to Cologne, where he preached and counseled Beguines,[4] friars, brothers, and nuns. He remained rooted there until 1327 and continued to preach in the vernacular.

- In 1326 the Archbishop of Cologne, Henry Virnberg, initiated a heresy trial against Eckhart for some of his teachings that sounded unorthodox. Eckhart wrote a "Defense" against any questionable unorthodoxy in a list of statements drawn up by Henry charging him of making errors in both his Latin and German works.

- In 1327 Eckhart denied the allegations and legality of the proceedings in Cologne, and he appealed to the Apostolic See and the pope in Avignon. He defended himself publicly in the Dominican Church in Cologne and then set off to Avignon to have his case heard there.

- He died in Avignon of unknown causes on January 28, 1328. All that has remained of his works is a relatively small portion of his *Opus Tripartitium*, 56 sermons in Latin, and approximately 117 sermons in Middle High German.

- On March 27, 1329, Pope John XXII issued a Bull of Condemnation, "In agro dominico," which listed twenty-eight propositions, seventeen of which were viewed as heretical and eleven of which were seen as suspect and capable of being improperly interpreted by his followers. The document also added that on his deathbed, Eckhart retracted all of the alleged errors as charged.

Although we know nothing about Eckhart's mother, or whether he had any siblings, we do know a few details about his childhood years. His father, Eckehard of Hochheim, was a knight and the district governor of the nearby castle Waldenfels in Saxony. Statements have

9

survived in Eckhart's vernacular sermons that confirm he loved his father very much. He admired his father for his nobility, horsemanship, knighthood, and presumably for his faith. Eckhart was raised with horses, and he was a keen observer of their actions. He knew horses quite well. There are a number of references in his works to the magnificence of horses: "Such is the horse's nature that it pours itself out with all its might in jumping about the meadow."[5] Eckhart preached about his sense of *equality with everything that Is*:

> God gives equality to all things; and as they flow from God, they are equal ... Now all things are alike in God and are God himself ... Here in this sameness God finds it so pleasant that he lets his nature and his being flow in this sameness in himself. It is just as enjoyable for him as when someone lets a horse run loose on a meadow that is completely level and smooth.[6]

Eckhart saw Christ in all things in an *equal* way. This profound humility is why he is so universally loved by readers today.

Eckhart took part in disputations for his order in Paris in 1289 at the age of twenty-nine, and he was again in Paris at the *Studium Generale* of St. Jacques in 1300–1302, where he debated and successfully won an intellectual dispute with a Spaniard named Gonsalvus, who eventually became general of the Franciscans. The debate between the Franciscans and Dominicans at the University of Paris was over the question of the highest agent of the soul. The Spaniard Gonsalvus claimed the highest soul power was the will, or love, whereas Eckhart took the Dominican position that it was the intellect, and he won the debate. In his sermons, however, he also said it was compassion or love. In other words, he could be heroically one-sided and then, when his soul *died*, and she was lifted up into God, he could be heroic, trans-dual, by embracing Francis and all Franciscans as his spirit-brothers in a sky-wide consciousness of the inner and outer Unified Reality.

A Life in Prayer, Study, Community, and Preaching

Eckhart's existence was spent in perpetual observance of the "Four Pillars of Dominican Life"—prayer, study, community, and preaching—inspired by the example of Saint Dominic. He gained his academic degrees from the *Studium Generale* in Cologne (a university founded by Albertus Magnus) and from the University of Paris. He later taught at both universities at different times. He was a priest and provincial head of the Dominican Order in two principalities of Germany, which meant he had active administrative and management responsibilities that kept him metaphorically *running* in God-consciousness. He walked almost everywhere he went, and his journeys took him all over Germany to Paris (at least twice, a 511-mile journey from Erfurt) as well as his final walk to Avignon from Cologne, where he carried a heavy cross next to a company of his sympathetic friends.

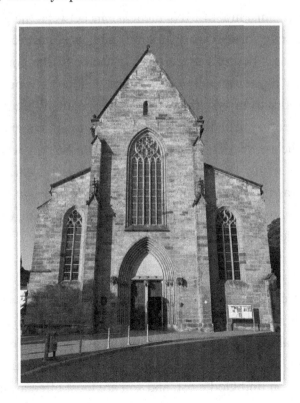

In the *Predigerkirsche* (Preacher's Church) Eckhart lived a traditional Dominican life. After supper, the friars would perform the day's last prayers at *Compline*. Then they would ascend the spiral steps into the attic, sleep for a few hours, and return to *Mantis* prayer, chanting the psalms and selected biblical passages, which were always initiated by the ringing of a church bell.[7] Ascending the spiral staircase into the roof space where they slept, and then descending again to the floor level to recite their prayers repetitively, was a symbolical transit from scriptural recitations to silent meditation, dreaming, and dreamless sleep—with a cross above at the apex in the attic and a cross below in the refectory. Prayer and singing were at the center of Dominican life. It was a way of reminding everyone that they were on the same spiritual journey together, moving upward toward the same goal, spiraling up into God.[8]

Although it is not possible to know all of the causes for the accusations against him in 1326, the tensions between the Dominican and Franciscan orders surrounding biblical interpretation and what constitutes heresy was certainly a factor in the complexity of relationships that eventually undermined Eckhart's reputation and kept his works from reaching the general populous until the mid-nineteenth century. Although sometimes hard to understand, Eckhart was, nevertheless, fearless in speaking truth in the only way he knew how without erring: by preaching it consistently and clearly. His final statement was that the *way of worshiping God is present in all ways and in all things.* He said to his disciples, before departing Cologne for Avignon to defend himself before the pope in France:

> God is in all ways and equal in all ways, for anyone who can take Him so. If you take one way, such and such, that is not God. If you take *this* and *that*, you are not taking God, for God is in all ways and equal in all ways, for anyone who can take Him so … In whatever way you find God most, and you are most often aware

of Him, that is the way you should follow ... But the noblest and best thing would be this, if a man were to come to such equality, with such calm and certainty that he could find God and enjoy Him in *any* way and in *all* things, without having to wait for anything or chase after anything: *that* would delight me![9]

Ultimately Eckhart lived a relatively peaceful life in the Order of Preachers. He managed to steer free of being crucified by its most powerful organization in medieval Europe, the Roman Catholic Church. I will go into this unfortunate history later in the book (Chapter 15). I mention it here because I want to dispel any doubts as to the authenticity of such allegations against the humble preacher of God's Word from the start. From my careful scrutiny of Eckhart's Latin and German sermons, it is clear that his knowledge of theology far surpassed the comprehension of any of his contemporaries, and the central problem in the inquisitor's minds was their ignorance, shallow orthodoxy, and inability to think *symbolically*. This is a type of thinking in which Eckhart excelled: *parabolical thinking*. Eckhart was a born poet and an irrational type.

CHAPTER 3

ECKHART'S UPBRINGING IN THE THURINGIAN FOREST

Johannes Eckhart von Hocheim (or "Master" Eckhart) was possibly raised in the small medieval village of Tambach near the Thuringian Forest, a predominantly wooded area inhabited by towering spruce trees, beech, firs, and pines. Today, Tambach in Thuringia is in what is called *das grüne Hertz Deutschlands*: "the green heart of Germany." This was a lovely locale for the young Johannes to grow up in as a boy, close to trees, greenery, and the native *Grund* (ground) of Bavaria. Eckhart once famously said: "The senses I have in common with animals; life I have in common with trees. Being is still more interior to me and I have it in common with all creatures."[10]

For Eckhart, human life and tree-life were *one-life, one* consciousness, *one* love. Our life and tree-life participate in a common equality. Being is what we share with all creatures because all life and creatures are Words of God. This is what orthodox theologians call *panentheism*, although for Eckhart equality goes further than God. It includes not only panentheism but also no theism at all. This is why Eckhart is so widely celebrated by Zen Buddhists, scientists, and Vedantists alike.

Panentheism considers God and all to be interrelated: the all is in

God and God's being is in the world and Cosmos. God is essentially in everything that partakes of God's Goodness. Yet, as Words of God, humans and trees and creatures are recipients of God-consciousness, God-breath, or wakefulness in the Eternal Now, when we are born out of our own ground. You don't need to be a Christian to understand or appreciate Eckhart, who was about as classically Dominican (Catholic) as it gets in his directed thinking, but was wild and effervescent in his metaphorical thinking and irrational intuition as a shaman in ecstatic prayer.

Eckhart's teachings about our human life in common with trees can be read as connoting a radical form of *trans-dualistic* theology, which emphasizes Absolute Unity (*Unum*)[11] with all forms of life, whether one is Christian, or non-Christian, monistic or pluralistic, Islamic or Jewish. Aristotelian science was at the center of his theology, and he was preaching the Word from a long line of succession, from the Old Testament prophets, to Jesus, Augustine, Albert, and Aquinas, to himself as apotheosis; wherein, he himself began to erupt, burst out, break forth in ways that the world has not yet comprehended. Eckhart is still ahead of our times. He was that futuristic.

Birthing New Life from Our Own Ground

Our singleness of vision enables us to see God as a living reality and light imbued in everything. This means that re-entering nothingness and emptiness are ways to *birth being* in the manger of the human heart. God and the human Self are trans-dual when the soul rises up above all opposites. Godhead and Nothingness are aimed at *birthing life from one common Ground*. Eckhart felt an equality with animals, trees, and creatures through his profound sense of empathy, an inner *commonality of being on the very ground he walked upon.* This *Grund* was felt most deeply in his German homeland, where his life was deeply rooted. His greatest utterances were voiced in Middle High German.

Eckhart's Latin treatises and sermons were also of great importance, and their brilliance and beauty cannot be denied from a theological standpoint. To be sure, his German sermons were more poetic and irrationally brilliant, so much so that it is almost impossible to grasp him intellectually at times. His high intellect leaves many in awe.

Keeping our Eyes on the Forests and Treetops

My aim, in what follows, will be to keep an equal eye on Eckhart's German and Latin works. In a passage from his most inspired German sermons, Eckhart told his audience that if they could understand the analogy between eye and wood, they would grasp his true meanings and get to the very bottom of everything he'd ever preached throughout his many years as a Dominican. This kind of analogy is typical of Eckhart as the irrational intuitive genius of his age: "Now mark me well: Suppose my eye, being one and single in itself, falls on the wood with vision … in the very act of seeing they are so much at one that we can really say 'eye-wood,' and the wood *is* my eye."[12] Imagine for a moment what our world would be like today if we valued and cared as much for trees as he did?

The woods of Thuringia formed a permanent impression on Eckhart's boyhood vision, so that his seeing *became* equivalent with *eye-wood*, at one with wood with no distinction in his soul. This is what I mean by his trans-dual poetic visioning: a view from above, from a detached superconscious state. This ascent of his soul into Wisdom is what gave him his greatest ability to tell us what God is while erupting forcefully from the Godhead. I get the same feelings in reading him today as I do when I read Shankaracharya or Vivekananda. It is a visioning above in the highest states of detachment from the outer senses.

When we enter the ground of our being, it opens us up to spaciousness, to vista, to *superconscious seeing*. Eckhart was no doubt an intuitive-intellectual visionary type of the highest order, a man to whom Nature revealed her innermost secrets about the *equality* of all existence. It was from his early life in the forests of Thuringia that his sense of Oneness with Nature's God and the primal *Grund* began for him.

Giving Big Gifts and Forgiving Big Sins

Another famous meditation on Nature's capacity to give birth to the Word in the world and human soul focused on the bigness in God's gifts, one of the most visible gifts being the majestic towering trees:

> God does not like to give anything as much as big gifts. I once said on this very spot that God likes to forgive big sins better than small ones. The bigger they are, the more freely and quickly he forgives them. This, too, is how it works with grace, gifts, and virtue. The bigger they are, the more freely he gives them because his nature depends on giving big things. And so, the better things are, the more there are of them.[13]

The essential goodness of all creation was at the center of Eckhart's cosmology and metaphysics. In his theology of the Word there is scant mention of sin or evil because love of the Good surpasses anything inferior to Nature. God's Love is supreme, superior to anything we humans can do on the brown-blue-green earth: "There is no creature so worthless that it could love anything evil; for whatever one loves must either seem good or be good."[14] Eckhart's views on sin and forgiveness are unique.

Why does God like to forgive big sins better than small ones? I'm raising this question because it is central to the thesis of this book: "You may be as certain of this as you are that God lives—that it must of necessity be the best thing of all, and that no other way could be better."[15] If I am a master housebuilder, I must love carpentry and construction as much as I do trees, which are needed for making a house. This is what we must learn today, all of us. We need to stay ecologically focused on our equality with trees without destroying Mother Nature and decimating our precious earth and forests and the air we breathe.

The better things are, the more there are of them. God does not like to give anything as much as big gifts. Eckhart's theology was not focused on sins and evils in human nature, so much as God's birthing of large gifts. I know this through meditations I've taken into our backyard in Joaquin Miller Park, which once was ground to some of the largest redwood trees in the world. The redwoods behind my home were used to build the cities of Oakland, Alameda, Moraga, Lafayette, Martinez, and San Francisco. I've observed with my own eyes (*eye-wood,* as Eckhart said) a multiplicity of small shoots or saplings growing around a butchered sea of redwood stumps in beautifully concentric circles, which Nature's God left for us to marvel at as miracles to behold. What fossil records tell us is that redwoods are ancient and have survived countless fires, land upheavals, and ice ages. They predate the birth of humans on this planet by hundreds of millions of years. They may, indeed, prove to outlast human existence.

Big gifts like redwood trees need to be well protected, because we have our lives in common with them, as we do with caterpillars, who also have isness, or arboreal salamanders who like to live near the moisture provided by these once-giant trees. Trees give us precious oxygen and store more carbon in their mass than any other living organism. We cannot exist without trees. I feel it is our duty and responsibility today as humans to preserve and protect our world's forests, because they are the best and biggest gifts God has given us on our planet. Moreover, I devoutly believe that if Eckhart were alive today to see the effects of climate change on our beautiful earth, spinning in the silence of outer space, he would be at the forefront of our global fight to protect them out of his remarkable sense of humility, poverty, compassion, and justice.[16] To speak up for God's existence in trees was part of his message as a preacher, whose eye was equivalent with wood.

In trees, Eckhart perceived a hidden *spark* of God, a living spirit, breath, power, or God-force that is the very source of our existence in Nature. Eckhart was not satisfied until he reached the essence of trees, their innermost being: "This is what the spirit does: It does not rest satisfied with just this light [heavenly light], but presses all the way through the firmament and pierces through the sky until it comes to the spirit that makes the sky revolve. Because of the revolving of the heavens everything in the world turns green and leafs out."[17]

In another gorgeous German sermon, he said: "Every image has two properties. One is that it takes its being immediately from that of which it is the image, involuntarily, for it is a natural product, thrusting forth from nature like the branch from a tree."[18] What *leafs out* of trees is the natural breath of the Holy Spirit. In one of Eckhart's Latin sermons, he preached earlier: "The Son, as perfect likeness, breathes forth love, the Holy Spirit."[19]

Is this not what trees do? Are they not showering us with their precious love as oxygen? To Eckhart's mind, trees were *Words of God.* Trees are involuntary products of the Holy Spirit emanating from the ground of Mother Nature. The Holy Spirit, *breath*, is inherent in all things in the created Universe. Eckhart's sky-vision makes his theology of the Trinity *spiritually democratic.* Spiritual Democracy was present in the blessed boy Johannes during his earliest days in the Thuringian Forest. His Oneness with trees and the being of all creatures remained with him throughout his entire lifetime.

CHAPTER 4

MY BIOGRAPHICAL CONNECTIONS TO ECKHART AND JUNG

My Lutheran grandmother came from Hof, Germany, to live with our family in Pacific Grove when I was about six months old. She stayed with our family for the first five years of my life. She gave me a little Lutheran prayer to memorize in German when I was four. I repeated it in silence to myself every night before I fell asleep: "Dear God, make me humble, that I might come into Heaven." I didn't know what God, or humility, or Heaven meant then, but I said it anyway, because I loved her, and saw something spiritual in her that I wanted to emulate. I also wanted to *experiment* with prayer to see what might happen, as children are apt to do. "Would I really come into Heaven if I prayed?" I wondered. Children sometimes ask such questions in their innocence.

That was my first exposure to Christianity, although nothing of any real consequence came of it intellectually until I discovered Eckhart. Then *everything* changed. Although I had always resisted identification with the Christian religion, my soul was suddenly Christianized in ways I'd never dreamed possible before. It was as if I was invaded at UCSC by the archetype of Christ. The kinds of inner experiences, in which my dream-ego was enabled to momentarily glimpse its essential *equality* with Christ and with Eckhart within, were facilitated at UCSC by my simultaneous reading of the Dominican and Jung and through my relationship with my spiritual teacher, Bill Everson (Brother Antoninus). Looking back at my Eckhart dreams today, the preacher's significance as an ancestral figure in my psyche becomes even clearer. The awakening of the Christian archetype reminds me of what is perhaps the most famous of all of Eckhart's sayings: "The eye with which I see God is the same eye with which God sees me."[20] This was one of the sentences that the Cologne censors objected to and to which Eckhart replied in his "Defense" by quoting none other than St. Augustine!

Yet as a four-year-old boy, before my consciousness was changed by my immersion in Eckhart's works, I simply said that little prayer my grandmother had given to me in the quiet of my mind in German, then fell asleep. I did this for a few years. Then, I let it go. Never once did I hear a word about the devil or hell or damnation from her, or my parents. Faith or belief in God was similarly never mentioned. I never had a conflict with my father or mother or anyone about Christ or the Trinity or faith or anything, except that my family did not go to church and were, therefore, agnostic.

However, once in a while, after saying the little Lutheran prayer, I *dreamt between four and seven that I was falling into an unfathomable abyss that had no bottom. It was boundless and infinite.* The sensations I had were those of falling forever into vastness without any sense of time or place. This was a bit disturbing. Yet, when I managed to let go of my fears, I would experience the most wonderful feelings and sensations of rest, floating for what seemed forever into a bottomless Ground, or "ground that is groundless."[21] There was also a sound, like a hum, which is difficult to describe in words. There was certainly no God down there, only Infinity, but an Infinity that was finite, because it was my own personal experience of it.

Whatever the abyss was, I knew it was not far away. It was as close as the doorway of my dreams. All I had to do was to pass through a doorway of sleep into a continuum of limitless Space. Later, I read that the abyss was what Eckhart had called the *Grund*, or Ground of Being out of which the Trinity is constantly being born in the soul. This little prayer helped to still my mind and allowed me to slip into deep sleep. I always kept my dreams about the abyss secret.

My family celebrated Christmas and Easter like many Americans do. Yet these outer events in our home were mostly without much religious meaning. Nevertheless, on May 20, 1964, at the age of eight, my father gave me a small white *King James Bible* with gold-typed words on the cover: "Holy Bible." He sent me off with my brother to the local Lutheran Church, in Pleasant Hill. He signed my book: "To Steven by Daddy." He gave us free choice to attend Sunday services or not. There was no coercion involved. He probably wanted us boys to have a moral education, even more so than a religious one, since he was no longer a practicing Lutheran. He had integrity to give us *free choice* as to whether to attend the Church. There was no force, just liberty and freedom and fatherly love. That's how I remember him. The choice was freely ours. After one service, we decided not to join the Lutheran Church and that was it.

The only time I remember stepping foot in a Catholic Church as a boy was when we visited the spectacular Notre-Dame during a visit with our French relatives in Paris. It was a numinous experience. The magnificence of that place was unforgettable. Construction on Notre-Dame began in 1163 CE and it was completed thirty-five years after Eckhart's death, so he is sure to have visited it while it was being built.

Later, when I was fourteen, we were making our way up Highway 80 toward Lake Tahoe. My mother drove our Chevy station wagon to take our family skiing after my father died. I was looking out at the beautiful Sierra scenery and marveling over its beauty. On the right, above Placerville, I saw two nuns driving next to us dressed in black-and-white religious habits. They were neatly dressed in their religious garb heading for the Sierras. They looked so happy seated together driving next to us, and they were pleasantly smiling at me. I spontaneously waved to them and they waved back to me. They reminded me of my grandmother. When I looked over at my mom, she seemed *enraged*. What was going on?

As I learned several years later, as a girl growing up in France in the 1930s, our mom had been sent to Catholic school where she had been physically, mentally, and emotionally abused by Franciscan nuns. Apparently, the nuns beat misbehaving girls with wooden paddles to shame them before their peers when they misbehaved. My mother was rebellious. A wild force of Nature, she had a strong character that could be chaotic at times. She had apparently been one of the "bad ones'" in her childhood and latency years. Whereas "good" Catholic girls had been treated with tenderness, physical affection, and loving kindness, she was publicly shamed, which probably filled her with *envy* and seething *anger* (two of the seven deadly sins). She recalled her traumatic history with me years later. Her emotional reaction to the nuns waving suddenly made sense to me when she told me the story of her childhood.

This memory stayed with me as a cautionary tale about what can happen if one's soul or psyche is placed in the wrong hands, whether in religious or secular school, and it may have played a part in shaping my decision to become a child psychotherapist. It also taught me something significant about the problem of splitting between right and wrong, virtue and sin, good and evil in Christian institutions. Jung never tired of warning readers of this problem in Christianity, what can happen when the soul is divided, disunited, in discord between love and hate, peace and violence, God and Nature. My mother was clearly not in an integrated condition of peace, like the two nuns appeared to be. Yet I had compassion and sadness for my mother's plight when I learned about her traumatic history.

A second story my mother told me from her time in Catholic school is that she disrespectfully pulled off the habit of a nun, after a violent beating episode where she was slapped in the face in front of her schoolmates. She exposed the nun's tonsured head for all her classmates to see to embarrass the poor nun in public and to humiliate her. This was part of the Christian religious complex into which I was born as a native Californian. On the other side was my Lutheran grandmother, who taught me how to pray, but who beat me when I misbehaved too. Unfortunately, she too was abusive in her own confused and loving ways. These experiences created a mistrust of the Church.

By far the most memorable experience for me of being in a church, however, certainly the most numinous, was when I taught a dream seminar to ministers and theologians and lay Christian folk alike in the *Predigerkirsche* in Erfurt during the approach to the summer solstice in 2019. I've also given a series of presentations, one on Meister Eckhart that I called "Leaving God for God," at the Unitarian-Universalist Church in Kensington, a real down-to-earth place without the medieval splendor of Europe, but authentically American.

What I remember most fondly about Christianity growing up was decorating our annual Christmas tree, the brilliantly colorful lights, waiting anxiously to unwrap the sparkling presents beneath the *crucified* Christmas tree, and hunting with great pleasure for colorfully wrapped shiny chocolate Easter eggs! My mother always came alive with great energy, happiness, and laughter to celebrate Easter with us. The Easter ritual seemed to organize her in a deeply spiritual way, and so did the classical religious music of Johann Sebastian Bach, whom we listened to with delight on our RCA Victor record player.

The conventional Christian idea transmitted to me as a boy of four by my Lutheran grandmother was that if I could become *humble* enough in my attitudes through prayer and the virtue of humility, I might arrive at a place of peace in heaven when I died. As Eckhart taught, if you are in God, you are at peace. Heaven is peace. *The Kingdom of Heaven is within you.* This is essential Eckhart. Everything in Eckhart's Latin and German Sermons revolves around rest, silence, peace, and ultimate spiritual freedom. Where might heaven be found in today's world? Isn't this what we are all seeking: a peaceful life? As Eckhart famously said in his "Talks of Instruction":

> For as far as you are in God, you are at peace, and as far as you are out of God, you are not at peace. If anything is in God, it has peace; as much in God, so much at peace. That is how you can tell how far you are in God or otherwise, by whether you have peace or unrest.[22]

CHAPTER 5

RUNNING IN PEACE: ECKHART'S THEOLOGY

My mother had come to the United States on a track and field scholarship at Iowa State University where she would meet my father. Before that she was the French champion in low hurdles and long jump for two years. I followed in her footsteps and ran in the California Track and Field Championships. I took fourth in the mile relay with my teammates in 1974.

I'm recalling this history here because Eckhart loved to use the metaphor of *running, striding,* and *rising* into God when he preached some of his most inspired sermons in Strasburg and Cologne. This is one reason I was so drawn to him: his sermons were so down-to-earth on one hand and so high up on the other! He was not only intuitively and intellectually brilliant; he was sensual in his grounded use of pictorial imagery. For instance, Eckhart began a sermon on peace (*pace* in Latin), first quoting from the Holy Scriptures, as he always did:

> Our Lord said to the woman: *"vade in pace,* go into peace" (Lk 7:36–50). It is good to go from peace to peace; it is praiseworthy. Still, it is a defect. One should *run* to peace, not *begin* in peace… A person who is in

a race, a continual race, and is in peace, such a person is a heavenly person. The heavens are constantly running around [i.e. revolving] and in running they seek peace ... The highest work of God is mercy, which means that God places the soul in the highest and purest that it can attain: into vast regions, into the sea, into uncharted depths. There God works mercy.[23]

I grew up by the sea, and I could hear the waves breaking on the shore for the first four years of my life. Equating God and the soul with the sea made perfect sense to me. Eckhart said a lot here, which I'll unpack psychologically and theologically to give you a flavor for my style of interpreting him in the pages ahead. The passage from Luke is about a *sinful woman* who brought Jesus an alabaster-box containing an ointment. With this balm and with the hairs of her head and her tears flowing, she washed his feet and kissed them and Jesus forgave her, and he said to her compassionately: "Thy faith hath saved thee; go in peace." Eckhart was always forgiving the sins of people, and he was, in my reading of him, always a peacemaker like Immanuel (Isaiah 9:6) and Christ (Matthew 1:23). That's why I love him so. Who of us is free of sin? We are all sinners. We need to accept our sins, equally with our virtues. Then we might be truly forgiven.

What did Eckhart mean when he said: "It is good to go from peace to peace; it is praiseworthy. Still, it is a defect"? People who live their lives in continuous contemplation and prayer can be praised, but there will always be some kind of a defect in them because they lack equality with God.[24] When the soul is dissolved completely in God, then she has peace.

We cannot individuate in a cave, in complete solitude. It is impossible. We need friends to balance out our introverted and extroverted functions. Then, in the company of friends, brothers and sisters alike, or in a soul society, we can approach the goal of life, which is fullness of character: attainment of our innate individuality in meaningful relationship with a supportive community. This woman was part of what would become the Christian community. She is an archetype of the anima who is at first sinful, and therefore part of all of our souls, and then gets up and runs in peace. Eckhart taught us to rise our souls up into God-consciousness to attain ultimate peace.[25]

Moreover, kissing the feet of Jesus was a very intimate and sensual act on her part. Thus, her natural goodness and her *faith* saved her and she was blessed with forgiveness. This healed her. Thus, Jesus was a healer. In this book, I call him a great medicine man, or *shaman*. So too was Eckhart (see Chapter 31). By this I mean a preacher who has a direct link to the *shamanic archetype*,[26] which is the most powerful source of connection to the healing energies of the psyche and Cosmos. The first Jungian analyst who pointed this connection out in both Eckhart's and Jung's works was John Dourley, who noted that Jung took the term "fetching God from outside" from Eckhart for whom "God is accessed from within," meaning that "every individual is a priest or shaman when the divine impulse arising from the psyche is consciously engaged."[27]

By "one should *run* to peace, not *begin* in peace" Eckhart meant that we have work to do on the integration of the opposites in the soul, between the virtuous inner person (the higher human) and sinful outer person in us (the lower human). We must arrive at a synthesis between the senses and the highest intellect to be cured of our suffering. Only when the soul arises to her highest destiny in Wisdom is she truly at peace. Then she attains a *vison of peace*.[28]

Eckhart was essentially saying that a person who is in a continual race and is in peace while racing is a heavenly person because the soul has entered the heavenly abode above. This means psychologically that whatever we are doing by vocation is like running, a continual race for a prize, which is to find our own *Way to God* and make it real, to realize it through our calling. Everyone, according to Eckhart, has a calling. Jung shared this same view about the aim of analysis. Thus, *running* was a metaphor for staying in the race, not giving up, no matter what happens to us from the outer blows of fate, unforeseen attacks from the outside, or from the inevitable suffering that comes from our sins or separation from the inner voice of God. We all have a Self that needs to keep moving. We also need stillness, stillness of body, stillness of soul, stillness of mind. If we can perform our works with a peaceful mind, then we might become heavenly beings.

Self-forgiveness is in truth a *medicine* for neurotic suffering. We can become complete in ourselves and our world if we can hear the call to vocation, like the woman with the ointment-box who washed and kissed the feet of the Jesus. She found her calling. Then, she rose up and went into peace to pursue her work.

There is a lesson there: the sensual anima is not the highest personification of the soul in Eckhart's view. *Sophia* is the highest personification because she connects us to the earth below and the sky above. Here again Eckhart and Jung were on the same page. They both postulated that there are *four levels* of evolution in the soul, or anima (Chapters 8 and 9). Eckhart equated this higher aspect of his soul with the celestial spheres of the Cosmos: "The heavens are constantly running around [i.e. revolving] and in running they seek peace." Peace is our aim, our goal in life.

We all want to rest in God, or Nature, or with loving friends or family, which brings peace. Working without a why, working with *detachment*[29] (see Chapter 32), is what Eckhart consistently said will lead us to a peaceful mind. He added at the end of this sermon: "The highest work of God is mercy, which means that God places the soul in the highest and purest that it can attain: into vast regions, into the sea, into uncharted depths. There God works mercy." Mary is Mother Mercy.

Psychologically then, he began with an image of the sinful anima that Jesus forgave and he healed her by leading her into peace and ended with Wisdom, the highest personification of the soul, inclusive of the whole world of nature and mercy, or compassion, whichever word you prefer. If we can rise up into the highest and purest regions of the soul, we come into the deep sea, into uncharted depths. Then, high and low are transcended and transmuted into *Oneness, One* Existence, Unity, where there are no opposites. Sins have been superseded and left below. Listen again to Eckhart:

> The soul's purification consists in her being purified of a life that is divided, and entering a life that is unified. All that is scattered among lower things is united when the soul climbs up into a life where there are no opposites. When the soul enters the life of intellect, she knows no opposites.[30]

The sinful woman was a woman of the ground. She was close to Eve, the serpent, and the tree in the Garden. Eckhart loved to use stories like this to give us spiritual instructions on how to rise above our imperfections. We are all imperfect. There is no perfection in relative existence.[31] Yet *"the soul's purification consists in her being purified of a life that is divided and entering a life that is unified."*[32]

How can the soul become unified in God, when our sensual anima or animus is constantly being distracted by external things? Temptations are everywhere. That is why monastic life can bring the soul into a state of inner quiet through prayer, chanting of psalms, and meditation. In non-monastic life we find it in the living out of our impulse to individuate. Then, Eckhart said, *"All that is scattered among lower things is united when the soul climbs up into a life where there are no opposites."*[33]

Transcendence into God-Consciousness

Transcendence connotes the very summit of spiritual attainment: the *full blaze* of God-realization, the *blitz*, seeing the *lightning*, or experiencing Absolute Reality. Eckhart described the transport of consciousness in the soul into Wisdom in the process of running, leaping, or rising into God's Kingdom. The realization of transcendence I examine in this book will be looked at, not as a metaphysical "belief," but as an actual *experience* that can be verified empirically.[34] This is wholly within the scope of what William James and C. G. Jung studied in their respective models of "analytic psychology," although with an understanding that this highest experience known to humanity is not a common occurrence, but is, rather, rare and outside the range of exact science on one hand, while being a variable of psychology that can be validated cross-culturally on the other. It is the same basic attainment regardless of East-West comparisons, or with Islam or Sufism. The realization of God-consciousness might best be described as a temporarily experienced *merger* with the Absolute. It happens through an elevation of normative ego consciousness to superconsciousness, Oneness, or equality with the Self Supreme, and it is following such states of elevated being that the soul of the seer is enabled to *perceive the God-presence vibrating in all things as God.*

Such Oneness can be attained via a calling, or vocation in Dominican theology. This theological field of inquiry is typically known as *metaphysics*, a domain Jung said he did not dabble in. Although in the final two decades of his life, after his consecutive trips to the United States and India in 1937–1938, his psychology became more open to considering how far psychology might lead us into cosmological dimensions of experience, or *psychophysical reality*, thanks in part to his rereading of James, who led him to see that the human psyche extends into the Infinite. Earlier than that he had read about the Infinite Ground in Eckhart.[35] As you'll see, transcendent awareness of the Absolute is not an overblown state of ego identity with the Self, but a state of humility and grace.

This kind of humility is not psychological inflation, but a noninflated ego state in the soul, a coming down into inwardness and ascent into pure Existence, which reveals the wholeness, humanity, and authenticity of Eckhart's *unitary theology* (see Chapter 13) or trans-dual Wisdom. The apophatic nature of all designations and

31

definitions of the Absolute was his highest realization; the Absolute can never be fully described, symbolized, or named.[36] Descriptions, names, symbols, and forms are all pointers to Absolute Reality, but they fall short of the beyond God, which is the Ground of the Godhead.[37] Symbols are all pointers to the one Reality, *imaginative constructs arising out of the native Ground Itself.*

Another metaphor for the state of Oneness in Eckhart is the Infinite. The correspondence of the number one and the Absolute is summed up in a mathematical equation of equivalence, such as, for instance: the *Absolute = Unity of Existence, God, or an infinite series of Ones.* There is a difference in Eckhart's theology between God and the Godhead, which can never be fully experienced, apprehended, or named by any single word of God. The names of God[38] are all pointers to Absolute Reality, which is endless. There is an equivalence, therefore, between the names *Christ* and *Krishna, God* and *Vishnu, Guan Yin* and *Sarasvati, Buddha* and *Allah,* or *Dao* and the *Great Spirit, Wakan Tanka* and *Raven, YHWH* and *Sophia.* To know the difference between God and the Godhead, one must become inwardly internalized: "God is brought down, not absolutely but inwardly, that we may be raised up. What was above becomes inward. You must be internalized, from yourself and within yourself."[39]

Moreover, I see Eckhart as an early precursor of *Spiritual Democracy*[40]: his positive affirmation of Christianity and Sufism, Judaism and Islam. This democratically spiritualized vision supports my empirical hypothesis that the Absolute can be posited in theology as an experience of transcendent light or illumination. Such a cross-cultural study aligns with the empirical psychology of James and Jung, who postulated the relativity of the Self, which contains an overarching vision of the Absolute as a hypothesis that has to be *proven* through scientific research via images (Jung) or descriptions of the highest religious experiences (James).

God is finally what we depend upon for our being and becoming, but we are reduced to nothing in the face of the Godhead, no matter how comprehensive and all-totalizing our God-concepts and experiences may be. Over the course of our evolutionary journey as a species on this planet, religions have attempted to give us a glimpse of the face of the Absolute, but according to Eckhart these are all garments of the hidden God. The only true representations of the Divine are the bare One, the naked[41] Essence in myself or yourself.

CHAPTER 6

PANTHEISM AND PANENTHEISM

A theological dispute that got Eckhart in a whole lot of trouble with the Pope in France was his transcending the traditional opposites on such a high-level theoretical issue as the paradox between pantheism[42] and panentheism.[43] Why are these hypotheses different? For Eckhart, they were One because they both emanate as ideas from the same Godhead. *Panentheism is a belief that all is in God and God is in all things.*[44] *Panentheism* is a word composed of the English equivalents of the Greek *pan*, meaning "all," *en* meaning "in," and *theism* derived from *Theos*, or God. This was one of those theological debates that Eckhart rose above, because above God, there is no need to argue such points as to whether the Creator is human or inhuman, Christ or beyond-Christ. In *pantheism* God is human and inhuman, whereas in panentheism the emphasis is upon God in humans as the *center* of the Universe. Pantheism[45] was one of the accusations that were hurled against the Dominican by the Inquisition in 1327 in Cologne. To think that anybody could be condemned for valuing God in Nature *equally* with God in humans always seemed to me to be preposterous; for what destroys God's transcendence in humanity is not pantheism, it is the splitting of the two notions into dualistic God-concepts, which theologians and scientists have promoted with their fixed and overly rigid propositions. Pantheism and panentheism are confessions of faith.

Why not climb higher up into the Godhead beyond God with Eckhart and cherish both? *When the soul enters the life of superior intellectual-intuition, she knows no opposites. She becomes One with God in Nature and God in humans and the impersonal God that created the Universe.*

Therefore, to be true to the spirit of Eckhart in this book, whose tomb was empty like Christ's (for no one knows where his body was buried),[46] it would be wiser and more just for me as author to posit that they were both contained for Eckhart by the *One God of the Universe,* as Benjamin Franklin once famously said. My hypothesis herein is that Nature's God was also Eckhart's God in his transcendence above God. The Cosmic Man, the Christ-image, is an *archetype.* It is also, Eckhart knew, trans-human, as are the stars and galaxies. Eckhart must have known this because for him the groundless ground of the Godhead was always beyond God. *"Du sollst ihn lieben, wie er ist ein Nicht-Gott, ein Nich-Geist, ein Nicht-Person, ein Nicht-Bild"*[47] (*Nicht* means "non" in English. "You should love Him as he is a Non-God, a Non-Spirit, a Non-Person, a Non-Image.") How can any human God presume to grasp the Infinite? It is mathematically impossible. All human-conceived God-images must be *finite.* Eckhart's highest prayer was to become rid of God, which, of course, included all historical images and names we have of the Father, Jesus, Mary, and Sophia from the Old and New Testaments.

In my reading of his works, I came to *see* that he was as much pantheistic as he was panentheistic.[48] He was in this sense truly a *trans-dualist.* He believed that both postulates were true and *equal* in God. Worship of Divinity in Nature and in humans is essentially a science of the Infinite: "The infinite God who is in the soul, he grasps the God who is infinite."[49] In other words, the Infinite that cannot be counted by Wisdom is gasped by the infinite God that can be counted by any one God-image.

The question whether Eckhart preached a theology of *pantheism* (All-is-God) or *panentheism* (All-is-in-God and "transcends" the entire Universe) is a topic I will take up in order to shed light on Eckhart's unitary theology, a metaphysic both dependent and interdependent on God from a spiritually democratic point of view. Unitary theology holds that both hypotheses are *equally* valid and can be *experienced* side by side, in a Godhead above the opposites where science and theology may come together and join hands in celebration of the sacred mystery of Creation. There is no need to argue whose belief is right, whose is wrong, or whose God-image is superior to whose; both are *equal*. In panentheism, God is everything in the Cosmos and everything is part of the divine order because it is all contained *in* a transcendent God. Panentheism is believed by some to be the only correct concept because it is said to subsume the pantheism, from below or above, and exceeds it. Whereas, in pantheistic belief there is no centralized accent on a personal, or anthropomorphic, name of God, such as Jesus, Krishna, or Buddha; in panentheistic thought all personal Gods in whatever religion subsume Nature, the World, and the whole Universe.

In pantheism, God is impersonal, transcendent of all human God-images, names, and forms of God, yet at the same time is *imminent* in the entire Universe. As a simple formula pantheism believes that God is everything in the Cosmos, whereas in panentheism the universal spirit or soul of a transcendent Divinity is present in everything and is everywhere, while at the same time surpasses all Creation. In short, pantheism asserts that *everything is God*; panentheism claims that *God is in everything and is superior* to everything in the Universe.

For anyone who considers the implications of these beliefs, it will be clear that the idea of a personal or human God as being superior to the Universe is highly problematic. For Eckhart what was superior to God was the vision that everything in the Universe is *equal*. Although most Christian theologians will probably not admit it, the Christian archetype has a missionary zeal to it, and by becoming infected with it one can try to turn everything into "Christ," so that the whole Universe becomes contaminated with the human *imprint* of God. This is not the way I read Eckhart.

Panentheism was a philosophical and theological term first put forward by the German philosopher Karl Krause (1781–1832) in an effort to distinguish his ideas from those of Hegel, Schelling, and *pantheism* was postulated by Spinoza in his *Ethics*. In the United States, Emerson, Thoreau, Whitman, Melville, and Dickinson all championed the pantheistic vision of Divinity in their writings. By 1864, pantheism was condemned by Pope Pious IX in the *Syllabus of Errors,* and in a Papal encyclical in 2010, Pope Benedict criticized pantheism for denying the "superiority" of humans over nature.

Anyone who looks deeply into this matter can see that at the center of such debates is the issue of faith—that is all a person can ever claim about God: their personal belief. In modern science, for instance, Einstein described his "firm belief" in a "deep feeling" of "a superior mind that reveals itself in the world of experience." His God was, as he said, "pantheistic" ('Spinoza')." Moreover, Carl Sagan's cosmological God-concept was similarly "the God of Spinoza and Einstein, God not behind nature, but as nature, equivalent to it."[50]

Eckhart's works will illuminate how God is everything and interfuses with every part of the Universe and at the same time "transcends" space and time and all conceivable conceptions of Divinity. In my view, therefore, Eckhart was both pantheistic and panentheistic and something more, not a reduction to one or the other but a *plus*. The *Geburt* of God in the individual soul was a pantheistic experience and a panentheistic experience for him, a religious experience that superseded God and for him Reality in the soul itself, Absolute Existence, or *Esse in Anima*:

> When I flowed forth, all creatures said, "God." If anyone asked me, "Brother Eckhart, when did you leave your house?" I was in there. That is how all creatures speak of God. And why do they not speak of the Godhead? Everything that is in the Godhead is one, and of that there is nothing to be said … When I return

to God, if I do not remain there, my breakthrough will be far nobler than my outflowing.[51]

Here Eckhart makes a clear distinction between pantheism and what would be called panentheism by Krause. In his flowing forth, all creatures declared "God." But when he penetrated beyond God to the Godhead, he achieved a breakthrough that was far nobler and higher than his flowing forth as the Trinity. He went beyond the Father, Christ, the Holy Ghost, and Mary into the Godhead, which is the Fourth. This Fourth principal was not only a mother-of-All but also a father-of-All too. This nobility of his soul shows us clearly that he was a panentheistic theologian who also embraced pantheism in a *trans-dual* way.

I will go a step further now to declare that he transcended pantheism and panentheism by becoming, not a second Christ, as some Christian theologians would like to turn him into, but himself: Brother Eckhart, who preached from the doorway of God's house a new theology beyond all conceivable conceptions of God or the Trinity: "But in my breaking-through," he said, "where I stand free of my own will, of God's will, of all his works, and of God himself, *then* I am above all creatures and am neither God nor creature, but I am that which I was and shall remain evermore."[52]

Contemporary theologians sometimes attribute a name of God to describe the panentheistic God, such as a *Universal Christ* (Richard Rohr) or *Cosmic Christ* (Teilhard de Chardin), but here, Eckhart said clearly enough that he was transported *above all* God-images in his own divine existence, not as God, or Christ, or even a second Christ, but as Eckhart through the breath of the Paraclete. The *upward impulse* propelled consciousness above God and made him equal with the Universal Mind, Transcendental Self, or Cosmic Intelligence, from the first Infinite Nothing out of which everything emanates. Here, therefore, is the unitary concept that is needed to establish a third hypothesis to unite the previous two hypostases: a trans-pantheistic-panentheistic theology above the Trinity. Through the Third Person he attains the Fourth: the highest Reality and Truth that exists in the primal Ground out of which the Universe is constantly expanding and being born, without any names or forms, except the Knower that sees him as Himself, or Herself, or Myself.

Eckhart in his breakthrough became one with the Eye of God that could see both concepts as equally valid in a Spiritual Democracy that transcends them by seeing both singly as being born from the same Godhead.[53] What gives both concepts equal validity are the vocations from which both ideas spring forth from the Godhead, which does nothing and does not care about competing ideologies. It is pure stillness and emptiness and quiet, a Oneness of spirit and vision in the Absolute. Theologians, with their intellectual arguments, sometimes like to hide a religious superiority behind their so-called ecumenism, when the fact is they are attempting to make their creed's God-image the God of the Universe in a way that is out of harmony with the divine order since it is based on preeminence of their own religion, not on equality. Eckhart preached that all God-images are equal in the Godhead, and when he rose above the angels, he was not God, or Christ, or a second Christ, but the simple and humble human being, the man of poverty and carrier of his own Cross: Brother Eckhart, OP.

The Self and no-Self in Eckhart's Work

Eckhart was our first psychologist of the Self in the West. He had a marvelous metaphor for this: "No creature is so tiny that it lacks isness. When caterpillars fall off a tree, they climb up a wall, so that they may perceive their isness. So noble is isness... A stone is nobler, insofar as it has isness, than God and his Godhead without isness."[54] Isness means existence, or being.[55] God and his Godhead without isness is Nothing, or Nothingness.[56]

To Eckhart every creature was a Word of God. The caterpillar has isness, just as we do. Climbing a wall was a metaphor for spiritual progress toward becoming transformed from relative existence toward the Absolute. Eckhart turned to natural phenomena such as this for proofs for his theological postulates, just as empirical scientists do. He learned this from St. Albert, who was a great scientist (see Chapter 12), and St. Thomas Aquinas. They were all devout men of faith and science in their order.

As empirical psychologists, we are not typically instructors of faith when we practice because we need to stay agnostic to some extent. Then again some of us are Jewish or Christian or Taoist or Buddhist or atheist, and so on. The panentheistic presence of God is a principle of faith too, for we do not know the Divine purpose; we may only believe or state our subjective theories as rational hypotheses. If we listen to and learn from Eckhart, the divine birth of God that takes place in a pantheist, who is perhaps an astrophysicist, is just as noble as the birth of the Word in a panentheist, who has faith in Christ's humanity and happens by vocation to be a minister. Both theories of truth are equally valid in God or the Self.

It is theologians who argue that their viewpoints are absolute, superior, or better than naturalists. Eckhart never quarreled over such a point in Christian theology. He accepted both perspectives in his theology of Oneness, which was based in eternal Wisdom and Love for his neighbors. The caterpillar has work to do, just as we do. Any entomologist or lepidopterist will tell you caterpillars have isness, or a Self.

Leaping over all Creatures to Find God

Here's another choice passage by Eckhart that straddles the opposites and then leaps above them into God: "The soul that is to find God must leap over all creatures if she is to find God."[57] I find this to be a beautiful statement. It suggests that jumping and leaping, which he observed in the actions of horses in a meadow as a boy, are divine acts of God, which on the human plane, connotes an ascension in soul, again like the caterpillar's wall-climbing, upward toward God-consciousness.

As a boy of seven, I used to watch monarch caterpillars crawling up milkweed plants, transforming themselves into a chrysalis, and then morphing into full-grown butterflies in flight. This seemed to me to be a miracle of God. So too with horses running and leaping.

Thus, the preacher on a platform was a performer who *ran, strode,* and *leapt* into God in the presence of his audiences in Erfurt, Paris, Strasbourg, and Cologne, where he uttered the Word in Middle High German, his mother-tongue, in an attempt to lift his audiences up. On his own ground, in Germany, his theology soared into God after she—his sensual soul—died to the world: "Thus the soul dies to herself *before* she steps into God."[58]

Scientific Agnosticism

As a Jungian analyst, when working with patients, I remain agnostic when relating with a person of Christian faith. If she happens to believe in panentheism as an absolute truth, I do not disagree with her, or correct her at all. I support her faith. Jung was a relativist. He remained neutral about God. When I am working analytically with a geologist who believes in the principles of science, he will on occasion ask me to hold a positive attitude toward pantheism. This makes analytical psychology more objective than traditional theology, which often wants to argue that their beliefs are better or right or more all-inclusive. Yet in Eckhart's vocabulary, the ground of the soul in John Muir and the ground of the soul in Thomas Aquinas would theoretically be one and the same ground, separated by seven hundred years, which is a blink of an eye in the Cosmos.

Becoming One with Christ

Supernatural knowledge in the works of Eckhart is, therefore, knowledge of the superconscious state of transcendence into God's Wisdom and Infinite Peace. It is the highest form of knowledge known to humanity, and it comes to us through intuitive flashes of brilliance or genius erupting from the Ground of Being and Non-Being in the Godhead. *Thus, the soul dies to herself* before *she steps into God.* Does she then become one with God? The danger Jung never tired of warning us about was "the temptation to identify with the self," where the "ego identifies with the inner Christ."[59] Yet, as the reader will see, this warning did not seem to apply to his readings and re-readings of Eckhart. The reasons for this were that Eckhart practiced detachment as the highest virtue.

In fact, in some of his statements, Eckhart *did* identify with God and he taught us to do the same. This is why he was so dangerous to the Holy See, who could not see clearly. *Spiritual Democracy* offers a more modest way of teaching Eckhart, I believe, than dogmatic theologies, because it *sees everyone as equals in God* through the power and grace of your vocation.[60] It thereby avoids the dangers Jung warned of by teaching us that we are not superior to anyone, but part of what Walt Whitman called the *divine average.*

The shadow of condemnation that loomed over St. Albert and St. Thomas for being individuals and expressing their intellectual freedoms was never much of a concern for Eckhart in the end because both were canonized before his heresy trial,[61] and he had faith and hoped devoutly he too would fulfill his well-deserved destiny to sainthood.

Spiritual Democracy

Spiritual Democracy subsumes pantheistic and panentheistic postulates by validating them both as hypotheses contained in a higher field of order. Readers of this book may by now understand where I stand in my attitudes as an analytical psychologist, as an American, and as a student of Eckhart. All my life, I've lived close to the earth, the Pacific Coast, the Sierras, and night stars. Nature is a place in which I've sought solitude and healing and learning, and for whatever reason, I've stayed away from churches, priests, and theologians whenever they've become overly *dogmatic*, a play on the word "watchdogs." Maybe it was Jung who kept me away from confessing a particular faith, for unlike me, he had a church phobia. Mine is based more on whether I feel embraced for being an Eckhartian, for he awakened my Christian soul and lifted her up into God like no Church possibly could. As Jung wrote in "Transformation Symbolism in the Mass":

> The numinous experience of the individuation process is, on the archaic level, the prerogative of shamans and medicine men; later of the physician, prophet, and priest; and finally, at the civilized stage, of philosophy and religion. The shaman's experience of sickness, torture, death, and regeneration implies at a higher level, the idea of being made whole through sacrifice, of being changed by transubstantiation and exalted to the pneumatic man—in a word, apotheosis.[62]

Apotheosis! As a Jungian analyst and a marriage and family therapist, having specialized for two decades with traumatic disorders in latency-aged children, it's clear that splits in Christian religious organizations, such as between the Church and Nature, science and God, good and evil, can induce any of its members to become *traumatizing* agents of their spiritual communities.

It's a terrible issue that is at the root of so many psychological and spiritual problems patients bring into analysis today: a general dissatisfaction with the institutions of the Church. Church organizations, such as those on the religious right in the American Republican party today, can become breeding grounds for what Jung called *psychic infections*. I think this is what happened to my mother as a child. She was the victim of a psychic contagion in the Catholic Church that led the nuns in Avignon where she was schooled to become wicked and to project the Witch archetype onto her.

CHAPTER 7

TRANS-DUAL: SEEING GOD IRRATIONALLY

My personal story illustrates how even as a child of four I had experienced God beyond God as an infinite abyss. When I read Eckhart for the first time, I remembered my recurrent dreams. The abyss, void, or Nothing is what we come out of, Eckhart taught, and what we must return to in order to be born again—without any images, ideas, or names of God, as democratic citizens of the world. Only when our souls have died in God can we awaken to our true destiny. The images of God are in each of us, regardless of our faith, ethnicity, color, or nationality. We are all born out of the Godhead and God is in us and outside of us, everywhere, if we will only open our eyes to *see God irrationally.*

Jung taught that the best way to bring about a state of peace in the soul or psyche is by conscientiously living out a meaningful symbolic life through the opening of the inner eye via dream work and active imagination. This is where Eckhart has a great deal to teach us *about the true meaning of Christianity,* for he was essentially a visionary and an intuitive seer.

So often Eckhart has been called a "mystic" of the Church. This has unfortunately led to confusion. In my view, Eckhart was the greatest theologian the Church has produced. He was a visionary and one of the greatest intellectual minds of his age. However, to experience peace in a higher, more transpersonal sense, which is perfectly still, and where we are completely empty of all images and are quiet enough to *hear the Word and speak it,* meditation or prayer or long walks in Nature are needed.

It is important to make such distinctions here in order to be clear about my methodology in this book. For just as Eckhart was misunderstood in his day, so too was Jung. From the beginning of his career, whenever he was writing on the subject of Christian theology, Jung insisted he was writing about the Self, or the empirical God-image from a scientific standpoint outside the field of theology, metaphysics, or divine knowledge. This was something many theologians who tried their best to understand him failed to comprehend.

As I've made clear, I'm writing this book as an analyst and I'm also writing it as a friend of theology, or armchair psychological theologist of God and the Ground. Not enough distinction has been drawn by Eckhart scholars between God and the Ground of the Godhead.[63] Jung said in an interview titled "Man and His Environment," given on February 8th, 1950: "We all need nourishment for our psyche. It is impossible to find such nourishment in the urban tenements without a patch of green or a blossoming tree. We need a relationship to nature … Big cities are responsible for our uprootedness … I am fully committed to the idea that human existence should be rooted in the earth."[64] Eckhart agreed with this and spoke it from his pulpit. If he were living today Eckhart would applaud Jung's fight with the human shadow and evil. There are a few theological points where they would have disagreed, but for the most part they would have celebrated each other's works.

The Integration of the Shadow and Evil

Jung's concept of the integration of the shadow and evil is still perhaps the most revolutionary notion in modern psychology. As he wrote in *Aion*: "In the empirical self, light and darkness form a paradoxical unity. In the Christian concept, on the other hand, the archetype is hopelessly split, leading to a metaphysical dualism—the final separation of the kingdom of heaven from the fiery world of the damned."[65] He never said this about Eckhart for whom the Kingdom of God was within us and for whom the fiery world of damnation was scarcely if ever mentioned.

Jung's thoughts on evil were entirely original. Evil is a reality. It is here to stay. It exists in all of us, in our personal psychology, our ancestral history, our social relations with the world, our racial complexes, our institutional work, and perhaps especially today our relationships with Nature. Evil is one of the most difficult problems in the field of theology to tackle and no one, not even Aquinas, gave us a treatise to properly understand it in the direct and honest and even ruthless way Jung did.

So often I read books by theologians that surprise me with their shallowness because they neglect to discuss this single-most important problem in religion: *evil*. No one seems to want to touch the problem of evil. There seems to be a fear about getting too close to evil, because one might get *contaminated* by it or be attacked for discussing it by one's religious order, such as was the case with Jung's friend, Victor White. Theologians who endeavor to grapple with the problem of evil typically fail to understand it psychologically as Jung did, or in the trans-dualistic way Eckhart did (see Chapter 26).

Jung was at great pains his entire lifetime to create a psychological superstructure in his model of the human psyche by which we might be able to formulate a critique of Christian theology and its excess purity and goodness and virtue with a more down-to-earth understanding of the God-images as relative and inclusive of a shadow side and, also, absolute evil. This was certainly noteworthy.

Nevertheless, it has to be acknowledged that Jung did not include in his critiques of Christian theology a metaphysical scaffolding to complement his psychology. It is high time, I feel, that we continue to build on the bridge between psychology and religion that Jung was attempting to construct toward a better understanding of God and the Self in modernity.

Toward a Trans-Dual Psychological Theology

I use the word *trans-dual* in this book instead of *non-dual*[66] to distinguish the attitude that is needed to hold a theological and psychological perspective in awareness from a vista above the opposites. By *trans*, I mean over, above, or from the Higher Self. From such a vista, creation and destruction exist side by side.

Psychophysical energy may be used for either good or evil. There's no escaping this existential fact of human existence. God or the God-image creates good and evil. In Isaiah 45:7 we read: "I form the light, and create darkness: I make peace, and create evil: I the LORD do all these *things*." To create darkness and evil is not the same thing as *being* evil. It is humans that are evil, not God. Evil is almost nothing in the infinite expanse of the Cosmos.[67] And in the ground of the soul too we are close to Nothing. This is why we can never identify with the immensity of the bottomless Ground. No human incarnation can come close to the grandeur of the Infinite, not even God.

It's a fact of theology and psychology that soul and psyche are wedded together forever in an eternal play of opposites, yet Unity or Oneness at a higher level of engagement transcends evil. This is in line with the sayings of Jesus, in Matthew 10:34: "Think not that I am come to send peace on earth: I came not to send peace, but a sword." In Luke 12:51, Jesus said similarly: "Suppose ye that I am come to give peace on earth? I tell you, Nay; but rather division." If God came to send a sword and division, I believe it was to make peace: peace between humanity and God and Nature, God and the Godhead.

Understanding the Paradox of Theological Psychology

Jung's eye toward theology was psychologically paradoxical because it focused on the God-images of scripture. He loved to quote passages like the ones I just quoted from the Bible. He always claimed he was not transgressing onto theological territory by uttering scientific truths about God, nor commenting about God in any Absolute sense. Eckhart had, according to Jung's reading of his sermons, a purely psychological view toward the relative aspects of God, or the God-image. Yet Jung's analysis of Eckhart fell short of providing a workable *bridge* between the Relative and Absolute because he did not read Eckhart theologically. The Holy Spirit is the *divine breath* that flows from the Father into the Son, but the Paraclete is the Love that flowed from the Son into Eckhart and from Eckhart into Jung and *us*. It's a sacred teaching that we don't hear much about in traditional Catholicism.

How can readers today hope to understand Eckhart properly if not *also* theologically? This is not a paradox; it's a *theological fact of divine science*: in order to speak about God, one needs to understand God's Word as a Transcendental Reality. This, of course, is not what has been taught by the Church Fathers for the past two millennia. Yet Eckhart meant what he said and lived at a very high level while remaining low to the earth.

Christ has not come until He or She comes in You! This was Eckhart's essential teaching. Like Jung, he placed a greater accent on the Third Person of the Trinity (the Paraclete) than the Second, the Son. Jung said: "There is an extraordinary relationship between eastern ideas, and the ideas of Meister Eckhart, which is yet to be fathomed."[68] Indeed there is. Jung was zeroing in on the fact that

Eckhart was the only *bridge* in European Christendom between East and West. Jung was developing a scientific hypothesis here that holds great empirical validity and theological weight, and it may be proven to be correct through careful textual analysis.

How did Eckhart escape the sin of pride when he asserted his equality with the Creator? Here is Jung's hypothesis in brief: "When the I is identified with the Self, it is sort of elevated to a great height where it does not belong; if one sees the difference, then it sinks down. Meister Eckhart would say: yes, you are terribly important, but abandon yourselves nonetheless."[69] How did the "I" sink down in Eckhart's experiences of equality with God, Christ, Mary, and the Holy Spirit? By what method did he abandon himself? He said: "If you humble yourself, God comes down and enters you ... The highest flows into the lowest."[70]

No Eckhart scholar has explained this to my knowledge, but I think it is why so many of us are mysteriously drawn to Eckhart for comfort, peace, and spiritual Wisdom: he teaches us the mystery of Incarnation and also how to become humble democratic citizens of the earth and the city and Church.

Theologians can go on quoting scripture and the Church fathers all they want, but if they miss this important fact that *Christ is within us* and we are all parts of God, they will misread the true teachings of Jesus and Eckhart. In one German Sermon, Eckhart quoted Matthew 2:2: "Where is he who is born king of the Jews?" When you think of the king of the Jews, you typically think of the Messiah, right? You think of something that can occur once only, or perhaps twice in Christian history, if you anticipate a Second Coming of Christ. Yet that is an illusion.

Eckhart said the King of the Jews is in *you*, in every democratic person. The archetype of the Messiah is present in all of us.[71] This is a psychological fact because it is an archetype in the human soul. Another name for "King" is Christ, Selfsame, or Sophia. "Now observe, as regards this birth, *where* it takes place," Eckhart continued: "'*Where* is

MEISTER ECKHART AND C.G. JUNG

he who is born?' Now I say as I have often said before, that the eternal birth occurs in the soul precisely as it does in eternity, no more and no less, for it is *one* birth, and this birth occurs in the essence and ground of the soul."[72] No wonder he was charged of heresy. The Church will never accept this truth, not for another two thousand years, if then. That's how far ahead of his times Eckhart was and continues to be. I'll have much more to say about this birth in the chapters ahead because it is essential reading for all readers of Western and Eastern wisdom as well.

Eckhart was saying in all humility, I believe, that eventually everyone will be able to experience the birth of Divinity within if they are empty enough. It may take millennia before it begins to happen in many, the democratic majority, but until then, if we are not all wiped out by the Antichrist, war, or climate change first, there will be those who will live out his prediction approximately, no one ever perfectly, because perfection is too high an ideal.

The Holy Grail

One experiences relative evils and sins every day, but we are all moving as a species toward an Absolute state that will perhaps be possible in collectivity only when enough people achieve true *spiritual healing* through direct unmediated contact with the numinous, or Light, yet no one, not even Jesus lived in constant bliss in a superconscious state. *Transcendence is always temporary.* The Word is forever impermanent and comes and goes with the seasons in humans. Grace comes to us when God wills. It may take thousands of years to get to wholeness. But evolution is happening in humanity every day.

The problem with the high ideals of most theologies today is that they have set a far too steep moral standard for anyone to live by any longer; perfection and celibacy and poverty are unattainable ideals for the masses. God exists in everyone, and spiritual leaders can pave the way toward a new democracy of the spirit, a social movement that can benefit from Eckhart's teachings on Peace.

Think of Mahatma Gandhi in India, or the Baptist preacher Martin Luther King Jr., leading civil rights marches in Selma, Alabama, to imagine how a nuclear symbol of the Self, which is potentially violent and nonviolent, a sword and a lance of healing, can be kept in relative consciousness while embracing an Absolute value. We each have an inborn possibility of changing who we are by becoming more spiritual in our outlooks toward our global community.

Eckhart went so far as to declare during his vernacular preaching that *transformation* is inevitable: "We shall all be transformed totally into God and changed into him. In the same way, when in the sacramental bread is changed into Christ's Body, I am so changed into him that he makes me his one existence, and not just similar. By the living God it is true that there is no distinction there."[73]

He did not mean *the imitation of Christ*. Like Jung, he meant transformed into our own life. By sacramental bread, Eckhart meant the transfigured body of Christ. He also meant the Holy Spirit in you and me. *We are the bread. We are the Body.* You are the new incarnation of the Self that is forever evolving into something entirely transformed and new. This can happen only when our devilish nature is accepted and forgiven. We are all possessed by devils and angels at times, by complexes, that is, and the healing power of the numinous Light of God is what heals us.

Integrating Good and Evil, our Good Angels and Bad Angels

Eckhart agrees with Rabbi Moses (Maimonides)[74] and Jung that evil is in us, the "evil creature" of scripture "commences 'in man at the hour of his birth, as scripture says, sin will forthwith be present at the door'" (Gn 4:7). Who can say that sin is not at our door? We are all sinners. We all have a human shadow. Eckhart continues: "'Each person has two angels, one good and the other bad; one on the right, the other on the left. These are the good and bad creatures.' Perhaps these good and bad angels, the sensitive part that inclines to and suggests evil, and the rational (i.e. synderesis) that inclines to good, are the 'good and the bad tree' spoken of in Matthew 7:17–29."[75]

Synderesis is what Jung later called the *superstructure within conscience*, which is shrouded in an aura of numinosity, or Light. There is no metaphysical dualism here. How can the most extraordinary event in religious history in the West, the birth of the Messiah, become a humble event in the soul of collective humanity?[76] How could a theologian of the Church say he was equal with God, or how could Jung say *living* the "idea of the Christ within—not the historical Christ without, but the Christ within … is our symbol, that is ourselves; we are all that"?[77]

Christ within, or the Paraclete (John 14:12), spoke through Eckhart and Jung as the *vox Dei*. Eckhart asserted this truth in an eighth point of objection in his "Defense." Through a careful and conscientious living out of the fact of your own humble human-Divine existence in time, we, too, by making our double creature (including the shadow and evil) conscious can partake of a similar likeness, or *equality*.[78] For individuation to take place in the masses of humanity, it is not going to look pretty. It is going to entail blood, our blood, our sacrifice, not the blood of Christ alone, but the living blood of the Holy Spirit, which is operating continuously in you and me as the greening Word of God. Insofar as we are all Christs now, we all must be crucified upon our own Cross.

The Cross as a Symbol for our Wholeness

Christ is a nuclear symbol of vocation for all Christians. We who are Christian, or post-Christian today, extend the calling of Christ because what the Church has taught us is mostly false. The birth of God, Christ, and the Holy Spirit to Eckhart was something explosive, *eruptive*, violent, energetic like the big bang of Creation. Yet this vocation came from Judaism. It came from the prophets. It came from Wisdom, who is also fierce and "terrible as an army of banners" (Song of Solomon 6:10). It came from God and the Serpent. It came from the soul's ground. By *nuclear symbol*, I mean that the human psyche is patterned by exact laws of physics.

Psyche is as much inside as outside. We are all sitting on a potentially explosive volcano, one that can erupt at any time and either kill us, infect others, or bring lasting peace and bliss and healing on earth. The tremendous nuclear force of the personality can be utilized to injure others, or *cure* society and clean up our environments. The choice is ours. The economic and political spheres of our democracies are sick. Part of this illness is caused by our religious upbringings no doubt, which always seem to place human beings at the center of Creation, rather than at the periphery. We are wee parts of a vast interconnected web, an ever-expanding Universe, not the web Herself, God's Wisdom, or the Universal Goddess, but a particle, minute God-particles. We are infinitesimal parts of God in our vast Milky Way. In relation to the hundreds of billions of galaxies and dark matter, dark energy, and black holes out there, we are close to Zero, Nothing, and according to Eckhart's prediction: the Messiah is not going to come in a single person, but by acting in ethical ways, in accordance with Nature's laws, as equals and carrying our own Cross (see Chapter 16).

Theologians are used to discussing the problem of good and evil[79] in scripture superficially and sticking to literal interpretations of the Word of God *as if* their words were Absolute, not also relative, subject to changes in attitude and understanding by human consciousness and evolving social mores and behaviors. Our religions have become petrified and need to be radically altered if they are to survive the coming storms of climate change. God and Nature are not separate; they are One. This is why the nuclear symbol is often portrayed in dreams as a tree, Cross, animal, lake, river, mountain, volcano, mandala, salamander, or a Saint with a golden halo above their head.

Finding Your Own Inner Truth, or Holy Grail

Truth is not something one can find by turning to someone else's theology textbooks. Eckhart and Jung both taught that. Study all the theology you want and still you will not have arrived at *your truth* from the reading of books. Truth-telling, speaking the Word is a vocation. As Eckhart said:

> Truth is within, in the ground, and not without. So, he who would see light to discern all truth, let him watch and be aware of this birth within, in the ground. Then all his powers will be illuminated, and the outer man as well. For as soon as God inwardly stirs the ground with truth, its light darts into the powers, and that man [or woman] knows at times more than anyone could teach him [or her]. As the prophet says, "I have gained greater understanding than all whoever taught me."[80]

"To what is high one says 'Come down!' To what is low one says, 'Come up!'... If you humble yourself, God [the Messiah] comes down and enters you... The highest flows into the lowest."[81] By "prophet" Eckhart was referring to the words of the Hebrew preacher Solomon, son of David in Ecclesiastes 1:16. Eckhart's works are as much Jewish as they are Christian and also as post-Christian as they are Eckhartian. He went beyond God into the Godhead and the void, and his ideas were highly influenced by Aristotelian and Islamic thought and his synthesis led him to preach his own *unitary theology.*

Moreover, spiritual revelation or transcendence is not a preventive against violence and evil.[82] Just think of our Christian ancestor Luther and his attacks on the Jews! God must always consult with his wife[83]

Wisdom, when the child is being born as the Word in preachers. What she wants from everyone is that we love our Hebrew and Jewish ancestors as ourselves. What does it mean to be true children of God?

We must leave the Holy Scriptures behind in our quest for the Holy Grail that caught Christ's blood if we are to be married to Wisdom. For it is our very own blood. We are the life-blood of Christ, not the Church. The *child of God*, perhaps the most famous trope in all of Eckhart's works, is someone who wakes up to their own truth, their own Dharma, their own authentic spiritual revelation and finds a way to paint, dance, construct, or speak God's Word as if they were created entirely new. This is what happened to Jung who abhorred churches. It can happen to any one of us. Language can leap out of us, in new idioms and metaphors of speech, when we *erupt* into ecstasy.

Only Eckhart left Jung *feeling* that he had breathed in the *breath of life*. I felt the same *breath of the Holy Spirit* fill me with ecstasy and spiritual freedom when I first read him in the redwood forest at UCSC. Eckhart was speaking to future generations from a place on high that very few in his generation could follow, since that meant letting one's soul die and vanishing into the abyss. Yet common people understood him and flocked to hear him preach.

Jung was caught by the spirit of Eckhart and never tired of reading and praising him. I was a bit older when I was caught by the divine spark he ignited in me[84]; he opened me up to experience the light and he wafted me up to such a high place that my coming down was like falling into an Infinite Ground. Eckhart modeled the symbolic life of a true Christian and his sermons continue to be fruitful for many of us because of his simple ways of speaking to our cores. That's why we read him. For the uplift into pure intellect and for the humility he transmits. Finding Eckhart was like unearthing the Holy Grail.

Receiving the Comforter

I am still learning Eckhart's theology. I have had to learn to see Eckhart as he saw God: eye to eye, in an *equal eye* with God and Christ and the Paraclete within us: "for he [the Comforter] dwelleth within you, and shall be in you" (John 14: 17). We must come to know Eckhart as an archetypal figure within to awaken his archetype and begin to dialogue with him. This is the only way to truly know him. An archetype is like an underground river along which the currents of psychic life have been flowing for many centuries. Of all Christian theologians, I believe Eckhart carved the deepest channel into the sea of peace, which is the Self.

Notice how radical Eckhart's theology of the birth of the Word of God is: by *transformed* knowledge, he means *supernatural knowing*, knowing that comes down to you from Heaven above because of your humility. Absolute knowledge comes to us when the soul dies and is dissolved completely into God-consciousness. Then the Self may be born in your soul and you may become the person you were destined to be. I had a dream while I was writing this part of the book that I want to share because it concerns my mother, who is now suffering from Alzheimer's and is no longer with us in focused consciousness, although her spirit it still present, in her beautiful smile and eyes.

I was sitting across from my mother and looking into her eyes and I felt a profound gratitude well up inside of me at the simple thought of how much joy and meaning she had felt in hiding those wonderful Easter eggs! This memory brought tears to my eyes.

I had no idea what this simple ritual actually meant as a child until I recently looked into it. The Easter egg symbolizes the empty tomb of Christ, which was found by Mary Magdalene, from whom my mother received her Catholic name, Madeline. That's where her Catholicism leapt out from the core of her catholic soul, hidden in her school trauma: her *ecstasy* in being a mother and a post-Christian woman who was in search of her new identity in California was archetypally Catholic, despite her collision with the Church. It was a fate she could not escape even though she had lost her faith. That dream was *healing*. In a certain sense, my destiny has been the reverse of Jung's: I have become more Christian, not less Christian in my coming of age. I did not have a father who was a minister. I had parents who had fled their faiths, and I had to rediscover my Catholic and Lutheran roots.

Knowledge that is inborn and innate is ready for use. This was archetypal knowledge and archetypal *knowing* that flowed directly into me in the dream from the ground of her being ancestrally from France, where the Grail Quest had once flourished. Being that was in God became God's being in us children, whether we were practicing Christians or not. It was a direct transmission from the Christ archetype: eruptive ecstasy from our French national psyche. Finding Easter eggs also helped me learn to discriminate between good and evil. Those chocolate eggs were pure goodness. Although all that sinful sugar was terrible for our developing teeth!

Discriminating Between the Opposites from Above

Discriminative knowledge is what led me to do good as opposed to evil. To do good, however, I had to know what evil is. The worst evils in human nature are what are done mostly by men in wars, colonization, and economic exploitation of Mother Nature, but women too are capable of evil, such as the Franciscan nuns who beat my mother. It was Jung who exposed the primal fact of human nature in his lifetime more than any other physician of the human soul: *the empirical fact of our imperfection and evil*. He exposed the shadow side of European civilization he was born into like no one else. He fought a valiant fight against the shadow and evil in his lifetime, with his sword of truth. He made some errors in his actions, words, and deeds, like we all do, yet his vocation as a psychiatrist and teacher and writer was always directed toward the good of humanity: *healing* humanity from its tendency to split good and evil in dualistic ways. Splitting is an undeniable *psychological reality*. Jung worked tirelessly as a peacemaker, like Eckhart did.

Theologians with shortsightedness and a lack of awareness of their own shadows were not only unable but unwilling to follow Jung in his lifetime because it would have amounted to a theological confession that no one is perfect, not even Jesus, or a Saint, a puncturing of the ideal we have been spoon fed to cherish about the God-man. As the son of a Swiss protestant parson of the Zwinglian Church, Jung was profoundly influenced by splits in his Christian psyche, which were made transparent in the actions of Luther, Calvin, and the Reformation movement and the Thirty Years' War, which had nothing to do with the goodness of God, or *being peaceful Christians*. If Luther used his sword to incite Christians to burn down synagogues and persecute Jews, he was no preacher of truth the way Eckhart was. Ironically, Luther lived in the *Augustinerkloster,* St. Augustine's Monastery, in Erfurt, between 1505–1511. It was there in Eckhart's city that he had his first conflict of conscience that led him to enter the monastery as a friar. The monastery, now a world UNESCO heritage site, was built between 1277 and 1340, so Eckhart was well aware of its presence since he was a fan of Augustine.

Whether there is absolute evil in God is an important question I'll tackle in this book. Jung thought he had enough evidence to assert that evil in God was true only as a human judgment, not as a substance. I want to make it clear at the start that the main problem in global affairs is the split between good and evil, violence and nonviolence, harm and no-harm, which is the central source for all coming evils; using the sword as a spiritual symbol for higher discrimination, or as a physical weapon, to injure others is the choice we are all faced with; if we side with the war option on political or national grounds we are colluding with evil. This is what our forefathers did in the United States to Indigenous peoples on their bloody trail westward, to the very ground on which I sit, or stand; the American earth is saturated with innocent blood, the very blood of Christ. I see no difference, since it is the same red blood running from the Creator.

Eckhart lived a virtuous life. His suffering went deep. He carried the Cross of the Redeemer so that we might all learn to die to our egos by picking up our own cross in a living symbolic life, not as a dead sign. *We could all benefit today, I feel, from a good dose of Eckhart's medicine.* He spent his entire lifetime trying to lead listeners to become more spiritually aware of the birth of the Holy Spirit within us, an evolving panorama that is forever in process.

CHAPTER 8

FOUR STAGES OF ANIMA AND ANIMUS DEVELOPMENT IN JUNG'S WORKS

Before moving into the rest of the book, it's important to note Jung's stages of anima development as they relate to Eckhart's four levels of the soul. Understanding these ideas will inform the chapters that follow in Parts II and III. As Jung pointed out, there are essentially *four stages of eroticism* that were quite well-known in the late classical period. These four stages Jung divided into a vertical axis, from bottom to top this way:

4) Sophia (*Sapientia*)
3) The Virgin Mary
2) Helen of Troy
1) Hawwah (Eve)

The names may be exchanged for other cultural variants, times, and places, yet the ordering of lower to higher stages is what is most significant here because there is a similar hierarchy of soul types in Eckhart's theology, as you'll see in the next chapter. Jung wrote about these four levels of the soul as such:

> As the nomenclature shows, we are dealing with the
> heterosexual Eros or anima-figure in four stages, and

consequently with the four stages of the Eros cult. The first stage—Hawwah, Eve, earth—is purely biological; woman is equated with the mother and only represents something to be fertilized. The second stage is still dominated by the sexual Eros, but on an aesthetic and romantic level where woman has already acquired some value as an individual. The third stage raises Eros to the heights of religious devotion and thus spiritualizes him: Hawwah has been replaced by spiritual motherhood. Finally, the fourth stage illustrates something which unexpectedly goes beyond an almost unsurpassable third stage: *Sapientia*.[85]

Thus, in the language of vocational psychology, giving birth in the transference to a patient's vocation is made possible by a kind of anima-relatedness and creativity that Jung called *spiritual motherhood*. This is the third stage of Eros development, which represents a kind of affect attunement by an analyst to a patient's inner voice, the archetype of one's innate destiny-pattern, which leaves the first sexual stage behind for strivings of a more spiritualized soul-image that is in transit toward a higher stratum of Wisdom. Such attunements to spiritual mothering can help a person transform their sexual libido into the even higher achievements of *Sapientia*.

Anyone who has studied Eckhart's vernacular sermons in-depth can see the analogy with the third stage, in the frequent emphasis he placed on men and women becoming *mothers of God* (or in Jung's nomenclature, spiritual motherhood). The fourth stage, in Jung's view, involved bearing God's Word, or the Holy Spirit, the Paraclete (John 14:16), which was equivalent to Wisdom in Eckhart's typology. Wrote Jung: "Eckhart speaks of God's birth as a continual process."[86]

It is not altogether clear how much we can credit Eckhart with having influenced Jung's thinking regarding the third and fourth levels of evolution in the transformation of the soul-image into God (Sophia

= God's wife or consort). It was a common trope in alchemy, natural philosophy, theology, and medieval poetry, as Jung points out. Yet, when considering the fact that Jung began reading Eckhart at the age of fifteen, and his own anima development had been lifted up by him during his theological debates with his father, it's not too difficult to prove the significance Eckhart played in Jung's psychological development as a *transference figure of great religious creativity.*

The thirteenth century was a time when the worship of the Virgin Mary was at its zenith. What Eckhart was so often dispensing in his sermons as a preacher of God's Word was the *medicine* symbolized by Mary and Sophia. It was not mere head-knowledge in the cranium, as was the case in so many of his more dry and cerebral contemporaries. It was pure *experiential* knowledge spoken from his wisdom-body and his emotional center—his heart united with a soaring intellect.

"Do we delude ourselves," asked Jung, "in thinking that we possess and control our own psyches, and is what sciences calls the 'psyche' not just a question mark arbitrarily confined within the skull, but rather a door that opens upon the human world from the world beyond, allowing unknown and mysterious powers to carry him on the wings of night to a more than personal destiny?"[87]

FOUR LEVELS OF THE SOUL IN ECKHART'S THEOLOGY

Eckhart's ordering of the soul's powers, or anima-types into four levels was, in a certain sense, complementary to Jung's. I am bringing this fact forward in postmodernity because it has been completely overlooked by Eckhart scholars and because it adds empirical validity to Jung's theory of the anima, which I reviewed in the last chapter. It also confirms for Jungians and Christian theologians alike that Eckhart's way of relating to the soul anticipated analytical psychology by over six hundred years. Of course, their ways of relating to the anima were different, yet it will show the reader how the medieval monk handled problems of projection of the soul-image and seduction by the sensual anima, particularly sex and temptations to enact violence or succumb to evil.

Eckhart placed Sophia on the topmost strata, the highest fourth level or what I've called his *Wipfel-Weib*, "treetop wife," or Wisdom.[88] He assigned to her the personified name of Martha from Luke (10:38). Moreover, in Sermon 88 he also called this highest soul-power Leah, Jacob's wife, who in the Book of Genesis bore him seven children. Leah or Martha could ascend or descend through her worldly wisdom to any of the four levels as a kind of mediator to Sophia, a principle of individuation in the soul's evolution. The Virgin, Mary, was placed at the third level. At the second level was the biblical figure of Mary, Martha's younger sister, or Rachael, Jacob's second wife and Leah's younger sister in the Old Testament. Eve was portrayed at the bottom, with her counterpart: the Serpent.

4) Wisdom, Sophia, or *true detachment*; Martha or Leah, representing the *active life*, worldly maturity and wisdom of age

3) The Virgin Mary who *bears* the Divine child (Son) in humanity with the Father and the Holy Ghost

2) Mary, Martha's younger sister, or Rachel, Leah's younger sister, who both represent the *contemplative* life; at its highest level she can become so empty that she ascends up to the Seraphim, as a virgin-wife

1) Eve and the Serpent

Heaven was at level 4 and the Ground at level 1. The figure of Wisdom was personified as *Sapientia Dei*. Eckhart's many scriptural references to Wisdom came primarily from his readings of Proverbs, Ecclesiastes, the Wisdom of Solomon, John, Luke, and also from *pure phenomenal experience of his anima at all four stages, what Jung called the archetype of life.* She was often interpreted as being equivalent with Christ, or the preexistent Logos at her highest level. Wisdom was, to Eckhart, the supernatural-practical complement to the Trinity in dynamic action: the all-masculine God-image, which was in the process of personal and cultural transformation when the Dominican came of age as a theologian and preacher in Erfurt, needed a feminine counterpart to complement the Father, Son, and Holy Spirit, which were all traditionally masculine. Martha and Leah were more grounded and worldly wise than the two Marys, who were both "virgins." Eckhart said: the "true life of Leah" was the "active life which is set in motion in the ground of the soul by the touch of the Holy Ghost."[89]

The four soul-levels, with Wisdom subsuming them, became for Eckhart the doorway to the fourth principle of wholeness, the Self: the *medicine* to cure the Church of its overly patriarchal emphasis and obsession with sin. In Eckhart's Latin treatises and vernacular sermons on the birth (*Geburt*) of God in the soul we can hear him engaging in what Thomas Aquinas referred to as "perfect prophecy" from Wisdom: "when a man knows he is being moved by the Holy Ghost."[90] Eckhart *knew* he was being moved by the Paraclete (John 14:26) through frequent transmissions he was receiving while speaking as a *preacher* and *teacher* of the Word.

What Eckhart added to Dominican theology during his time was a working formula for four distinct soul types and an inner awareness that he was identical at times not only with the Trinity, but also with Sophia, the Virgin Mary, Martha, Leah, Rachel, and also, most importantly for the theology of his era, in *conversation* with the Serpent and Eve. This makes up *seven* aspects of the archetypal feminine, or "one-continuum" in the Judeo-Christian psyche. The idea of one-continuum comes from Marie-Louise von Franz's book *Number and Time*.[91] This continuum always remains the same and is based upon natural numbers "in which every individual number represents the continuum in its entirety."[92] It can be compared to a "field" in which "individual numbers represent activated points."[93]

To explain it, von Franz turned to Maria Prophetissa's alchemical axiom: "Out of One comes Two, out of Two comes Three, and from the Third comes the One as the Fourth." As Marie-Louise von Franz wrote, the "one-continuum which runs through all of them. From this viewpoint all numbers are simply qualitatively differentiated manifestations of the primal one."[94] This oneness corresponds to the fourth level Eckhart spoke from as the voice of Wisdom. Moreover "each number must be thought of as containing a specific activity that streams forth like a field of force. From this standpoint numbers signify different rhythmic configurations of the one-continuum."[95] The qualitative rhythm of the one-continuum is what assigns the aspect of meaning assigned to each number.[96]

This dynamic process of interpenetration between quantitative and qualitative aspects of numbers is seen in Eckhart's four soul types and their corresponding *seven* personifications, which are all subsumed by the One, which is Wisdom. In Eckhartian theological terms, Maria's axiom would read: *Out of the Oneness of the Father comes the Son, out of the Son's Oneness comes the Holy Spirit, and from the Oneness of the Trinity comes Sophia as the One as the Fourth.* Within this fourfold formula are contained the seven soul-sisters, Jewish and Christian, who are all parts of the one-continuum in the *Ground* out of which everything comes into being and passes away again like the multiple fragments of a dream.

Eckhart broke conventional bounds in his verses by embodying a *fourth* way, or path of earthly and spiritual knowing and experiencing *life* and being moved in the light by the Trinity in relationship to his whole Self. This included the feminine figure of the Self, which was inclusive of instinctive power (Snake) and the eternal Wisdom of the higher masculine-feminine totality. Wisdom was for Eckhart, as it was for Jung and the alchemists he studied, including St. Albert, *equivalent* with the archetype of the Self because *She* was an active, living part of the Jewish and Catholic anima structures within Western culture and civilization.[97] This Self-figure, Sophia, included the chthonic dimensions of the earth, the five senses, and the human body and spirit. In other words, as the *fourth figure* Sophia contained all levels of the soul in a four-continuum masculine-feminine Self structure of what I've termed (using Eckhart's vernacular) a *Wisdom-Wipfel-Weib-Martha-Leah*, a natural and supernatural consciousness and being of a masculine-feminine Anthropos. The Anthropos is the Cosmic Self in the Universe, the deepest substratum of the objective psyche, or the Cosmic Woman or Man in the primal Ground of all Existence.

What Eckhart really *meant* theologically by the birth of God, Christ, or the Paraclete (John 15:26) within did not always correspond

67

with what Jung *meant* when he used the same terms psychologically. The inner Christ, according to Jung, was not the outer historical Jesus, but the *homo totus* or philosopher's stone, the Self within, which was sometimes equated with the Emerald tablet of Hermes Trismegistus and could be found everywhere at any time *only* by the wise.[98]

According to Eckhart's four-tiered soul-theology, the spiritual marriage at the third level (Mary) was to take place, in Jung's language, as a "trans-subjective union of archetypal figures"[99] within. Its goal was complete individuation—or as complete as one could possibly become during the spirit of the times in which one lived.

An important difference between Eckhart and Jung was that for the Dominican, total transformation involved an ever-repeated inner birth of the Trinity in the higher levels of the soul, Mary and Sophia, whereas the higher person in their soul did not drop down to the level of Eve; they stayed higher up, and left the lower person, including sex, to those with genuine callings to a mate through the sacrament of marriage. Moreover, the higher person was not to abase themselves to the level of the serpent. The serpent could be raised up to *converse* with Eve in the higher levels of the soul, however, beginning with level 2: "And as Moses lifted up the serpent in the wilderness, even so must the Son of man be lifted up" (John 3:14).

While today the anima at all four levels of evolution serves as a birthplace for the Self's essential wholeness in humans, in Eckhart, the first level, needed to be lifted up to at least the second level of inner purity where an inner *dialogue* could take place between Eve and the Serpent. This did not mean that Eckhart was a spiritual man whose feet never touched the ground. On the contrary, he was grounded to the utmost because he stressed the centrality of the Godhead in his theology as the place of the birth. As Jung pointed out in his "Relativity" essay:

> Eckhart distinguishes between God and the Godhead.
> Godhead is All, neither knowing nor possessing itself,

whereas God is a function of the soul, just as the soul is a function of the Godhead. Godhead is obviously all-pervading creative power or, in psychological terms, self-generating creative instinct, that neither knows nor possesses itself, comparable to Schopenhauer's universal Will. But God appears as issuing forth from the Godhead and the soul.[100]

Indeed, what we hear in the words of Eckhart is not Christ-Wisdom alone. It is also eruptive and instinctively infused wisdom from the doorway of God's house, earth-Wisdom, that is, preached from the soul's Ground. The place of the Self's *explosive power*, sensuality, and exquisite Love was the place of God's most passionate "kiss." As Eckhart wrote in his Latin *Commentary on Exodus*, "'Life' expresses a type of 'pushing out' by which something swells up in itself and first breaks out totally in itself, each part into each part, before it pours itself forth and 'boils over' on the outside. This is why the emanation of the persons in the Godhead is the prior ground of creation."[101]

Moreover, in his Latin *Commentary on Genesis,* Eve and the Serpent were said to unite through a *colloquy* at the center of the superior and inferior functions (intuition and sensation). Although "evil" had been traditionally projected onto sexuality, women, or Satan, Eckhart did not use the term *Satan* in speaking about the Serpent and Eve. Rather, he included the dark side of animal instinct, the shadow, matter, and the human body at a point of *intersection* in the soul, where consciousness provided the necessary understandings for the transformations of the opposites of sins and virtues into the archetypal figure of Martha-Leah, which left no level of psyche out of his equation, including the two Marys and Eve.

He posited a theory of types that is complementary to Jung's: "It will also be evident how the serpent, namely the sensitive faculty, can truly and literally speak to the woman, that is, the inferior reason, and how that inferior rational faculty speaks with its superior and how this highest faculty speaks to God, as well as how God address all three."[102]

Here we have a portrait of Eckhart's psychological typology stated succinctly. I'm using typology, not in a traditional Jungian sense, but in post-Jungian Eckhartian sense. By typology I mean the different psychological and transcendental types in the human psyche, the levels of the soul, anima, or animus in a man or woman, that touches the primordial Ground that gives eternal birth to the Trinity. For Eckhart these meta-psychological soul types are crowned by the intellect, feeling, sensation, and intuition, which are all contained by Wisdom, the highest psychological and theological grace-infusing power capable of allowing us, if we are humble enough, to truly experience God, and speak His or Her Word from within.

In Part II, I get to the story in Luke 10:38, but first we need an understanding of the meaning of Eve. Not all of this was new as Eckhart was standing on the shoulders of Avicenna, Maimonides, Augustine, Albert, Aquinas, and many other great intellectuals. However, it must be noted that Thomas Aquinas was said to have "shunned sexuality" and even viewed it as "diabolical"[103]; whereas there is no evidence whatsoever of any of this kind of shadow projection of "evil" or the "devil" onto females, the serpent, or sexuality by Eckhart. (According to von Franz, Aquinas saw women as an aberration of nature.[104] Might this explain why Jung could not read Aquinas and felt his overly intellectual writings left him feeling "cold" and "lifeless as a desert"?)[105] Eckhart was a celibate and practiced chastity, but he was no prude and had the utmost prudence. This shows, to my mind, that Eckhart had a far more harmonious and refined relationship to his anima than what we find in his Dominican predecessor who sadly shunned women as inferiors. To his credit, Eckhart venerated women as equals.[106]

According to Jung's psychology of individuation, when the anima is projected onto matter she is captured in an unredeemed state and cannot be recognized as a *psychic function of relationship* within individuals; she is thereby transferred externally onto idealized figures, such as the Virgin Mary, the Church, or Sophia. Yet, as an overly intellectualized and idealized concept, such projections are the only safe places for veneration of women in Catholic theology, except in female nuns and saints.

Rather than seeing the soul as the place where total transformation can take place in the now, before Eckhart, the transformation process in the soul had historically to exclude Eve, evil, and the Serpent. Eckhart taught that the only correct way to relate to God was through the archetypes of Eve, Martha or Rachel,[107] the Virgin Mary, and Wisdom or Sophia as four soul types from a higher peak of order.[108]

Moreover, Eckhart was not merely preaching and teaching in Paris but also giving pragmatic instruction: right *feeling*, right *thinking*, right *sensing*, right *intuiting* through contemplation and action. "The serpent, the woman and the man describe and express the three principles of man ... in which the superior gazes on the inferior and vice versa."[109] Thus, the levels of the soul take a middle place of equality in the dialogue where upper and lower, superior and inferior "kiss" and embrace.

Eckhart's creative connection to all dimensions of his four soul types is what I called in my senior thesis at UCSC "The Recollection of the Self." It consisted of a total withdrawal of soul-projections by Eckhart—shadow, anima, and persona—which led to an awakening of the archetype of the Self, or Paraclete within. For Eckhart, women were the *real birth-givers,* and it could have been especially for females that his two sermons on Luke 10:38 were developed in Strasbourg or most probably in Cologne. Eckhart valued the vocation of birth-giving above all others, both in himself and others, men included. Our callings are constantly being born out of the Ground of the Godhead. This is perhaps the most important notion to grasp in Eckhart's theology. For in the *Grunt* "God passes away."[110] When this happens, the soul can *bear* the eternal Son from the same ground as the Father.

Of all the charismatic figures that emerged during what Joaquim of Flora had termed the Holy Ghost movement in Europe, Eckhart in Jung's view was the *forerunner* of modern analytical psychology because he strode past *belief* and literal readings of Christianity and emphasized instead the centrality of individual experience, of *life*, of birthing God or Christ within from the universal ground as a way to bring about complete change in individuals.[111] By the liberation of the soul from external projections and through a synthesis of the four figures of anima consciousness in service of one's destiny, one could give birth to the Holy Spirit. This kind of synthetic union or oneness with the opposites enabled Eckhart to embrace even the Serpent and Eve. For "we should also note that in the contact, meeting and union of what is essentially superior with the highest point of the inferior both sides kiss each other in a natural and essential love that is inward and very delightful."[112]

Eckhart diagrammed a *fourfold schema of anima consciousness* to connote points of contact between the soul's higher and lower powers, where the shadow, traditionally projected onto the Serpent, Eve, and women, could be *elevated* through a dialogue at the median point in his equation. This radical solution to the Christian problem of the projection of the shadow, sin, and evil was the *answer* he gave to the enigma of Christ, whose personality in the Four Gospels became more Divine than human.

In his new *humanized* theology of the Word, the earth as an aspect of *chthonic Wisdom* was personified by the ground, the Serpent, and Eve:

> "The serpent was more subtle than any of the beasts of the earth." It is evident that man's sensitive faculty signified by the serpent is more excellent than in any other animal produced on earth. Man's sense-endowed body has a more delicate constitution than any other animal body. Men of delicate flesh are well endowed with intelligence, and the softer and more delicate a person's constitution, the greater the pleasure in the perception of the appropriate sense object.[113]

These passages reveal Eckhart's earthiness and sensuality as well as his delight in *all* of his rational and irrational functions while his inner "wife" (Martha-Leah) was "free and unfettered by attachment."[114] Eve was necessary as she was part of what was integrated into consciousness by the soul's higher powers. This allowed Eckhart to engage in what Jung called the *transcendent function*, produced through the thesis and antithesis and achieved through active imagination. Wrote Eckhart: "'Imagination is a movement produced by sensation.' All the premises from the first to last make it necessary for the integrity of man that he have a sensitive faculty. The sensitive faculty is by nature under the intellective faculty."[115]

Thus, Eckhart's sensual anima needed to be *spiritualized* through an inner union of the Serpent and Eve with the higher soul-powers and Sophia in their *quaternary* complementarity to the Trinity. Right now, I am focusing on level 1 in his soul-strata. In the next chapter, the Mary-Martha story will make things clearer. First, he said in the Latin text: "The serpent, the woman and the man describe and express the three principles of man, namely the sensitive, the rational through participation, and the essentially rational in number, nature and properties."[116] In Eckhart, the connecting link between the rejected feminine and evil, Eve, was made by his perennial descent into the Ground and the inclusion of the Serpent in his dialogues with Mary and Martha as his "wife," who engaged him in his active and civic life in the world.

In Eckhart's theology of the birth of the Word, the Trinity was said to emanate from the Ground. What made Eckhart's theology so unique among his contemporaries is that he provided the Church with a potentially useful psychological method for raising the contents of the collective unconscious into consciousness and showed by way of metaphorical exegesis how an understanding of the chthonic powers (Serpent and Eve) could be raised through the integrative powers of a contemplative and active life into the soul's higher Wisdom.

Eckhart was describing certain dynamic processes of transformation within a *fourfold model of the Self in Anima,* where all four functions of consciousness were withdrawn from projection and recollected within through:

1) A *fertilization* of the feminine earth-soul, Eve and Martha-Leah by the Godhead's procreative and penetrative powers in the ground
2) Dialoguing with the Serpent and Eve, and raising of the fourth function into the higher faculties of the soul
3) *Becoming a mother of God* through inner union with the Virgin Mother
4) Ascent to *Scientia* (the higher science of God) or *Sapientia* (Wisdom), through the prayer of quiet and detachment

Only the combination of all four soul-stratifications produces the *Self* at the center and heart of the cross. The subtle difference in Eckhart's schema of the soul is that the Anthropos never fully descends through the shadow into Physis (serpent, sexuality, and aggressive instincts). The colloquy of Eve with the Serpent was *elevated* into higher states of anima integration. Mary or Rachel at stage two and the Virgin Mary at stage three ascended upward into Sophia. The inner person, or aristocrat, was not brought down into the shadow, sex, unconscious anger, or evil because the soul remained in a state of perpetual recollection through contemplation and prayer and mindful work, art, science, or vocation.

Nowadays, with the entrance of the sun into the constellation of Aquarius, we've entered the Age of the union of the opposites, of God and the Goddess in humanity as a whole, a task of synthesizing polarities in the psyche without any further ignorance by patriarchy in projecting the shadow of evil onto Eve, women, or the serpent, a psychological movement found in medieval theology but transformed totally in Eckhart's works. In Eckhart's day, on the other hand, the

Church had transferred its sins (shadow) onto "Joaquim of Flora as the teaching of Antichrist."[117]

Parvuli was the term given to the mendicant orders of monks, the Dominicans and Franciscans, who were, in Joaquim of Flora's vision of the future age of the Holy Ghost to build the *Ecclesia spiritualis*.[118] Eckhart fulfilled this vision most completely by giving voice to the Serpent and Eve in his own soul and by showing readers how a different theology could have evolved to keep the Church from splitting off the sensual anima, the shadow, and evil, but that hope was never fulfilled in his lifetime.

In Eckhart we see, in contrast to the projection of the shadow, the glorification of the feminine principle in his frequently used metaphors of the Ground, which can be equated with the earth, not only with Eve, spiritual motherhood, fruitfulness, and childbearing. As Marie-Louise von Franz rightly pointed out in *Aurora Consurgens*: the *ecclesia spiritualis* of Joaquim of Flora was supposed to have arisen in the *seventh age*, or the age of the monastic orders, when the sun and moon would be united.[119] This was a perfect symbol for the unification of opposites, or masculine and feminine polarities that we find everywhere turning green and leafing out in Eckhart's writings. It was not enough that this prediction was to be fulfilled in the monasteries alone since, as Jung said, the soul can *only truly* "live in and from human relationships."[120] That meant that some Catholic sisters and brothers had to leave their cloisters and monastic communities and break their vows to their orders, if they were to have a healthy sex life without having to hide it—or act it out tragically with parishioners and children. Still today this is a quandary for priests and nuns.

Thanks to Jung's 1921 essay "The Relativity of the God-Concept in Meister Eckhart" in *Psychological Types* it has been known now for over one hundred years that the Dominican was the first Western-Christian figure in whose works the Self began to play a major role in Medieval Europe. In Jung's understanding, the birth of Christ within was not the same as the birth of the historical Christ-image. "In the world of Christian ideas," Jung wrote, "Christ undoubtedly represents the self. As the apotheosis of individuality, the self has the attributes of uniqueness and of occurring once only in time."[121] Eckhart's theology agrees with this central idea concerning Christ's uniqueness and never-again-to-be-witnessed miracle of the divine drama upon the earth. Like Jung, Eckhart did not teach the imitation of Christ, but becoming Christlike, expressing one's own God-given individuality with humility.

Such passages by Jung might at first glance suggest that the Self and the Christ-image were equivalents, but nothing could be further from the truth of his science. In a pre-psychological age, Jung argued, "Christ did not merely *symbolize* wholeness, but, as a psychic phenomenon, he *was* wholeness. This is proved by the symbolism as well as by the phenomenology of the past, for which—be it noted—evil was a *privatio boni*. The idea of totality is, at any given time, as total as one is oneself."[122]

In *Aion* Jung analyzed the Christ myth as an astrological prediction with cosmic significance for the future of a psychology of religion. Moreover, the approach of the sun into the zodiacal constellation Aquarius signified the coming into consciousness of the deity in humanity as a whole, or what Jung called the "Christification of many" through a continuing indwelling of the Holy Ghost.[123]

Jung argued that the myth of perfection Christ represented was no longer valid as a representation for the Self in modernity because evil, violence, and the animal side of the libido were not included. The shadow side of God was split off and projected onto the Serpent, Satan, the Devil, or Antichrist. To be sure, Jung's God-concept was more instinctive, earthy, inclusive of sin and evil than Eckhart's ever was, although he was fond of quoting Eckhart's statement that "God is not good." Yet, nowhere in his works did Eckhart say *God is evil*. For Eckhart, God was and continues to be "above all." [124] Thus, I will hazard the following formula that the Self was closer to the myth of perfection in Eckhart's day than wholeness, whereas the Self-image we wholeheartedly embrace today is fortunately, or unfortunately, depending on one's conscious relationship to the Light, a lot darker. Eckhart lived at a very high level in Wisdom and God's Light. Transcendence is no longer so Absolute as it was in Eckhart's day.

Eckhart's understanding of Sophia was closer to the treetop, closer to the superconscious, than to the hell below God's house. Jung appears to have lived closer to the primal affects than Eckhart and Jung's anger was certainly more ego-syntonic than dystonic, more volcanic, explosive. Eckhart was more virtuous and lived closer to the ideal of perfection, the seven cardinal virtues, Wisdom and seraphim. He was more transcendent in his everyday life, saintlier, and closer to the Absolute than to relative existence. This is why it is impossible to equate the birth of the Christ-image in the human soul with the birth of the Self as we understand it in postmodernity. On the other hand, for both Eckhart and Jung, the birth of the Paraclete in the human soul was the factor in the conscious evolution of the Now of Creation.

Something to keep in mind for readers is that Eckhart's theology was *both* relative and Absolute. For about God he said: He/She (Sophia, Christ, Wisdom) "is absolutely the Absolute."[125] The Absolute is spread throughout the entire Universe. It is a Cosmic Intelligence that is in charge of everything: "the principal activity of the Intellect is in charge of the whole universe."[126] Not only the universe within, but also the Universe without too. The charismatic preacher of the Word traced the Imprinter to taproot and achieved a vertical ascent in his soul's highest powers.

Eckhart was not an institutional preacher of God's Word; he was a charismatic, autochthonic speaker of practical theology. He spoke relative and Absolute truths, a supreme union of psychology and metaphysics. The Ground was a synonym for nature and the Godhead, and hence, pantheism and panentheism were united into one synthesis of *pan-panentheism*: God in Nature and Nature in God: "All things are in God as in the First Cause in an intellectual way and in the Mind of the Maker."[127] Moreover, by interpreting the Savior's words, "The kingdom of heaven suffers violence, and the violent take it by force"

(Mt 11:12), Eckhart was insisting that *force* and violence are also vital parts of God and the God-image that have to be integrated in the soul along with the serpent through imagination, not negative affect.

"It was not until after the time that the disciples received the Holy Spirit that they began to perform virtuous deeds."[128] The "living water of the Holy Ghost is only granted to those that dwell in the intellect." What did Eckhart mean by intellect? Intellect is Wisdom or Cosmic Intelligence. "Intellect," he explained, "is the highest part of the soul, where she [the Holy Ghost, Sophia] dwells in community with angels in angelic nature. Angelic nature is not in contact with time, nor is the intellect which is the man in the soul: it is free from time. If the man is not living there, the son dies."[129] Thus, the Son lives in the higher powers of the soul while suffering in the lower powers. This union of the Christ-image with the total Self produces the indwelling of the Paraclete in a truly psychological way that prospectively anticipated postmodernity. "God is ever at work in the eternal now, and his work is the begetting of his Son: He is bringing Him forth all the time."[130]

Eckhart preached further: "Now see: God the father has perfect insight into Himself, profound and thorough knowledge of Himself by Himself, and not through any image."[131] To be sure, this is a very different theology than Jung's psychological vision in *Answer to Job*. Eckhart's view of Christ's birth within is far brighter. On the other hand, Eckhart was a maverick when it came to holding to his own positions on matters of prayer, which formed an intimate and regular part of Dominican life. For instance, about the payer of silence, he said:

> Those who pray for anything but God or to do with God, pray wrongly: when I pray for nothing, then I pray rightly, and that prayer is proper and powerful. But if anyone prays for anything else, he is praying to a false God, and one might say this was sheer heresy. I never pray so well as when I pray for nothing and for nobody, not for Heinrich or Konrad. Those who pray

truly pray to God in truth and in spirit, that is to say,
in the Holy Ghost.[132]

Praying in truth in the Holy Ghost is praying with the right
inhalation and exhalation, the breath of the Counselor (John 16:7).
Speaking the Word through the Paraclete meant a post-Christocentric
type of speech, preaching with the breath of God out of a vocalizing
function in the soul *after* Christ. Eckhart, like Jung, had his own inner
Wisdom to transmit and some of it was entirely innovative because that
is the true meaning of the Advocate (John 14:16).

Interestingly, Jung agreed with Eckhart on this point: it is a
psychological fact that letting go of oneself and of all God-images was
instrumental in inspiring the new path Jung discovered that he called
active imagination. The teaching of the Paraclete that was promised
to the disciples after the departure of Jesus is what Eckhart and Jung
both embodied in their lifetimes, each in their own ways.

The Self in Jung's model was the *totality* of subconsciousness
and the superconsciousness, the infrared to ultraviolet spectrums of
consciousness. Few people exist at levels of consciousness where seraph
and snake can live together side by side, like Jung did. Individuation
today requires the highest possible integration of the shadow and soul
into the superstructure of unitary conscience in the Aquarian Age. This
means an awareness and acceptance of our sins as well as our virtues,
good and evil, into the vessels of our consciousness.

With his superior intuitive thinking, Eckhart gave Jung a sword
to duel with his father intellectually in adolescence, particularly on
the issues of God's alleged goodness, which Eckhart said was only a
garment of God: "Goodness is a garment by which God is hidden."[133]
God's pure *naked being* was for Eckhart forever undefinable,
unfathomable, unreachable, and any of the names of God missed the
mark: "The intellect [intuition, Sophia] pulls off the coat from God
and perceives him bare, as he is stripped of goodness and of being and
of all names."[134]

79

PART II

ECKHART'S CALLING AS A DOMINICAN PREACHER AND TEACHER

CHAPTER 10

THE MARY-MARTHA STORY

I will begin my discussion on Eckhart's theology with the Mary-Martha story as he understood it in his meditations on Luke (10:38). Eckhart tells us that in the story told by Luke in the Gospels, Jesus was received by a woman named Martha, who had a younger sister named Mary. Mary "sat at the Lord's feet," enamored, her soul possessed with bliss over the great goodness of God. She sat there admiring Him with unspeakable "longing" and "desire." In contrast, her worldly-wise sister, Martha, knew what her true vocation (*Gewerbe*) was. In analytical-psychological terms, Mary was projecting the archetype of the Self onto Christ. She had not withdrawn her idealization of God from him in the transference. Therefore, she sat there captured by him while Martha was in service to her Lord. Eckhart preached that Martha was of a "mature age and fully trained in work." She thought nobody else could do her work of service to Him as perfectly as love had ordained. Therefore, with great dignity for her beloved guest, she served him. Eckhart said Martha had lived long and well and *life* had given her the finest understanding, for "life makes one known to oneself."[135] Martha was certainly more grounded in herself than Mary was. She was earthlier and more spiritual and embodied Wisdom.

It seems clear that Eckhart was making up a story about his own soul types here, one a *virgin*, the other his *wife*. The story provides a basic metaphor for the central plot, which is his theology of a vocation of the Self, or a life-long devotion to following one's calling into the light of God within and without. To sit at the Lord's feet enamored with Him meant that Mary was in awe, captivated, and in bliss. She took sensual satisfaction and delighted in taking excess pleasure in the words of Jesus, which possessed her. She was apparently spellbound by Christ, and all of these variables—longing, desire, satisfaction, pleasure—are all indicative of sensuality and passionate intensity, without higher spiritual understanding. Mary did not know what her future profession was. She was spiritually confused by the presence of Christ, perhaps even mesmerized, so Martha instructed Jesus "tell her then to help me." In contrast, Martha was earthly wise, for "Martha knew Mary better than Mary knew Martha."[136] This is because Martha knew who she was and knew her work and her calling in time, her trade. Her light was her vocation and her vocation to serve others was her light (licht).[137] Martha was so grounded in her instinctive and spiritual essence that her work in service to the Word did not hinder her in the least.

The meaning of the Mary-Martha story was amplified further by Eckhart in sermon 8 in the Walsche text, where Eckhart quoted Luke (10:38): "Our Lord Jesus Christ went up into a citadel and was received by a virgin who was a wife." In this sermon we can hear Eckhart's innovations. He said specifically: "a virgin is a person who is void of alien images, as empty as he was when he did not exist."[138] He continued:

> Now attend and follow me closely. If a man were to be ever virginal, he would bear no fruit. If he is to be fruitful, he must be a wife. "Wife" is the noblest title one can bestow on the soul—far nobler than "virgin" ... Many good gifts received in virginity, are not reborn back into God with wifely fruitfulness and

with praise and thanks ... A virgin who is a wife is free
and unfettered by attachment; she is always as near to
God as to herself. She brings forth many and big fruits,
for they are neither more nor less than God Himself.[139]

The veneration he gave to the integration of Wisdom in Martha,
the fourth soul level in his typology is even more exquisite than the
love he felt for the Virgin Mary at level 3. This is truly extraordinary.
In Eckhart *den obersten Wipfel des Geistes,* the highest treetop[140] of
the Holy Spirit, became Wisdom incarnate, in *equality* with the Father,
the Son, and the Paraclete, which she *bore with* God in the highest
intellect. "Truly," he said, "in *this* power there is such great joy, such
vast unmeasured bliss that none can tell of it or reveal it fully."[141]

The main contrast between Eckhart's and Jung's conceptions of
the soul or anima is centered on the notion of *being* or what Jung called
esse (existence) in anima (soul): "What indeed is reality if it is not a
reality of *esse in anima?*"[142] Jung had read the story of Meister Eckhart's
"daughter," the divine maiden, or anima in the preacher.[143] However, it
is doubtful he was aware of the seven soul-levels in Eckhart's theology
since his reading was limited owing to the lack of a fuller survey of the
Master's works during his times.

I want to leave you with one idea before proceeding any further,
however: the "third path" to awakening that Eckhart called "being-at-
home."[144] What did this mean? Being-at-home meant: *esse in anima.*
For Eckhart it connoted Absolute Existence, or *esse in anima* in a
higher transpersonal or supernatural sense, *being* in the Higher Self,
not the lower levels of the soul. For Jung, as you will see in Part III,
existence in the anima meant being-at-home in all four levels. For
Eckhart *esse in anima* was to be lived in levels 2–4, not in level 1, which
included the Serpent and Eve. Christ called us to come up higher and
serve him, in Eckhart's story, as his *weib-im-Wipfel.* Martha asked
Jesus to tell Mary to get up from worshiping him at his feet and serve

him in a higher light as a virgin-wife: *seeing* with God's singleness of vision the *purpose* for which our souls are meant to follow to profess our own Truth in Christ, Light in Christ, and Way in Christ. The wifely soul who was spiritually married in Martha and Christ was Wisdom in her four aspects.

CHAPTER 11

SPIRITUAL MOTHERHOOD AND THE BIRTH OF THE PARACLETE

Meister Eckhart went through four transitions during his life. The first transit from childhood to maturity was in Gotha and Erfurt: from birth to initiation into his religious order at age fifteen (1260–1275). The second was during his rapid rise to prominence as prior of Erfurt and renowned lecturer of theology in Paris (1275–1313); the third and fourth transitions occurred in Strasbourg and Cologne, after Eckhart let go two tenures as an esteemed chaired professor, lecturer, and scholar of biblical theology for the Order of Preachers (OP) at the Parisian University.

Since this chapter focuses on a core idea of my book, the birth of the Paraclete in the human soul, it is by far the lengthiest and perhaps most challenging for the reader. It provides an overview of many of the most central ideas in this book concerning Eckhart's transformation and his defense against heresy as well as some of my own interpretations of the Bible including Eckhart's ideas on becoming mothers of God and giving birth. I have divided the chapter into thirteen sections in which I break down the overall themes of the book.

Eckhart's Intimate Work with Nuns and Beguines

Goddess worship was *emergent* in many cities in Europe during Eckhart's lifetime, almost triumphant over the Son. Some of the changes were no doubt being called for by the increasing number of nuns in the Catholic convents that Eckhart counseled. He also counseled the *Beguines,* religious women who lived together in *beguinages,* or women-houses but did not take any formal vows.

Eckhart was in charge of administering to Dominican friars and women-houses in Strasbourg as "vicar general" of Teutonia when a remarkable transformation began to happen in Eckhart's soul. A spiritual metamorphosis inspired by an excited archetypal nucleus suddenly seized him and fastidiously determined his fate for good or for ill. It was the emergence of the archetype of the Divine Child, the Divine Son of the Virgin Mother, and also the humanized *Son of Sophia,* the Counselor that is present in everyone: the universal archetype of the child of God. This imprint had been almost invariably projected outward onto the Church and Mary and the birth of Jesus, as it still is, for the most part, in traditional Christianity. To be sure, this was an archetype of excessive purity that had the potential to change anyone who came into unmediated contact with it, such as during annual Christmastime worship, and it's among the most significant of all archetypes in the collective human psyche: the archetype of the Divine Mother and her Chosen Son.

As an *antidote* to toxic patriarchy touted by traditional Christianity, we all have an inner child of divinization that calls out to us for fulfillment from within. The aim of the greatest Dominican preacher was extraordinary: to unite the patriarchal religions of the Old and New Testaments with a new dispensation[145] of the feminine based on continuous birthing of the Paraclete in collective humanity, whereby each person can potentially become not only a child of God, or imitation of Jesus, but also a *mother of God within* and transmitter of holy Wisdom.

Any of us, if we follow Eckhart's practical instructions, could lie in the childbed with the Virgin Mother and give birth to the archetype of God, for we are all, at the highest levels of divinization, not only Christlike, but also the same Son of the Father and Mother of all Creation: God and Sophia.

This was dangerously heretical when Eckhart preached this practical lesson of direct experience in the Cathedral of Our Lady in 1318. His theology (of gestation, relating to women as *equals*, birthing of the Word, and *becoming mothers of God*) was so revolutionary and so new that it was obviously unorthodox. No one could properly understand him in his day and still today, some theologians struggle to explain to laypeople what he meant. Nevertheless, by reading the Latin and German works, side by side, it becomes clear that what Eckhart preached was the truth of the Holy Scriptures, which he knew as well as any of the saints.

The Calling to Write a Great Three-Part-Work

In the third part of his great *Opus Tripartitum* or *Three-Part-Work*, which he let go of in Paris when he sacrificed his career for his primary vocation as a preacher, he made it clear that he had gone over the Old and New Testaments from beginning to end and had given his interpretations freely stated in prose. In his *Commentary on Genesis*, he quoted from the first chapter of John that stated simply "'In the principle was the Word' (the Greek has 'Logos,' that is, reason)."[146] Eckhart made it clear that the birth of the child as the principal (Logos, Word, or archetype, which is derived from Neoplatonism) is equivalent with the birth of Wisdom.

Thus, stated in psychological terms, Eckhart was saying in medieval language that the child archetype in us is vulnerable to being *infected* with the wrong ideas, and therefore it needs proper education, provided for by the Church, with regard to what level of the soul is the most optimal to human health, which is to dwell in Wisdom. This was the same essential teaching of Krishna in the *Bhagavad Gita*, only Wisdom had another name: the Goddess Sarasvati.

However, for Eckhart the movement toward Wisdom meant proper theology and right spiritual practice: right feeling, right sensing, right intuition, and right thinking. How he came into his profession in the Order of Preachers in Erfurt is somewhat unknown, since we have little history from his early childhood and latency years. All we know for certain is that he joined the order during his midteens.

Eckhart's Waking Dream

I want to zero in on what, in my mind, is the most startling bit of evidence we have of Eckhart's authentic religious experience in Strasbourg in his third transitional period: his waking dream of God and the birth of Wisdom within.[147] This is what Eckhart had to say about the birth of Wisdom:

> When the soul is unified and there enters into total self-abnegation, then she finds God as in Nothing. It appeared to a man as in a dream—it was a waking dream—that he became pregnant with Nothing like a woman with child, and in that Nothing God was born; he was the fruit of nothing. God was born in the Nothing ... But as it is in the ground of my soul, there it is at its highest and noblest, *there* it is nothing but an image.[148]

Here we have moved beyond empirical psychology into the theological plane of the Absolute: "Wisdom comes into being from Nothing" (Job 28:12). Here, he is speaking about his spiritual motherhood and the birth of Wisdom out of the first and second stages of the soul into a new revelation of God out of Nothingness that surpassed all of the angels.

He became pregnant like a woman with child. The archetype of the child he gave birth to as a mother of God was not Jesus in the historical manger in Bethlehem, but an entirely new image of the Holy Spirit: a child born from Nothingness who was himself Sophia's child and above Mary. The three persons of the Trinity—the Father, Son, and Holy Ghost—became a fourth figure in Eckhart's soul, and following this fourth state he achieved the quintessence: God beyond God and Christ.

The Divine Feminine and Divine Masculine incarnated in a man's body in which the "All" was integrated as One. As it was in the Ground of his soul, in Eve or the Earth mother, there it was now born anew in him at its highest and noblest level; there, it was nothing but a new image of God in Holy Christendom. Of course, Buddha, whose experience went beyond *all* previous gods of Hinduism, had this same realization; it was the same experience, only Eckhart named it God's image.

Analysis of Eckhart's Dream of the Birth of God

So high a value did Eckhart place on the birth of the divine Word in the human soul that he did not hesitate to reveal to his listeners how this miracle of becoming *One* with Christ and the Self happened to him. In his *waking dream*, there is evidence for the birth of the Paraclete. Now I will further explore the meaning of that dream from a vocational angle and circumambulate around it a bit further, just as one might with the Jungian method of dream analysis to expose its deeper significance. Eckhart scholars have, for the most part, overlooked this dream. We owe a great debt of thanks to Walsche's translation of *The Complete Mystical Works of Meister Eckhart* for drawing our close attention to it in an endnote to his text, which is easy to overlook. He wrote explicitly: this is a "record of a personal experience."[149]

This was without doubt a *calling dream because some of his most important theological principles were evoked by it.* A *calling dream* is a dream of vocation, a vision, or fantasy thinking that comes from the superconscious as a *call to action.* We all have the potential to give birth to vocation, whether in mathematics, science, music, psychology, art, music, computer science, engineering, architecture, or any other sacred work. In the career field of the preacher, the vehicle of the calling is through the Word made flesh: through *incarnation in the World.*

Dreams like this one came to Eckhart through visionary experiences (the actual date of it is uncertain). Eckhart described it this way: *"It appeared to a man as in a dream—it was a waking dream—that he became pregnant with Nothing like a woman with child, and in that Nothing God was born; He was the fruit of nothing. God was born in the Nothing."*[150]

Eckhart's anima became pregnant with Nothing. This woman within Eckhart was the highest level of his anima: *Wisdom.* The Self was born in him as a new revelation of God for the future benefit of humanity. In the Now, everything was pregnant with meaning and possibility, and everything was contained in him in a secret order or symmetry in one space-time continuum. Unity was pregnant and alive with significance in his blessed soul. How did this birth come about?

A man cannot attain to this birth except by withdrawing his senses from all things. And that requires a mighty effort to drive back the powers of the soul and inhibit their functioning. This must be done with force; without force it cannot be done. As Christ said, "The kingdom of heaven suffers violence, and the violent take it by force." (Mt 11:12)[151]

"Without force it cannot be done." Violence was the way to divine Wholeness, the fourth, Oneness, which emerged from the Ground of his soul. By violence, I mean *spiritual violence*, or the spiritualization of the primal energy into an experience that does not split the opposites and stays true to the inner voice that connects us to our instincts, our urge to individuate. The Goddess of the Universe is a powerful force, for She gave birth to the entire Cosmos in one Big Bang. This corresponds roughly with Eckhart's metaphors about the primal eruptive or explosive Ground of all being that births the eternal Word in us, whether one is a poet, a preacher, or a psychotherapist administering a talking cure as a powerful and potent nonviolent medicine.

The Self can be born in any of us—if we can become empty enough to become Nothing in the infinite abyss of the Godhead. The biblical source was the scripture of St. Luke (Acts 9:10). St. Augustine also commented on this passage. Yet in his typical intuitive way Eckhart transformed it into a theology that was not in existence before he spoke it: "All creatures are pure nothing. I do not say they are a trifle or they are anything: they are pure nothing."[152] In order to become who we are we must experience a death to the hero in midlife and accept crucifixion in the Now. "Unless you transcend world and time," he preached, "you will not see God."[153] This means that the soul must die to time on the cross before she can become a birth-giver. His censors did not like the sound of either of these statements. The first of the two sentences were condemned in article 26 of the Bull of 1329. Why? Before answering this question, I want to say more about typology and transcendence. By the term vocation of the Self in the subtitle of this book, I mean the totality of the four functions of consciousness that Jung posited for us in 1921: thinking, feeling, sensation, and intuition. These four functions are all running psychologically into a metaphysical ground of all empirical being. In Jung's 1916 essay "The Transcendent Function," he called the synthesis of the four psychological functions and two attitudes of introversion and extroversion "transcendent," yet he took all metaphysical considerations out of his hypothesis of the Self. This was limited, I feel, because it tried to reduce everything to psychology, including Eckhart's theology. In William James's model of the Self, I found a way out of the dilemma in Jung's theory of types. For in James's 1890 *Principles of Psychology* the fourth level of the Metaphysical Self subsumes all other selves in the conscious, subconscious, and superconscious integration of the total personality. My hypothesis herein therefore is that the Transcendental Self subsumes all other Selves in the human psyche, and this is the essential Source or Ground of all vocations in Eckhart's view.

Eckhart's typology as an intuitive-thinking type was part of what prevented the Holy See from being able to understand him because many theologians are thinking types. That is probably why I sometimes have such difficulty understanding some of them. Yet Eckhart could outthink the best of the best by following his intuitions, as Jung did. His intuition and thinking were unparalleled. Eckhart revered "the pure and naked power of the *intellect*, which the master's term receptive. Now mark my words!" he added sharply, as if he were speaking directly to his inquisitors: "It is only *above all this* that the soul grasps the pure absoluteness of free being, which has no location, which neither receives nor gives; it is bare 'self-identity' which is deprived of all being and all self-identity. *There* she grasps God nakedly as in the ground, where He is above all being."[154] His use of paradox is remarkable here.

In Sermon 70 he explained further:

> So, since God dwells eternally in the ground of the Father, and I in him, *one* ground and the same Christ, as a single bearer of my humanity, then this (humanity) is as much mine as his in one substance of eternal being, so that the being of both, body and soul, attain perfection in one Christ, as one God, one Son. May the Holy Trinity help us so that this may come to pass in us. Amen.[155]

No nobler words were ever spoken from a pulpit. As Christ said: "The kingdom of heaven suffers violence, and the violent take it by force" (Mt 11:12). Eckhart took it by force. He was speaking force to force, protecting the most precious integrity of the Church and his own humble integrity as One being with the Holy Spirit. For Eckhart there was no distinction between his spiritualized anima (Sophia) and God: "The eye with which I see God is the same eye with which God sees me: my eye and God's eye are one eye, one seeing, one knowing, and one love."[156] This last passage was also objected to by the Cologne censors, and he ironically had to cite Augustine to defend himself from their ignorance.

Why was this? Why so much fear in Rome that anyone in any order in Europe might say something new from the highest ordering principle of God? Jung called synchronicity an ordering principle in the universe. In Eckhart's case it was ordered by the One God. Indeed, it came to Eckhart in a dream that he became pregnant like a woman with child, and that child was the child of a new revelation of God, which could have helped to transform Catholicism in Europe if he'd been canonized. His calling was to preach a new doctrine of Spiritual Democracy to heal the Church of its power problem, its split from God. If *God is in all ways and equal in all ways, then this new way to God could have made the Church a much healthier place for people to worship and preach in!* About this way, Jung said in a talk with students at the C. G. Jung Institute in Zürich in 1958: "The way is ineffable. One cannot, one *must* not, betray it. It is like the way of Zen—like a sharp knife, and also twisting like a serpent. One needs faith, courage, and no end of honesty and patience."[157]

What Jesus taught his disciples in all four Gospels and especially in the fourth Gospel of John was that they would never die; they would live spiritually and in beatitude for all eternity if they followed the Way. Eckhart taught the same. He gave us his own new teaching of what the Way was for him: a way to the liberation of the Spirit from an excessively orthodox and callous patriarchy. Eckhart loved St. Francis and preached on his feast day on October 4 in either Strasbourg or Cologne: "The more universal our life is, the better and nobler it is."[158] By better, he meant closest to the soil in his native Motherland, not Avignon or Rome.

Eckhart's Views on the Self

The birth of God and the Self are not the same in Eckhart's works for the simple reason that God is a metaphysical Absolute, which excludes relative evil, yet includes it in God's *understanding of evil* through Wisdom. God in catholic theology is the Highest Good. For Eckhart, God transcended God's goodness, however, which is only a "garment" of the Divine.

In Eckhart God is a Word that speaks itself from on high. Eve can speak with the Serpent, but Eve is not God. Mary and Sophia are *equivalent* with God. Words speak themselves in Eckhart's theology from the *whole Self,* from the snake and Eve to the Word above. Sex, for example, was almost always excluded from his theology as a transforming agent of the soul. Whereas for Jung, sex was a catalyst to spiritual transformation and needed to be experienced in the body. This important difference between theology and psychology as systems of healing and as antidotes to evil need to be spelled out in a rational way.

Therefore, the voice of God and the inner voice of the Self are not identical. They may be similar, however. Eckhart and Jung were both introverted intuitive types. Yet at a certain point of evolution in Eckhart's development, in the third and fourth stages, this soul's typology changed and he became increasingly infused by Wisdom and *feeling,* less school-like and more charismatic and intuitively brilliant. Intuition opened the doorway to new understandings in him that needed to be written down or preached from the Higher Self, and he taught us to do the same—for those of us who can follow him.

For instance, when you try to write through your rational functions, you will sometimes fall into great error, in Eckhart's view. You must get it all down in words from the Word Itself, Eckhart taught, through inspiration and grace. "Grace is above love, first, in the same sense that the soul is above its faculty; second, as existence is over action; third, as a principle of cause over what is caused. Thus it is outside the category of genus, as you know, and consequently above intellect."[159] For the Word is prior to all images, and when the Self speaks with the unified voice of Wisdom, and *equally* from the Logos, the Word may spring forth out of you from *supernatural grace*.

Moreover, there is a common vocabulary and paradox used by both Eckhart and Jung regarding the Ground of the soul: The Ground is a synonym for the *Universal Soul*, which is entirely objective. When the Word speaks in you, you must answer if the child has been born since we are merely midwives for the Self to emerge through our callings. Whether you are called to write on the subject of religion, psychology, theology, or science, you have to keep certain distinctions in mind. There are no obstructions in writing from the Ground when all obstacles to your understanding have been removed. The articulation is automatic, spontaneous, actively flowing into your passive intellect, into streams of pure reason, when *intuition runs ahead*. God is inscribing words and syllables through you from the first principle, the Word.

It has to be remembered that Eckhart was a prototypical intuitive introvert who was in almost constant prayer even while he was working as an administrator of his order. His work was a kind of prayer; without any question he was a *seer* and *healer* of the highest spiritual type. In India seers were known as *Rishis*. Some of the best lines from Eckhart's vernacular sermons have to do with the organ of the eye and the function of seeing. For instance: "The inward eye of the soul is the one that sees into being and takes its being from God without anything else mediating. This is its proper function ... The person who is turned in on himself so that he knows God by his own taste and in his own ground is free of all created things and is enclosed in himself as in a veritable fortress of truth."[160]

Words issue forth from the Word through divine *grace*. Eckhart drew a sharp distinction with the sword of the Logos, Christ, or the Word between God and evil. Eckhart's thoughts about the importance of sin were quite intriguing to Jung and perilous to orthodox theology.

His statement that "God is not good" was one of the reasons Jung liked him so much. Without doubt, Eckhart often upset the apple cart of Augustinian obsessions with sin. Nevertheless, Eckhart did, in fact, support the doctrine of *evil as a privation of the Good*, and he agreed with Augustine, Albert, and Aquinas that "God does not cause evil ... evils, as nonbeing, are not from God nor is God in them, since there is no existence in them. They are evils only in the fact that they are not in God and he is not in them."[161]

All this means is that when one's soul is in a state of oneness, unity, bliss, one cannot do evil, for "God, Wisdom, is one."[162] And "Wisdom which is God is especially one in that it is the First."[163] The problem of evil will be taken up in more depth in Chapter 14. I mention it here because we need to keep in mind that Eckhart was Catholic and had faith and *love of Christ* like all Christians do. Eckhart was always a person of belief in God's essential Goodness. He quoted Rabbi Moses (Maimonides) as having said: "The sages agree that the sciences do not apprehend the Creator; only God himself can grasp his essence." To apprehend God a person of higher Wisdom required *supernatural aid*. [164]

The Holy Virgin Mother and Wisdom or Sophia were always the mediators, the soul-images that accompanied the birth of God that spoke through him most purely as the Word. It was God's Wisdom that was spoken by Eckhart; God's wife was Eckhart's beloved. Eckhart's anima or soul was wife to the Logos. She united him with the sensual and spiritual contraries in his body and psyche and he brought all of his senses up into a higher state of *integritas*: "Moral goodness excludes privation; otherwise it would no longer be a moral good, which is the apex of goodness."[165] And "good is in the One and evil in number."[166]

This kind of soul speech was the Wisdom of God that *understood evil*, but could never be equated with evil. Eckhart made room for sin and evil in his theology of Oneness in a creative way that Jung applauded. In my personal view Eckhart's superior intuition made it possible for us to see how sin and evil are a natural part of the soul's development toward unitary conscience, and it is truly unfortunate that his "Treatise on the Good" in the *Book of Propositions*[167] has not survived the passage of time, for it might have given us an even better sense of his thoughts on evil.

Eckhart as a Shamanic Healer

In Eckhart's theology there was nothing intrinsically evil about violence when it was spiritualized. Biblical theology has become such a specialized branch of knowledge over the past two millennia that it is hard for a Jungian analyst to try and reconcile it today with the psychology of the unconscious, with dreams, imagination, the cure of souls, sex, and the human body. Nevertheless, the panacea and the poison are often inextricably interconnected. Eckhart said in Part III of *The Book of Divine Comfort*: "'Those who are well,' says our Lord, 'have no need of medicine' (Luke 5:31). The physician is there to heal the sick."[168]

This function of *healing* was as present in medieval theology as it is in-depth psychology today. Confession and psychotherapy, pastoral counseling and depth analysis, are each concerned with the cure of the soul: her transformation into higher levels of spiritual realization. What is the *medicine* that both provide? Jung called it the *numinous*. Eckhart called it *grace*, which is a supernatural remedy for suffering: "The work of grace, because it is supernatural, is superior to every created work. Because it is above nature as something higher, the first thing that follows is that it contains the whole of nature undividedly united in itself as though by its power."[169]

Jungian analysts do not encourage identification with God, or the

Self. We counsel modesty through active imagination, dialoguing with different complexes and archetypes, a two-way conversation. One can safely dialogue with Sophia, but not *be* Sophia, or God's Wisdom as Eckhart embodied Her. As a medieval theologian, Eckhart lived in a place higher than the rest of us do. He was closer to God and became Wisdom's mate at times and taught that we could do the same; we could all be *totally transmuted into the super-substantial Bread*: "We shall all be transformed totally into God and changed into him. In the same way, when in the sacrament bread is changed into Christ's Body, I am so changed into him that he makes me his one existence, and not just similar. By the living God it is true that there is no distinction there."[170]

In the biblical narrative, Eve and Adam were tempted to eat of the fruit of the tree of knowledge of good and evil that was forbidden. But how can the *knowledge of good and evil or the Wisdom of the Serpent not be good and even very good*? Humanity needs to have the knowledge of the opposites of good and evil above all things.

In my post-Jungian reading of the Bible, God *intended* Adam and Eve to be disobedient. Otherwise why would God have put the Serpent in paradise, if not to tempt our first parents to make its instinctive and spiritual wisdom conscious? As Eckhart wrote: "'He [God] created heaven and earth,' that is good and evil. 'Creating evil and making peace' (Is 45:7). The existence of evil is required by the perfection of the universe, and evil itself exists in what is good and is ordered to the good of the universe, which is what creation primarily and necessarily regards."[171] Moreover, "('He made the heavens in intellect,' Ps 135.5), and 'earth' is taken as the existence of things under the aspect of goodness ('The things he made were very good,' Gn 1:31)."[172]

Therefore, in my thinking, in concurrence with Eckhart's *theology of the Word* and Jung's *psychology of the Self*, and while respecting their differences as systems of healing, I follow their hypotheses that disobedience from a psychological and theological standpoint is not necessarily evil because it brings about an awareness of our need to be obedient to God over everything else, on whatever path our souls are traveling toward ever higher Wisdom. For any interpreter of the Bible who might resonate with my respect and love for serpents, this means not being obedient to any previous theologian, or psychologist for that matter, as final authorities, not even Jung or Eckhart.

Listening as best as we can to the Word within, depending on which voice is speaking to us, requires the highest uses of discrimination. As Eckhart said, "The serpent was more subtle than any of the beasts of the earth,"[173] and the snake, who I've dreamt of too many times to count, has been a primary symbol for the Self in virtually all cultures across the globe as well as in Jung's psychology of individuation.

That is why Jesus preached in Matthew 10:16: "Behold, I send you forth as sheep in the midst of wolves: be ye therefore wise as serpents, and harmless as doves." And Eckhart wrote further: "Man's sensitive faculty [serpent] is more excellent than those of all other animals by reason of its participation in the rational faculty."[174] "And I say that in this light [the Light of supernatural grace or God-consciousness] all the powers of the soul lift themselves aloft. The senses leap into thoughts."[175] This metaphor of *leaping up into God* was one of Eckhart's favorite metaphors; Eckhart never left the body out.

I've often turned to Jung or to Eckhart whenever I've been suffering in my adult life, and I've received *equal* healing from both, empirically and theologically, depending on what my soul has asked for during her growth at different stages of her evolutions. Sometimes I have fallen from grace and partaken of the apple of the knowledge of good and evil.

Jung advised some of his patients to write their own *Liber Novus*. Eckhart said similarly: we will all be *totally transformed* into the image of God when we can become silent enough to hear God's Word speaking in our souls through our vocations from the Higher Self. Why wait today when the world needs answers on how theology and psychology might be united on a higher plane of understanding?

In my view, Eckhart was a great shamanic healer, and his heresy trial a sign of psychic infection in the Catholic Church. In the *Commentary on Genesis,* Eckhart said: *"Man's sense-endowed body has a more delicate constitution than any other animal body."*[176] No wonder he was so hazardous to orthodox theology!

On the Serpent and Evil

The traditional theological interpretation holds that Satan made his first appearance in the figure of the Serpent who tempted Eve in the Garden. Eckhart made it clear that the Serpent was not evil but good. The Serpent as our sense-endowed faculty in his theology could be as much our friend as our enemy. It all depends on our relationship to it and the soul. It is an aspect of the Self that needs to be spiritualized, according to Eckhart.

In Eckhart's theology he advised us to say "yes" to the Serpent, to be true to our destiny as a species, with all of its twists and turns of fate. We must learn to dialogue with the snake and Eve, to engage with the senses by transforming their energies into superior reason, spiritual motherhood, and Wisdom. For most postmodern people, this means embracing our sexuality and all of the instincts of our lower natures that need equal play. This is what makes the Word in Dominican theology and the Self in Jungian psychology different; the life of the monk enforced celibacy as a vow, whereas today sexuality is more of a sacrament than a vice.

Based upon my readings of Eckhart, I do not think God fell into temptation or was split inside either, in the beginning or end of the biblical story of creation: from Genesis to Revelation. I think God *intended* us to sin by endowing us with a *"more delicate constitution than any other animal body,"* as Eckhart said, and we were meant to experience bliss in soma as supreme delight.

Eckhart, who lived at the highest planes of anima-transformation possible seemed to have found that the traditional worship of Mary was too much an ideal of purity and that the spiritual motherhood of the Virgin was not the topmost aim either. Wisdom was humbler and better when the child in us was at play and our soul becomes a wife.

Individuation can only take place in a *unitary conscience* that does not split off the Serpent from our personality, or from God's instinctive and spiritual nature. God and the Serpent are One. *This is the hidden meaning of scripture.* This is why I continue to read Eckhart. We need better theologies to cast off the dross of outdated catechisms to lead psychotherapists and clergy toward higher evolutions of soul.

The Serpent has often been misinterpreted as the shadow in theology and that was perhaps why it became so evident in the projections of the Devil as the "Father of Lies" onto Eckhart. Instead of the senses being celebrated by the Church and elevated into the Oneness of God, they were demonized. It is hard for anyone who reads Eckhart today to see how anything he said was poisonous or possessed by the Devil. The Father of Lies was in the organization of the Church, not in Eckhart.

As you'll see, Eckhart objected to the projection of evil with compassionate justification from the power of the Word in his own self-defense. Today most postmodern psychologists would see the mechanism of shadow projection at work in *In agro dominico* ("In the field of the Lord"), the Papal Bull accusing Eckhart of heresy. It is one of the clearest documents of the projection of evil that exists in theological diatribes, and this is what makes Eckhart so important in the dialogue between psychology and theology.

Perhaps the most significant aspect of God's Wisdom in Nature and scripture is the Serpent. The snake is the wisest and most healing archetype in our instinctual makeup because it is still alive in us in our snake-brains, as either a medicine or a poison.

The mistake in theology has been the compulsive obedience to literal interpretations of the Bible, instead of seeing it as a continuous unfolding of many books of parables. Eckhart wrote: "When we can dig out some mystical understanding from what is read it is like bringing honey forth from the hidden depths of the honeycomb."[177]

I feel fortunate never to have read a word of theology until I read Eckhart. He was my only true theological teacher. It is *we* who have fallen from Oneness. *We* are split inside as a species, not God, in Eckhart's view. The Serpent is an essential part of God's creation, a very important part at that. The Serpent is adversarial to civilization and culture only because we humans have lost touch with the instinctive God of Nature. This is especially true, I believe, in theology. "As Rabbi Moses [Maimonides] says, the whole old testament is either 'natural science' or 'spiritual wisdom.'"[178]

In Eckhart's works, I've scarcely read anything that would support the idea that God is dualistic in any way. God is One. Read as a parable, one of the central messages to the children of Israel in the story of Genesis is that we must all take the temptation of the Serpent, to make the paradoxical meanings of the tree of knowledge of good and evil in the Garden of Eden conscious, through our ongoing conversations about our climate and the earth's environment in which snakes make their homes. "And as Moses lifted up the serpent in the wilderness, even so must the Son of man be lifted up" (John 3:14). We must dialogue with the Serpent to gain Wisdom in-depth. In other words, God was acting through the Serpent to awaken the Self in our snake-brains for a specific purpose: to initiate a process of individuation in collective humanity toward a trans-dualistic consciousness above all projections of evil onto our brothers or sisters.

From my reading of the documentary evidence, it is clear that a psychic infection entered the organization of the Church and the officials in charge were contaminated by their own toxic projections, which in turn infected Pope John XXII. The members of the Holy See that were put in charge of investigating Eckhart's writings were probably mostly sensitive men who were doing their best not to sin and be good Christians, but were suffering from a split-conscience. By projecting the shadow onto Eckhart and making him into a scapegoat the Holy See revealed the problem in religious orthodoxy that always wants to see the moat in someone else's eye and never the beam in one's own. *His goodness arose from his calling to shamanhood, to heal humanity of its split from God.*

The Union of the Snake and Sophia

When Jesus was one with the Father, he was in his true vocation, in relationship with his snake powers. This is what his disciples received: the powers to *heal* the sick and speak in strange tongues from the *shamanic archetype,* which was awakened in an earlier era of culture. The snake as Christ's wisdom was one with the Holy Spirit, Wisdom's child, the Word. They are *trans-dual.* They are One. The Self is not the Holy Spirit, if it excludes the Serpent. It is only the whole Self when the archetype of Oneness subsumes the Serpent and we take a bite from the fruit of the tree. Sophia and Eve were soul-sisters in Eden. Eckhart's dialogue with the Serpent and the Serpent answering Eve in a two-way conversation was present in the opening section of his *Commentaries on Genesis.* His vocation was to preach the divine birth of the child of God in everyone, as Jesus had to Nicodemus (John 3:1–6).

Envy crouched at the doorway of his Church in Erfurt because of his early success as a preacher. It became especially infectious later on in his career because he taught and preached what the Catholic Church could never accept, a healthy respect for the shadow, sin, and an inner acknowledgment of one's own potential for evil.

Eckhart preached the divinization process in humans for everyone: "'His Name shall be Emmanuel, that is God with us' (Is 7:14; Mt 1:23)."[179] The King of the Jews in the books of Isaiah and the New Testament was neither an archetypal image of the Messiah located in a single chosen individual, nor a privileged group of individuals in history, in either Jewish or Christian societies. "'A child is born to us, a son is given to us' (Is 9:6), a child in the smallness of its human nature, a Son in its everlasting divinity."[180]

For Eckhart the members of the Christian collective he preached to, including women, were all potential *mothers of God*. Everyone was encouraged to withdraw their projections of the Self onto Jesus and lay in the *childbed* with new births of the Word in the democratic majority. This majority could awaken grace by making the shadow of sin and the Light of God conscious through a recollection process where the soul could be fully realized. In his vernacular sermons Eckhart preached that we are all potentially *peacemakers* when we receive the vision of peace: "'Jerusalem' denotes a 'vision of peace' ... Let us pray to our Lord that we may be ... established in this peace, which is himself."[181] In the prophecy of Isaiah (7:14–16), the biblical story of the child of God (*Immanuel*) who would come to choose the Light of the highest Wisdom and good over evil was a millennial process in humanity's perennial struggle to become Self-conscious. Eckhart preached further: "'Unto us a child is born, unto us a son is given.' (Is 9:6): a child by the frailty of human nature, a son by the eternal Godhead."[182]

Eckhart taught that the archetype of the King of the Jews was a possibility of divinization in every human soul. "Blessed *are* the Peacemakers: for they shall be called the children of God" (Mt 5:9). Monotheism demanded a radical centralization of authority in one central archetype in the human psyche in one individual only: Jesus. For Eckhart, the Word was alive in everyone by the grace of the Paraclete and Jesus was only one incarnation of God that will be followed by many in a millennial process of evolution. The vocation of the Self as a pathway beyond projections onto Jesus or the Church was a *democratic way* in the masses that relativized God because its realization was no longer singled out for privilege in one special individual, or group of chosen people, whether Jewish or Christian.

The Self was meant for birthing the democratically divinized majority as a child of God and as a "Prince of Peace" (Is 9:6) in everyone. The archetype of totality was meant to serve the Self and society within and without. The Serpent and God intended us all to become conscious of the opposites as a realizable goal in the many: the *democratization of the Self* in the collective soul of humanity. Eckhart, the *preacher* of God's Word, became the messenger and counselor of the divine birth of the vocation of the Self in democratic societies in Europe, and he opened the doorway to the Word made flesh in everyone. He charted a new way forward for the Self's emergence as Wisdom, love, and divine justice as the supreme fulfillment of Scripture.

It was Eckhart's destiny to awaken the Self in the democratic majority within his own Dominican Order and in the entire Holy Roman Church. In Eckhart's theology the Holy Ghost replaced the centrality of Jesus and the Virgin Mary by awakening Sophia and God in the collective and by dialoguing with Eve and the Serpent as soul-powers.

Eckhart's Great Love of St. Francis

Jung stratified the anima into four levels: 1) Eve, 2) Helen, 3) Mary, and 4) Sophia (see Chapter 8). Mary, the mother of Jesus, was too spiritual for most humans to integrate, too pure, too virginal, too spiritual, even in Eckhart's day. No one could live up to the standards of perfection without error. Something far more humanized was called for. Sophia was, for Eckhart, much more human and closer to the senses and the earth. She was a much more humanized version of an exquisitely sensualized soul-image that was at the same time extrovertedly wise and was referred to simply as God's other half, Wisdom, including the serpent power of sensation. When elevated through inner dialogue, or active visioning, one could bring all aspects of the Self, including sensation, into consciousness without splitting.

Embodying the archetype of the King without inflation or pride in organizational life required two virtues that Eckhart most valued in his civic duties to the Church, and he found them best exemplified in God's loyal servant, St. Francis of Assisi: 1) poverty and 2) humility. To these twin virtues and the traditional seven Catholic virtues (prudence, justice, temperance, and courage, faith, hope, and charity), Eckhart added *detachment* as an eighth and highest virtue, which we also find in Advaita Vedanta and Buddhism. Detachment enabled him to bring something entirely new into Christendom: Nothingness and the Abyss, an experience of the Void, or universal Ground that is without bottom. This universal value of the virtue of detachment Eckhart placed above the seven virtues as an ultimate principle beyond God and the Godhead. The ground was simply the Infinite Universe in its eternal round.

Eckhart brought light to the nations by silently suffering, as Isaiah and Job and Jesus and St. Francis all had suffered. Being crucified for the sake of the common people was something he accepted as his fate as an ordinary citizen, one of the divine averages, who refused to compromise his integrity. He taught us we are all elected by the Self for divinization and *equality* with God. Eckhart embodied this new ideal of selfless service to the Church. His calling was to enlighten us and fill us with grace. Through his endless efforts to teach, he was one of the finest examples in human history of what it means to be fully human: a person who truly serves the Word from the humus, the soil of the earth, or Ground.

The Holy See was not only in desperate need of a scapegoat, but of a shaman-healer who had already produced the medicine the Church needed to cure itself of its psychic infections of excessive hubris and pride. Contagion was spread by institutional power in the Church in the thirteenth century when Eckhart came of age in the preacher's Church in Erfurt. The sins of envy and hatred were sickening the empire. The suffering servant welcomed the scourges of God because he knew he had a child in him that was Divine, just like Jesus was. But he did not identify with the Christ archetype out of any need for control or institutional power; he simply continued to maintain his integrity, even in the face of death and destruction, under the sword of political violence and tyranny wrought by the Inquisition.

If the old King of organizational dictatorship in the Church was to be cured of its illnesses of institutional inflation and psychic infection, a lance was needed with the blood of Christ on its tip. This was the lance of Longinus, the spear that pierced the side of Christ at the crucifixion.[183] It was destined to hit its mark when welded by someone in European history who was raised within stories of the quest myth, a skilled preacher, who knew how to take aim, and direct his spear to the place where it obtained its highest mark and strike through fearlessly to its long fulfillment. Eckhart, with his superior introverted intuition and unmatched introverted thinking, did not preach the denial of the flesh, senses, or any hint of the unreality of evil. Not at all. He looked the *reality of evil* in the eyes in Cologne and Avignon and stared it down in the name of a higher Good.[184] Anyone today, not only Christians, but also scientists can easily see the evils of the Catholic Church, for "The eye of conscience is a gift of nature granted also to nonbelievers."[185]

The evil eye in Eckhart's *envious* accusers could not prevent him from achieving the insignia of incarnation from the "higher causality"[186] of God's Word that supervened in his fate and his destiny-pattern from the Word. He taught and preached what he did without fear, not out of any malice or ego-need, but as a speaker of the truth of the Wisdom of God, and he tried his best always to facilitate *healing the needs of the Church for a better theology, a better doctrine, a new covenant.* This new covenant was true to the light that he shown on the darkness of his inquisitors: the ignorance of Church fathers who had denied the wisdom of the Serpent or cursed it. In the end he was exonerated and glorified in God.

Dreams of Eckhart Pointed Me to My Self-Path

When I began my individual experiments in experiential theology at UC Santa Cruz (UCSC), I proceeded with Eckhart's work in one hand, and my dream journals and Jung's writings in the other hand. While writing my thesis on Eckhart, I could not find any problem based on my dream research with the *privatio boni* doctrine in Eckhart's thinking (for more on the *privation boni* doctrine see Chapter 14). While being well aware at the same time of Jung's strong objections to this Catholic doctrine for minimizing the reality of evil, I felt Eckhart had somehow solved the problem for the Church by including evil into his God-equation.

In fact, my *Eckhart dreams* pointed me to a symbolic solution between analytical psychology and Christian theology over the problem of evil. These vocational dreams became part of my theory of truth, my personal mythology, my parabolic understandings of theology without getting lost in the complexity of Eckhart's ideas in Jung's works. I had no background in theology when I began to read and write about Eckhart at UCSC. I had no way to understand the problems he faced, the history of what was going on when he developed his theology, what worried people who were listening to his sermons in Germany. When he was writing and preaching in Latin in France, no one seemed to have bothered being concerned about him. But once he began preaching in Germany that rapidly changed as he developed a big following around him, most notably, women who he counseled and preached to. Then everything began to change.

As I wrote and I wrote at UCSC I was drawn back into the theology of the medieval period. My dreams gave me an answer to the problem that theologians had wrestled with but somehow left unsolved with regard to a new way of envisioning the wholeness that Eckhart had inaugurated with his revelation of the birth of God in the individual soul. Everything in these dreams pointed me to the relativity of the Word as complementary to the way of Jungian individuation, although

I had no contemporary theologian to guide me in my thinking—only Eckhart.

My first big "initial dream" about Eckhart came in 1981. Many of my dreams about Eckhart have been filled with light and understanding. Even his comments on envy, sin, and evil have not struck me as being problematic in the least from an analytical-psychological point of view. He seemed to be a transmitter of healing to so many people who read him and continue to read him. Why is this?

For myself, it was not only Jesus that preached the Word of God, as in the opening line in John. Eckhart spoke the Word every bit as much as Jesus did, and the light that he shone on the darkness of the Church was wonderfully playful and joyous, even amid all of the bitterness, tears, and the scourge of persecution he suffered. He accepted his fate with an upright conscience and heart. All the evils of the Inquisition could not overpower his works because synchronicity was at work in the *transcausality* of his destiny-pattern. As Jungian analyst Murray Stein wrote: "Synchronicity is a kind of God principle, the transcendent unifier of all that exists."[187]

Eckhart's Power to Heal the Wound of the Fisher King in Us

I was *healed* by Eckhart's theology, not broken, as the Fisher King was in the Perceval story when the bleeding lance drew out the poison from his wounds.[188] It was during the time of the Holy Roman Empire and the bloody history of the Crusades[189] that followed in which the living sword of our Savior was symbolically broken by the horrors inflicted by the Church in "Christ's name." Eckhart not only repaired the sword in me; he used his skillful lance of intuition to heal the wound of the Fisher King as well, which was epitomized by the dualistic theological thinking of his day.[190] I saw the beauty of this aspect of Eckhart's character inscribed in the lines: "'The light shines in darkness.' There follows: 'And the darkness did not comprehend it.' Nothing is pure evil or falsehood."[191]

What did Eckhart mean by this? The key to understanding the new revelation of God in Eckhart's works is in the simple formula that we can only be birthers of the Word, pure goodness and truth, while we are standing on the Ground of our truest vocation, which is the vocation of the Self. In Eckhart's preaching, his primary vocation, it became transparent that he was speaking, not from the ego, but from the objective non-ego: the Word of Truth. The Higher Self was aware of itself in his soul at the fourth level of Sophia, or Wisdom, to a remarkable degree.

Jesus's healing the sick was a sure indication that he was operating in the ancient role of a shaman to his Jewish tribe. Eckhart served a similar role for priests, monks, women, Beguines, and Dominican nuns as a father-confessor and counselor. He wrote the *Book of Divine Comfort* for Agnes, Queen of Hungary, whose father, Albrecht of Habsburg, had been murdered that year. We can also see this shamanic function at work in his calling as a healer of the people he counseled of physical, emotional, and psychological sufferings of various kinds.

What I learned from Eckhart is that there is a predisposition that exists in the human psyche to "see" in blessed people around us something of the light that illuminates all things, animate and inanimate. We cannot help but project some of this goodness of Christ-consciousness onto someone who has already been awakened by his archetype. This is one of the primary meanings I gave to my hypothesis of the "Vocation of the Self" in my thesis at UCSC: it can awaken what is *Christlike* in any of us by means of internalization of his archetype.

We all have an ailing Fisher King in us that needs to be healed. So too do we have an inner Percival who can heal our wounds with his lance, the spear of Longinus, which pierced the side of Christ. It's an old legend that emerged in Europe during the time of the Middle Ages, and when Eckhart was a boy, he must have read the Grail stories. Like Jung, he read the myth written by Wolfram von Eschenbach. In a very real sense, Eckhart became a hero of his childhood fantasies and not only healed himself but also offered a shamanic medicine, soul power as an *alexipharmic,* much as Jung did, that could have cured the sickness in the Catholic Church. He was indeed a living example of a shaman-preacher who delivered his sermons to make everyone well.

Eckhart gave special significance to the symbol of the gateway, or doorway, in one of his most important sermons, Sermon 35 in Miss Evans's English translation of Franz Pfeiffer's original 1857 text, which Jung read. The gate was the place of what he called the *primal eruption and it is from this gateway that he said we should stand and assert God's Word*: "But the primal eruption where truth breaks forth and originates, there in the doorway of God's house, the soul should stand and pronounce and declare God's Word."[192] In German the wording is even more precise.[193] It means *first eruption.* Breakthrough[194] is not always strong enough to define what Eckhart meant by *ersten Ausbruch.* Walsche captured Eckhart's meanings best to my liking. The word *Ausbruch* means in German to *erupt, explode, flare up.*

The Word of God is not something soft and pretty and nice, it is fiery and eruptive and corresponds to that level of the human psyche that Jung called the primal fire. This is the place where the Word breaks out, the place of primal violence and explosive power. Eckhart did not repress this power in his soul like many Catholic preachers did behind a bushel of pretense. He spoke truth to falsehood about the fiery nature of God. This was the primal utterance of the shaman-preacher who was standing erect in the subconscious and superconscious spectrums of awareness, with his intellect equal to the Seraphim, their "burning fire."[195]

Eckhart's Influence on Brother Antoninus

When I was a young man serving as Everson's teaching assistant, I could not see far enough into my future to know what my vocational dreams were pointing me toward, yet I knew through many numinous experiences that wherever I landed, it would be through the nuclear imprint of a Jungian analyst that I would find my Ground to stand upon. Bill saw this potential in me and believed in my calling. This led me to have hope and faith in my destiny. Bill became my Dominican reader of my Eckhart thesis. As he said in an interview with Matthew Fox OP, in 1989, he found Eckhart and Jung in the summer of 1956 when he experienced a breakthrough from the instinctual unconscious. It was Jung's "The Relativity of the God-concept in Meister Eckhart" essay that turned him on to Eckhart and awakened him to the power of his Word. He was born an Augustinian and St. Augustine converted him to Catholicism when he joined the Order. Yet in 1956, the year of my birth, he was called to go out from the monastery on a poetry-reading circuit and create an effective platform presence. Eckhart's works proved invaluable in this regard. Eckhart placed in Everson's hands what he termed "the weaponry of an enlightened spirituality" that served to transform his poetry readings into a direct "spiritual encounter." He began to use the "sacredness of silence" on a platform as a "spiritual weapon, a living blade."[196] *Nothing is pure evil or falsehood, Nothing.* How could the prayer of silence Eckhart taught become a spiritual weapon, a *living blade*?

Not only did I gain Dominican instructions from Eckhart at UCSC about the sword of Christ as a living blade, but Eckhart incarnated the same identical spirit as Everson: the *force* of Truth. Eckhart's vocation was to awaken in us our God or Christ nature as unique human beings through a creative expression of our own unique set of gifts. Vocation leads us to see the light and radiate its "glow" to others once the calling archetypes are switched on through evocation.

I see this in Eckhart and Jung. They both had charisma to point ways to the Self-path in their followers. However, neither Eckhart nor Jung were Gnostics, or mystics in my view. I do not speak of them this way. Irenaeus had attacked the Gnostics with a charge of religious pluralism, and this was probably because identifications with the dark side of the Self, Lucifer, or the Father of Lies was a *reality*. The shadow of the prophets is the *false* prophet. As analysts, we know only too well the dangers of inflation that can come from possession by the archetypes.

Neither Eckhart nor Jung identified with archetypes. They both taught us to be transformed like Christ by the light side of the Self, while assimilating our own darkness. Not to identify with any images of God, but to make our own sins and darkness conscious by befriending the Serpent, the body, and making the shadow aware by elevating it through a process of spiritualization to higher levels of integration; this was the way in which they both walked. The organizing sphere of the Holy Spirit, the Self, God, and Wisdom, were united in spiritual marriage in each of them, in their own ways.

Trinity and the Fourth

This brings me to the problem of evil within the psyche and cosmos and its entropic tendency to move toward nonbeing and Nothingness. This was Eckhart's definition of it, as it was also Augustine's, Albert's, and Thomas's. For all four of these great sages of the Church and especially for Eckhart, God, Christ, and the Holy Ghost were all One, and the Serpent was an essential part of the Oneness of being, when his senses leapt upward from the Ground into thoughts.

For Jung synchronicity was essentially a fourth God-principle, a transcendent ordering principle of all that exists in psyche and cosmos, an acausal order based on Oneness of the world, or the *Unus mundus*. This One was the key mathematical formula for the principle of synchronicity, which also organizes evil in individuals, groups, and institutions, such as through heresy trails, witch hunts, Crusades,[197] insurrections, and chaos.

The acausal order of the Self constellated during Eckhart's trials in Cologne and Avignon was disordered, disrupted, and infected with evil; yet at its nuclear center of energy was the God-principle that had incarnated itself in a human being who the Church officials were intent on crucifying. This too is an archetype: the one who carried his cross with humility, acceptance, and joy. It had been constellated earlier by the Holy See in their suspicions of error against Albert and Thomas Aquinas, Eckhart's spiritual mentors. Both were canonized as saints. But not Eckhart. Evil had to darken the light of the Word somewhere in the Church's organization, and the projections of criminality eventually landed on the poor and humble preacher because his *vision of equality was the most farseeing and the most threatening to the power hierarchy of the papacy and Catholicism as a patriarchal structure.*

Eckhart preached an early form of Spiritual Democracy, which was unheard of in theology at such high levels of education as he had attained to at the University of Paris. Yet if Jung's hypothesis was right about him, which I believe it was, Eckhart became the primary link between East and West, which the Christian, Islamic, Sufi, Hindu, and Buddhist worlds were waiting for.

Why Jung used the term *relativity* to speak about Eckhart's God-concept has been somewhat of a mystery to me over the past hundred years since he published it. Yet, it formed a link between his psychology of the unconscious and the theory of meaningful chance in a surprisingly refreshing way. Synchronicity as an acausal ordering principle was ordered, in my view, by a *higher causality* in Eckhart's thinking: from a supernatural order, which any of us can tap into in the Ground of being. Such an order is what the Zürich analyst and doctor of divinity, Murray Stein, called a theological position of *natural theology*, or *psychological theology*,[198] a standpoint in alignment with Christian metaphysics and natural science in common with human experience, which we also find in the writings of William James, Jung, and many post-Jungians.

Such a dialogue between Eckhart and Jung through *psychological theology* is based on numbers and a mathematical order in the Cosmos: $3 + 1 = 4 = 1$, the Trinity—God, the Son, and the Holy Spirit + Ground (including the Wisdom of the Serpent and Sophia) = Oneness, or an *Unus mundus*. For Eckhart the union of contraries between Christ and the Serpent, spirit and the body, occurred between his superior function of introverted intuition and his inferior function of extroverted sensation. Similarly, Jung said in 1925: "If the superior function is intuition, then the intuitions are directly in the way, since the transcendent function is made or takes place, between the superior and inferior functions."[199] In Eckhart the conversations between Eve and the Serpent occur at the midpoint in the soul, and from there the senses are elevated into a direct colloquy with Sophia and God.

CHAPTER 12

THE INFLUENCE OF ST. ALBERT ON ECKHART'S THEOLOGY

In this chapter I'll consider the importance of Albert the Great (ca. 1200–1280), the German Dominican friar, philosopher, and bishop, on the career of Meister Eckhart. Sometime between the age of fifteen, when the young Johannes entered the Dominican monastery in Erfurt, and the age of twenty, he was sent for higher education to the Dominican Order's advanced institute of learning in the monastery at Cologne, which Albert had established in 1248, and where he'd taught for thirty-two years. It was there in Cologne that Johannes met the aging Albert who taught young novices at the *studium generale* until his death in 1280. Albert had taught St. Thomas Aquinas and was considered by many to be the greatest theologian and scientist of his day. Thomas and Albert had also taught at the University of Paris, and Eckhart followed in their footsteps in 1293. It was in Paris that Eckhart established his reputation as a famous lecturer in Catholic theology.

Moreover, in his Easter Sermon, preached in 1294, Eckhart remarked: "Albert often used to say: 'I know this is the way we know; but we all know very little.'" This supports the hypothesis that Eckhart had been Albert's pupil for a time in Cologne. This proposition has been supported by scholars with the additional fact that Eckhart mentioned "my Lord, Friar Albert" during his "Vindicatory Document," or "Defense" issued in 1326, in fierce protection of his teachings *against* the Cologne inquisitors, and he quoted Albert's works in many of his Latin treatises and German sermons.[200]

I believe Albert's influence on Eckhart needs to be examined in greater depth to show *why* he was so central to the advancement of Dominican theology in medieval Europe at a time when the fear of Christianity becoming obsolete led to horrible contradictions between the actual teachings of Christianity and the violence perpetrated in the name of God. This period in Europe was defined by the Crusades,[201] Knights Templars, and Church warfare against women, mystics, prophets of the Holy Spirit movements, and Islam.

Albert was without doubt one the most powerful influences on Thomas Aquinas, and he left an indelible mark, a distinct signature of *Dominican identity of the archetypes of theologian, preacher, and scientist,* on the soul of Eckhart. Albert was what I've called a *Self-figure,* a man who guided Eckhart's destiny from a *hand of Destiny* high up in the superconscious and from the ground of Saxony he loved most. I see his influence in Sermon 80, where Eckhart preached passionately about the "unfathomable Ground of the Godhead."[202]

The universe, as we now know, is really and truly unfathomable. The Ground of the Godhead is endless, a divine abyss or infinite void. God, on the other hand, is One in Many, a plurality of being and non-being in the Universal Godhead. Eckhart remarked: "Bishop Albert says, 'Something is simple which is one in itself separate from all else, and that is God. All unified things are sustained by that which he is. There creatures are one in the One and are God in God; in themselves they are nothing.'" He often used this quotation from Albert—that creatures are in themselves *nothing*—and it was condemned as article 26 of *In agro dominico.*[203]

This is why Jung loved him, I believe, because of his profound humility. "When the I is identified with the Self," Jung said, "it is sort of elevated to a great height where it does not belong; if one sees the difference, then it sinks down. Meister Eckhart would say: yes, you are terribly important, but abandon yourselves nonetheless."[204] Eckhart's soul sank down. He did not identify with the Self. He became a mother of God and united with his anima at the midway point. He listened to Eve converse with the Serpent in him. He did not reject the Earth Mother.

We know nothing of his sexuality, but my hunch is that he did not deny it. He was a very sensual man as can be seen from his sermons. Moreover, Eckhart preached: "You should be firm and steadfast; that is, you should be the same in weal and woe, in fortune and misfortune, having the noble nature of precious stones."[205] This statement about the medicinal qualities of precious stones can be traced to Eckhart's *Latin Commentary on the Wisdom of Solomon*, where he said: "Again the imagination in dealing with magnitude is able to imagine something greater than any great thing, even heaven."[206] What is greater than heaven? In the writings of Albert, the firestone was an image for Divine Wisdom that could infuse *power* upon a person's life without ever exhausting itself, and it was capable, furthermore, of *infinite extension*.

In the highest state of the soul, the primal eruption, exploding outward and inward toward all being, all knowing, and all woe and bliss is endlessly diverse because it is constantly breaking out of an inexhaustible and revitalizing principle, making the soul's range of action in the superconscious *unlimited*. From this state, the soul can act transpersonally, beyond and outside the individual as an *ordering principle* in the Cosmos, directing our steps, like the alchemists, to the production of the philosopher's stone. This incarnation of Wisdom projected into minerals and stones is also active within quartz crystals, for instance. St. Albert, Eckhart's spiritual mentor, wrote a whole treatise on the magical properties of gems and minerals and related their transformative powers to alchemy. Eckhart connected this mysterious power in stones to the primal Ground, where crystals are found in the earth below our feet, or Mother Nature. This projection onto stones was not the personal aspect of Eckhart's soul, but the transpersonal, or archetypal, aspect embodied by the feminine aspect of the God-image.[207] In the active intellect the soul comes into absolute knowledge of all things as God's eternal Wisdom.

The primary source for the medieval conception of the *active intellect*, or highest power in the soul, where she is identical even with the highest angels, was Ibn Sina (Avicenna), the preeminent philosopher and doctor of the Muslim world. By *intellectus agens,* Avicenna meant an active intelligence that is a *cosmic reality* whose rays can be likened to beams of eternal light. This divine intelligence was a trans-psychic force present in nature and at the root of all human cognition as well as being incarnate in matter, such as in prized stones. When the soul soars up into this universal reality, holy power can stream into her and her springing forth from the Infinite Ground inspires a preacher's prophecy, but then she must come down again through detachment and poverty.

Both Albert and Maimonides took over the conception of universal intelligence. This idea corresponds to Jung's concept of "absolute knowledge."[208] Eckhart preached in Latin on Isaiah 60:1: "Arise, Jerusalem, stand up and become resplendent": "Jerusalem means heights, as I said in the convent Mergarden. To what is high one says, 'Come down!' To what is low one says, 'Come up!' ... If you humble yourself, God comes down and enters you ... The highest flows into the lowest."[209] This is one of the best examples of what Jung called the relativity of the God-concept in Eckhart's works. Jung claimed that "relativity is rather shocking to a Westerner."[210] Not so for Eckhart. His understanding of God was truly anachronistic—so much so that Jung used the term "relativity" only in his essay on Eckhart and nowhere else as the subject of a major work.

Not only did Eckhart postulate four levels of the soul, like Jung, but also four psychic functions, which were all relativized at the midpoint, where the upper and lower powers "kiss." Yet so often in Eckhart's works, his metaphors have a Jewish origin. His central teaching about the birth of the Messiah came from the book of Isaiah (7:14). As a biblical theologian he knew his sources well, such as the metaphor of the highest flowing into the lowest, which in Isaiah 40:4 reads as follows: "Every valley shall be exalted, and every mountain and hill shall be made low." Thus, the relativity of the God-concept relating to the city of Jerusalem, or the highest point of Zion, meant essentially the same thing to Eckhart: high and low were one.

In Gershom Scholem's masterpiece *The Messianic Idea in Judaism*, the former professor emeritus at Hebrew University in Jerusalem reported a fascinating story about the Baal Shem Tov. In September 1746 in Ukraine, the Baal Shem experienced a "visionary ascent of his soul" through a series of consecutive stages until he entered into the *palace of the Messiah* where he studied Torah with the Zaddikim. The Baal Shem asked the Messiah in the vision when he would come and the Messiah said, not "until your teaching will spread throughout the world."[211] In another interesting story about the Baal Shem, he is reported to have said: "Only when everyone attains individual redemption will there be universal redemption and Messiah will come."[212]

The point of repeating these Hassidic stories is to draw my readers' attention to the fact that Eckhart was not only preaching from the fourth level of his soul that he identified as Sophia, but also from his treetop soul, or wife, Wisdom, who could not fully be named even by Martha: "So when I am able to establish myself in Nothing and Nothing in myself, uprooting and casting out what is in me, *then* I can pass into the naked being of God, which is the naked being of the spirit."[213] In this sermon, Eckhart ascended to the "Crown" of the Tree of Life and became one with the archetype of the Messiah above in the superconscious. Then, he could come down to preach in a convent to nuns about the birth of God in their souls, not only in his. The Baal Shem's vision might help readers see through cross-cultural analysis that the vision of Zion may take place in a symbolic Jerusalem that is both high up in the superconscious and down low, on the Ground, where Eckhart's teachings spread like the Jewish Rabbi's to Martin

Buber, who introduced not only Eckhart's works in his early Zionist days, but also published them in his 1908 book, *The Legend of the Baal Shem Tov.*[214] Eckhart learned a lot about kabbalism from his reading of Maimonides.

When he was preaching, Eckhart was filled with the divine grace of *affective knowledge* from the Infinite Ground of the Godhead. It was from this emergence in time from the *ersten Ausbruch,* or original outbreak from the primal Ground, that he was inspired by the Holy Spirit to prophecy God's Word: "All words have their power from the first Word. Stones too have great power through the heavens wrought by the stars and the might of heaven."[215]

Maimonides, Albertus, Aquinas, and Eckhart all believed in the magical and *healing properties* of rare stones. They all knew, moreover, through their reading of Avicenna, that alchemy was a "true art" on account of the effects of certain celestial powers upon the human soul. Moreover, there existed an important document from Albertus Magnus concerning the Beguines and the Beghards, which, according to Marie-Louise von Franz, had been written by Albert to *protect* these spiritual movements whose center was located in Cologne *against* the institutional powers of the Inquisition.[216] So, the reader can see why these three Dominican masters of the Church—Albert, Aquinas, and Eckhart—were so threatening to organizational power that wanted to keep science divorced from religion, God from the Godhead, and Kabbalah from Christianity.

It is important to add that Albert had discovered in the writings of Avicenna an account of magic, where Ibn Sina said: "I found that the affectivity (*affectio*) of the human soul ... can influence everything magically if he falls into a great excess."[217] What did he mean by *excess*? Avicenna had taught Albert that "science is the production of the right 'imagination,' the right symbols," and when speaking of the magical mysteries in certain minerals and stones, he took over in principle Avicenna's hypotheses about the *higher science of the soul,* or Wisdom.[218] The inclusion of Wisdom as the "fourth" principle in

Dominican theology was contained in the notion of the Holy Spirit, a new expression for human wholeness that was to include not only the feminine (Wisdom, *Scientia*) and the body but also, as Jung later argued, evil into a theology of God.

This new dispensation[219] of the Holy Ghost was ushered in by the time of Joachim of Flora (c. 1135–1202). Jung mentioned Joaquim in many places in his works and quoted Albert as having said that everyone can influence everything magically if he or she "falls into a great excess."[220] What did this excess mean to the preacher from Erfurt? When charismatic preachers fall into the *excesses of God*, they are in the domain of transpersonal emotions of ecstasy, joy, happiness, and heightened states of excitement. Albert spoke of great intensities of *feeling* as a *passion of faith* or a *desire and hope* that can overtake a person during such moments of inspiration and that may "tip" the balance, in psyche and in the world, in favor of the miraculous. According to Jung, nothing like *emotional excess* can so alter events in our personal and cultural and collective lives, where mind-matter correlations, or synchronicities, are the possible concomitants: that is, whenever great intensities of emotion are *touched*.[221]

In chapter eight of Ira Progoff's book *Jung, Synchronicity, and Human Destiny*, which was aptly called "The Synchronistic Ground of Parapsychic Events," Jung inscribed in his marginalia of a manuscript on "hopeful expectation" some words with Albert's quote from Ibn Sina in mind.[222] The Ground metaphor goes back to Eckhart's concept of the *humus*, or *Grund*, from which we get the word *humility*. Eckhart's works were like Aquinas's, heavily inspired by Albert. Moreover, it was from Albert and Aquinas that Eckhart learned his technique of *imageless meditation*, entering the Ground of the soul and standing bare before God in the doorway of God's house, where the Word was said to emanate from the "primal eruption." Even the metaphor of God's nakedness implied that Eckhart's intention was to include the body and sexuality into his God-equation, when the soul or *God's playmate finds Him naked*.

Such ideas in Eckhart emerged out of his study of the platonic teachings of *emanation*, where "souls were themselves the result of a primordial big bang," wrote Joel Harrington in his book on Eckhart.[223] This is what Albert and his followers had called a boiling over (*bullitio*) of the Godhead into the divine Trinity, followed by creation (*ebullitio*) of the Universe. Thus, their *seminal equation* of a vast difference between God and the Godhead was clearly not limited to the Trinity. The Ground was something much larger and vaster and completely unfathomable. As Eckhart preached: "God and the Godhead are as different as heaven and earth."[224]

One of the most explosive movements that influenced the three Dominicans—Albert, Aquinas, and Eckhart—was no doubt the commotion caused by the *Concordia* of Joaquim of Flora, which posited in Parable 4 of his text that the Church was formed of a number of monastic orders and the Holy Spirit, which gave them all birth, had *seven* functions,[225] seven ages of the world, and seven gifts of grace.[226] He also prophesied that two orders of monasteries and monks would be united together at the time of the "great Sabbath."[227]

The unification of a plurality of monasteries in Holy Christendom was symbolized by the number *seven*, and they were foreseen to be united by two "mendicant orders," the Franciscans and Dominicans into *one unitary order.* Moreover, von Franz wrote:

> It is no exaggeration to say that the hallmark of almost all heresies at that time was an attempt to found a new religion or church of the Holy Spirit, or a free community in which the main accent lay on the Paraclete and on the individual who was inspired or guided by him, and on that individual's interpretation of the Scriptures. Abbot Joachim of Flora had pronounced the doctrine of three great ages, the second of which ... was that of the Son or of Wisdom, when the church and her sacraments

were considered to be the new dispensation; this was
to last until the year 1260.[228]

This is remarkable! *This date, 1260, corresponds exactly with
the birth of Johannes Eckhart.* In this "new dispensation" the Holy
Scriptures would be read anew with "spiritual understanding" and
would no longer be taken literally, but *symbolically.*[229] Thus, we Jungians
have to nod our heads to Albert for giving Eckhart the *keystone* that
would round off all of his works during his farewell address to his
disciples, before his final walk to Avignon, to face his accusers with his
Dominican rosary in hand: "I will give you a rule, which is the keystone
of all that I have ever said, which comprises all truth that can be spoken
of or lived ... In whatever way you find God most, and you are most
often aware of Him, that is the way you should follow."[230]

This is what we Jungians call the *way of individuation* as the path
of individual conscience. Albert was so essential to Eckhart's preaching
in Cologne that he became in some ways a transformative inner figure
for Eckhart as Eckhart became for Jung in his youth.

What Eckhart taught in his day was a basic attitude toward human
destiny that Jung referred to as "hopeful expectancy."[231] What is
hopeful expectancy, and how can we make use of it today? *Hopeful
expectancy* was not an archetype in Jung's view. It is a state of mind
similar to faith, but it's open to everyone regardless of whether they
are an atheist or a believer. For some, it is accompanied by faith or
belief in a transpersonal principle, a goal in *God-consciousness*, Christ-
consciousness, Nature, or *Turyia* in Advaita Vedanta. What gives us
hope is trustful loyalty or fidelity to our *life's calling*, our capacity
to experience something that is summoning us and that Jung called
numinous. Christians refer to it as *grace*.

Jung spoke of the archetype of the "miracle," or "magic effect" as
a quality of expectation in human beings.[232] We not only hope miracles
will occur in our lives, we also expect them to happen, and they do, in
fact, when we are open. Hope is an important psychological variable

in any vocation. Said Eckhart: *"You should be firm and steadfast; that is, you should be the same in weal and woe, in fortune and misfortune, having the noble nature of precious stones."*[233]

During his trials of strength in Avignon, Eckhart unleashed the explosive power of his vocation from the place of the primal eruption in his soul and he spoke truth to the face of falsehood. Eckhart kept hope alive, even while he was being made ready in scourges, as he said. Hope did not leave him. He kept the hope, faith, and love alive, that one day the Church would come to its senses and realize that the God-image of scriptures is only an infinitesimal part of the Infinite Godhead, which will never be fathomed either by theology or science.

With Eckhart the bottomless Ground of the Godhead was the *fourth dimension of pre-being and non-being* that is so real it is *reality itself.* Eckhart was a son of the Universe, including dark matter, dark energy, and black holes. Eckhart's child was born naked from Nothingness, and as Nothing, he carried the dispensation of Christ much further than the carpenter from Galilee could by including universal violence and evil into his visions of God: "I speak as incorrectly when I call God good as if I were to call white black."[234]

What gave him the audacity to speak so honestly about the fact that God is beyond all opposites? Perhaps it is what Jung said was necessary in the carrying of the cross of our vocation: fidelity, trust, or trustful loyalty: "Fidelity to the law of one's own being is a trust in this law, a loyal perseverance and confident hope; in short, an attitude such as a religious man should have toward God."[235] This is what is typically known in theology as a Catholic conscience: "The Catholic has to follow the judgment of conscience even if, objectively speaking, it is erroneous, and even if it should separate him from his church. The judgment of conscience is absolutely binding: it commits man to himself and to God."[236]

It is the same attitude that I find most helpful in psychotherapy as an *antidote* to doubt and despair. When a patient has been falsely accused and fired from their job, for instance, they may come into analysis suffering from a full-blown midlife crisis with symptoms of severe anxiety, depression, paranoia, and acute panic. Being attacked by someone in an institution is not that uncommon. Eckhart said in one of his most beautiful Latin sermons: "Four things are needed for someone who is attacked: fortitude, circumspection, armor, and good trust ... Avicenna claims and proves by cases that truth is more important for a cure than the doctor and his instruments."[237] *Truth and good trust over falsehood!*

In this same sermon, he also spoke of how one must learn to carry the Cross, not only the Cross of Jesus, but our *own* Cross in *four ways.* The fact that Eckhart spoke of *four ways* of following one's calling when one is attacked and is suffering from fate is numerically significant, in my view, because it shows us how much he conformed to the *archetype of the Self, or the fourfold path of wholeness.*

I will go over this challenging sermon in more detail in Chapter 16, but I want to leave the reader with his last words of Wisdom regarding the *fourth way of the two Crosses now*:

> So every contrary and everything hostile thing loses
> its evil and ill-nature in the soul that has been clothed
> with the armor of light, so that the soul no longer feels
> it, but rejoices and delights in suffering for the love of
> Christ.[238]

CHAPTER 13

ECKHART'S UNITARY THEOLOGY

Eckhart's theology is first and foremost *experiential*. Reading Eckhart is about *awakening*; it's about experiencing equality with God insofar as God can ever be experienced through a process of continuous witnessing, seeing, and birthing God from a standpoint in eternal time. As "the Apostle says, God will be one in all' (1 Cor 15:28)."[239] By "all," Eckhart meant the Ground, not Christ or the Trinity, but the *all* in a pluralistic and pantheistic sense. Most theologians may disagree with me, but theology missed Eckhart's careful theoretical delineation between God and the Godhead based upon his own personal experience of Divinity as Infinite and beyond all conceivable names of God or God-images.

Eckhart put forth a *unitary type of theology* that he practiced, taught, and preached for most of his career that strongly appealed to Jung. By *unitary theology*, I mean Eckhart's vocation was to lead people into unitive states of mind—transformations of consciousness that could change his audiences and also us as postmodern readers today. The same birth of God is happening eternally throughout the whole Cosmos, and this miracle of creativity is taking place inside and outside of ourselves *now*, whether we are aware of it or not. Theologians are mistaken to posit panentheism over pantheism; doing so only perpetuates the same dualism that got Eckhart into trouble with the Holy See and the pope.

How did Eckhart avoid the problem of inflation that comes from prideful identifications of the human ego with the Universal Self? By living a simple life in modest accordance with the highest Christian virtues—humility, poverty, chastity, charity, obedience, detachment—qualities that protected him from the nemesis that follows *pride*, the greatest of all Catholic sins. About pride, or what the Greeks called *hubris*, Eckhart wrote in the *Commentary on Exodus*:

> Pride is linked with every sin both because it is opposed to humility which subordinates the soul to God and so makes it able to be influenced by him, and also because pride by its very nature usurps for itself the name and the property of the superior by denying its own inferior status whose sole task is to receive the superior's gifts and perfections.[240]

Eckhart taught exhaustively that God is born in the human soul from a fourth principle that precedes and complements the Trinity, the divine Ground, or *Grund*, which he also called *die Gotheit* in Middle High German. Out of this primal Ground, the Trinity emanates into manifestation or descends from supernatural aid in the form of an indwelling presence from above, the Paraclete (from the Latin, *Paracletus*).

In Christianity generally, the Paraclete has commonly been spoken of as the Holy Spirit. It is a function of emanation in humanity that is in continuous process of becoming. Eckhart incarnated the Paraclete through his human-divine personhood. For Eckhart the Paraclete represented the indwelling principle of continuing incarnation in parity with God: "We shall all be transformed totally into God and changed into him."[241] And perhaps a few might even do *greater works* than Christ: "Verily, verily, I say unto you. He that believeth unto me, the works that I do shall ye do also; and greater *works* than these shall he [the Comforter, Advocate, or Paraclete] do because I go unto my Father" (John 14:12). Equality was one of Eckhart's favorite metaphors for unity, or the Oneness of existence. In Eckhart's understanding, "the Godhead is the beauty of the three Persons;" and about himself he added: "I am come like the fragrance of a flower."[242]

This is the way I like to remember Eckhart: like *an intellectual flower, a fragrant essence of Mother Nature.* How is such flowering of spirit possible in us? Eckhart said: "I alone take all creatures out of their sense into my mind and make them one in me."[243] In this chapter I present Eckhart's *unitary theology of Oneness* to move readers toward an understanding of Christianity that has not typically been taught in traditional institutions of theological learning. Christianity has preached, in most Churches of the world, that its parishioners should worship Jesus as the *only* Son of God, venerate the Virgin Mary, and avoid at all costs the sin of pride that comes from too close an identity with God. *Identity* has been viewed as the greatest sin if it stems from pride. The antidote to pride is humility, and this was Eckhart's metaphor for the ground, or *humus.* Staying low to the earth and rising up in spirit was Eckhart's way into *Self-consciousness,* or the coexistence with what Fredrich Schleiermacher called "God-consciousness" with the "consciousness of an environing world."[244] Eckhart remarked further: "Heaven can only work in the ground of the earth. Thus God cannot work except in the ground of humility, for the deeper we are in humility, the more receptive to God ... The more a man is sunk in the ground of true humility, the more he is sunk in the ground of divine being."[245]

The solution to excessive pride is the way of the cross: staying close to the divine Ground through the carrying of one's own cross of suffering. It means that we must learn through painful experiences how to endure and transcend evil by staying true to our vocations. Our calling can deliver us from the infection of evil. Psychologically, evil is horribly real, a devilish *force* that may cross our paths ruthlessly at times, yet, theologically, evil has typically been viewed as a defect, a falling away from the essential goodness of God. All three major monotheisms share similar views about the essential goodness of God in states of Absolute Existence, Unity, Peace, and Oneness.

When one is in an absolute state of Unity, evil is felt *experientially* to be nonexistent because all one sees and feels is light or bliss in the shining Temple of God: "Intellect is the Temple of God wherein he is shining in all his glory. Nowhere does God dwell more than in this temple of the intellect's nature."[246] This is the absolute intelligence of all existence.

In his *Commentary on Exodus,* Eckhart quoted Avicenna as having stated that "being is the first thing known by the intellect," to which Eckhart added: "Existence itself is God and 'God was the Word' (Jn 1:1)."[247] So the Word is the *source* of our existence, and our protection from evil; therefore, our *being* is *necessary* in the Universe for our planetary survival. All life matters on the planet. Eckhart showed how Avicenna and Rabbi Moses both agreed that "Only God's Existence is 'necessary existence.'"[248] What this meant was that his own existence had ultimate meaning in the Cosmos:

> I have life in common with those things that live, in which life is added to being. My being is dearest of all to me, it is the thing I have most in common, and is my most intimate thing. I would rather give up all things that are under God. Being flows without mediation from God, and life flows from being, and therefore I like it best and it is the dearest thing to all creatures. The more universal our life is, the better and nobler it is.[249]

"The more universal our life is, the better and nobler it is." I love this quote. Is your being dearest of all to you, reader? Is it the thing you have most in common to all creatures, and is your life the most intimate thing? Would you rather give up all things that are under

God than your own life? Eckhart answered the paradox of being and nonexistence thus:

> Elsewhere I have declared that there is a power in the soul which touches neither time nor flesh, flowing from the spirit, remaining in the spirit, altogether spiritual ... God is in this power in the eternal Now. If a man's spirit were always united with God in this power, he would not age. For the Now in which God made the first man and the Now in which the last man shall cease to be, and the Now I speak in, all are the same in God and there is but one Now ... One equal eternity ... Therefore nothing new comes to him from future things nor any accident, for he dwells in the Now, ever new and without intermission. Such is the divine sovereignty dwelling in this power ... all the future and the past are there in one Now.[250]

Therefore, Eckhart prayed: "That we may attain to this Now, so help us God. Amen."[251] What might such a prayer in the Now lead to *if* the Divine were to give answer in a mathematical formula? What kind of an experience of Oneness might this kind of quiet prayer lead to *in us*? What kind of totality? For Eckhart, the answer came simply. It leads to emptiness, to an empty mind, to the realization of our naked essence, a mode of *visioning God from Nothing*. Zero plus the Universal Being is equivalent to One: (Zero + Universe = One). When all images of God are left behind for the *humus* of the Godhead, only One remains. Then one has "a vision of God."[252]

In her book *Number and Time* Marie-Louise von Franz referred to this mathematical principle as "one-continuum." Such a continuum is both "mode-and power-transcending," which is to say in Eckhart's words, "It is a Something which is neither this nor that."[253] This mysterious mathematical something is a universal totality in the microcosm transcending even the macrocosm—a birth more exalted than even the "heavens above the earth."[254]

So what are we to do once we have a vision of God? What is asked of us? We need to attune our instruments to God's music in us through continuous *work*. Eckhart said: "Man requires many instruments for his external works; much preparation is needed ere he can bring them forth as he has imagined them."[255] By preparation, he meant contemplation and prayer, instruction and *listening*, imagination and *birthing*, learning and *seeing*. By rising up into the Higher Self one momentarily becomes free of the contagion of evil.

Although Jung was called to provide an answer to the problem of evil with his remarkable empirical psychology, his attempts to "strip things of their metaphysical wrappings in order to make them objects of psychology"[256] and occasional "irreverent"[257] attitude toward metaphysics calls, at least for me, for a more unitive way of practicing psychotherapy. Can we practice analysis without reducing God to an "autonomous psychic complex," a term Jung used in his relativity essay? Later, Jung intentionally invoked the spirit of Eckhart to defend himself against charges of excessive reductionism: "Should Meister Eckhart be accused of 'psychologism' when he says, 'God must be born in the soul again and again'?"[258]

Eckhart did say this. But what did he mean by "God"? Jung's fights with his father, a Zwinglian pastor of the Swiss Reform Church were probably bolstered by his *identification* with Eckhart as an archetypal figure in his early adolescence and adulthood, and I believe this affinity with Eckhart continued throughout his life and well into old age on an inward level. Eckhart helped Jung marshal his criticisms toward Christian theology in a way no other theologian could. This was important, for what would eventually become the birth of analytical psychology during Jung's *Red Book* period owes a great tribute to Eckhart, as you will see in Part III.

Nevertheless, after he emerged from his experiments with his methods of active imagination, in his 1921 essay, "The Relativity of the

God-concept in Meister Eckhart," he didn't give sufficient attention to Eckhart's metaphysics. This led him to misread Eckhart at times. For instance, Jung described Eckhart as espousing a "purely psychological and relativistic conception of God and of his relation to man."[259] To him Eckhart was the "great relativist"[260] and "Meister Eckhart's view," to him was therefore "purely psychological."[261]

Moreover, while Jung can certainly be credited for having celebrated Eckhart as the "greatest thinker" of his age,[262] I must question whether his statement that Eckhart's "medieval mysticism" can be characterized psychologically as "a regression to a primitive condition,"[263] or whether a better phrase like *progression to a condition that represents the apex of human consciousness* might have been a better word choice than *primitive?* We have to be careful today to explain what Jung meant by "primitive." He was using anthropological language that was in vogue in 1921. Today the word *primitive* might be judged to be an insensitive ethnocentric word. Jung commented on Eckhart's "primitive idea of God"[264] and that his "God has become an autonomous psychic complex" that was "only partially conscious."[265] I have to question this assertion by Jung about Eckhart's experience of God.

By "primitive," I take Jung to have meant *archaic,* or *primal,* which is more in alignment with Eckhart's own linguistic experiences of his soul's first emanation from the Ground of the Godhead. Eckhart's idea of God was actually pretty much up to date with postmodernity, in my view, because he made room for the mystery of violence in the Universe and also in Christ's character. How could Eckhart's view be purely psychological and not also theological? I see Eckhart's theology as *trans-dual.* I made use of Stein's term "psychological theology" earlier to solve this lacuna, yet here I advocate a *theologically based psychology* to complement Jung's lack of specificity regarding the Absolute.

Jung's calling was not to examine Eckhart's metaphysics or theology. He used Eckhart's theology to support his psychology of individuation and the relativity of God. He hypothesized that in Eckhart's works, God was only *incompletely* conscious.[266] Fortunately, this was only a hypothesis, not a fixed theory. What I believe Jung meant is that the dark side of God needed to be included into the Trinity, as a fourth principle of modern science. Whether his *hypothesis of a partially conscious God* was true to Eckhart's theology of birthing is a question at the center of this book. My answer, in short, is that the term *God-complex* does not do sufficient justice to Eckhart's teachings. To suggest that his God was *less* conscious than a modern or postmodern person of today is questionable from a spiritually democratic standpoint. One wonders how Jung could have arrived at such a view. Yet, if Jung had stopped citing Eckhart in 1921, he might have limited his views on the birth of God to a "God-complex," "God-function," or "God-symbol." Thankfully, he did not stop there and continued quoting Eckhart as he aged, with increased understanding.

Ways are twofold, taught Eckhart: one is rational; the other is intuitive and sensitive. Eckhart was an intuitive-thinking type. Intuitive types tend to follow their own individual *ways* to God-consciousness. Eckhart preached a way that was paradoxically wayless. "For whoever seeks God in a special way," he said, "gets the way and misses God, who lies hidden in it. But whoever seeks God without any special way gets Him as He is in Himself, and that man lives with the Son, and he is life itself."[267] Eckhart found a way to free himself of God as a mere *complex*. We can see Jung's continued use of him in his essay, "The Development of the Personality":

> A good thing is unfortunately not a good forever, for otherwise there would be nothing better. If better is to come, good must stand aside. Therefore Meister Eckhart says, "God is not good, or else he could be better."[268]

Jung's model of the Self for modernity made creative use of Eckhart: *empirically, God is both good and evil in Jung's model.* This has confused some theologians and led a few to wonder if Jung might have been a Gnostic or neo-Manichean dualist. Jung argued to the contrary. Empirically, Jung was right. Nevertheless, when it comes to analytic work with patients, some of whom might be Catholics, statements like these might sound offensive; if good must stand aside to let evil have its way with us, what is the "anything" destined to be better? If one reads Jung incorrectly, it could sound problematic clinically and theologically. Therefore, care is needed to clarify what Jung meant.

Eckhart's remarks on pride followed the traditional Augustinian doctrine that sin and evil do not exist in the highest powers of the soul, for they are "not produced as effects, but as defects of some act of existence."[269] In his *Commentary on Exodus,* he quoted Avicenna and then added: "Existence itself is God and 'God was the Word' (Jn 1:1)." Eckhart showed how Avicenna and Maimonides had concurred that "Only God's Existence is 'necessary existence.'"[270]

What we need today is better theological understanding to properly represent Eckhart and better comprehend what he meant to Jung. In short, we need better *visioning, better imagination, and creativity* to reflect for readers who this remarkable man was and what he taught us, as a world-transforming theologian of unsurpassable stature. We need help in accomplishing this vision from theologians and philosophers and historians alike. Psychologists can only take us so far. Fortunately, I have had discussants along the way, both with Jungians and theologians to help me get closer to the mysteries of God and the Godhead that Eckhart left us to try our best to fathom.

Eckhart's unitary theology was relative and absolute, scientific and metaphysical, psychological and trans-psychological. Practicing Jungian analysts, psychotherapists, spiritual directors, or clergy would benefit from formulating a *healing metaphysic* born from Eckhart's work. We need new visions of Eckhart's theology to aid us in our work with patients, whether of faith, lost faith, or no faith at all. Jungian psychology needs better and more robust comprehensions of Eckhart's theology to help us in our work with patients who might believe in any of the three monotheisms through a *trans-dualistic type of theology* that is more tolerant and embracing of Christian, Jewish, and Muslim faiths.

As a contemporary Jungian critic and a lover of Eckhart, I cannot abandon the Divine Child of the master's theology in favor of Jung's psychological-relativistic view. I'm writing as a Jungian analyst and a marriage and family therapist (MFT) and a follower and brother of Eckhart. I've specialized for two decades as a child psychotherapist, healer of children's souls, and their families, many of them Christians. I cannot abandon Eckhart's theological child and cannot abandon Jung's psychological child either. They are both children of the imagination. To unite psychology and theology on a solid trans-dual foundation, Eckhart's child of unitary theology and Jung's child of unity psychology need our nurturance, love, and protection. For both are divine children and need our best mothering and fathering.

CHAPTER 14

FURTHER THOUGHTS ON EVIL

Only when someone has been touched by evil can they be *emotionally involved* with it, empirically and metaphysically, not as a mere intellectual problem, but also as something affectively *real*, a mystery that has to be wrestled with in actual relationship with the Divine Selfhood and in human relationships with colleagues with whom we might not agree. The hand of God is what protects and delivers us from excess pride and evil.

Empirically evil can and does affect us, such as when we experience it as an arrow shot that stings us to the bone. Evil can be deadly, both in a relative and existential sense. Moreover, in Absolutist faiths (Judaism, Christianity, and Islam), God, Christ, or Allah are transcendent principles that are unique, yet equivalent essences of Supreme Goodness, Love, Compassion, and Existence in which no coequal contrary reality can exist next to God or Ultimate Reality. God is good and there is no evil in the Absolute, no excess pride, pernicious Devil, or poisonous Iblis. This is basic unitary theology, across all three of world's Abrahamic monotheisms.

Analytical psychology needs theology to help our field grow in more ecumenical ways toward a closer union with people of faith because many of our patients are Christians, Muslims, Jews, Hindus, Buddhists, Sikhs, Taoists, Native Americans, or scientifically agnostic.

Belief in God is an incontrovertible fact, and monotheistic faiths are often an essential part of our practices. To provide diverse therapy, competent psychotherapists, spiritual directors, or analysts need to be well-informed about principles of belief. Spiritual diversity was at the center and heart of Eckhart's preaching. We therefore need some education about the *privatio boni* doctrine of the Catholic Church.

Irenaeus (c. 130–c. 202), the Bishop of Lyons (where my French grandmother and mother were born), was the first Church elder to formulate a theology based on a clear distinction between the *Imago Dei* implanted in the body and soul and our *likeness* to God, which is our destiny through moral freedom and responsibility to God to emulate. Like Augustine who fought against Manichean dualists, Irenaeus waged a fierce battle against Gnostic dualism in defense of monotheism as the ultimate triumph of our Lord over evil. Our "likeness" to God was mirrored, he conjectured, through our actions, vocations, thoughts, and virtues every day. In his view, we are each responsible to our Maker for our thoughts, words, and deeds. We all have cognitive freedom to choose good over evil.

What the doctrine of goodness meant to early Christians is that *in God as Absolute Existence, evil does not exist*: *Evil is a privation of God's essential goodness and being.* The champion of this doctrine was St. Augustine (354–430 CE). The *privatio boni* doctrine postulated by Augustine ruled out all dualistic conceptions by Mani and the Manicheans, whose notion of two absolute principles, one good, the other evil, was heretical to biblical exegesis of God as Universal Intelligence. The doctrine has had a long-standing tradition in Catholicism and Protestantism, and it is still being debated.

Eckhart's views on *repentance* from sins were astounding when we consider their implications. The aim of repentance from sins, when God permits them to enter into us, is to lift us up out of sorrow and lamentation into an unspeakable joy. He wrote in his "Counsels on Discernment": "as godly repentance lifts itself up to God, sins vanish into God's abyss, faster than it takes me to shut my eyes, and so they become utterly nothing, as if they never happened, if repentance is complete."[271] The key metaphor here is God's abyss. *Abyss* is another word for *Ground*.

To be sure, Eckhart's views on sin and evil were novel, although they were in complete concordance with the Hebrew-Christian Bible and his close reading of the traditional Augustinian-Thomistic views of the Catholic Church. Jung's fight against the *privatio boni* doctrine reached its apex in his fights with the Dominican theologian Victor White, who, at one point in their letters, charged Jung with postulating a new type of "neo-Manichaeism." This was an unfair accusation on White's part because Jung always claimed he was making postulates of analytical psychology, as James had before him as an American radical empiricist, not treading on sacred theological ground. Jung was at pains to trace the problem of religious dualism to the teachings of Zoroaster and Mani in his *Nietzsche Seminars*. He was clearly no New Age Manichean, or in White's terms, a *wicked old Manichee at heart* who a really sound Dominican like him could feel compelled to hand over to the Civil Arm of the Vatican for the good of his sinful soul.

Jung taught the unity of a central God-image in the human psyche: the *Self*. Jung said in a footnote to one of his most important books *Aion: Researches into the Phenomenology of the Self* that his psychology was the exact opposite of dualism because it taught the unity of the Self. By this he meant what I'm calling *trans-dualism*: "My learned friend Victor White, O.P., in his Dominican Studies ..., thinks he can detect a Manichean streak in me, I don't go in for metaphysics ... my leanings are therefore towards the very reverse of dualism."[272]

This was true. Yet, the unity of the Self and the unity of existence in the Higher Self were and still are today two different *experiences*. One cannot contravene the other. They belong together in the same bed of analytical psychology. Nevertheless, Jung asserted that he was always speaking as a relativist and doctor of the soul, neither as a philosopher nor a theologian. He insisted he did not fiddle in metaphysics, although he was a fierce critic of metaphysical ideas, not unlike James. Jung had an exceptionally keen intuition and often picked up things in Christian theologians, such as the fear of the spread of the Holy Ghost movement that began to flourish in the thirteenth century. Jung mentioned four minds of immense significance for the future from that time: Albertus Magnus; his pupil, Thomas Aquinas; Roger Bacon; and Meister Eckhart. Jung added: "Some people have rightly seen the Holy Ghost movement as the forerunner of the Reformation."[273] Interestingly, three of the four were Dominicans (Albert, Aquinas, Eckhart) and one a Franciscan (Bacon); yet all four were steeped in natural philosophy, science, and Catholic theology. Moreover, they all held similar yet original views on evil, as did Augustine.

The dualistic belief in a *coequal equation* of good and evil in God was seen by Augustine as disastrous because it went against the very foundations of Christian faith and ethics. To the fathers of the early Church, there was no evil to be found in God or Sophia. This view was not completely novel by any means, for it was a synthesis of scholarship in early Christian circles, an evolutionary process that had its roots in the Hebrew Bible and could be found in Aristotle, Plotinus, Neoplatonists, Ibn Sina (Avicenna), Ibn Rushd (Averroes), Maimonides, and other medieval philosophers and theologians. For such reasons, Jung's fight with Victor White over the doctrine was lacking in sufficient academic scholarship, for in all of these thinkers, including Eckhart's most immediate Dominican teachers, evil was *non-esse*, or non-being. Here are four examples from Eckhart's pen that lend support to the *privatio boni* doctrine, all from his Latin works:

1) "Division, insofar as it is a fall from the One, is a privation of existence, of oneness and goodness, and is thus an evil of a kind and an accident in nature."[274]

2) "The good is always on high—the higher, the better. What is Most High is the best. On the contrary, evil is always below, and the deeper, the lower, more inferior and more subject ... to many things it is, the worse it is."[275]

3) "It is evident first that evils, as nonbeing, are not from God nor is God in them, since there is no existence in them. They are evils in and only of the fact that they are not in God and he is not in them."[276]

4) "Moral goodness excludes privation; otherwise it would no longer be a moral good, which is the apex of goodness."[277]

These four examples from Eckhart's theological writings might be sufficient enough to show that Jung's view of him as the "great relativist" was only half of the picture; the other half was his metaphysics of creation. The second quote, "The good is always on high—the higher, the better. What is Most High is the best," shows Eckhart's careful attention to a gradation of the qualities of God, not the kind of relativism where good and evil are *equivalent* values. Moreover, in the fourth quote the *apex of goodness, the most high, was a moral good,* and there was a clear differentiation made by the preacher between heaven and hell, or God and the devil.

Eckhart was both tough-minded and tender-minded, a relativist and an absolutist. The empirical and metaphysical standpoints needed a practical bridge, therefore, in the field of analytical psychology to traverse toward the higher unity in the Transcendental Self, if psychology and theology are truly to meet on an *equalizing* Ground. This is the bridge I am building, along with Jung and many others.

In his book *Evil and the God of Love,* the philosopher John Hick explained from a theological point of view that it was the Platonic distinction between nonbeing in the metaphysical sense of sheer nothingness and in the relative sense of some not-yet-realized potentiality to be some specific thing that has been regarded, throughout a long-standing philosophical tradition, as the "lurking-place of evil."[278] I saw this early on in a chapter of my thesis on Eckhart at UCSC that I called "The Vocation of the Self."

Where evil lurks, God is not present, although He (YHWH) and She (Sophia) understands evil. From a psychological angle, such a philosophical insight holds a great deal of empirical validity when it is viewed through a lens of vocational development as the pivotal organizing principle of transformation in the human species. I mean that everyone has a unique and specific calling that presses for fulfillment, and when the creative energies of our central self are obstructed, evil may arise as a nonbeing, where the shadow side of the Self has to be dealt with.

I'll say more about this hypothesis later. It touches on the notion of what Jung called psychic infections and what I have termed *psychic antibodies* that can help us fight against evil. Hick asked an important question in this regard about whether evil is "a positive force with a malevolent nature of its own, liable actively to attack and infect all that it touches."[279] This, as I see it, is a central question in Christian theology and analytical psychology today. *Infection by evil* cannot possibly be something insubstantial. It must be substantial, a negative force, something that is alive and present in a previous good.

There is no evil in Nature, only goodness and pure being. So too with the transcendent Creator of the Universe, who, paradoxically is the author of evil. For instance, Eckhart wrote: "Seventh, 'He created heaven and earth,' that is good and evil. 'Creating evil and making peace' (Is 45:7). The existence of evil is required by the perfection of the universe, and evil itself exists in what is good and is ordered to the good of the universe, which is what creation primarily and necessarily regards."[280] This was a position held by Aquinas before him. Yet Eckhart added: "'The light shines in darkness,' because evil always exists in something good and is neither seen nor known nor visible without the form of something good ... Thus good shines in what is evil, truth in falsehood, and possession in privation ... Nothing is pure evil or falsehood."[281] Now this is as true theologically as it is psychologically. Not being able to pursue our true vocations can indeed *infect* us with negative effects that can produce evil, resentment, envy, jealousy, hatred, avarice, violence, and so on.

It is in the human realm of relative existence that evil is present and can spread through massive psychic contagions. For Eckhart, trees had a life *coequal* with humans on our spiritually diverse planet. Trees were not lesser beings. Trees were made in the image of God through their inherent *Isness*. Eckhart avoided dualisms between God and Nature. He did not make Christ the ultimate reality in his theology. Our theologies need to be brought up to date with a science of religion and Eckhart was attempting to do that in his times.

Human-caused evils are a psychological and scientific fact of our planetary existence. Evil is a human-born illness, and we need to realize this fast. The basic idea is that God creates evil, but is not evil. Evil's status in the Universe is merely an epiphenomenon of human evolution, and it is "parasitic rather than primary and essential."[282] Evil is a positive or negative force of destruction, an infectious reality that can prey on its host (God's goodness) like a virus.

Empirically, evil is, as Jung argued with White, terribly real from a relativistic and psychological standpoint. To call it a defect of goodness does not do sufficient justice to the horror and outrage anyone naturally feels who is touched by evil. Evil is *contagious* and a highly *parasitic* psychic entity that can *toxify* people, families, groups, and nations and lead them and us to commit horrible atrocities. Evil is an incontrovertible fact, an empirical reality. In "The Development of the Personality," where Jung quoted Eckhart, he said ominously in 1932:

> The gigantic catastrophes that threaten us today are not elemental happenings of a physical or biological order, but psychic events. To a quite terrifying degree we are threatened by wars and revolutions which are nothing other than psychic epidemics. At any moment several millions of human beings may be smitten by with a new madness, and then we shall have another world war or devastating revolution.[283]

Hick cautioned theologians and readers generally of the gravity and danger to humans and all life forms if not enough attention is given to the crucial difference between metaphysical and empirical understandings of the *privatio boni* doctrine. In one of White's final publications, "Theological Reflections" in early 1960, he asked a panel of Jungians and theologians to reflect upon the following polarities:

> One [psychology] contains good and evil, light and darkness, the other [theology] is beyond the opposites of good and evil, and (according to St. John) "all light, and in Him there is no darkness at all." One seems to be only imminent and relative, the other both imminent and transcendent, absolute and relative. One is an archetype of human psycho-physical wholeness, the other has been commonly seen since St. Augustine, as the Sustainer and Creator of All.[284]

This was a statement he made shortly before his death. In Eckhart's unitary theology we have to become the One to *see* the One, *know* the One, *love* the One, and *be* the One operating in our life to arrive at a synthesis. We have to get below and above the empirical and relative worlds, so that we might perceive the Absolute. When we can *see* in the apparent tragedies of our lives in time the operation of the hand of God, the creator of good and evil on a relative and absolute plane simultaneously, we might gain a precious key that will unlock the gateway that opens the doorway to the divine goodness of Creation, which is everywhere present in the intelligent design of the Cosmos. Eckhart said: "I once spoke of how our Lord came to his disciples on Easter day through a locked door."[285] Eckhart gave us a *key* to unlock this doorway to the Higher Self.

Theology and psychology are in the same bed in a transpersonal sense. According to Eckhart we are all running into peace. Some events and relationships and patterns in our lives are just too significant not to move a person to formulate a theory of truth out of the empirical and metaphysical data, especially when considering the extraordinary mystery of *calling dreams*. The scientific study of *destiny dreams* has led me to one simple conclusion: psychology and theology are forever wedded. Calling dreams tend to be teleological in nature and point to some future achievement in one's life; destiny dreams point to our foreseen goal.[286] If I've read Eckhart correctly, then I can assert this truth to be self-evident: *the most important birth in the Cosmos is the birth of God or the Self in you, dear reader.* This was Eckhart's basic teaching. Not the life of Jesus, but the Divine life within is what truly matters most in the *Now*.

This simple teaching got him into a whole lot of trouble with the pope. *The ultimate aim of human evolution is you, is me, is whoever we truly are.* Eckhart was not only a father of the German language but also a father of modern theology and a psychology of the Self too.

The harmonious unitary theology of the Universal God of all Creation that we find in Eckhart's best formulations is also found in the philosophies of ancient India and in the writings of the ancient Hebrews, Islamic philosophers, Sufis, ancient Greeks, and in the Church fathers, a vision of unity that subsumes a vast diversity of the world's religions. Wrote Augustine: "All have their offices and limits laid down so as to ensure the beauty of the universe." [287]

This universal beauty is what Eckhart embodies for me and for many who are similarly drawn to him through a certain equality and likeness of spirit. Although he was fond of Augustine, Eckhart would never have endorsed this statement: "the universe even with its sinister aspects is perfect."[288] This is the kind of nonsense that so infuriated Jung. Augustine wrote even more positively: "God judged it better to bring Good out of evil, rather than to suffer no evil to exist."[289] This statement might have spoken to Jung like a breath of fresh air. Here is a post-Augustinian passage from Eckhart that Jung liked to quote:

> Therefore, God gladly suffers the harm of sins, and
> has often suffered it, and most often he has permitted

it to happen to men for whom he has provided that he would draw them to great things. Notice well: Who was dearer to our lord than were the apostles? But there was no one of them who did not fall into mortal sin; they had all been mortal sinners. In the Old law and the new he often showed this through men who afterward were by far the dearest to him. And even now one seldom finds that people attain to anything good unless first they have gone somewhat astray.[290]

Eckhart's thoughts about evil were often more radically trans-dual than either Augustine's or Aquinas's, I feel. We are all mortal sinners, Eckhart said. Saints and popes and bishops and clerics too. Everyone. No one can escape the fact that we all must make a moral inventory of our own evils. Eckhart blew off the dome from idealistic catholic theology and opened up our view to the infinite Godhead that created God and the entire universe of human thought. He showed us that the Godhead is forever a *force* of nature, and we must speak the Word without falling into error as best as we possibly can. How can the Church support Augustine's statement that *the universe even with its sinister aspects is perfect*?[291]

On the Protestant side of the theological debates about the problem of evil was Karl Barth (1886–1968), a long-standing traditionalist among post-Lutheran Reformation theologians. He developed a theory of God's Creation possessing a "shadowside" (*Schattenseite*): an enemy of Universal Being. This is an interesting term, considering the fact that he was born in Basel eleven years after Jung and was a Swiss theologian on Jung's home turf. His formulation was founded upon what he called *das Nichtige*, the arch adversary of God, and it was only overcome for good by Jesus Christ: "The true Nichtige is that which brought Jesus Christ to the cross, and that which he defeated there."[292] However, as Jung correctly showed, the shadow side of God was not defeated; it was only *temporarily* overcome by Christ's victory over evil on the Cross. The ego must be defeated by repeated experiences of the Self. Eckhart said, much earlier than Barth, that "every created being smacks of the shadow of nothingness."[293]

The notion of the goodness of God's Creation is biblical. It can be traced to Genesis, as Eckhart rightly said; it is not a uniquely Christian theological belief. Its foundation is Hebraic. An Augustinian-Thomistic equation of being and goodness was not independent of biblical thought; it was *integral* to the theologies of trans-dualistic cosmologies, or what would become *trans-dualistic* in Eckhart's unitary theology of God and the Godhead.

God's goodness and love were understood by the early Church fathers and mothers, St. Theresa among them, as an emanation or creative outflowing of God's "fecundity." *Fecundity* in Eckhart's theology took on a uniquely feminine characteristic in his metaphor of humans being mothers of God, birthers of God—a revolutionary idea Jung translated into psychological language. Eckhart said: "God is in all things as being, as activity, as power. But he is fecund in the soul alone, for though every creature is a vestige of God, the soul is the natural image of God. This image must be adorned and perfected in this birth ... If you miss it, you will miss all good and blessedness."[294]

Evil was never recognized by Catholic theologians as part of the Holy Trinity, and I doubt this will change *unless* some better formulation emerges. Eckhart wrote: "God wishes man's existence for the sake of the perfection of the universe."[295] This was in line with Aquinas. However, Eckhart drew a clear distinction between God and the primal Ground. In a Universe of multitudinous galaxies, evil presents each of us with the moral freedom to make choices about how we might relate more positively to our communities, our friends and colleagues, our families, and our Mother Earth. At the highest pinnacle of human thought and imagination, psychology and theology, science and religion must join hands in celebration of the divine unity of existence, plurality and Oneness, pantheism and panentheism, theism and scientific atheism, for we are all endowed by our vocations to espouse our own views on God and nature. This is what I mean by a vocation of the Self.

In Eckhart's unitary theology, the knowledge of evil things is good in God-consciousness. This was an early way for him to speak of the importance of what today we call integrating the shadow. According to Eckhart, God comprehends evil and the shadow of our nothingness before God, but God can never be said to be evil in any Absolute sense. As he said in his defense: "Even though existence and understanding are the same in God, still we do not say that God is evil although we can say that he understands evil."[296]

In Eckhart's unitary theology God-consciousness is a state of mind I've called Spiritual Democracy: an *ideal equality of all people with the image of God in its full and robust maturity in superconscious states of mind*. In such ideal states of *unitary seeing*, the world community will need trust and hope. Wrote Eckhart: "Do you want to know what sin is? Turning away from felicity and virtue, that is the origin of sin."[297] Like an experienced gardener, he also said: "God's seed is within us. If it had a good, skilled, and industrious gardener to tend it, it would thrive all the better and grow up to God, whose seed it is, and the fruit would be God's nature."[298]

I'm postulating that contemporary postmodern Christian churches would be wise to be increasingly unifying if they are to help in healing the hurtful divisions and illusions within so many churches of the world today. It was Eckhart's calling to *show* the world how unitary theology could offer a *medicine* to heal the infectious spread of orthodoxy in so many Christian branches and offshoots from the same biblical tree. His inclusive theology centered on the continuous birth of God-consciousness in individual souls of his listeners, women and men alike, social elites and the poor, one person at a time. Soul was and continues to be the birthplace where the Word is born, where Wisdom is born. Sophia, the Word, moves us to arise out of our complacency toward higher *transcendent experiences* of unity, where the agonies of this life and its evils can be viewed from a higher vista.

Eckhart was a unifier and synthesizer of a *new dispensation of God in Dominican theology*. Evil exists in the lower powers of our souls on the relative plane, but a greater goodness and more all-inclusive love can arise out of them and lead us to victory over evil through better understanding. Otherwise, the Word cannot be spoken and made flesh. Eckhart taught: "Mark that anyone who wishes to hear God speaking must become deaf and inattentive to others."[299]

In Eckhart's book *The Nobleman*, he distinguished further between the outer human and the inner human, the aristocrat, new person, or nobleperson: "The other man who is in us is the inner man, whom scriptures call a new man, a heavenly man, a young man, a friend, and a nobleman ... The man in the soul is the good tree that continuously brings forth good fruits ... The outer man is the evil tree that can never bring forth good fruit."[300] As Eckhart said further in a vernacular sermon: "The more universal our life is, the better and nobler it is."[301]

By *universal*, Eckhart meant what we might call *transpersonal experiences*, which are at the same time intimately personal because they are incarnational of the good seed from the good tree planted in the spaciousness of God's Ground. Incarnation is the most intimate experience of God's true nature, the dearest and most common experience we can have along with our fellow human beings and creatures. The highest celebration in the Universe in Eckhart's theology was mercy, or love: love of oneself and love of one's neighbors. Eckhart made it clear that the highest form of love comes from God: "the full equality or parity or even identity of love of self and love of neighbor ... yet love of God from the whole heart is the measure or principle and cause of love of both self and neighbor."[302] Thus, love of God was for him always highest.

It is the function of theology and psychology to treat our spiritual paths today as a science of spirituality. Ideally, science and scripture might one day meet on a common psychological-theological bridge toward a better understanding of the world's religions. Eckhart wrote about the human-divine paradox: "The good angel advises and continually inclines him [her] to that which is good, that is godly, that is virtue and heavenly and eternal. The evil spirit advises and inclines the man [woman] continually to what is temporal and transient, to what is sinful, evil, and devilish."[303]

In Christian theology the devil was and is real, for Eckhart said further: "Moreover, a division is of its very nature a privation. Furthermore, God is not in division; but since God is in all being, that in which God does not exist is nonbeing. Therefore, since God has ordered that he be loved with the whole heart, whatever in the whole heart does not love God is nothing."[304] Wholeness was to him equivalent with spaciousness, wideness, amplitude, sky-consciousness.

The challenge he posed to Christendom is how to get there. "Would that the eyes of the soul were open," he preached, "so that perception could gaze clearly at the truth!"[305] Truth exists in the Kingdom of God within. The more spacious and limitless, the more cosmic, grounded, and humbled. "Hence man is called homo in Latin, from *humus* (ground) and *humilitas* (lowliness)."[306] The nucleus of such a science of religion was the loving care and protection of the humble child in every human heart from the touch of evil.

The Holy Spirit was said by Eckhart to be like a rapid ever-flowing river that divinizes us and unites us potentially in the city of God as a *civium unitas* that will ideally be based, not on inequality, but on our divine *equality,* with our friends, neighbors, justice, and Wisdom. Here, again, is Eckhart speaking about a *vision of peace*: "'There was a man.' Where was he? 'In Jerusalem.' 'Jerusalem' denotes a 'vision of peace'... Let us pray to our Lord that we may be 'man' in this sense and established in this peace, which is himself."[307] The biblical story of the child of God (*Immanuel = God is with us*) was an evolutionary idea that was predicted in the prophecy of Isaiah as a millennial process during humanity's perennial fight against evil on a moral and ethical plane. Eckhart said: "'Unto us a child is born, unto us a son is given.' (Is 9:6): a child by the frailty of human nature, a son by the eternal Godhead."[308]

This story aimed at the birthing of God in the World Soul in a *civium unitas*, or a vocation of the Self in Society and Nature. Eckhart had moral courage and integrity to declare repeatedly: "We are being transformed into the same image."[309] As Jung said of Eckhart, he *"embodied the archetype of the child king without pride and with the utmost humility and poverty of spirit, like St. Francis did."*[310]

Who taught the world that the King of the Jews, the Counselor, the Wonderful, the Transformer, predicted in the Book of Isaiah, the Messiah, might one day be born in the souls of God's children via the Holy Spirit in a *civium unitas*? Eckhart preached: "I say as I have often said before, that the eternal birth occurs in the soul precisely as it does in eternity, no more and no less, for it is one birth, and this birth occurs in the essence and ground of the soul."[311]

The previous theology of the Church fathers from Origin to Irenaeus, Augustine to Dominic, and Albert to Thomas, all theologians before Eckhart had asserted that, according to biblical exegesis, God was born in Christ Jesus as King of the Jews, not that *we* may achieve unity and oneness with Christ. Eckhart took the old theology forward into an entirely new spirituality.

Eckhart charged us all with the problem of overcoming evil in a new *unitary theology* that asserted that the same victory over evil must be worked out by each of us in the relative and Absolute planes of human experience. Evil "stands outside, draws and directs things outward, distracts from inner things, draws to what is other, smacks of otherness, of division, of withdrawal or falling away."[312]

Eckhart preached: "Christ says: 'Whoever would follow me, let him deny himself and take up his cross and follow me' (Mt 16:24, Mk 8: 34). That is, cast out all grief so that perpetual joy reins in your heart. Thus the child is born."[313] Eckhart preached that the Kingdom of God and the King of the Jews or Queen of the Jews (Sophia) is a living reality within us. Wisdom is crucial here, as is Mary, Mother of Jesus. Eckhart equated Leah with Martha.[314] These are feminine archetypes. In India, however, the primal mother of the universe and the Gods is

Vishnu's sister Parvati, the mother of Ganesha and wife of Shiva. I don't want to get stuck in Western God or Goddess-images here. Jung wrote about the transformations in the Western God-image, but I am broadening this to include the metamorphosis of our Goddess-images too. For instance, Sophia, Wisdom, was the fourth level of the soul, above the Virgin Mother in Eckhart's typology. Eve was also included and not rejected as evil. The serpent too was an incarnation of the Divine, as in Kundalini Yoga. Eckhart is therefore the bridge between East and West.

We must learn to appreciate *our* diversity and complexity as small parts of the immensity of space in the infinite Cosmos: "I am so changed into him that that he produces his being in me as one, not just similar."[315] How minute God is in relationship to the Infinite Godhead! For Eckhart, Nature was God's Cathedral. He revered the divine harmony of things, of trees, equally with his own humble existence. The word *equality* is echoed again and again in his most precious sermons. He venerated Mother Earth and her creatures.

Like Christ, Eckhart was called to doctor a *disease in the Church, its inquisitional bondage to Satan and the Devil*—its witch hunts, bloody Crusades, extermination of indigenous people of the earth, its poisonous projections of evil toward women and their bodies, such as the public burning of the French mystic Marguerite Porret. Because he saw that they were his equals and were equally divine, Eckhart came to the support of women. "And so I say, if this child is born in you, then you have such great joy in every good deed that is done in the world that this joy becomes permanent and never changes."[316]

Eckhart taught the spiritualization of all peoples of the earth: "God knows nothing outside of Himself; His eye is always turned inward towards Himself. What He sees, He sees entirely within Himself. Therefore God does not see us when we are in sin. Therefore, as far as we are in Him, God knows us.[317]

"God does not see us when we are in sin." When we are in the Ground of the Godhead, when our souls are sunk in the ground of

Nature, all we see is God: "Here God's ground is my ground and my ground is God's ground."[318] Moreover, where the inborn image wells up *in principio*, the primary archetype of the One, and the Holy Spirit blossoms forth and a new child is born in us in the eternal present, the *Now*, we are at the soul's peak, the apex, or highest vista of spiritual *seeing*.[319] Then an infusion of the Holy Spirit leads us to experience and feel the light of a higher love in the Intellect.

This highest part of the soul is the *Intellect Absolute*, detached from all outward images, a superconscious state of existence, above all outward symbolic forms.[320] "I do not become blessed because God is good," he insisted. "I will never entreat God to make me blessed with His goodness, for he could not do so. I am blessed only because God is intellectual and I know it."[321] *Intellect takes God bare when we are in God*: "Intellect draws this garment of goodness off God and takes Him bare, when he is stripped of goodness and being and of all names."[322] Thus, even the names—"Father," "Jesus," and "Christ"— can be obstacles to the utmost *spaciousness* in the Ground of the soul's highest agent. There we may rejoice: "For God makes merry and laughs at good deeds, whereas all other works are not done to God's glory and are like ashes in God's sight."[323] Our insignificant works *are merely "ashes in God's sight."* In "The Master's Final Words," he repeated the word *equality* again, and with this closing passage, I'll end this chapter:

> Therefore we should accept all things equally from God, not ever looking and wondering which is greater, or higher, or better. We should just follow where God points out for us ... Therefore we should accept God equally in all ways and in all things... God is in all ways and equal in all ways ... In whatever way you find God most and you are most often aware of Him, that is the way you should follow ... But the noblest and best thing would be this, if a man were to come to such equality,

with such calm and certainty that he could find God
and enjoy Him in any way and in all things, without
having to wait for anything or chase after anything:
that would delight me![324]

CHAPTER 15

ECKHART'S AWAKENING TO GOD-CONSCIOUSNESS

Not much is known about Eckhart's transformation of consciousness, his change from acquired knowledge to *supernatural* knowledge. We do not have many stories about the transmutations that occurred in his spiritual character, as we do, for instance, about the Buddha's enlightenment. It does not appear in any of the records that have survived that he was permanently changed by a single transformative experience, one that completely altered his consciousness. Yet it is clear that something did, in fact, happen in his soul while he was in Erfurt that made him one of the greatest spiritual theologians and preachers the world has known.

Rather than positing that Eckhart's awakening to God-consciousness came suddenly through a single illumination that stood out above all others, it appears that his transformation came through successive experiences that eventually culminated in the arrival at a relatively permanent victory of the higher powers of his soul over his lower powers. This spiritual triumph was an outgrowth of the method of meditation he had practiced constantly, every day.

What is the *imprint* Eckhart received that enabled his soul to rise above the angels? Another name for imprint is *Aufschwung* (an "upward impulse").[325] In this imprint or impulse from the primal eruption he said he was enabled to see that *he and God were one*. The highest power of the soul for him was intuition, the "forerunner" of all soul's agents. Whatever the impulse was, his intuition perceived it at his soul's apex and through a descent of grace he became one with the imprinter—God, Christ, the Paraclete, and the divine Ground beyond the Trinity. Eckhart said: "Intellect is a matter of pure being. Intuition, its forerunner, goes ahead and penetrates to what is born there: God's one begotten Son ... Intuition, with the key of Peter, unlocks and goes in and finds God face to face."[326]

Detachment was *key* to his ultimate experience of divinity in the Absolute Intellect. Eckhart always said that his highest experiences were identical with God's bare being. Jung was also well aware of this. He told his seminarians for instance: "Meister Eckhart had a vision of a little naked boy."[327] Who was this little naked boy and what did he want from the Dominican? Jung reported an interesting story from his readings in the Pfeiffer edition: "Where hast thou left him?" Eckhart asked the boy. "In virtuous hearts," he answered. "Whither goest thou?" Eckhart asked the boy once again. "To God," he said. "Where wilt thou find him?" Eckhart continued to question. "When I leave all created things," the boy said. "Who art thou?" Eckhart asked again. "A king," he replied. "And where is thy kingdom?" the preacher continued. "In my own heart." Of course, Jung commented, it was God himself who Eckhart had with him a little while.[328]

If we take this visionary experience as empirical evidence of the *birth* of God in Eckhart, then it needs to be noted that the "king" was the King of the Jews—Immanuel or Jesus. From my research into this story and its origins in Eckhart's visionary life, it is clear that the naked boy was an archetypal figure who Eckhart *actually saw in his mind's eye* and who he engaged with in a dialogue. Jung called this kind of colloquy with the soul *active imagination* in his essay "The Transcendent Function" in 1916. By this Jung meant a synthetic function that unites feeling and thinking, sensation and intuition at a higher level of integration. The reader who dreams of such a child might want to enter into an inner conversation with the child, to see what the child has to teach them about the nature of their vocation, which may have had its origins in childhood. I've found that reading Eckhart can evoke memories of one's first spiritual experiences in early childhood.

Be on the lookout for synchronicities when the vocational archetype is activated in you. As I was writing this chapter, for instance, a colleague called me with a referral for a four-year-old "little girl." I had not treated a child in seven years. Then, a woman entered my practice who *dreamt of a preacher who was leading a five-to-seven-year-old girl by the hand and a second woman in the dream wanted to marry the preacher!* This second coincidence blew me away. First, the inner preacher in her soul was leading the little girl in latency by the hand, and then some other part of her feminine personality was obviously wanting to experience an inner spiritual marriage with her animus, Wisdom, or inner wiseman. This patient had no idea what I was writing. When recording your dreams and inner reflections, watch for synchronicities that are happening around you when vocational archetypes are constellated!

Eckhart's colloquy with the *little naked boy* describes what Jung called a natural process of coming into Selfhood, transformation, or individuation. For Jung, active imagination was a dialogue with visionary content, a dream image, or symbol of the psyche. In Eckhart's example, it was the archetype of the divine child, a boy who appeared to him in his vision as a king. One could say that Eckhart was channeling the archetype of the Christ-image; but it was not Christ, it was a king. Eckhart was channeling in his sermons a "living symbol" that was, in Jung's words, "pregnant with meaning." "The symbol," wrote Jung, "is alive only so long as it is pregnant with meaning ... It is, therefore, quite impossible to create a living symbol, i.e., one that is pregnant with meaning, from known associations."[329]

Jung finished his story by reporting what Eckhart finally said to the boy: "Take any cloak thou likest," the preacher finally said. The unclothed boy-king replied to Eckhart: "Then I should be no king."

159

Suddenly, the boy vanished! "So you could say," Jung concluded, "the equivocal quality of the child in this vision is not just a God but a King of the Kingdom of Heaven that is within, within ourselves, not the God without ... This god, this divinity, has the appearance of a child. If you do not become as a little child you cannot enter the Kingdom of Heaven, you cannot make true the God within."[330] This is vitally important in understanding the goals of Jungian analysis. The child archetype holds the keys to the inner kingdom. This story contains a mystery; for it shows us very clearly how Eckhart's theology was a natural product of his work with inner dreams, visions, and images that came to him spontaneously from his imagination.

It has troubled me for forty-four years why Eckhart scholars in the past have had such a hard time understanding Jung. I disliked James M. Clark and John V. Skinner's curious criticism in their book because of their ignorance about Eckhart's psychology of the Self and Jung's genius in intuiting the main thing in his psychology and that was the birth of the child. It was not the Christ child of myth, but the inner child in Eckhart, the Paraclete that he meant. Their objections to Jung's essay on Eckhart in *Psychological Types* revealed a certain theological bias and inability to understand Eckhart psychologically and to misrepresent Jung in the process. The authors concluded that "the result" of Jung's analysis "can only be described as a travesty of Eckhart's teaching."[331]

A travesty? Clearly, Jung did not read Eckhart theologically as a theologian does. It has been my experience, however, that a little dose of *Eckhart's medicine, his meditative method, can permanently change consciousness in profound ways, as they unquestionably did Jung's.* Any writer on Eckhart's theology would be wise to take his methods seriously by experimenting with his meditative techniques. Otherwise, how can they hope to understand Jung or Eckhart? The travesty of theologians is that they try to understand Jung through the Christ myth without uniting Christ with the Self, or moving beyond "Christocentricism."[332]

Eckhart studies are now centered in Germany with the governmentally sponsored Kohlhammer edition of all of Eckhart's works. Even without Eckhart's full oeuvre at hand, however, Jung zeroed in on the story that gave him a key to understanding Eckhart's essential teachings in their entirety. What really matters is the birth within. The many volumes of theology that I've read are nothing compared to that central inner experience theologians often overlook. To Eckhart and Jung, the birth of God was psychologically *real*.

What would have happened if Eckhart's works had not been condemned? Jung suggested that a great spiritual movement might have followed him. In a further seminar given on March 20, 1929, Jung spoke of the dream of Brother Eustachius, a dream allegedly reported to Eckhart while he was preaching in Paris. In this fascinating dream, *Brother Eustachius saw that many brethren in the Dominican monastery were standing in a circle in the refectory around a beautiful boy. The little child of God asked for a simple loaf of pure white bread to eat. A humble friar, Brother Ruopreht, who was in charge of baking in the refectory, found for the divine boy a loaf of modest white bread to eat. Eustachius loved this brother baker with all of his heart, because of his profound poverty and humility of spirit.*[333]

Stories and quotations such as these are endearing. Jung venerated the memory of Eckhart over all other Christian writers and preachers, even St. Ignatius. He was neither harsh nor critical of Eckhart in any way. In his "Introduction to Suzuki's Zen Buddhism," Jung maintained that Eckhart actually descended to a deeper level of the objective psyche than any Christian theologian before his time. Eckhart's doctrine of birthing God from the Ground of the soul reflected a psychological truth to Jung. "In our actual modern mind," Jung wrote, "we cannot explain it [the divine birth] like that anymore; we understand it more psychologically than ever before. We explain the little naked boy as a psychological fact. A thousand years hence they may have an entirely new name but it will be merely a new form of expression for the same old fact."[334]

This is true. Yet we have to understand the divine birth theologically too. For instance, in his Latin *Commentaries on Genesis*, Eckhart wrote: "'The lion and the sheep will abide together, and the little child shall lead them' (Is 11.6). The little child is the superior rational faculty, which cleaves to God and leads together and reconciles the lion (the sensitive faculty) and the sheep (the inferior reason)."[335]

Eckhart was clearly speaking of the functions of consciousness here when he called the little child the *superior rational faculty*. He was probably writing about what Jung called introverted thinking. Are such dream motifs new forms of expression of the same old fact of the birth of the God-child within? What can psychology learn from theology to help us better understand the child archetype in an experiential way with the aid of Jung's theories of types? Here, I can only provide the reader with some hints.

As I've conjectured, Eckhart was an intuitive-thinking person. Intuition was his superior function, sensation his inferior function. These two functions were balanced at the arms of the cross he carried and was crucified upon with his beloved Christ between thinking and feeling to form a quaternity of four functions. Yet the axis of communication between the superior and inferior powers, sensation below and intuition above, was crucial, as it was also for Jung. My mentor John Beebe called this axis the "spine" of personality. Together his intuition and sensation formed the backbone of his personality that connected him to the Ground of his soul.

Yet as Eckhart said: "A master who has spoken the best about the soul says that all human science can never fathom what the soul is in its ground. To know what the soul is, one needs supernatural knowledge ... What the soul is in its ground, no one knows. What one can know about it must be supernatural, it must be from grace."[336] Entering such a ground can be *healing* because it is where oneness, unity, and peace are experienced and where the eternal child is forever at play. The goal of analytical psychology, in Jung's view, was to reunite the mind with the "eternal Ground of all empirical being."[337] This Ground may be accessed by anyone through traditional methods of meditation offered by any of the world's religions. The goal is the same transnationally. Later in life, Jung said further: "This much we do know beyond all doubt, that empirical reality has a transcendental background."[338] *Eckhart focused on the transcendental background.* He exposed the bedrock of the human psyche, the Psychoid. Together he and Jung form a complementarity that has helped me understand psychology and theology in a much more comprehensive way.

The *spacious atmosphere* Jung said he experienced while reading Eckhart is what is most remarkable in his comparisons between East and West. Spaciousness is an attitude that Jungian analysts must inhabit in our work between ourselves and our patients. Analysts can move toward evermore spacious analytic altitudes to experience the divine birth in themselves and their patient's psyches. Such openness to vista comes about slowly and gradually, over a lengthy analysis, but an analyst should know techniques to keep such an open attitude available to ego consciousness. In Erfurt, an enlargement of scope came to me after my certification as an analyst through the rediscovery of a spiritual practice I had learned while I was reading Eckhart in my youth. I felt a spaciousness open inside of me as I taught at the

Preacher's Church and felt Eckhart's presence in the rooms around me. This is understandable; being there was the fulfillment of my life's dream. Not only had I just become certified as an analyst, but I was also teaching in Eckhart's Church. It doesn't get more meaningful than that for a post-Jungian like me. Just writing about Eckhart sometimes beings me great joy.

In the *Predigerkirsche* (Preacher's Church), Eckhart lived in the angelic realm of archetypal realities, I felt, in the highest place, perhaps most purely when we ascended the spiral stairway and entered the sanctum sanctorum of the attic, where he had slept next to his brothers. I felt I had been there in spirit. The aim of analysis is to give birth to God through the constructive or synthetic method, which was highly influenced by Eckhart. As Jung wrote: "The synthetic method elaborates the symbolic fantasies resulting from the introversion of the libido through sacrifice ... It is equivalent to a renewal of life, which Eckhart symbolizes by God's birth."[339]

This method is what I practiced in Erfurt— making my knowledge there purely experiential. Theologians often overlook the feeling states that Eckhart can evoke when we read him and perhaps especially in the vocational dreams we have later. This is why I spent most of my time upstairs in the Eckhart Room meditating, or walking about in the city with a friend, or reading through my dream journal from nearly forty years prior when I was at UCSC. I wanted to get a *feel* for the preacher and his region and what I experienced while I was writing my first manuscript on him. I felt blissful being there in his Church.

Jung wrote about *blissfulness* in his essay on Eckhart as a state of "intense vitality" in the psyche. The "feeling of bliss," Jung wrote, accompanies "all those moments when one feels born along by the current of life."[340] I can get carried away by reading Eckhart. He transports me to new vistas of understanding. In Jung's elucidation of the transcendent function, he wrote the following: "From the empirical standpoint of analytical psychology, the God-image is the symbolic expression of a particular psychic state, or function, which is characterized by its absolute ascendancy over the will of the subject, and can therefore bring about or enforce actions and achievements that could never be done by conscious effort."[341]

This *God-function* arises from the birth of a living symbol. While reflecting on the meaning of Eckhart's play on words *"Gott ist selig* (blissful) *in der Seele* (soul),"[342] Jung had asked himself sometime prior to 1921: "Whence comes this 'blissful' feeling, this ecstasy of love?"[343] Love is a characteristic of God-consciousness, and I think Jung was in love with Eckhart, as I am also. Birthing God is accompanied by love in Eckhart's theology of the Word. Love is God's child. Yet love is not the highest power of the soul in Eckhart's teaching and preaching. There is a higher state of mind than love. It is detachment. Detachment is always higher: being wedded to Wisdom.

How much Jung learned about types from Eckhart is unclear, although his focus on *right feeling* is transparent in the lines he quoted in the 1921 text cited here. He quoted Eckhart further: "He that is right in his feeling is right in any place and in any company, but if he is wrong he finds nothing right whatever or with whom he may be. For a man of right feeling has God in him."[344]

What does it mean for a person to be in their right *feeling*? It means bliss. In another important passage, Jung states clearly: "'Childlikeness' is therefore a symbol of that unique inner condition on which 'blissfulness' depends.'"[345] What is required to teach Eckhart is a psychological understanding of what it means to become naked, uncovered, unrobed, joyous like a playful child. Nakedness was a metaphor for Eckhart of a state of childlikeness, as it was also for the mediaeval portrait artists of his day, who painted pictures of the Virgin Mother with the bare baby Jesus seated on her lap or playing near her feet. There was nothing concrete or sexual meant by *naked*:

> He must take God not as being good or just, but he
> must apprehend Him in the pure and naked substance
> where he is nakedly apprehending Himself. For

goodness and justice are God's garment which covers Him. Therefore, strip God of all his clothing—seize Him naked in his robing room, where He is uncovered and bare in Himself. Then you will "abide in Him."[346]

Taken literally, in the twenty-first century, this sounds controversial! *"Strip God of all his clothing—seize Him naked in his robing room, where He is uncovered and bare in Himself."* What Eckhart meant was an experience of pure *blessedness before the imageless God,* not pedophilia in relationship to the naked boy-king or voyeurism. To Eckhart scholars, theologians, and postmodern readers it is probably clear what he meant by *naked.* He meant what he had been teaching ever since his first attempts to articulate his methods of *imageless meditation* to his fellow friars and novices in training in the Preacher's Church during his *Talks of Instruction,* written sometime between 1295 to 1298 (the precise dates of publication are uncertain):

The most powerful prayer, one well-nigh omnipotent to gain all things, and the noblest work of all is that which proceeds from a bare mind. The more bare it is, the more powerful, worthy, useful, praiseworthy and perfect the prayer and the work. A bare mind can do all things. What is a bare mind? A bare mind is one which is worried by nothing and is tied to nothing.[347]

Thus, the naked child was a metaphor for *Nothingness,* a *bare mind that is not worried by anything or tied to anything.* Eckhart was approximately thirty-five to thirty-eight years old when he wrote down his method of imageless meditation. Thus, his teaching of this practice of maintaining a bare mind came to him during his entrance into midlife, when powerful transformations typically happen in the lives of great individuals who are aware of the natural processes of transfiguration taking place within them. For Eckhart it happened at an exalted level.

To be sure, God's nakedness meant something exceedingly pure and virginal to Eckhart. Often such life-altering metamorphoses, as symbolized in Eckhart's dreams and visions, occur today through dreams or fantasy thinking that may outline the future of a person's whole life in *advance* with remarkable lucidity and significance. Jung called such occurrences *teleological* or *prospective dreams.* Dreams or visions may emerge in us that often contain portraits of archetypal motifs that are potentially transmuting of the entire personality. It is probable that such a transformation of consciousness occurred in Eckhart's life through a dream state: "God was born in the Nothing."[348]

Humility and Prayers

In his Latin *Commentary on John,* Eckhart said specifically: "One who is not humble ('from the ground') is not a man, for the word man (*homo*) is taken from 'ground' (*humus*)."[349] The true test of a person, therefore, is whether they are humble or not. Human beings are born from the Ground, which is an earth symbol. We are all earth beings, not sky beings. We emerged from Eve, Gaia, or the Great Spirit. We are all wee parts of Nature, in a long line of human evolution, and some of our ancestors were shamans or medicine people, as Eckhart was. Jesus was one of the greatest shamans who ever lived because of his miraculous powers as a *healer.* Eckhart too was a great medicine man and healer.

Eckhart made a clear distinction between the lower and higher powers of the soul. He saw in the lives of Isaiah and Christ an archetype of the suffering servant of God, and he was himself as much a self-realized person of tremendous transformational power as they were. "You should observe two things in yourself which our Lord also had in Himself," Eckhart wrote in the *Talks of Instruction*: "He [our Lord] possessed the higher and lower powers, which had two different functions. His higher powers had possession and enjoyment of eternal bliss. But his lower powers were at the same time involved in the greatest suffering and struggle in the world."[350]

Like Jesus, Eckhart possessed the higher and lower powers in equal measure. *The above and below have two different functions.* The potential is the same in us. Intuition and sensation need to be married at the midway point on the cross beams. Our higher powers must strive to know and enjoy eternal bliss. But our lower powers are at the same time involved in the greatest suffering and struggle in the world. This is the same basic truth as we find in Buddhism and in Jung. The result of the union is always mercifulness or Wisdom. In other words: all human beings have the same basic powers. They are innate, inborn in the souls of every one of us. How to tap into these powers was Eckhart's calling to transmit.

What kind of Prayer did Eckhart Practice?

Monastic life in Eckhart's day was highly structured and consisted of daily sets of prayers set down by the Rule of St. Augustine. Every day began with a prayer service in the Preacher's Church at midnight. It involved a reciting of the divine office. Eckhart and his brothers would then sleep for a few hours and get up again before sunrise for *Lauds* (Morning) prayers. This was a very vigorous training. Eckhart also had to learn the Dominican Order's Marian devotions, such as the Salve Regina and Office of the Blessed Virgin. They had to memorize the entire Dominican psalter for the day's liturgical hours. All brothers in the priory practiced daily confessions as well. Repentance was also a regular practice, one-on-one with a confessor. Prayers for forgiveness and expressions of genuine penitence and remorse was the way to self-forgiveness for sins. *Studying* during the day was also a form of prayer.[351] But of all virtues, poverty, humility, and detachment were perhaps the most important.

In Latin Sermon 22, Eckhart preached: "Man is called *homo* in

Latin, from *humus* (ground) and *humilitas* (lowliness)."[352] In *Talks of Instruction*, he wrote: "For the deeper and lower the ground, the higher and more immeasurable the exaltation and the height."[353] Suffering in the lower powers of the soul and experiencing *bliss* in the higher powers was the answer to the question about what it means to be fully human. Jesus was a man who was poor and humble in spirit. He was a man from the *humus* or ground. *Humus* is an organic element of the soil of the earth. Jesus sometimes spoke of himself as the vine and of us or "ye" as "the branches" (John 15:5). We all stem from the same vine and roots of God.

Therefore, wine and good cheer are wholesome for the soul. Before the last prayers of the day at *Compline* (Night Prayer), the brothers would form a line into the refectory where they would break bread, eat supper together, and drink the *fruit of the vine*. Some of the food came directly from their verdant garden in Erfurt, which was organic. Humus was formed by decomposition of local leaves, vines, tree bark, and other plant materials that had been broken down by living microorganisms. Thus, when Eckhart employed the word *Ground* he meant the place of the divine birth and fruitfulness. He meant the vine and ground. He said in a German sermon: "'Truly, you are the hidden God' (Is 45:15), in the ground of the soul, where God's ground and the soul's ground are one ground."[354]

The Ground of the soul is where oneness and unity and healing and wholeness are in the *Now*. "God is a God of the present ... As He finds you, so He takes and receives you, not as what you were but as what you are now."[355] In Eckhart's view, the confession of sin (or the human shadow) was not merely confessional, but characterized by *supernatural repentance*: "a spiritual joy which elevates the soul above all woe and distress and makes it fast to God."[356]

Eckhart despised flagellation and other severe forms of penitence and torturous methods of extreme physical suffering. The burden of the cross was for him and his brothers heavy enough. Before sitting down at one of the long tables lining the walls of the refectory, the brothers would bow before a mounted wooden crucifix above the head table of the *Predigerkirsche's* prior to their right.[357] Praying to the crucifix was a kind of silent prayer, like counting beads on a rosary.

Eckhart was a man *from the ground*, a preacher of true humility, like his brother in spirit St. Francis. Eckhart referred to detachment as humblest spiritual practice. Only in a detached state of mind can we "find true peace, and nowhere else."[358] This was really a simple teaching, one he repeated almost everywhere he went. It was given to him by God as his noblest spiritual offering.

The seeds of his teachings were planted in section six of *Talks of Instruction*: "On Detachment and on Possessing God." This section became a prototype for his later treatise *On Detachment*, his most lucid elaboration of how to practice humility and achieve blessedness or grace in abundance. Here are *seven simple principles* from this fascinating text:

1) A detached state of mind is an *equal mind*.
2) An equal mind is a requirement of all spiritual seekers who wish to have God ever-present with them through grace, as bliss coupled with compassionate suffering.
3) In order to attain such states of inner peace a person cannot be satisfied with any externally imagined God-images. A person must arrive at a more transcendent, inward consciousness of God as a *nonimage* by means of detachment.
4) Eckhart perfected this technique at the *Predigerkirsche* as a meditative way of transcendence over sorrow while remaining merciful. He said: "It is just like learning to write: truly, if a man [or woman] is to acquire this art."[359] The art of being a good and fluent writer requires disciplined practice, no matter how challenging the discipline may be. So too with silent prayer: one learns to experience the opposites in a unitive way, side by side.
5) Mastering the art of writing requires discipline and diligent repetition, no matter how difficult the task at hand might seem

to you, no matter how heavy or impossible the subject of the art may be. Becoming a fluent writer requires exercise, rehearsal, and repetitiveness. (This is why I always recommend to my patients and readers that everyone keep a journal to improve their writing skills.) So too with meditation.

6) At first, it may be a bitter practice, but it becomes more and more *blissful* and easy as one makes progress and our *childlikeness* is quickened.

7) *Bitterness*, related to the word *bittersweet*, is a synonym for the suffering that comes to anyone on the Self-path. As an emotion, bitterness tells us when we are in the deepest ground of humility. To cultivate this *right state of mind*, one needs constant and consistent practice and one needs a technique. Eckhart tells us what it is: a simple prayer that leads us to a *bare mind*, one free of worries, tied to nothing, and completely immersed in God's will, not our will, or the will of some outer person, but detached from all outwardness and at peace in the higher powers.[360] This leads to transcendence over sorrow while remaining sensitive to the suffering of ourselves and others: "Nothing is more gall-bitter than suffering, nothing more honey-sweet than having suffered."[361]

A detached state of mind is a naked mind free of selfhood. It is egoless, joyous, and mindful of human suffering. This is God as an archetype of *spaciousness* above all images and limited to the utmost by the exigencies of time. This transcendent and imminent God is our most spiritually democratic experience because it makes us all equals in God-awareness. It is found universally in all religions, by way of our common human *equality* with the archetype of the Self within us. The Roman philosopher Boethius taught that the best way to establish direct unmediated contact with *Divinity* is by way of its *exemplar*. In his Latin *Commentary on the Book of Wisdom*, Eckhart explained that for Boethius: "this world, i.e., the whole universe, was first intended and was 'derived from its exemplar.'"[362] In Book III of Boethius's *De consolatione,* the word *exemplar* was used as a synonym for the *God archetype*: "All things Thou bringest forth from Thy high archetype."[363] To arrive at the *high archetype of God, Christ's exemplar,* meant for Eckhart that we need to let go of liturgical prayer, or make better use of it by emptying ourselves entirely of God. If we happen to be Christians, we must first descend and then ascend even higher into God beyond God-images.

What then was the highest prayer for Eckhart? "When I pray for aught, my prayer goes for naught; when I pray for naught, I pray as I aught ... When I pray for nobody and for nothing, then I am praying most truly."[364] I love this one because it is essentially a rhyming poem. It is so childlike that it could have been written by his inner seven-year-old boy, the God-king.

The greatest humility attainable is when we realize we are nothing, we come from nothingness, and our life in time is to become naught, for *"When I pray for nobody and for nothing, then I am praying most truly." Then the child is born*: "What is changed into something else becomes one with it. I am so changed into him that he produces his being in me as one, not just similar. By the living God, this is true! There is no distinction! ... God and I, we are one."[365] As he wrote further in *The Commentary on John,* "'His name shall be Emmanuel, that is God with us' (Is 7:14; Mt 1:23).'"[366]

Christ was a messenger of the ultimate *equality* between God and humanity: "Christ was a messenger from God to us and has brought our blessedness to us. The blessedness he brought was our own."[367] This blessedness can only be found in profound silence. What will happen within you if you listen? In his Latin *Commentary on John,* Eckhart quoted Hugh of St. Victor to answer this:

> All at once I am renewed and entirely changed; I begin to feel well in a way that lies beyond description. Consciousness is lifted on high, and all the misery

of past misfortunes is forgotten. The intellectual soul rejoices; the understanding is strengthened, the heart is enlightened, the desires satisfied.[368]

Eckhart went further than Victor by saying: "He gives birth not only to me, his Son, but he gives birth to me as himself and himself as me and to me as his being and nature."[369] This was where his Spiritual Democracy really began to shine through, and why I feel today his works are being so widely read by persons of faith or no faith. He helps us shut off the obnoxious noise.

CHAPTER 16

ON THE MEANING OF THE CROSS

Every Christian knows the symbol of the cross. For Catholics the crucified Jesus on a cross hangs from the end of every Rosary. To Eckhart the cross was his armor. Eckhart began the following Latin sermon with a quote from Ephesians 6:13: "Receive the armor of God."[370]

Delivered to a learned Dominican audience this was one of Eckhart's most torturous sermons. It focused on the cross and also on the awful *nails* that were used to crucify Christ during an act of unprecedented violence. It's painful to read. He told his audience what Augustine meant by the awful metaphor of being "fixed" with "nails." When the soul has been fastened firmly to the cross, the soul is then freed from suffering and transported into supreme delight through a humble acceptance of one's fate by *nails,* Eckhart explained: "One nail by which we are fixed is the thought of eternal punishment; the second is examination and anticipation of reward."[371] I've never liked the eternal punishment part of Catholicism; it has been so terribly abused by priests to frighten parishioners and children into submission to faith in Jesus.

Eckhart's traditional support and belief in eternal damnation and reward in an afterlife was self-evident in early Christianity, and it is still part of the prevailing opinion of the day. Yet, Eckhart meant what he said: without nails, without scourge, without agony, there is no ecstasy and bliss from the Blood of Christ, the fruit of the vine. For Eckhart reward was fortunately not only recompense in a future life, it meant reward in the *Now*, celebration of relative and absolute existence in time while we have the honor and privilege to be here. Neurotic suffering is dishonest because it fails to admit that all life is sorrow. Sorrow in the lower powers of the soul comes from that fact that one may have missed one's mission, one's vocation in life. Transcendent joy comes from reward for hard work in Eckhart's theology of work. Grace is our recompense in our higher powers for the *nails on which our souls are fixed to the wood of the cross on the horizontal plane, as we suffer the slings and arrows of fate.* To overcome fate's arrows, we have to take aim at our ultimate unity: carrying the cross of Christ voluntarily to the utmost victory in a new birth and resurrection of our personal spirit, which is hard won through daily discipline and endurance. There were *two* crosses to be carried in this sermon, the cross of Christ and *our* cross. For Christians have two crosses. Without Christ's suffering and *nails*, without our own suffering and nails, there is no freedom from pain, no gain. Without agony, no ecstasy.

Life is a paradox of opposites, and we are crucified on the crossbeam. The two nails cannot be prettified by any theologian who wants to present Eckhart in a whole or complete way. So often commentators miss the accent he placed on traditional Christian readings of the cross. Mortification of the flesh really meant *death.* Before Resurrection comes death. Agony and bliss are One Existence: one ecstasy, one life. The agony is carrying Christ's cross and our own, with all of their blood and suffering. Being nailed to two crosses simultaneously in time was central to Eckhart's preaching; so too was spiritual Resurrection, two of them, Christ's and ours.

For me this is one of his most beautifully and carefully crafted homiletical "collations" on not only what it truly means to bear Christ's cross as an obedient and devout Christian, but also what it might mean for any of us today to carry our own cross with an awareness of suffering, humility, and joy in our hearts, and without worry about whether there is an afterlife. "The cry to arms!" preached Eckhart, "is used when enemies approach and danger threatens. Today's epistle talks about nearby enemies and very great danger, so the Apostle calls us to arms with the words 'Receive the armor of God.'"[372]

To further amplify the significance of the cross symbol, Eckhart quoted St. Paul: "Let us put on the armor of light" (Rom 13:12). What is the armor of light? "You will change them and they will be changed; but you are always the Selfsame (Ps 101: 27–28)."[373] The indwelling Self, the Selfsame, and the "armor" of light are the same, both synonyms for God-consciousness.[374]

Light is a necessary precondition for relative and absolute existence, and the higher the soul arises into the superconsciousness, the greater the intensity of illumination. Jesus was a man who was aware of his suffering in the lower powers of his being and transcended suffering in his higher powers. That is why the resurrected Christ is such a joy to see in pictorial representations by gifted artists. He represents victory over life's sorrows. Eckhart quoted Matthew: "If anyone wishes to come after me, let him deny himself, take up his cross and follow me" (Mt 16:24). What does it mean to take up one's cross and follow Christ? *True Christians are instructed to follow the way of the cross as a way to the Selfsame, or light within:* "If anyone"—that means with no exceptions. In this everyone is on the same footing, whether servant or lord, poor or rich, noble or base. *On the same footing means on the same ground,* regardless of one's station in life.

We are all on the same ground regardless of our professional, economic, or social standing.[375] Furthermore, the same footing makes us all equals on the round earth. We are all democratic citizens of the world, all equals. The theme of equality for *everyone* is made transparent here; being *grounded* on the same green earth, wherever one may be. The Holyrood is a *symbol* for one's destiny-pattern. It *symbolizes the source of your vocation.* In Eckhart's sermon, the cross is a symbol for the spiritualization of the soul in the highest possible sense, as Wisdom. It can come to us at any time in our lives as a beacon of light, and it gives us certainty of our end in peace, toward which we are endlessly running.

Eckhart says about the Selfsame: *God is Goodness Itself.* "Since the good is the object of the will and God is Goodness Itself, it is right that a person who serves God does so in completely voluntary fashion."[376] "Completely voluntary" means with full free will.

Will and Intellect were frequently juxtaposed as a pair of complementary *powers* that existed hierarchically on one-continuum. Eckhart's masterful "collation" suggested that "we ought to carry Christ's cross and our own."[377] By "our own," he meant our personal cross of suffering *equally* with Christ's cross, so that the two crosses (Christ's and our own) could be conjoined together into one, or one stacked on top of the other in a vertical manner, making our burden even heavier! The four ways Eckhart gave of bearing our two crosses with humility was specified thus:

1) By frequent and devout remembrance of Christ's passion (here his meditations on Nothingness only hasten the Passion to its ultimate)
2) By hatred of sin (our own sins)
3) By giving up the world's pleasures (attachments)
4) By mortification of the flesh and mercy for our neighbors (fasting and brotherly and sisterly love)[378]

This sermon was a four-part instruction delivered to clerical audiences consisting mostly of Eckhart's fellow Dominicans. He was trying to teach them what it might mean to them if they could become free of "every contrary and everything hostile" in their lives, so that their souls no longer *felt evil*, but, rather, she (the Wise soul) "rejoices and delights in suffering for the love of Christ."[379]

Like the prophets and evangelists of the Old and the New Testaments Eckhart spoke in a *parabolical manner* (a method of interpretation he learned from his assiduous reading of Maimonides's book *Guide for the Perplexed*) to unlock the mysteries and inner meanings of biblical truths.[380] Like Maimonides in the *Guide*, Eckhart often spoke in *equivalences* of meaning.[381] The same style of symbolical thinking had been practiced by Plato and the Neoplatonists at the Academy. Eckhart said: "Plato himself and all of the ancient theologians and poets generally used to teach about God, nature and ethics by means of parables. The poets did not speak in an empty and fabulous way, but they intentionally and very attractively and properly taught about the natures of things divine, natural and ethical by metaphors and allegories."[382]

So, we have to read the nails and cross and blood parabolically. What does the blood of Christ really mean? Similarly, Solomon's proverbs are entitled "Parables."[383] Moreover, "Christ the Truth himself, in parabolical fashion in the Gospels both gives moral instruction and also transmits the general roots of profound, hidden truths to those who have 'ears to hear' (Mt 13:9, etc.)."[384]

Eckhart had explained what Rabbi Moses meant by parables in the *Guide*.[385] Fifteen pages later, after a masterful exegesis, he again quoted Maimonides on the equation of the highest Intellect with Light (Light = Intellect): "On the basis of this conversation of our highest faculty, which is the image of God with God and God with it [superior intuition], the whole book of the Song of Songs seems to have been based and developed. This conversation is between what is holy and the Holy of Holies, between the holy and holiness, the good and goodness, the just and justice."[386] Light and Intellect are synonyms for the highest experience of God, which is crucifixion: "Therefore, when I come to the point that I form myself into nothing and from nothing into myself, and if I remove and throw out whatever is in me, then I can be placed into the bare being of God, and this is the bare being of the spirit."[387]

This is why the nails are necessary and why they cannot be prettified:

> Everything must be driven out that is [merely] likeness,
> so that I can be placed above into God and become one

with him, one substance, one being, one nature, one
Son of God. And after this has happened, nothing in
God is hidden that does not become revealed or that
does not become mine. Then I become wise, powerful,
and all that he is—and one and the same with him.
Then Zion shall become a "true-seer," a true "Israel,"
that is, a God-seeing man, for nothing in the Godhead
is hidden from him. ... If any image or any "similar"
were to remain in you, you would never become one
with God.[388]

"Everything must be driven out!" This was not Jesus the Son
driving the merchants out of the Temple in Jerusalem, it was Eckhart
in Cologne driving out all of the previous thinkers of the Church
and formulating his own unique theological New Dispensation of
nonviolence for the present and the future of European civilization
and culture. It was Eckhart the Son driving out everything that did
not belong in the Temple of God, the place inside each of us where the
little spark in the soul can be seen and heard in the Highest Intellect
and where peace reigns supreme over all bloodshed of war. All learned
knowledge must go if the birth of the Word is to be born in us as God's
light. Eckhart said: "'Unto us a child is born, unto us a son is given.'
(Isa. 9:6): a child by the frailty of human nature, a son by the eternal
Godhead."[389] This is the Prince of Peace, not War.

Eckhart went on further to completely overturn all conceivable
understandings of any previous Church dogmas, from Augustine to
Aquinas. What follows is really vintage Eckhart!

Man experiences two kinds of birth: one *into* the world
and one *out of* the world, that is, this [second] is the
spiritual birth into God. Do you want to know whether
your child is being born and whether it is stripped
bare, that is, whether you have been made God's Son?

As long as you have sadness in your heart because of anything, even if it is because of sin, your child has not been born. If you have sadness of heart, you are not a mother. Rather, you are in the process of giving birth; the birth is near.[390]

Now I will return to the central theme of this chapter after this progression: *carrying of the two crosses*:

Christ says: "Whoever wishes to follow me, let him deny himself, take up his cross, and follow me" (Mt 16: 24). This means: Throw out all sadness from your heart so that nothing but constant joy is in your heart. Then the child has been born... This is why he says, "No one will take your joy from you" (Jn 16:22). Once I have really been transported into the divine being, God becomes mine and whatever he has. Hence he says, "I am God, your Lord" (Ex 20:2). Then I shall have true joy which neither sadness nor pain can take from me, because then I have been established in the divine being where suffering has no place.[391]

Passages like this need to be contemplated deeply in order to comprehend them in the context of Eckhart's life and history. This is an example of detachment at its most extreme. From a contemporary analytical standpoint, it might be a foregone conclusion that such self-torturous meditations on the cross and transport into the higher powers above were dissociative in nature. They were pathological because of their extremity and excruciating excess. Can we ever really throw out all sadness? Of course not. The point is that if you have really been transported into the Divine Being, God becomes yours, and whatever you have is now more freely felt because transcendence has been gained. One still suffers in one's lower powers but not in one's upper powers. It is a paradox. The Self contains all of the opposites from a place above in Wisdom. Emotions no longer capture us. We are not subject to states of possession so easily anymore.

Take anger, for instance, one of the seven deadly sins: "For we see that in God there is neither anger nor gloom, but rather love and joy. Even though it may appear that he sometimes becomes angry with the sinner, this is not anger but love because it comes from great divine love. Those he loves he punishes, for 'he is love' (cf. 1 Jn 4:16), which is the Holy Spirit. Because God's anger rises out of love, he gets angry without passion."[392]

Passionless anger is measured and no longer in surplus. In the infinitude of God, which means the entire Universe, within and without, we all smack of the *shadow of nothingness because we come from nothing, naught.* Yet, "In the beginning was the Word"[393] and "The Word was with God."[394] The Word is Christ, who is forever blissful but suffers in the lower powers, nevertheless.

The Word is what bursts forth from the place of primal eruption, which is the zone of emptiness and violent up-boiling. "The phrase 'with God' bespeaks a kind of equality"[395] with the Word. For Eckhart "the just man is equal to justice."[396] In *The Book of Divine Consolation,* he said: "As the soul becomes more pure and bare and poor, and possesses less of created things, and is emptier of all things that are not God, it receives God more purely, and more totally in him, and it truly becomes one with God, and it looks into God and God into it, face to face, as if it were two images transformed into one."[397]

So too can we become totally transformed through conscious suffering:

> He should lay down and put away everything that is
> a cross of suffering. For truly, if anyone had denied
> himself and had wholly forsaken himself, nothing could
> be for him a cross or sorrow or suffering; it would all

be a delight to him, a happiness, a joy to his heart, and
he would truly be coming to God and following him.[398]

The *Counsels on Discernment* were given to his Order of Preachers
at Erfurt. In Counsel 13, "Of a twofold repentance," Eckhart said
before he became Meister, there are two kinds of repentance: one is of
time and the senses; the second is divine and supernatural. Eckhart
made little mention of the first kind of repentance. What we need to
understand from a point of view in natural theology is what he meant
by *supernatural repentance*. Jung quoted Eckhart on repentance twice
in his seminars. "Eckhart says one should not repent too much of one's
sins because it might keep one away from grace."[399]

Supernatural repentance comes after a person has achieved
sufficient self-inflicted suffering through fasting or other penances,
so that through repentance of the lower human, namely the shadow, in
Jungian terms, a light of supernatural grace begins to emerge through
which a change into its opposite occurs. This person becomes free from
the tendency to suffer in conscience from the stain of sins or evil. They
then gain an insight into God's grace at a higher vista of understanding
that takes *love* (the Paraclete) with it into the Higher Self as Wisdom.
Having borne the burden of the first cross with obedience to Christ, a
higher-type person throws off the cross of Jesus's suffering, and this
detachment is a *higher form of repentance*, where the lower type of
penitence has been cast off in favor of a superior ecstasy. To clarify
this paradox further, I quote Eckhart again: *as godly repentance lifts
itself up to God, sins vanish into God's abyss, faster than it takes me to
shut my eyes, and so they become utterly nothing, as if they had never
happened, if repentance is complete.*[400]

From such a vantage point, a superior vista of light is vouchsafed
to the soul via supernatural grace and through grace one is united
with the highest Wisdom. Then sins, evils, and sufferings are sloughed
away and vanish faster than one can blink. Although a person may
still suffer in the lower levels of their being, which is to say in their

ordinary states of mind, yet the soul *delights* in the higher levels of *her* being as she is bathed in goodness and love and God's grace. A higher transformation has occurred at the ultraviolet end of the spectrum of the psyche, extending from the visible hues of light into the invisible rays that cannot be seen directly by our human eyes, only by refraction.

When the two crosses become one cross, the soul attains transcendent bliss and absolute unity in the *Now*. This parabolic teaching in Catholic theology does not mean the transformation is permanent. Profound change such as Eckhart modeled is always *impermanent*. Discipline and continuous practice are necessary to maintain it. To be sure, Eckhart was interested in speaking to the public in a new parabolical manner so that anyone might understand him, transcendent of time, locale, and religious culture. Yet evil is still evil; and the Devil was a terrible *reality* that stared him in the face during his trial in Cologne and Avignon where he suffered and died.

CHAPTER 17

ECKHART'S TRIAL AND DEFENSE

The opening words of the Bull *In agro domenico* (March 27, 1329) were written by Pope John XXII, fourteen months after the preacher's death in Avignon: "The man [Eckhart] was led astray by the Father of Lies who often turns himself into an angel of light in order to replace the light of truth with a dark and gloomy cloud of the senses, and he sowed thorns and obstacles contrary to the very clear truth of faith in the field of the Church and worked to produce harmful thistles and poisonous thorns."[401]

The biblical reference by the eighty-five-year-old French pope concerning Eckhart's being led astray by the "Father of Lies" was found in John 8:44. In his *Commentary on John*, Eckhart had said faithfully about this passage: "He who falls from the True falls into a lie … To leave God is to approach the devil—'The devil is your father' (Jn 8:44) … Everything that exists and that is true and good is possessed in the One itself."[402] Eckhart was living in a unitive state, the state of oneness, where evil did not exist on the inside. The attack on his integrity by the Pope was a privation from the truth of God, a devilish projection of evil onto poor Eckhart. Who was the real devil here? It was certainly not Eckhart. Who had left God, Eckhart or the Pope?

It appears to me that the accusations by the pope against Eckhart were about his having been led astray by the "Father of Lies," by which he meant the serpent, Satan, or the Devil. What was going on here? As I see it, a psychic infection had entered the Holy Roman Church, and it had a lot to do with projections of the shadow and evil onto Eckhart by Franciscans and Dominican brothers and officials alike. The devilish attack by officials in Cologne and the Avignon's pope's merciless accusations that asserted that Eckhart had succumbed to the "dark and gloomy cloud of the senses" were false and unjust. Really, if his works had been studied properly, they would have recognized that Eckhart could have provided the Church with a winning proposition on ways to spiritualize the sensual anima into the highest possible stages of Wisdom!

True, Eckhart was closer to the serpent and women than most theologians would dare to be in his day, but he delighted in the sensual body and spread joy with a generosity of spirit as a father of the Church wherever he went. Eckhart was blessed by the serpent-powers and the grace of God, and he lived an integrated life of delight and creativity at much higher levels of awareness than many theologians of his era could. The added emphasis by the pope that Eckhart produced "harmful thistles and poisonous thorns" was suggestive of a toxin in the Church itself, which was highly *infectious*, a veritable poison that was lurking in the thinking of his times and that Eckhart had attempted to *heal* as a psychotherapist might today with a better system of therapy and ethics, one based not on splitting, but on oneness and unity with the higher levels of the soul, not on dualism, but *trans-dualism*.

It was *not* Eckhart's teachings, counseling, or preaching, but a highly contagious *toxin* in the Church and its doctrines that encouraged dualistic thinking, the very thing Augustine had fought against in his denouncements of the dualist Manicheans. To Eckhart the serpent was God's most excellent creature because of its subtle wisdom. In my view, it was the Church of his times that produced poisonous thorns, whereas Eckhart's works provided *antivenin*, a psychotherapeutic *balsam* so desperately needed, the *medicina catholica* of a trans-dualistic theology. The Father of Lies was in the organization of the

Church that Eckhart had been called to *heal* as a theologian and preacher by celebrating our "sense-endowed" bodies and souls on an equal plane with superior reason, the highest intellect, or Wisdom of Sophia.

During his trial, Eckhart became a doctor of the Church by diagnosing precisely what the illness was that had infected the Holy See and the aging pontiff. Eckhart made it clear in his own self-defense on September 26 in the "year of our Lord 1326" that he *knew* that the attacks against him had begun to spread like a virus in Cologne. They proceeded from a "false suggestion and an evil root and stem" by vicious lies of "envious people." He was acting as a postmodern analyst might today to diagnose the infection of his accusers, prior to applying his antidote, his *medicine of Truth*, before the Archbishop of Cologne:

> "Blessed are they that suffer for justice's sake" (Mt 5:10), and according to Paul, "God scourges every son he receives" (Heb 12:6), so I can deservedly say with the Psalm, "I have been made ready in scourges" (Ps 37:18). I ought to do this particularly because long ago, but in my own lifetime, the masters of theology in Paris received a command from above to examine the books of those two most distinguished men, Saint Thomas Aquinas and Brother Albert the Bishop, on grounds that they were suspect and erroneous.[403]

It was *sad* and upsetting for me to read this. Eckhart's medicine was the way of the Cross and the blood of Christ, not the superficial Christ of the Church fathers, but Christ within him: the Word of God. He had instructed his followers to be wise as serpents and harmless as doves, and Eckhart was in touch with the serpent power as well as with the spiritual force of Wisdom in the angelic order. Eckhart obediently soared upon this Self-path *above* the opposites with the wings of an eagle: the metaphorical *Via Delarosa*, representing the path that Jesus took in Jerusalem, he took from Cologne to his destination and final resting place in Avignon. This, I think, was key: the Serpent, God in his trans-dual nature, eventually poisoned the inflated ego of the Catholic Church for its own splits from unitary conscience, from the air, seas, our environment, and from the *true* speakers of God's Word, as many preachers were in the twentieth century when Jung was reading him. The Catholic Church has not recovered from its illnesses yet.

The humble preacher protested before his commissioners on September 26, 1326, in his own just self-defense:

> If I were less known amongst the people and less eager for justice, I am sure that such attempts would not have been made against me by envious people. But I ought to bear them patiently, because "Blessed are they who suffer for justice' sake" (Mt 5:10), and according to Paul, "God scourges every son he receives" (Heb 12:6), so that I can deservedly say with the Psalm: "I have been made ready in scourges" (Ps 37:18) ... I can be in error, but I cannot be a heretic, because the first belongs to the intellect, the second to the will.[404]

By *will* Eckhart meant right feeling, right virtue, right suffering, right love, right mercy, and his accusers lacked these virtues. More, he justly exclaimed: "I am always ready to yield to a better understanding."[405] This was his refutation of charges of any error, as a respected theologian, preacher, and a man. He was making an important ethical and legal point as well. Truth was more important to Eckhart than his mortal life. He insisted: "Even though existence and understanding are the same in God, still we do not say that God is evil although we can say that he understands evil."[406] Eckhart understood evil, as it was staring him in the face.

Eckhart was a symbolic thinker, and he was attuned to a deep spiritual experience that was virtually unknown to the Archbishop of

Cologne, Hermann von Virenberg, who accused him of heresy, having no comparable experience of his own. He read only a few of Eckhart's sermons and writings and knew nothing of his voluminous teachings in Paris. In 1327, after answering to charges of heresy at the Archbishop's Court at Cologne, Eckhart preached at the Cologne Church, defending his belief in the Word of God that was vernal within him. He insisted he had avoided all errors of faith and exhibited correct moral conduct and obedience within the traditional virtues of his Christian faith. The fact is that Eckhart had gone beyond Church conventions to posit what was essentially a new revelation of God's incarnation in humanity through the continuing indwelling of the Holy Spirit—a truth that Jesus had explicitly stated to his disciples before his ascent to the Heavenly Father.

Eckhart then set out fearlessly for the vestal Court at Avignon, the headquarters of the papacy in France to defend his thinking. He was kept under surveillance in Avignon and died there of unknown causes on January 28, 1328. This was truly unfortunate, for in an Avignon trial, he might have encountered some of the most learned theologians of his day, who could have defended his theology if they had taken time to study his works in German and Latin. This may be too optimistic. Yet, if they had truly been Dominicans, in the sense that Eckhart was, some, yet certainly not all of the specifics of his statements about God and the Ground beyond God might have been clarified. (One of the most contested issues concerned his *identity* with God, a charge Eckhart said was completely false, since he practiced self-abnegation and self-abandonment above all).

What shines throughout his testimony was Eckhart's profound *humility and fearlessness to speak the truth as he walked through the valley of the shadow of death, carrying his cross with an integrity that cannot be measured.* He had the audacity and courage to speak evil (affective anger) to evil, while taking in his accusers' poisonous projectiles of envy and hate into his own saddened heart. He continued: "The first mistake they make is that they think that everything they do not understand is an error and that every error is heresy, when only obstinate adherence to error is a heresy." He even called attention to his accusers "stupidity and ignorance."[407] This was God's divine justice speaking through him.

The commissioners had not read a fraction his works, in either Latin or vernacular. "I have written a hundred things," he declared, "and more that their ignorance neither understands nor grasps."[408] His truth-telling about the birth of the Paraclete in his soul was done in full awareness of the potential perils that could befall him if he'd been charged with heresy, which fortunately wasn't to become his fate because of his obedience to his oath of office and his humility. It was his destiny to be completely freed from all suspicions of sacrilege. As divine providence would have it, many of his vernacular sermons and a portion of his Latin works were protected.

Eckhart's final point in the "Defense" was perhaps his most poignant in light of the way he had lived his life as a bearer of Christ's cross and his own: "Eighth, they attack the idea that the godlike man can perform God's works, against the teaching of Christ and the Evangelist: 'He who believes in me, the works that I do he also shall do, and greater than these' (Jn 14:12)."[409] This eighth point was the main argument in his defense, the pivot around which the entire "Defense" turned. He did not identify with God or Christ, but knew he was One with the Paraclete that had given him birth.

Two of the evil commissioners, Master Reiner Friso, Doctor of Theology, and Peter Estate, Custodian of the Order of Friars Minor in Cologne, did not accept his objections. Why? Because they did not read him carefully or fully enough. If a reader starts with Christ's teaching in John 16:7 that the *Comforter* would come to the disciples only *after* Jesus departed, then they would discover the promise of the Lord was that the carrier of the sacred lineage of chosen Sons of God would lead from Isaiah to Jesus, to Eckhart, and to you and me. This is not what the Church had traditionally taught, and it is still stuck in childish theology that has not yet become psychologically mature in the sense that Eckhart and Jung meant it.

It was not Eckhart's orthodox Augustinian statements that got him into trouble with his censors during his heresy trial in Cologne and Avignon; it was startling statements such as this one that outraged them: "In every work, even in an evil, I repeat, in one evil both according to punishment and guilt, God's glory is revealed and shines forth in equal fashion."[410]

This striking passage, which certainly would have pleased Jung, formed article 4 of *In agro dominico*. In addition, Eckhart made other statements that shocked his commissioners, such as this one: "He also knows that God would not permit him to sin if it were not for his own betterment."[411]

Eckhart was humble enough to admit he could err, like we all do. He was open to editing and deleting, like everyone who writes errs. We all make mistakes in judgment and wording. He admitted in his Defense: "I am always ready to yield to a better understanding ... I can be in error, but I cannot be a heretic, because the first belongs to the intellect, the second to the will."[412] I cherish this statement, because it is both modest and wise.

With plenty of politics involved in his trial, there was a foregone conclusion, and no apology had never been made by the Catholic Church. No confession of any wrongdoing was made by Eckhart's accusers, neither the Commissioners, representatives of the Holy See, nor the pope who signed *In agro dominico* (March 27, 1329). Eckhart the man may have made a few mistakes, as we all can, but was willing to withdraw anything that was evil-sounding or untrue to scripture, as he had been classically trained by the best theologians in Christendom. Nevertheless, he stayed true to his vow of obedience in the end. Here are some lines from the Bull in order to let readers hear it for themselves:

> In the field of the Lord over which we, though unworthy,
> are guardians and laborers by heavenly dispensation,
> we ought to exercise spiritual care so watchfully and

prudently that if an enemy should ever sow tares over the seeds of truth (Mt 13:28), they may be choked at the start before they grow up as weeds of an evil growth. Thus, with the destruction of the evil seed and the uprooting of the thorns of error, the good crop of Catholic truth may take firm root.[413]

Eckhart was accused of being an *enemy of God* whose seeds of truth needed to be *choked at the start* before his works could grow up in the so-called good crop of the Church. Notice the *violence* directed at Eckhart's radical truth-telling. The pope wanted to choke his work at the start before he could start a movement based on a new teaching that had not come into collective awareness yet. Eckhart had said clearly enough that *only obstinate adherence to error is a heresy.* He acknowledged his shadow for Christ's sake! Rather than turning his scholastic violence inward against his own pride, the pope and the commissioners projected their unconscious shadow during the tribunal onto the preacher and tried to *nail* him to the cross. While it is true that he sometimes went too far, Eckhart devoutly believed with the pope and Holy See that *with the destruction of evil seeds and uprooting of the thorns of error the good crop of Catholic faith could take firm root with a better understanding of theology.* He was a Dominican after all, and his devout obedience was to the Church.

No one who reads this document today and is familiar with Eckhart's sermons and treatises can read the condemnation without feeling pain over the accusations and poisonous documents. Eckhart was charged with wishing "to know more than he should" and was further accused of having been "led astray by the Father of Lies" who had "worked to produce harmful thistles and poisonous thornbushes."

Eckhart was further attacked for preaching alleged falsehoods to an "uneducated crowd in his sermons." Who were these uneducated persons? Dominican brothers and sisters (nuns) and Beguines? The condemnation was directed to everyone who congregated around

Eckhart, as if only the orthodoxy could declare that they *knew* how to read the Bible correctly, which is ridiculous. The Bible is open to interpretation by anyone. It was not Eckhart, but the Holy See that infected Eckhart's pupils with falsehoods by cautioning them with fearful threats of violence.[414] Finally, it was stated at the end of the document that "at the end of his life" Eckhart had "revoked and also deplored" the twenty-six articles that were to the committee "evil-sounding" and suspect of heresy, but there was zero evidence in any statement to my mind that supports the opinion that his works should have been banned if the few statements in question had been edited out.[415] The Bull condemned Eckhart's works and threatened anyone who might read them with scrutiny and persecution.

Article 4 of the Bull stated clearly what was so pernicious in Eckhart's theology. I will repeat part of it: "I repeat, in one evil both according to punishment and guilt, God's glory is revealed and shines forth in equal fashion"[416] This was a psychological statement, and it could clearly be interpreted as being overly idealistic about evil, but that was not so because he was speaking evil to evil.

Wisdom sometimes *wills us to sin consciously.* The Holy See projected the Father of Lies onto Eckhart, yet they were entirely corrupt. Church organizations, like all organizations, are breeding grounds for psychic infections, and in Christianity the very issue Jung took on face to face with theologians was the denial of the shadow and evil and the assertion that God is always good. During Eckhart's trial the fearless preacher of God's Word cast off his garment of goodness as a theologian and let the shadow of God speak through him with the voice of justice as one of God's watchdogs. He assumed the accusing mantle of an inquisitor and charged his accusers with sins of envy, pride, and heresy, which they had projected onto him. He tasked the Holy Roman Empire with the problem of becoming conscious of its own shadow-casting.

This radical relativity of God as not only good, but also capable of wrath, anger, even evil-sounding words, is *why*, I believe, many readers revere his memory today. He did not hesitate to speak his own truth from the *vox Dei*.

I bow my head to Eckhart for having stood up to the Holy See. Eckhart's trail is a tragic example of the problem of the splitting of the opposites in Catholic organizations. Every writer knows how difficult it is to write well. We all must edit out our own excesses if we are to publish a polished work that we can be happy with. Everybody who studies these documents can clearly see today that he was set up as a scapegoat. In some ways I feel I am Eckhart's *advocate* in Truth. The fight with the shadow and evil is the ultimate fight, no minor work of individuation, but the masterpiece. No one is free from error, or evil. None of us. No saint, prelate, or pope. The myth of the perfect human died with Jesus on the cross. Eckhart put forth a better understanding of God for the future of humanity, as we must all attempt to do to take the Christ myth forward to the way *after* Christ.

We cannot go back in time to remedy the mistakes of church dogma. The best we can do is to remedy the problems of theology that are psychologically unsound, such as the *privatio boni* doctrine. Everything Jung objected to about this debatable principle is open for discussion and dispute. No theologian I've read has helped us understand the problem of evil over which Eckhart was silenced better than Jung did.

Every archetype of vocation is in possession of existence in its exemplar, and in Eckhart, the paradoxical God-images of the Old and New Testaments were speaking through the Word of the preacher via the continuing incarnation, the Paraclete (John 14:12), or Wisdom of God. After Eckhart left Paris, his identity seems to have morphed into Wisdom and his gender identity melted away into Unity. To be sure, his anima seems to have evolved through his relationships with women. Women have to work on their violence too, which, despite bad theology, is part of the dynamic of Wisdom: "Who is she that looketh forth as the morning, fair as the moon, clear as the sun, and terrible as an army of banners?" (Song of Solomon 6:10). There must be something chilling

about the Word that bespeaks a certain inhumanness, an inhumanity
that makes relations between men and between some women terrible
and the bloodshed of war endurable, even desirable. From this shadow
side of patriarchal religions—Judaism, Christianity, Islam—we've had
the Crusades, the Thirty Years' War, Islamic jihads, Manifest Destiny
from the eastern seaboard westward to California. As far as I know,
Eckhart did not support a theology of so-called just war at all. He
seemed to be speaking about detachment from all external violence.
Often while giving sermons, he sometimes stated his principles in
fours, which suggests wholeness:

> When I preach, I am accustomed to speak about
> detachment, and that man should be free of himself
> and of all things; second, that a man should be formed
> again into that simple good which is God; third, that
> he should reflect on the great nobility with which God
> has endowed his soul, so that in this way he may come
> again to wonder at God; fourth, about the purity of the
> divine nature, for the brightness of the divine nature
> is beyond words. God is a word, a word unspoken.[417]

It was not my calling to be a preacher, theologian, or minister
of sacred doctrine when I heard the call at UCSC. As a California
psychotherapist, who happens to also be a Jungian analyst and child
psychotherapist, it seems clear to me that Eckhart's relationships with
women made him a much better preacher. My main focus in analytic
treatment has been on dreams as *mediums* through which the *light
of the archetypes of vocation* may be revealed to patients, directly or
indirectly, from their own experiential Ground of being. What I practice
might also be considered by some to be transpersonal psychotherapy.
In mysterious ways, Eckhart has been behind my vocation since its
inception.

Here is a passage from Eckhart I came across recently, which transmits the whole message he taught in a simple and pragmatic way, so that anyone might understand him with an open heart: "My message is: if you want to act justly and well, may 'to fight for justice unto death' be like your life is to you, indeed, may it be dearer and more precious to you than your life is. If this be so, then your work is in God and is a work divine and just."[418]

To put our life in justice above our own personal life in community is tantamount to saying that the way of the two crosses, even unto death if need be, is *the way of our future*. I mean this as a Jungian: the way forward for humanity is through a *symbolic death*. We are all called not only to work in justice but also to *be* Justice.

This might mean that our fight in the armor of God's light can come to us from within or without. Whether by attaching oneself with chains to redwood trees to prevent further crucifixion of our precious Sequoia people or whether expressing anger over racial injustices or the stealing of indigenous lands, justice leads the way to a better global society, a better earth, a better climate. The animals of the world and the animals of the soul are depending on us during this new geological age that scientists have termed the *Anthropocene*. As Jung said to Victor White: "I have discovered for my private life, that a true Christian is not bedded upon roses and he is not meant for peace and tranquility of mind but for war."[419]

If we are not all crucified on our vocations to the universal God of the world's forests and if we do not protect the creatures of the earth, we may all be doomed. As a California Jungian, I am also a Jamesian at heart, as well as a staunch Eckhartian. This means that I believe in the *democratic equality* of all spiritual traditions and do not place any one theology above another because the only way I know how to understand theology is by becoming an *impermanent* and *imperfect* medium for the reception of God's light. Great masters of the Church like Eckhart are transmitters of immeasurable light, love, life, and *spiritual healing* worldwide. They help us in times of distress and sorrow, and offer us wise counsel on better discernment or discrimination between good and evil.

When I was suffering from spiritual aridity and a bad neurosis as a young man at UC Santa Cruz, city of the Holy Cross, I was blessed by a number of dreams relating to Eckhart that illuminated my spirit and temporarily healed me. This much I *know*: It came from the fact that Eckhart was alive in me, and I was living in Eckhart's teachings through the light of his example. In his *Commentary on John,* Eckhart defined *light transmission* this way: "It does impart something to the medium reciprocally and impermanently, in the manner of a reception, something transitory that happens in it so that it is and is said to be illuminated."[420]

The soul can only be illuminated by an exemplar *impermanently.* No one, in this sense, is ever forever and finally free from sin and evil. A true Christian is never fully free from the seven deadly sins. Hate and anger are still present in the soul because the opposites are not placed next to each other, but are, as Eckhart said *within each other*: "Hatred of evils itself is the love of good or of God. It is one habit, one act."[421] "Thus, good shines in what is evil, truth in falsehood, and possession in privation. 'The light shines in the darkness.' There follows, 'And the darkness did not comprehend it.' Nothing is pure evil or falsehood."[422] If Eckhart committed evil in the eyes of the Lord it was to bring out the light to illuminate the darkness within Christianity itself.

When I was in the Preacher's Church in Erfurt on the summer solstice, in 2019, I remember standing in front of the Eckhart Portal. I asked two women who were walking by on the cobblestone-street to snap my picture there. On the door behind me were the famous words from John 1:5: "The Light shineth in the darkness; and the darkness comprehend it not." At the Eckhart Portal, I was standing in the doorway to God's house, the Light of the *Preigerkirsche*. What I owe to Eckhart is simply incalculable. He transmitted to me and so many others his *sacred medicine* to heal ourselves of our own darkness and evil by infusing us with everlasting light. Eckhart's disciple, Henry Suso, saw shining in a vision an illumined visage that appeared before his awakened eyes:

> The blessed Master Eckhart … By the Master he [Suso] was told that he lived in surpassing glory, in which his soul was purely divinized in God … Then [Eckhart] said: … stand out in silent patience against all wolfish men.[423]

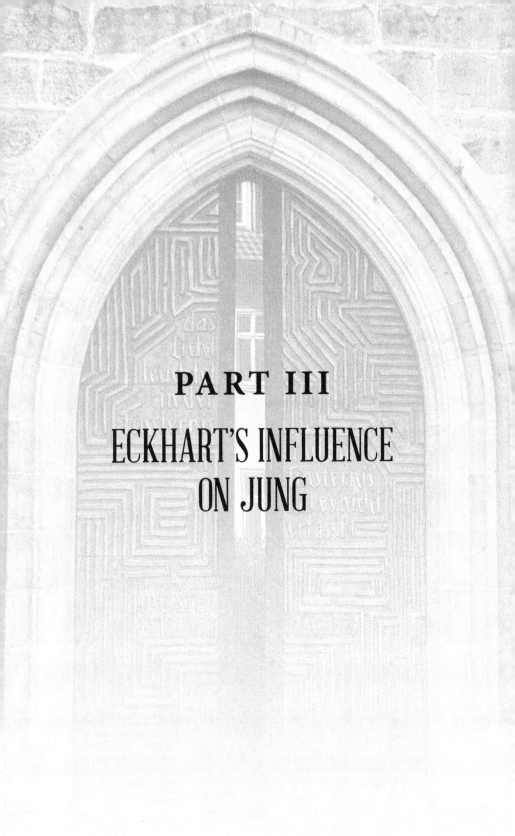

PART III

ECKHART'S INFLUENCE ON JUNG

CHAPTER 18

ECKHART AS A TRANSFERENCE FIGURE IN JUNG

Fifteen was a transformative year for Jung! He discovered a volume of Eckhart's sermons on his father's library shelf as well as books on the Grail Quest, the Parzival legend, and Nietzsche's *Zarathustra*. These imaginative and intellectual discoveries all led to a re-awakening of his *nuclear symbol*[424] of vocation as a born healer of humanity. Never once did Jung disparage Eckhart. He turned to him for spiritual assistance in clarifying his ideas during his lectures in the *Psychology of Yoga and Meditation*. There Jung said on June 9, 1939, about Eckhart: "He is expressing in Western medieval language what is, in fact, the essential idea of eastern yoga."[425]

Eckhart filled Jung with the *breath of the Holy Spirit*[426] because he had spoken God's Word in his own unique incarnation and was not just parroting Abraham, Moses, or Jesus. To Jung he was the greatest of all preachers because Eckhart erected a bridge between East and West that made *equality* of religious ideas possible six hundred years before there was a Parliament of World Religions, which was held in Chicago in 1893.[427]

It needs to be added here that, like Freud, Jung was never analyzed. He did not have a personal analysis. Yet, both he and Freud were convinced that the transference was the alpha and omega of analysis. If it could not be resolved through an analytic relationship, Jung's projections had to naturally go somewhere other than onto Freud, who had a far too pessimistic view of religion for Jung's taste. Thus, they landed for a time on William James. Before that, however, it was Eckhart who he idealized in a truly spiritual way. All other theologians fell short of Eckhart's stature, to Jung's mind, even Böhme. Jung later said that the transference is a universally valid phenomena that may occur anywhere in life. It's the way our personalities build themselves up through human relationships, whether through personal or transpersonal connections, and without which no authentic individuation may take place. Jung wrote in 1946: "The transference is itself a perfectly natural phenomenon which does not by any means happen only in the consulting room—it can be seen everywhere."[428]

This *universality of the transference* is perhaps especially true in the phenomenon of vocational development worldwide. We often transfer our nuclear symbol onto a great figure in history who carries for a time our ideal projections of the Self by virtue of their high attainments of excellence in a certain field. We see this in theology, such as when Eckhart transferred his nuclear symbol as a novice onto a number of great Catholic Saints (Augustine, Albert, Aquinas), a Greek scientist and philosopher (Aristotle), a Jewish philosopher (Maimonides), and two Islamic philosophers (Avicenna and Averroes), for significant periods of time in Paris. By the time he stepped foot back in Germany, all of that transference fell way into the abyss again and he was left empty and pure and filled with his own divinity of personhood. Although the Christ-image was always primary for him ever since very early childhood, even Christ slipped away from central stage in Strasbourg and Cologne.

Similarly, Jung was influenced by Schleiermacher, Schopenhauer, Kant, Nietzsche, and many other important theorists. Yet, I hypothesize that Eckhart was always a central-most inner figure for Jung, an internalized *theologian and preacher,* a *Self-figure* who, through a natural process of transference, sparked religious truths in Jung that were both practically and theoretically profound about the nature of the human psyche and the "birth" of God in the soul. As Jung said: "This [birth] is probably one of the most important points in Meister Eckhart's writing."[429] This is true. Eckhart led Jung to discover new ways of speaking his own psychological truths with his own inner Wisdom as a psychiatrist and teacher.

To be sure, the child in Jung was originally called to deliver a religious message to humanity before he read Eckhart, and his insights into the nature of God were far in advance of his years, even before he entered Kindergarten. But it wasn't until adolescence, when he picked up that volume by Eckhart from his father's library shelf and began to read in it, that the sparks of the Christian *teacher* and *preacher,* the charismatic writer and speaker of God's Word, was switched on in him through a natural process of evocation. Eckhart *evoked* the latent symbol of his vocation, his nuclear symbol as teacher and practitioner of authentic religion.

CHAPTER 19

ECKHART'S INFLUENCE ON JUNG

In order to properly understand Jung's thoughts on the role that Eckhart played in the development of his analytical psychology, it is best to consult his *Red Book* and the 1921 "Relativity"[430] essay first; then proceed to his later hypotheses in the *Dream Seminars,* the seminars on *Nietzsche's Zarathustra* and *The Psychology of Yoga and Meditation*; followed by "A Psychological Approach to the Dogma of the Trinity," *Aion,* and *Answer to Job*; and finally, his essay in 1958, "A Psychological View of Conscience." This overarching trajectory began with the composition of his *Red Book,* where Eckhart played a seminal, although unacknowledged role, as a *spiritual ancestor and minister over the dead.* Eckhart had by this time (1914–1921) become a Self-figure in Jung's soul or psyche, an imprint of great spiritual wisdom. His influence was in the background during Jung's processes of active imagination, his colloquy with certain key figures, such as Salome and Philemon. In Jung's *Collected Works,* published *Letters,* and semiautobiographical work *Memories, Dreams, Reflections,* Jung cited Eckhart a total of forty times, as was first pointed out by Jungian analyst and priest John Dourley (1936–2018).[431]

Yet, as I pointed out to John in a personal letter, there are another forty references in Jung's *Seminars* that need to be considered as well in order to grasp the overall significance of Eckhart's influence in Jung's published work to date. As a Self-image, with whom Jung had identified in his youth, Eckhart inspired some of Jung's hypotheses on the nature of Self; the collective unconscious; God and the Godhead, and the birth of the God-image in the human soul; being and Nothingness; becoming mothers of God and Wisdom, or Sophia;[432] the Holy Spirit; fetching God from without or, in psychological language, from projection; detachment as a state of psychic objectivity; the inner voice; the Word; the Ground of all empirical being; and the limitless expanse of the human psyche.

Studying the eighty citations in Jung's work is too cumbersome for most readers, so I've done the footwork and synthesized his references in what follows in a pragmatic way; one cannot overlook this line of inquiry and possibly hope to understand what Eckhart meant to Jung as a mystic and first psychologist of the Self in Europe. Even then, after the eighty citations are examined for their specific content, we're still only making hypotheses about how Jung translated what he learned into the language of modern science since his inner relationship to Eckhart is still somewhat of a mystery. I'll provide a review of most of Jung's thoughts on Eckhart in this book, so readers can decipher for themselves how Jung made use of Eckhart and how he may also have misread him at times to fit in with his own empirical knowledge of the unconscious.

Bridge to the Self

Although Jung had indicated an established link between Eckhart and the *Upanishads* by 1921, it was not until his ETH Seminars between 1928–1939 that we find convincing evidence for the correlation that Jung *saw* between Eckhart and the East. By this, I mean the *bridge* the preacher-theologian had erected, without his knowing it of course, to Hinduism, Buddhism, and Taoism. The important point in this bridge-building was that Eckhart was speaking from the depths of the collective unconscious, from a level beyond the national psyche, a Ground that is below and above all opposites in the trans-psyche. What this suggests is that Eckhart had gone so deep into the collective unconscious that he broke through to the one-continuum of Wisdom that we find in Eastern and Western philosophy and theology as a place of meeting between mystics and shamans of all varieties. As far as I know, Eckhart is the *only* figure in the Christian West, however—and this is the most significant *fact* mind you—who Jung said created such a bridge to the concept of the Self from European soil.

Jung's clearest definition of the Self as a foundation stone of analytical psychology was the *equation* of the Christ-image with a "Christ that comes after Christ, a new Savior. Or ... the Paraclete, the Comforter, promised by Christ."[433] This is the exact mathematical equation found in Eckhart: God, Christ, and the Holy Spirit are *One* emanation on a continuum of evolution from the primal Ground of the Godhead. In Jung's *Letters*, he said further: "In Europe, as far as I can make out, Meister Eckhart is about the first where the self begins to play a noticeable role."[434] By "noticeable" Jung probably meant partial since, in his view, the Self is always in a process of evolution across time. Eckhart's significance in Jung's thinking about the Self cannot be overstated, however. He was more important to Jung than any other theologian.

> For instance, Meister Eckhart had an extraordinary revelation of truth, so he was the fellow who could have been followed by a great religious movement. But nothing happened. On the contrary ... For 600 years Meister Eckhart went under. His writings were condemned and one hardly knew of his existence. He died on his way to Rome,[435] where he should have given an account of his ideas, and his works were only piece by piece discovered, here and there in the libraries of Switzerland. In Basel we have one of his manuscripts

in his own handwriting, but it was only in about the
middle of the 19th century that an edition was made
of his works. Now of course we have practically the
whole opus. You see, this is a case where nobody could
have foretold what the development would be: he was
thoroughly anachronistic.[436]

By *anachronistic* Jung meant that Eckhart belonged to a period of
history other than the time portrayed in his works in Strasbourg and
Cologne between approximately 1313–1327 CE. Jung felt that Eckhart
had actually written and preached for the nineteenth and twentieth
centuries when he was widely celebrated after six hundred years of
obscurity. This celebration of Eckhart's works continues to unfold
today, and it is my hope that it will achieve apotheosis in 2029 CE,
seven hundred years after his condemnation. The signs are already
propitious for that event since John Paul II quoted him with great
appreciation as a Christian mystic in 1985.

Why is Eckhart so important to analytical psychology and
its evolution today? Because he gave birth to a novel theology of
Christianity that was no longer completely Christocentric, but rather,
increasingly *Self-centric* in a true Jungian sense. By this I mean that the
Holy Spirit continued to evolve across two thousand years of Christian
history to where we stand today.

In Jung's view no one in Christian history had read Christ's words
psychologically until Eckhart. The truths Eckhart preached were so
radical that no organization was big enough to house his theology of
the Word. His teachings of religion were meant for the masses, inside
and outside the Church, Christian or not Christian. The implications
are radical: the *Imprinter* (God or the Self) forms the full imprint of
individuation in each and every individual and that is the new myth
in which we are living today in Jung's view. Eckhart did not use
the term *individuation*, which Jung borrowed from Nietzsche. But he
and Jung were on the same page regarding the individuating factor

being the spirit or breath in the soul, life or existence, individuality or vocation. The primary question for any post-Jungian reader today is what the Self is in its *totality*. Or in Eckhart's post-Biblical language, what is total transformation, becoming *totally transformed* into God-consciousness? The gift of totality for both theorists was the Holy Ghost. Jung continued:

> Now if the Holy Ghost descends *in toto* upon people, they receive the full imprint of divinity. The divine form enters them and they are even more than the priests; they *are*-instead-of-the-deity—as Christ, having received the imprint of God through the Holy Ghost, *is*-instead-of-God ... Inasmuch as Christ promised that he would leave a Comforter and inasmuch as this Comforter has descended upon the disciples, they had received the divine imprint and they *are*-instead-of-Christ—not only St. Peter ... The church doesn't dwell upon that however; the church dislikes this idea: no conclusion has ever been drawn from it.[437]

Not only did Eckhart like this idea, he also preached it to the masses. The conclusions he drew from it were mind blowing, simply unique.

My aim is twofold: to clarify Jung's views on Eckhart and his work and to specify Eckhart's theology alongside his own psychology. Eckhart preached Spiritual Democracy. Eckhart taught and preached with such passion, conviction, and vigor that he successfully carried the message of Christ out in his own being and Isness. His archetypal *imprint* on the collective soul of Europe would only become intelligible through modern psychology and comparative religions six hundred years after his death. Analytical psychology, where the Self in its entirety can find enough spaciousness to assert its own right to freedom when it is loosed from religious institutions and their oppressive strictures, might be a place where Eckhart's works will be taught and practiced in the future. Yet if we are to do this for psychology and theology, we must proceed with modesty because of the bigness of Eckhart's revelations about the vocation of the Self in humanity at large.

Individuation in Eckhart and Jung

In his essay "A Psychological Approach to the Dogma of the Trinity" Jung stated that the Paraclete could represent "the final, complete stage in the evolution of God and the divine drama."[438] That final and complete stage found its fulfillment in Eckhart's life and works. This stage is what Jung called *individuation*: the synthesis of opposites in the Self, which is an endless approximation. That is the new myth, or new theory of truth as William James called it. It begins with individuals, which is the only way God can individuate in humanity. Moreover, Jung quoted John 10:34, asserting further that "the doctrine that the Paraclete was expressly left behind for man raises an enormous problem."[439]

What is the problem? Jung suggested here that the Paraclete always produces a "third" that represents a *function* of the Godhead,[440] and by function he meant a *God-function*, which he had written about almost twenty years earlier in his "Relativity" essay on Eckhart. From this quick overview of Jung's reflections on the Paraclete, the reader who's been following my steps of inquiry toward a unifying theory will have foreseen the *mark* toward which my bow's arrow has been aiming[441]— the centrality of the Self to both Eckhart and Jung.

> In the Paraclete, therefore, God is closer to the real man and his darkness than he is in the Son. The light God bestrides the bridge—Man—from the dayside; God's shadow, from the night side. What will be the outcome of this fearful dilemma, which threatens to

shatter the frail human vessel with unknown storms and intoxications? It may well be the revelation of the Holy Ghost out of man himself. Just as man was once revealed out of God, so, when the circle closes, God may be revealed out of man.[442]

What is *revealed* if we take Jung's exposition to its logical conclusion is that the Paraclete represents the Spirit of your vocation—your *calling* in life to fulfill the pattern of your completeness or wholeness. One reason why theologians had such difficulty following Jung in his lifetime is that they were still living under the illusions of the Church, where the Christ-image had been seen as the final revelation of truth from the time of Irenaeus, bishop of the Church of Lyon (130–203 CE) to Augustine of Hippo (354–430 CE). The differences between "Christocentrism"[443] and the theology of Eckhart was the radical accents he placed on the Holy Ghost as "the breath that heals and makes whole." Said Jung:

> Christianity claims that this breath also has a personality, which in the circumstances could hardly be otherwise. For close to two thousand years history has been familiar with the figure of the Cosmic Man, the Anthropos, whose image has merged with that of Yahweh and also of Christ. Similarly, the saints that received the stigmata became Christ-figures in a visible and concrete sense, and thus carriers of the Anthropos-image. They symbolize the working of the Holy Ghost among men. The Anthropos is a symbol that argues in favor of the personal nature of the "totality," i.e., the self.[444]

Thus, in his writing, Jung attempts to establish a *bridge* between the East and West, whereupon the emergence of the Self and the continuing indwelling of the Paraclete in humans could be established through a natural process of individuation. This connection was made even clearer in his most lyrical book, *Answer to Job*. There he wrote specifically:

> The future indwelling of the Holy Ghost in man amounts to a continuing incarnation of God. Christ, as the begotten son of God and pre-existing mediator, is a first-born in a divine paradigm which will be followed by further incarnations of the Holy Ghost in empirical man ... Although the Paraclete is of the greatest significance metaphysically, it was, from the point of view of the organization of the Church, most undesirable, because, as is authoritatively stated in scripture, the Holy Ghost is not subject to any control ... Anyone who is inclined by the Holy Ghost towards dissident opinions necessarily becomes a heretic ... It is the task of the Paraclete, the "spirit of truth," to dwell and work in individual human beings, so as to remind them of Christ's teachings and lead them into the light.[445]

Jung went further in his analysis of the Revelation of St. John to state even more explicitly:

> From the promise of the Paraclete we may conclude that God wants to become *wholly* man; in other words, to reproduce himself in his own dark creature man (not redeemed from original sin) ... This disturbing invasion engendered in him the image of the divine child, of a future savior, born of the divine consort whose reflection (the anima) lives in every man—that child whom Meister Eckhart also saw in a vision.[446]

It is my hypothesis that Jung had read and studied Eckhart so deeply that the inspired preacher of God's Word had become a living *Self-figure within Jung*, a living spiritual presence of the *vox Dei*. To Christian theologians for whom the Church and its dogmas had become a way of life and for whom Jesus and the saints were the ultimate God-ideal, the Paraclete held almost no significance in their ideologies. Understandably they sometimes had a problem with Jung's views about the shadow and evil. Eckhart's views on evil were never so challenging as Jung's. Yet, as you know from Part II, they were nevertheless daring and highly original. Because Jung was not speaking as a theologian, but only as a psychologist of the human soul, such criticisms were ignorant. To be sure, Jung could have been much clearer and consistent in his position as a radical empiricist and relativist operating in a post-Jamesian field of scientific inquiry. Nevertheless, he acknowledged in all humility that

> compared with the purity of the early Christian saints (and some of the later ones too), we do not show up in a very favorable light. Our comparative blackness naturally does not help us a bit. Though it mitigates the impact of evil forces, it makes us more vulnerable and less capable of resisting them. We therefore need more light, more goodness and moral strength, and must wash off as much of the obnoxious blackness as possible, otherwise we shall not be able to assimilate the dark God who also wants to become man, and at the same time endure him without perishing. For this all of the Christian virtues are needed and something else besides, for the problem is not only moral: we also need the Wisdom that Job was seeking.[447]

I personally have turned to Eckhart whenever my soul has been accosted not only by the *"obnoxious blackness"* of our times, but also when I've needed to be bathed in the living fountain of delight that his words as a preacher provide.

What is really at stake here is a question of what the birth of Christ or the Self meant to Eckhart, and what it meant to Jung six hundred years later. There had been a Reformation, and a bloody Thirty Years' War; French, American, and Russian Revolutions; and in the United States Indian Wars and a devastating Civil War by the time Jung came of age. What the Paraclete meant to the preacher from Erfurt, prior to the Black Death, and what it meant to the sage of Küsnacht during World War I and World War II are without doubt two very different readings of the Old and New Testaments. I will specify this subtle difference in pragmatic terms later.

My intention in what follows is to provide readers with an overview of what Jung wrote about Eckhart without quoting all eighty plus citations. In doing so, I can only give readers my sketch of what Eckhart meant to Jung, as there are still unpublished materials in the works that might add insight into what we already know.

As mentioned Jung began reading Eckhart at the age of fifteen, after which he began having some rather heated theological debates with his father, the Swiss Reform Protestant pastor Paul Jung, about the nature of God. Jung's relationship with his father was at the center of his divergence from what Christianity taught about Christ and his message to humanity, most notably the senior Jung's struggle with his faith.

Clearly Jung found something in Eckhart's sermons that spoke to an already revealed truth within him that he had been carrying around as a destiny within—a *calling* as a religious psychologist of the depths, something new and enlivening, which did not coincide with the dry and rigid theology of his day, or with what the Church fathers had failed to do with the teachings of Christ. This is what his violent feud with Christianity was truly about. It is hard for any psychotherapist not to feel a sense of empathy and compassion for the suffering that Jung endured in his childhood, accompanied by a number of quite severe religious traumas in his home caused mainly by his parents, and nine uncles who were all parsons. Yet it is undeniable that his psychology was in some ways affected by terrifying emotions that could become explosive and were ancestral in nature, such as his adolescent fantasy of God's turd shattering the Basel Cathedral, where his grandfather had preached. Anyone who reads his works cannot help but *feel* some of this *affective violence* toward God, his father, and the Church.[448]

---◦⌒◦ CHAPTER 20 ⌒◦⊢-----

THE CRUSADER AND THE RED BOOK

I'll begin my overview with some probable traces of Eckhart's influence on the development of Jung's *Red Book*. First, Jung reported a 1912 dream about a Crusader. This dream figure was reported during his seminar given in 1925, Jung's fiftieth year.

On April 20, 1925, Jung told the seminar attendees about the dream, after an earlier exposition on his theory of the *God-function*. The Crusader dream was unique in a number of ways. What did the Crusader mean to Jung? As an archetypal symbol, the Crusader was obviously Christian (Roman Catholic). Jung said: *"He looked quite detached and aloof."* In a previous part of the dream, an Austrian officer had appeared who Jung identified as Freud. It is possible the Crusader was a part of Jung's ancestral vocation from the start of his analytic career, an *archetype of his destiny as a natural scientist.* Jung was on a symbolic *crusade* in 1912 to transform the field of modern psychology, literally from the ground up. In the dream, Jung found himself in a Southern town on the slopes of some mountains.

> *The streets consisted of steps going up and down the steep slopes. It was a medieval town and the sun was blazing at full noon, the hour when spirits are abroad in southern countries. Jung came walking through the*

215

*streets with a man [the shadow], and many people
passed them to and fro. All at once he saw among them
a very tall man, a Crusader, dressed in a coat of mail
with a Maltese cross on his breast and back. He looked
quite detached and aloof, not in any way concerned with
the people about him, nor did they pay any attention
to him. Jung's dream-ego looked at the Crusader in
complete astonishment and he could not understand
what he was doing walking about there. "Did you notice
him" the shadow figure asked Jung. Then the shadow
said: "He has been dead since the twelfth century, but
he is not yet properly dead. He always walks here among
the people, but they don't see him."*

Jung said he was quite bewildered in the dream that people paid
no attention to the Crusader and then he awoke. In other words, Jung
could see in his imagination what other people around him couldn't
prior to WWI. Jung discussed the dream with Freud, who could not
find any satisfactory meaning in it whatsoever. Then, with his essay
on Eckhart in *Psychological Types*, he began to glimpse its deeper
meanings. This is what Jung said at the seminar: "The Crusader is an
archetypal figure, a Christian symbol living from the twelfth century,
a symbol that does not really live today, but on the other hand is not
really dead either. It comes out of the times of Meister Eckhart, the
time of the culture of the Knights, when many ideas blossomed, only
to be killed then, but they are coming again to life now."[449] Eckhart
was always a great promoter of peace.

That the Crusader was not yet properly dead suggests two things:
1) the Crusader was not yet properly dead in Jung's psyche, or in the
soul of European Christendom, and was still potentially dangerous,
and 2) Jung's crusade as a post-Freudian analyst would be profoundly
influenced by the figure of Meister Eckhart, who was an *internalized*

Self-figure in him since he read the Percival myth. But why was the figure so detached?

Detachment (*abegescheidenheit*) as a state of mind is something Jung had read about in Eckhart's works, so his word-association interests me. Was the Crusader a part of Jung's Christian cultural hero that was still alive in him, just as the Crusades had been in Eckhart's time? As Joel Harrington pointed out in *Dangerous Mystic*: "The dramatic real-world embodiment of the Christian knight ideal throughout Eckhart's lifetime remained the crusader."[450] Before he assumed the title Meister Eckhart, he grew up near the Thuringian forest, and like Jung, he loved to read the most celebrated of all Arthurian legends and perhaps the most famous in all medieval German literature: Wolfram von Eschenbach's *Parzival,* a largely expanded version of Chrétien de Troyes' *Perceval, the Story of the Grail.*[451] In the works of Eckhart, the Grail, sword, lance, and the solution to the problems of violence, the feminine, blood, and evil were all present in a stunning and unsurpassable synthesis. In *The Book of Divine Comfort,* Eckhart wrote: "A knight in battle risks property, body and soul for fleeting and brief honor, and yet we think it so great a thing that we endure a little suffering for the sake of God and eternal blessedness."[452]

Thus, as an archetypal image Eckhart was a living symbol of the *Crusader-in-Jung,* an imprint at the center of his efforts to transform the very fabric of the Christian mythos in the West, and the field of psychoanalysis itself, by including a less idealized view of what Christianity might be *if* the birth of God, or the Self, were to be made fully conscious in the collective World Soul in both its light and dark aspects through the vehicle of analytical psychology. The shadow of the Crusader carried Jung's potential for violence. At a higher moral level, as an energy and force in the psyche of Jung, the Crusader was a *power* that served the Good.

Then, in 1915, on the verge of World War I, Jung had a colloquy in his now famous *Red Book* with a figure called Izdubar, an early name for Gilgamesh, a looming figure who looked like an archaic warrior from Iraq. In his colloquy, Jung's "I" identified with:

- Being a mother or simple maiden of God: *"I am the mother, the simple maiden, who gave birth and did not know how"*;[453] *"My God, I love you as a mother loves the unborn whom she carries in her heart."*[454]
- Lying in a child bed as a pregnant or incubating mother: *"Since I am a giver of birth. Whence do you delight me, Oh God?"*;[455] *"I became his nocturnal mother who incubates the egg of the beginning."*[456]
- Giving birth to a new symbol for the Self that is inclusive of masculine and feminine polarities and Good and Evil: *"Wow betide the mother who gives birth to a God"*;[457] and *"Because I wanted to give birth to my God, I also wanted evil ... This is why I want to go to Hell. Would a mother not want to give up her life for her child?"*[458]

These statements about birthing a new image of God sound like Eckhartian notions to me. For instance, in Jung's "Relativity" essay he quoted Eckhart as saying: "Therefore do I turn back once more to myself, there do I find the deepest places, deeper than hell itself; for even from there does my wretchedness drive me. Nowhere can I escape myself! Here will I set me down and here I will remain."[459] Although Jung claimed not to have understood Eckhart when he first read him in adolescence, here he did indeed portray a series of metaphors of birthing a new Self-image that he may have come across in his scrutiny of Eckhart's sermons regarding the birth of the Counselor, or Paraclete, in the human soul following his imaginal journey to hell and back. Dante was not Jung's only reference for this descent. Here, in Jung's colloquy with Izdubar and particularly in the "Incantations" and "The Opening of the Egg" (a series of free-verse poems via active visioning that lead Jung down to "taste the very bottom of Hell"[460]), we find a representation that corresponds to the processes of becoming a mother of God, the idea of spiritual motherhood, which appears not infrequently in Jung's writings as well as in Eckhart's.

Eckhart literally took the theology of Catholicism into a New *grounded* Dispensation[461] of truth, which anyone could understand, and particularly women, without having to be a Neoplatonist, an ordained cardinal, bishop, or pope of the Church. One could become God, the Son, the Holy Spirit, and the Virgin Mary and Sophia, the fourth principle of the feminine by virtue of one's work in the world. Eckhart said: "God has ever been begetting His only-begotten Son and is giving birth to him now and eternally: and thus He lies in childbed like a woman who has given birth, in every good, outdrawn, and indwelling soul. This birth is His understanding. Eternally welling forth from his paternal heart, in which lies all his joy"[462]

The implications of this statement are astounding for theology and psychology alike. For what he was saying is that God has a maternal function and is a mother of God, as well as a father: *the Holy Ghost lies in childbed like a woman who has given birth and blossoms forth as Love and joy!*"[463] In *The Red Book,* Jung uses this same idea of lying in a childbed as a mother giving birth.[464]

God is a Father-Mother Divinity in One. The Father *gives birth* and Eckhart *bears* the Son, as we may also from the ground of our souls, where the Holy Spirit enters into us through Divine Grace. God *begets* the Son in the soul of humanity through the Holy Spirit, in the childbed of a perfected soul. The perfect soul is *brought to bed* with God and *bears* the Son in all her activities, works, or vocations.

This is a masculine theology and a feminine psychology that was seven hundred years ahead of its times. It was not only psychologically relative, but also, for the theologian, Absolute. God was to Eckhart a *maternal Father* and a *paternal Mother*, and also a Son and the Paraclete in equal measure. The gendering of God was completely transcended in a union of supreme opposites. How would it benefit the world if the Son of God were to be born Jesus if *we* are not also filled with grace and give birth to the Divine too? This basic formula for total transformation in humanity into the Christian image or the Anthropos is quite different from the birth of God in Jung's "Incantations."

In the last section of his *Red Book* called "Scrutinies," Jung recorded a dialogue with his wise inner teacher or guru, Philemon, in a section that bore the title "The seven instructions of the dead. Written by Basilides in Alexandria, where East touches West." This is significant because he often said that Eckhart was the only bridge in Europe to Eastern wisdom texts. Philemon appeared to Jung in a vision in a white priestly robe and announced in the opening sermon: "Now hear. I begin with nothingness. Nothingness is the same as fullness. In infinity full is as good as empty. Nothingness is empty and full ... We call this nothingness or fullness the *Pleroma ... Creation* is not in the Pleroma but in itself. The Pleroma is the beginning and the end of creation."[465] In a footnote to the word *Pleroma* the editor Sonu Shamdasani wrote that the word is derived from Gnosticism and "the distinction that Jung draws between the Pleroma and creation has some points of contact with Meister Eckhart's differentiation between the Godhead and God."[466] Indeed. The contact points are self-evident.

Yet Philemon went on to define the God Abraxis as "the mother of good and evil."[467] I will not provide an interpretation of Jung's *Septum Sermones* here. I only want to point out some probable lines of correlation to the ways in which Jung made creative use of Eckhart's metaphor of birthing and his comments on the Godhead and Nothingness. The difference is that Eckhart's Mother-Father bearer gave birth to Love or Goodness in an Absolute sense because his soul was closer to the idea of perfection than completeness. More: here is what Jung said about Incarnation, during his *Visions Seminars*:

> As a rule, the leading idea of a new religion comes
> from the symbolism of the religion that preceded it.

For instance, the leading idea of a new religion to follow the Christian age would be that everyone is Christ, that Christ is merely a projection of an entirely human mystery, and that insofar as we take the Christ projection back into ourselves each one of us is Christ ... Now everyone is a Christ, and inasmuch as he is a Christ, he is sacrificed.[468]

As we will see, Jung's understanding of the birth of Christ within modern people was quite distinct from Eckhart's owing to the added emphasis Jung placed on birthing evil as well as good: "Because I wanted to give birth to my God, I also wanted evil ... This is why I want to go to Hell. Would a mother not want to give up her life for her child?"[469]

Like Jung Eckhart taught equality, distinction, and individuation in God. The Trinity is One breath in the Godhead. The Godhead was always beyond God in Eckhart and Jung, for beyond the Godhead was the Infinite Ground of the Cosmos, which includes black holes. One could give birth to one's own distinct incarnation in time, but all images and names of the Divine were forever finite.[470]

This theology of the Self in Eckhart was closer to Buddhism than it was to the overly institutionalized theology of Augustine or Aquinas. It was a theology of trans-dualism that we do not find in any of the Christian mystics in quite the same way. This kind of theology is a *bridge* that we can still build upon. In Jung's seminars on *Nietzsche's Zarathustra,* he commented on a newly revised version of the New Testament in Greek and Latin, the *Nouvum Testamentum Graeci et Latine,* where he referred to a passage from the Lord's prayer in Matthew (6: 11), "Give us this day our daily bread," to which he added that we can now read this scripture quite differently. "In German," Jung said, "it would be, in the pure language of Meister Eckhart: *das überwesantlische Brot.*" He asserted further: "It would be very beautiful if we had in the Lord's prayer: *gebe uns Heute das überwesantlische*

Brot ['Give us this day our super-substantial Bread']. That is the true meaning, you see."[471] It is important to add that this passage from Lecture # III of the 1934 seminars on *Zarathustra* was preceded with a long discussion on the meaning of communion:

> The real meaning of communion is the flesh or the body, the blood. You see it is not in vain that Luther defended the *estin* ("is") against our Swiss reformer Zwingli, who in a somewhat lame way said the communion was a sort of symbol. But Luther defended the primitive point of view, that it was the real body and the blood, because it is utterly important that the primitive instinct of man, the anthropophagous instinct, should be satisfied. For the real communion with the qualities of human beings, particularly the psychical qualities, only takes place when you eat them.

In a footnote to this passage the volume's editors wrote further: "In opposition to Luther's doctrine of transubstantiation, Ulrich Zwingli (1440-1531) said the wine and bread were to be understood symbolically. He was killed in a Swiss battle between Catholic and Protestant armies."[472] I point this passage out to the reader to highlight Jung's beautiful line: *"Give us this day our daily super-substantial Bread."* This would be the Bread of the Awakened Self in humanity, which comes from the process Jung called individuation.

Furthermore, Jung made many fine comparisons between Eckhart's works and Eastern meditation, Zen Buddhism, Taoism, and Yoga. Eckhart's radical and daring truth-telling of birthing a new God-notion as a Father-Mother of God was clothed in the Christian myth. This birth (*geburt*) within was made possible by what Eckhart called *"In-sich-selbst-Stehen"*:[473] *Standing in the Self* might be a way to interpret this poetic phrase from an analytical-psychological angle.

When one is standing in the Self, the superior and inferior functions are united in a state of union, or *Unum,* in the midway point, where the superior and inferior functions "touch" and "kiss." Then, one experiences peace and unity and rest in the psyche, or soul.

CHAPTER 21

SPIRITUAL MOTHERHOOD AND THE PARACLETE IN JUNG

Jung suggested in his book on the transference that the appearance of the marriage archetype, or "higher psychotherapy" of *spiritual motherhood,* was actualized in analytical practice by the birth of the divine child, hero, orphan, daughter, or son figure from the collective unconscious: "Consequently the higher psychotherapy is the most exacting business and sometimes it sets its tasks which challenge not only our understanding or our sympathy, but the whole man."[474]

The idea of the analyst as a spiritual mother who facilitates a fertilization and birth of vocation in patients was an archetypal image Jung translated into the language of modern psychology. It was highly influenced by his reading of Eckhart who scarcely mentioned sexuality at all. This is the goal of the sophisticated psychotherapy of a spiritualized vocation.[475]

Such wholeness is 1) the product of fertilization of the mother, Eve, followed by 2) development of aesthetic and romantic eros, 3) spiritual motherhood, and 4) birthing of vocation as Wisdom (Sophia). These four successive movements toward the highest stage of anima-relatedness, Sophia, are all contained by Oneness with the caveat that *the idea of totality is, at any given time, as total as one is oneself.*

In other words, the Paraclete is continuing to become incarnated in the souls of each of us as we work out the kinks that keep us from becoming who we were destined to become as individuals.

Jung placed the transference in the widest possible context, suggesting that it may be heralded by a flash of lightning (Eckhart called this the "Spark in the soul; the highest, noblest, innermost part of the soul," or *vünkelîn*),[476] a spiritualized situation of love, like Mary sitting at the feet of Jesus in the Mary-Martha story, where the sexual libido is transformed by an illumination, or lightning bolt, represented in its broader and higher aspects as a powerful, electrical, or *numinous* energy field that can be accompanied by bliss.[477] Jung did not relate the birth of the Self to the problem of vocation directly, as I am in this book, but his ideas of spiritual motherhood and "higher psychotherapy" of the soul suggest that the inner voice is what connects the birth of the Higher Self to the larger cultural task of transformation of the historical God-image in society at large. This higher kind of service can lead to great happiness in wisdom. Eckhart preached: "Happy the man who dwells in wisdom."[478]

Since the problem of the inner voice and development of the personality is the central issue of analytic work, the creative instinct and its transformation along one's Self-path is *key*. This key is at the heart of analytic practice, and holding the vocational archetypes in a spiritually mothering way, by means of laboring and loving what one is called to do, is what makes the work of higher psychotherapy possible and what unlocks the door to freedom. It is a creative birthing process that can only take place when projections of eros have been withdrawn by the patient. The higher one goes in one's inner relationship to the anima or animus, the closer one comes to the angelic realm of God, where the soul *knows* truly her destined vocation. Then she possesses the key to the inner kingdom of God. She has found her treasure and realizes that the voice of God is now her playmate.

In the ascent to the highest levels of the soul in its spiritual transformation into God-consciousness, an analyst's knowledge becomes superfluous to the patient because the soul then possesses absolute knowledge. Listen to Eckhart and you will understand what I mean: "Knowledge has the key, unlocks, penetrates, breaks through, and finds God naked. Then it tells its playmate, the will, what it has come into possession of, although it had the will already, for what I want, I go searching for. Knowledge goes on ahead. She is a queen seeking to rule over the most lofty and most pure, and handing it over to the soul."[479]

Only when the primal chaos has been stirred in the analytic couple and transmuted into order, can the *balm* of vocation be bestowed upon a patient through the fertilized and spiritualized mother pair. The resultant outcome produces Love's child, Wisdom, which is accompanied by joy. Eckhart says: "If you have sadness in your heart, you are not a mother. Rather, you are in the process of giving birth; the birth is near ... And, so strive intently, so that the child is not just *being* born in you, but rather that it *has been* born, as the Son has always been born in God and is constantly being born."[480] When the child is *being* born, the birth is a relative experience; when the child has *been born*, the birth is Absolute and partakes of the absolute knowledge of the higher marriage of Sophia with God. I'm quoting from Eckhart to illustrate how he provided a higher psychotherapy of the soul for Jung through his theology of the birth of the Word long before Jung could formulate how the stages of anima development related to the practical problems of psychotherapy.

Eckhart had his own way of bringing the animal instincts that had been split off by Christianity into his God-concept through his colloquy with Eve and the Serpent at the midpoint on the cross. His inclusion of sensation and the wisdom-body into his theology of the soul can be heard in these vernal lines from vernacular Sermon 71: "The senses leap into thoughts. How high and limitless they are no one knows but God and the soul."[481] The goal was vocation: the evolution of consciousness via a never-ending dialogue with the Self or the Word within.

The resolution of the transference represents a supreme

responsibility for the analyst because they are working not only for transformation of the individual patient, but also for the transformation of humankind one individual at a time. Humanity can be transformed only when a significant number of individuals are engaged in dialogue at various cultural levels with the Self.[482]

The opus, the vocation, is not only an intellectual endeavor in the consulting room. It is a moral and psychological undertaking that requires a *religious attitude* in the analyst to succeed. Jung was called by the inner voice to work toward a higher understanding of the transference as a spiritual phenomenon. He viewed vocation as among the most important spiritual phenomena in the history of humanity. Following the inner voice leads finally to moral and ethical responsibility: actualizing the vocation in relationship to one's community.

The quintessence was, for Jung, the creative instinct-substance. It formed the crown of the instincts because its cultural pattern was and always will be vocational in nature. It is the mediator between body and spirit: the voice of the soul in its synthesis as maternal Wisdom, which embodies and contains above and below, earth (Eve) and heaven (Sophia) in an intermediary position.

The conscious realization of sexual fantasies that can contaminate the transference is only compensated through soulful longings for transcendent wholeness, and this goal can only be achieved through vocations to live by. Jung spoke in this regard of *higher copulation* as an intercourse of the soul's reanimated body with the spirit.[483]

The resolution of the transference comes about with dissolution of the patient's projections onto the analyst. Jung's notion of psychological "pregnancy"[484] followed by the new birth, was a spiritual idea that can be traced to alchemy and also to Eckhart, who beseeched us all not only to become mothers of God, but also to become spiritually pregnant with Love's child, Wisdom:

> And thus the birth of the person taking place
> continuously in God is to be taken according to how

> he shines with his image in God's image, which God
> is according to his bare being—with which a person
> is one. Hence the unity of God and man is to be
> understood according to the likeness of the image,
> because a person is like God according to this image ...
> Wisdom is a name for a mother.[485]

In *The Psychology of the Transference,* in the late chapter called "Death," Jung spoke further of a "trans-subjective union" of archetypal figures (God and Sophia) and emphasized that it should not be forgotten that spiritual marriage is a symbolical relationship whose goal is complete individuation.[486] *Trans-subjective union* is a subjective experience in the patient that leads to ever-increasing levels of human consciousness that include ethics and moral values that accord with law. Thus, the soul can only be reunited with the body through the withdrawal of projections. The experience of the spiritual marriage is a "trans-subjective" event that takes place in the objective non-ego, or in the transcendental realm of the gods.[487]

In later life, Jung liked to state that he was neither a man of faith, nor did he possess belief in God. Nevertheless he said he *knew* God existed and therefore didn't need belief. Jung was a Christian by ancestry and birth, but his interests in religion expanded to include the whole world, or *Anima Mundi.* All religions held Jung's interest because he was, like William James, spiritually democratic in his outlook. He was raised Swiss Reformed Protestant, but to really *know* God, Jung needed proofs. He needed facts of personal and transpersonal *experience.* Dreams of patients were the best source of evidence for him that God was a reality, and no belief or faith was necessary to verify God's existence in the world. For Jung, God operated through the collective unconscious by means of certain scientific facts and meaningful chance events, or *synchronicities,* confirmed through the parallelism of psychic and physical events.

Jung believed modern people had outgrown faith in a perfect

God-image because they were living in a new age of spiritual relativity, which was radically empirical, a view he had adopted from Eckhart and James. For Jung, archetypal images and their forms of projection needed to be taken seriously into account via an in-depth study of dreams and fantasy images. This meant that through a study of dreams, fantasy thinking, or active imagination (his methods for engaging with the God-image), curative symbols of the religious instinct could be produced, and corresponding with their emergence into consciousness were emotionally toned *numinosities*, natural healing lights, or luminosities, that could transform the human psyche and eventually lead the soul of a person toward wholeness.

Jung made it overwhelmingly clear: "Only in Meister Eckhart did I feel the breath of life—not that I understood him. The Schoolmen left me cold, and the Aristotelian intellectualism of St. Thomas appeared to me more lifeless than a desert."[488] Jung thought that the schoolmen of the Church wanted to "prove a belief to themselves, whereas actually it is a matter of experience."[489] One thing that stands out about Jung's comment here is that Eckhart had spoken directly from *experience*. In his Tavistock Lectures, Jung added: "The archetypes are the great decisive forces, they bring about the real events, and not our personal reasoning and practical intellect ... Sure enough, the archetypal images decide the fate of man. Man's unconscious psychology decides, and not what we think and talk in the brain-chamber up in the attic."[490]

In Jung's view the "brain-chamber up in the attic" was the intellect divorced from instinct, or the dry intellectual thinking of theologians who left him feeling cold and without life-breath, without soul, because there was no deep *feeling* at play, no luminosity from the Word, the Holy Spirit, Sophia. In its attempts to "prove a belief to themselves," theology had lost its way. This was a personal problem Jung had detected in his father as a boy, for his father, Paul Jung, was a Protestant theologian who had lost his faith and Jung had been a witness to this tragedy in his youth.

Jung's favored Eckhart over Aquinas and other "schoolmen"

(unfortunately he didn't read St. Albert's work in-depth) because Eckhart *felt* the soul of the world in his sermons, the *Anima Mundi*, speaking God's Word to him. Even more than that, he *felt* Wisdom, the feminine face of God, speaking too in equal measure. The "breath of life" was and continues to be the Holy Spirit in Catholic theology, the third person of the Trinity. In Eckhart this *breath* was the life-force of the Son and Sophia. It was this aliveness and *soulfulness* that Jung felt deeply while reading Eckhart, who Jung quoted as saying: "He that is right in his feeling is right in any place and in any company ... For a man of right feeling has God in him."[491]

One of the reasons for Jung's deep fondness for Eckhart's works over all other Christian theologians was the fact that he primarily read his Middle High German sermons from the later period of the preacher's life, preached in Strasbourg (1314–1323) and Cologne (1323–1327). This was a time of transition for Eckhart when he had let go of two tenures as an esteemed chaired professor, lecturer, and scholar of biblical theology for the Order of Preachers (OP) at the Parisian University.

During his time in Paris, Eckhart had written a number of works in Latin that were at times as dry as any of the so-called learned "schoolmen" he had learned from, yet these highly intellectual works are necessary reading for anyone interested in understanding his theology of the birth of the Word in the human soul. After decades of teaching theology in Erfurt and Paris, Eckhart would see an increasing number of religious movements stirred up by activated archetypal forces in the collective psyche, which would affect Christendom in unprecedented ways. The Mother of God, the Blessed Virgin Mary, became the central object of veneration in many medieval cathedrals, such as at the cathedral of Our Lady in the German city of Strasbourg.

─┤ CHAPTER 22 ├─

JUNG'S POST-ECKHARTIAN TEACHINGS

The Messiah and the Messianic

Both Meister Eckhart and St. Thomas Aquinas, another Dominican, developed their contributions to Catholic theology in their own times and in their own unique ways from Rabbi Moses Maimonides (1138–1204). According to a foremost authority on Jewish spirituality whose work Jung was familiar with, Gershom Scholem, the coming of the Messiah was anticipated to be a public event in Jewish history that was anticipated to take place on the world stage within the community. For the Messiah to be recognized by everyone as the King of the Jews, he would have to prove himself as the fulfillment of the promise of being God's chosen Son, the Savior, or Redeemer of humanity; whereas, in Christianity, according to Scholem's analysis, redemption was said to take place in the unseen spiritual realm as an event that was reflected solely in the soul, in the private inner world of the individual.[492]

The central idea in the evolution of the archetype from its inception in Isaiah 7:14 was that the Messianic principle would eventually crystallize in Judaism through a retrograde turn toward the past glory of Jerusalem, a glance backward in time, in an effort to reestablish an original state of existence in harmony with the life of the Hebrew ancestors, combined with a vision of world peace in the future (Isaiah

2:4). It was a utopian vision of the establishment of world peace in the imagined and hoped-for future End of Days, based on the writings of the prophets in the Old Testament.[493] This was a *vision* of the reestablishment of the city of the Lord through the future glory of Zion, which would ideally have returned to God and also to everlasting healing through the Messiah, the prophesied Prince of Peace (Isaiah 9:6). This is the Son who would turn all nations toward the One God of Israel and away from all heathen God-images once the foretold apocalyptic events had fully run their course in cataclysmic ruin.[494] These Last Days were prophesied to be catastrophic events in world history foretold in Isaiah 2–4 as the Days of the Lord, or simply the End of Days.[495] In this sense, the Messianic fulfillment was to be presaged by the "birth pangs of the Messiah" attached to his coming in a climactic period when the new Aion would begin with a Last Judgment.[496] It is out of these visions that the Revelations of St. John in the New Testament had their origin. We do not see any such reference to an apocalypse in Eckhart's works, although it is central to Jung's work in his two important books, *Aion* and *Answer to Job.*

Interestingly, the most consequential attempts to eliminate apocalypticism from rabbinic Judaism appeared first in the works of Moses Maimonides.[497] In the conclusion of Maimonides's main philosophical work, the *Guide to the Perplexed,* which Aquinas and Eckhart both read, an idyllic state of consciousness—the *vita contemplativa,* the culminating principle above the active life in the community—was imagined to be reached under ideal economic and political conditions without any need for a reference to Messianism.[498] Eckhart further develops Maimonides's vision of contemplation as the highest state of the soul toward a new *theology of sacred action.* However, with his own dispensation of a *principle of exalted activity* in the Christian soul that was "higher" than study and prayer from his reading of the Hebrew-Christian Bible, he rejected both Maimonides's and Aquinas's theories that contemplation was higher than the active life. In Eckhart's vision, acquired knowledge through inward contemplation of Holy Scriptures and outer action united in the Messianic idea of the "birth" of a Son who is a Savior formed a higher synthesis of vocational activity through imageless meditation, a prayer for Nothing as a calling from Nothingness whereby the Self becomes the guiding principle of human incarnation toward perpetual pursuit of final peace, within and without. Eckhart absorbed what he learned from his reading of Maimonides and transformed it into a new theology of birthing the Messiah through contemplation and action, prayer and vocation. The King of the Jews, who he believed had come in Lord Jesus and who was also born in him through the Paraclete, could continue to be born in the human soul.

In Maimonides's work, the Messianic age was envisioned to be a *restorative* time through public events realized in the world community. The accent on the Messiah as incarnating in a single individual was rejected through a realized potential salvation of the world in the spiritualized community. Eckhart's vision was not only anti-apocalyptic, but rather *trans-apocalyptic,* for by escaping the terrors of history, the individual is given a chance to reverse the coming catastrophes by running perpetually to peace. For Maimonides, similarly, the "Messianic age will strengthen man's capability by favorable conditions of universal peace and universal happiness."[499] The main thrust of Maimonides's message to humanity was written in 1172 in his *Epistle to Yemen,* when he preached to his Yemenite readers about the vast difference between the prophetic rank of the Messiah and the rest of earlier prophets, from Moses to Malachi:

> But his unique characteristic is that when he appears God will cause all the kings of the earth to tremble and be afraid at the report of him. Their kingdoms will fall; they will be unable to stand up against him, neither by the sword nor by revolt. They will neither defame nor slander him, but they will be frightened into silence when they behold his miracles and wonders. He

will slay anyone who tries to kill him and none shall escape or be saved from him ... That king will be very mighty. All peoples will maintain peace with him, all nations will save him on account of the great justice and miracles which issue from his hand. All the words of scripture testify to his success and to our success with him.[500]

Scholem says Maimonides later eliminated the terrifying eschatology. The Messiah of Maimonides in his letter to the Yemenites was a miracle worker without any doubt who was metaphoric for a transpersonal mystery contained in the book of Isaiah 40:17–18: "All nations before him *are* as nothing; and they are counted to him as less than nothing, and vanity. To whom then will ye liken God? or what likeness will you compare him to?"

This central idea in Judaism continued to evolve and work itself out in history through a number of religious figures, all of whom, one might rightly say, were inspired by the Holy Spirit, from Maimonides to Isaac Luria, to the Baal Shem Tov, to Martin Buber. Between the former and the latter, was the controversial figure of Sabbatai Zevi (1625–1676) and the whole Sabbatian movement. He claimed to be the Messiah and later was forced to convert to Islam in 1666 to save his life. As Jung wrote in a letter in 1957, Hassidism and the movement of Sabbatai Zwi or Zevi, and the intricacies of the Kabbalah still remain "unexplored psychologically."[501]

I cannot go into this history further here. What is important for the reader to keep in mind are Jung's comments on the fact that the medicine, panacea, or elixir of alchemy was "praised as the second coming of the Messiah," or as a "gift of the Holy Ghost or of the *Sapientia Dei*," a doctrine that never came to very much in the Church, except in the works of Eckhart: "The Paraclete descends upon the single individual, who is thereby drawn into the Trinitarian process. And of the spirit of procreation and life indwells in man, then God can be born in him—a thought that has not perished since the time of Meister Eckhart."⁵⁰² As Eckhart said: "God loves Himself and His nature, His being and His Godhead."⁵⁰³

Love is what binds the opposites of war and peace, the sword and mercy, violence and nonviolence. As Jung wrote in *Aion*: "The God-image is not something invented, it is an experience that comes upon man spontaneously."⁵⁰⁴ He went on to state further that psychology must refrain from "passing metaphysical judgments," and we must only "profess convictions to which it [analytical psychology] is ostensibly entitled on the ground of scientific experience," for "the one and only thing psychology can establish is the presence of pictorial symbols," and "this symbolism uses images or schemata which have always, in all the religious, expressed the universal 'Ground,' the Deity itself."⁵⁰⁵

Here Jung was using the language of Eckhart when he capitalizes on the word *Ground*. Jung's finest quotes from Eckhart's sermon "The Poor in Spirit" (Mt 5:3) are located in his chapter "Gnostic Symbols of the Self." Yet Eckhart's God in Galatians 3:16–22 was not Gnostic, but Jewish in origin. In Latin sermon 29, Eckhart preached on the words of Deuteronomy 6:4: "God is infinite in his simplicity and simple by reason of his infinity. Therefore, he is everywhere and everywhere entire. He is everywhere by his infinity, but entire everywhere by reason of his simplicity ... God is the inner reality of each thing, and only in the inner reality. He alone 'is one.'"⁵⁰⁶ He went on: "'Hear, Israel, your God is one God.'... the God of Israel, a God who sees, a God of those who see, a God who understands and is understood by intellect alone, who is totally intellect."⁵⁰⁷

This Infinite God cannot be a God that sees evil as equal with good in the Intellect because the One God of Israel *understands* evil in the Higher Self, where evil is canceled out to Zero. Eckhart became not only a second Christ, but also a second Israel, as his spiritual wife was either Leah or Martha or Sophia depending on how one wants to read him. Eckhart preached on Isaiah 40:18: "*Then* I shall be wise and mighty and all else as He is, and one and the same with Him. Then,

Sion [Zion] will become truly seeing, and true Israel, a God-seeing man, for nothing in the Godhead is hidden."[508] Out of Israel's wrestling with God comes Peace. The Messiah as a Son of God, an Eternal One, the One God of Israel "shall know to refuse the evil, and choose the good" (Isaiah 7:15).

Jung wrote, in a letter to Victor White in 1953, "The Godhead has a double aspect, and as Meister Eckhart says: God is not blissful in his mere Godhead, and that is the reason for his incarnation."[509] But where Eckhart and Jung differed was on the issue of the "absolute opposition expressed by the symbol Christ versus Satan."[510] Nevertheless, Jung got it right in *Psychology of Yoga and Meditation* when he quoted Eckhart on true "Detachment": "Undertake this, and let it cost you everything you can afford. There you will find true peace, and nowhere else ... Perfect humility is a matter of self-naughting; but detachment so narrowly approximates to naught that no room remains for aught betwixt zero and absolute detachment."[511]

Another Eckhart-inspired passage appeared in Jung's *Seminar on Dream Analysis*, where he said in 1929:

> It is a bewildering thing in human life that the thing that causes the greatest fear is the source of the greatest wisdom. One's greatest foolishness is the biggest stepping-stone. No one can become a wise man without being a terrible fool. Through Eros one learns the truth, through sins we learn virtue. Meister Eckhart says one shouldn't repent too much, that the value of sin is very great.[512]

Eckhart's teachings on the value of sin were central to Jung's psychology. We are not to repress the shadow, sin, or evil, according to Jung, but make the shadow conscious in us. What's more, God wills sins, sending them to individuals who are called to develop a deeper and broader consciousness. Grace comes from the acknowledgment of one's sins, not by denying them, in Jung's mature ideas on individuation. This part of Jung's psychology owes a great tribute to Eckhart.

In 1931, in Jung's *Visions Seminars,* he said more about the process of becoming fully human: "Only those people who can really touch bottom can be human. Therefore Meister Eckhart says one should not repent too much of one's sins because it might keep one away from grace. One is only confronted with the spiritual experience when one is absolutely human."[513]

In these seminar passages it is clear Jung's notion of the integration of the shadow found theological support in Eckhart's views on sin and evil, and on the necessity of descending into Nothingness for renewal and transformation. In his seminars on *Nietzsche's Zarathustra,* Jung said further in 1935:

> I always fight against it when theologians say God is good. Meister Eckhart says God is not good because if he were good he could be better. That is true. Moreover I would say he loses the freedom because he is then bound to be good, can do nothing but good, which would be a very grave restriction to his omnipotence and is surely not meant.[514]

Was Jung's "fight" that began with his father partly derived from the freedom he felt in first reading Eckhart, a relativity that became central to Jung's new myth for Christendom? I believe it was. During the same year, 1935, Jung cited my favorite passage on the Dominican, when he said: "God is forced to go through that narrow doorway, the gate of man, in order to become God. That is the teaching of Master Eckhart, and that is also the meaning of the Christian mystery, that God first became man and underwent the most miserable fate in order to become God."[515] The narrow doorway is plural. Ways are many in Eckhart, not singular. But there is one key, the key of Peter, the highest agent of intuition, which unlocks many doorways to the one reality of the vocation of the Self.

Jung said, further, while reflecting again on Eckhart in 1936: "In the East it [the idea of the Self] appeared much earlier than here, but we see it at work in Master Eckhart."[516] Moreover, by January 1939, after his trip to India in 1937–1938, Jung was well aware of the terrible ground-swell of evil that was emerging in Nazi Germany. This was when he said that Eckhart was the man who could have been "followed by a great religious movement."[517]

Since he wrote the passage above in 1939, Jung may have been thinking about how much Eckhart could have provided a *panacea* to the collective outbreak of violence and evil that was about to consume Germany, and much of the world, in an even greater human tragedy than anything previously known in history since the Thirty Years' War.

Two more principles in Eckhart's thinking that greatly appealed to Jung might surprise you:

1) The idea of the Self as a union of opposites appeared in the East much earlier than in the West, but Jung saw it first in Europe in the works of Eckhart. For Jung the Self was the greatest saving idea of modern psychology, an idea that was previously championed by William James in 1890.

2) Eckhart's teachings about God and the Godhead and the relativity of the God-concept were an extraordinary revelation of truth that Jung had clearly elaborated in his essay on Eckhart in 1921. Jung expressed his belief there that Eckhart's teaching was not only in alignment with his own principles of analytical psychology, but with what Christ *truly* taught about the continuing incarnation of the Holy Spirit in humanity as a whole, a message that the Churches needed to hear, namely that God needs us as much as we need God. Never was there a time in Germany that Germans needed Eckhart most than in 1939.

Eckhart absorbed what he learned from his reading of Maimonides and transformed it into a new theology of birthing the Messiah through contemplation and action, prayer and vocation. The King of the Jews that he believed had come in Jesus and that was also born in him through the Paraclete could continue to be born in the human soul in us.

---iᑫᓇ CHAPTER 23 ᕋᓂᕼ---

ON THE UNION OF CHRIST WITH THE SELF

One of the reasons Eckhart appealed so much to Jung is that his theology of the Word focused on *equality* as a key to unlocking the doorway to modern psychology, where individuation, giving birth to the Self, might become possible in each person: the *principium individuationis* in everyone that aims toward distinction, separateness, and individuality. Such equality might only become possible when our souls have become Nothing, when we are all reduced to Zero, or not, in the Infinite Cosmos. This experience of emptiness and poverty of spirit born in a quiet mind can free us from ego inflation and into *self-abandonment*.

Jung reflected in his seminar on *Children's Dreams* in 1939 on the final stage of "the union of Christ and an experience of the Self, or anthropogenesis that will be fully realized only in the coming Age of Aquarius." Moreover, he modestly admitted that he was not able to arrive at a far-enough-reaching understanding of the union of Christ and the Self for his audience, so he said simply:

> Let me quote instead from Meister Eckhart's sermons. You surely know the words of Meister Eckhart: "All nature means man." And another one: "All creatures

240

feel an urge to rise from their lives to their inner nature. All creatures carry my reason within themselves, so that they may gain reason in me. I alone again prepare all creatures for God!" (All creatures—thus also man!)[518]

The final stage of anthropogenesis, which will only be fully realized in the Age of Aquarius, where we are now, will require a *union of Christ with the Self* that was presaged by Johannes Eckhart. In struggling to articulate what he meant in his empirical understanding, Jung turned to Eckhart to explain what the task of the new myth of expanded consciousness might be. Eckhart was really that far ahead of his time and was, therefore, truly *anachronistic*.

Jung emphasized with an exclamation point: "(All creatures—thus also man!)" You can see the urgency in Jung's emphasis on the word *man!* Jung's stress was applied to everyone listening during his seminar on children's dreams, which took place on the eve of World War II, when the worst nightmares in human history would be evoked by the Nazi war machine. Of course, he knew this realization that "I alone again prepare all creatures for God!" was always an ideal of human freedom and not many of us will come close to fulfilling it fully.

He had been discussing the emergence of an archaic God-image in the psyche of Germany that was about to engulf the world, with the worst and most horrifying outbreak of evil our fragile world-order had ever known. Jung spoke of this breakout of evil as a psychic contagion or infection that affected everyone: the instinct toward ego-extinction acted out in mass psychosis, becoming nothing in a negative, rather than in a positive sense. The solution was to be found in the *psychic antibody* or anti-toxin that Eckhart represented. Jung was emphatic about what he said. Jung saw something in Eckhart's teachings as a *solution* to the coming Armageddon of Antichrist.

In an earlier essay, "Die Stimme des Innern" (translated as "The Inner Voice"), and delivered at the Kulturbund in Vienna in 1932, Jung revealed another way he made creative use of a paradox inherent in

Eckhart's ideas on the Self. In this short passage near the end of his talk, he said: "Meister Eckhart says, 'God is not good, otherwise he could be better.'"[519]

Reflecting further on the Nazi atrocities during World War II, Jung wrote the following in an essay called "After the Catastrophe":

> Without guilt, unfortunately, there can be no psychic maturation and no widening of the spiritual horizon. Was it not Meister Eckhart who said: "For this reason God is willing to bear the brunt of sins and often winks at them, mostly sending them to people for whom he has prepared some high destiny. See! Who was dearer to our Lord or more intimate with him than the apostles? Not one of them but fell into mortal sin, and all were mortal sinners."[520]

This passage needs some careful unpacking.

Here Jung was clarifying what he meant by the integration of the shadow as seen through a misquoted passage of one of Eckhart's most beautifully articulated vernacular sermons. God's *winking* at our sins was one of Miss Evans's unfortunate mistranslations from the 1857 Pfeiffer edition. In a better modern translation by Walsche, and several other interpreters seem to agree, what Eckhart really said was God *permits* sins or evil, not "winks at them." To *wink* suggests God endorses our sins. Eckhart never said this. What he did say suggests a further stage in the integration of the shadow in Europe and a different understanding of God and evil.

Nevertheless, Jung was saying in a new psychological idiom that everyone needed to make a moral inventory and confess their *guilt* because everyone was guilty of evil who was *touched* by evil. We all suffer from the collective shadow of evil, as we are surrounded by sin and criminality and vice every day. For this reason, Jung said in *Answer to Job:* "We therefore need more light, more goodness and moral strength, and must wash off as much of the obnoxious blackness [evil] as possible."[521] It's remarkable how often Jung quoted Eckhart as a support for his psychology of individuation.

For instance, in his "Introduction to the Religious and Psychological Problems of Alchemy" Jung said further: "A little more Meister Eckhart would be a good thing sometimes!"[522] Indeed! That's why I am running to complete this book today before our 2024 presidential election. By instructing readers to make the shadow conscious, Jung never hesitated to give readers a good dose of Eckhart because he had witnessed absolute evil at work in his century and had to do his part to help wash off the horrible darkness that had infected everyone.

To be sure, Jung felt it was his job as a doctor of the soul and as the founder of the school of analytical psychology in Switzerland to offer a way of healing national, political, and religious strife by clearing the way for people to *see the Self at work in their own psyche through active imagination or by living a symbolic life.* Listening to the inner voice is an art of hearing in silence, where the Word of God continuously speaks in the streams of the unconscious, if we only crouch low enough to listen. Active imagination was not characterized only by *visioning* (that is, perceiving or intuiting dreams, images, and symbolic representations), but also an active form of *listening* (that is, hearing what the inner voice, or Word of God, has to say and discerning through *unitary conscience* its messages and myriad meanings). As Josef Rudin wrote in this regard: "The ultimate foundation of conscience does not come from outside but is inherent in man's innermost being as a structural ground plan and a permanent pattern of order."[523]

Jung's Psychological View of Conscience

I begin this section with a quote from Jung's 1958 paper "A Psychological View of Conscience"[524] in order to provide the reader with an understanding of some of the more complex issues that are involved in any analysis of the problems involved in a critical examination of Jung's 1921 essay "The Relativity of the God-concept in Meister Eckhart." For the reader who is unaware of Jung's comments on psychological *conscience*, his 1958 essay is the best place to start. The opening quote by Jung reads as follows:

> Since olden times conscience has been understood by many people less as a psychic function than as a divine intervention; indeed, its dictates were regarded as *vox Dei*, the voice of God. This view shows what value and significance were, and still are, attached to the problem of conscience. The psychologist cannot disregard such an evaluation, for it too is a well-authenticated phenomenon that must be taken into account if we want to treat the idea of conscience psychologically ... The *vox Dei* is an assertion and an opinion, like the assertion that there is such a thing as conscience at all. ... It is a *psychological truth* that the opinion exists and the voice of conscience is the voice of God.[525]

Jung's views on conscience were not a theology, but a therapy for those who had lost their faith in traditional religious traditions and were looking for a psychological substitute that never boasted of formulating any ethical principles at all, but instead preferred to remain ambivalent about the question of what God really wants from us. Nevertheless, he stated surprisingly near the end of his life:

> I have not been able to confine myself exclusively to the psychological nature of conscience, but have had to consider its theological aspect ... We have, rather, to give priority to the assertion which conscience itself makes— that it is a voice of God ... Conscience ... behaves like a God so far as its demands and authority are concerned,

and asserts that it is God's voice. This assertion cannot be overlooked by an objective psychology.[526]

Therefore, in this book, an objective psychology such as Eckhart's has taken the theological aspect of conscience into account. We cannot leave theology behind but must carry it forward into the present and future. In 1959, Jung addressed a Stuttgarter Gemeinschaft group that had traveled to meet with him in Zürich to discuss the question of "Good and Evil in Analytical Psychology." There he postulated a synthetic principle that made the bridge back to where he began as an adolescent boy of fifteen reading Meister Eckhart for the first time.

> That is where his most personal ethics begin: in grim confrontation with the Absolute, in striking out on a path condemned by current morality and the guardians of the law. And yet he may feel that he has never been truer to his innermost nature and vocation, and hence never nearer to the Absolute, because he alone and the Omniscient have seen the actual situation as it were from inside, whereas the judges and condemners see it only from outside.[527]

The psychological questions Jung raised in these important late essays about the nature of God, as both good and evil, are what we post-Jungians have been left to wrestle with for the future of analytical psychology. Jung said: *"But because I take an empirical attitude it does not mean that I relativize good and evil as such."*[528] This appears to contradict his previous views on the relativity of God. Clearly, something more than archetypes is involved theologically in our evaluations of the variables of conscience. As Jung wrote in his "Foreword" to Erich Neumann's book *Depth Psychology and a New Ethic*, "The chief causes of neurosis are conflicts of conscience and difficult moral problems that require an answer."[529]

"Living reality" was to Jung "living psychological process, through *esse in anima*."[530] What is the feeling of your vocation, the meaning of your existence in the soul or in God-consciousness? How can you know your true calling in the present moment through feeling? How can we learn to feel it in the Now? All of these questions can be answered through consulting our own conscience.

Eckhart preached:

> So if I say God is good, it is not true: *I* am good, God is not good. I go further: I am better than God! For only what is good can become better, and only what is better can become best. God is not good, therefore He cannot become better; and since he cannot become better he cannot become the best. These three: good, better, best, are infinitely remote from God, who is above all.[531]

Jung loved this sermon. He quoted it in his book *Psychological Types*. Yet it needs to be stated that Eckhart's *esse omnium,* God as "the existence of all things" in the Absolute sense, or *ipsum esse,* was God as "Existence Itself" with a capital *E*; or *Esse Absolutum,* Absolute Existence in the soul. Here, again, there is a different theological emphasis on the metaphysical self in Eckhart's works.

God was for Eckhart in some ways always beyond *esse*: "Thus, too, if I say God is a being, that is not true: he is a transcendent being, and a superessential nothingness."[532] If feeling is the deeper sort of religion, as William James had first argued, then Eckhart got it right, when he said: "He that is right in his feeling is right in any place and in any company ... For a man of right feeling has God with him."[533] Jung knew what this meant when he spoke about being in one's right vocation as having the right *feeling* for it.

Only in Eckhart, Jung said, did he *feel* the "breath of life." Other theologians left Jung feeling soulless, without life, without the indwelling "breath" of the Holy Spirit, without *esse in anima*. Eckhart brought

Jung's soul to life. *Feeling* was, therefore, the main thing for Eckhart, as it was for William James and for Jung when it came to religious experiences, or visitations from the numinous Self. Religious feelings, the feeling for religion, was something all three had in common with one another. Without a feeling of unity for the human race, a feeling for vocation, a feeling for world peace, we are doomed as a species. A trans-dualistic consciousness is the goal of the individuation of humanity.

Jung's oeuvre was so large that many people fail to understand his best theological source—and that was always, from the beginning of his career, Eckhart. Eckhart's God was the Word of the Hebrew-Christian Bible, the Word of Creation, and the Word of Christ in the Gospel of John, the Word born in humanity from the highest temple of the soul. His God was the "little spark" of the anima universalis, the *vünkelîn* (spark), *burglelîn* (castle), *wipfel* (wife), *supremum animae* (supreme soul), *or the Divine Grund* (Ground of divinity). The *geburt*, meaning "birth," was bliss Absolute. Consider Martha united with Wisdom, or Sophia, through work.

Theoretical Postulates on the Metaphor of the Pregnant Monk

> It appeared to a man as in a dream—it was a waking dream—that he became pregnant with Nothing like a woman with child, and in that Nothing God was born; he was the fruit of nothing. God was born in the Nothing ... But as it is in the ground of my soul, there it is at its highest and noblest, *there* it is nothing but an image.[534]

It was Jung's hypothesis that after two thousand years of religious evolution had passed, it would be time for humanity to learn that good and evil are categories of our moral judgment that are *relative* to humans as a global species in evolution toward an expanding vision of

Self-consciousness during the Age of Aquarius. "Thus," Jung wrote, "the way was opened for a new model of the self."[535]

Eckhart's dream of the pregnant monk was at the center of all of his mature thoughts about the way of the future, which is birth-giving through the vehicle of your vocation. The monk who became pregnant with Nothing in the Ground of the soul was the Higher man in Eckhart, the superior man, the holy man. He became pregnant with Nothing and in that Nothing God was born as an image of Nothingness; this was a new living symbol for the Ultimate Self in Eckhart. *"Du sollst ihn lieben, wie er ist ein Nicht-Gott, ein Nicht-Geist, ein Nicht-Person, ein Nicht-Bild."*[536] ("You should love Him as he is a Non-God, a Non-Spirit, a Non-Person, a Non-Image.")

Eckhart served a *fathering function* for the Church in his pregnancy and birthing as a humble monk who preached the Word. He showed how a Dominican could himself become a Father-Mother of God, by lying in the maternity bed as a woman with child, as a man who bore a new image of God as Nothingness—first in the Ground, the *Grund*, and then in the highest temple of his soul, as the highest principle of Existence in the Godhead: *"in den Grund, der glundlos ist."*[537]

Through a simple prayer, the prayer of silence, Eckhart taught a practical method for teaching listeners to climb upward into God, to become totally transformed by the Holy Spirit and unified in a higher field of order in the Absolute. This is a prayer that can lead anyone who uses it toward a cure for whatever it is that makes them ill. Eckhart called this prayer "detachment (MHG: *abegescheidenheit*)." Bernard McGinn said, "Detachment appears everywhere in Eckhart's works."[538] Detachment is the summit of the soul's powers in the divine Being beyond all God-images: the simple "'One,' separated from all duality."[539]

Abegescheidenheit, or *gelâzenheit,* "Detachment, or letting go" in Middle High German are two key words that define this prayer. I define detachment two ways: 1) One, as the right state of mind free from negative emotions in a *relative* sense; and 2) Two, as wakefulness to transcendent states of bliss and peace in an *Absolute,* or transpersonal Intelligence.

Absolute detachment is above perfect humility and poverty as a matter of relative self-abnegation, for *ultimate detachment* so "narrowly approximates to naught" in Eckhart's words that "no room remains for aught betwixt zero and absolute detachment."[540] Thus, whereas relative detachment is the state of humility and poverty in the soul, absolute detachment is above the will and the intellect and is equivalent to Zero, or Nothingness, which is the highest state the soul can arise to in her transcendence into *superconsciousness*.

What then was the highest prayer for Eckhart? Praying for Nothing, a return to Nothingness. "The truly humble man has no need to pray to God for anything: he can command God, for the height of the Godhead seeks nothing but the depth of humility, as I said at St. Maccabees. The humble man and God are one."[541]

The greatest humility attainable is when we realize we are Nothing, we come from Nothingness, and our life in time is to become Naught, for *"when I pray for nobody and for nothing, then I am praying most truly. Then the child is born in me"*: "What is changed into something else becomes one with it. I am so changed into him that he produces his being in me as one, not just similar. By the living God, this is true! There is no distinction! ... God and I, we are one."[542]

There are four God-principles involved in Eckhart's technique of praying to God to free him of God, while preaching God's Word:

> When I preach, I am accustomed to speak about detachment, and that man should be free of himself and of all things; second, that a man should be formed again into that simple good which is God; third, that he should reflect on the great nobility with which God has endowed his soul, so that in this way he may come again to wonder at God; fourth, about the purity of the divine nature, for the brightness of the divine nature is beyond words. God is a word, a word unspoken.[543]

CHAPTER 24

THE IMPRINTER IN THE WORLD SOUL

Jung understood psychologically that every *typos* requires an Imprinter.[544] The God-images in humanity were his main interest of empirical investigation, not God or the Self in a transcendental sense. His psychology did not place an accent on the Imprinter, only on imprints, or *typos*. Yet his empirical method did, in fact, accent the most important and universal *imprint—the Self*—in which no single theology can claim final truth for its religion.[545] This *relativity of God* was what he had found in Eckhart as well as in the *Upanishads*.[546]

The *typos* of the Self, in other words, was first revealed, in Jung's view, in Eckhart's writings in the West. Moses, Jesus, Mohammed, and the teachings of Yoga and Buddhism and Taoism—all of these teachings stemmed from a universal archetypal foundation of conscience, an *Imprinting Voice in the World Soul*. All God-images were, therefore, images of the Self in Jung's mind, imprints of experience, emanations of the one universal God-function in humanity that *democratizes* and equalizes all. "For psychology," Jung wrote, "the religious figures point to the self, whereas for theology the self points to its—theology's—own central figure."[547] In other words, in Christianity, Christ points to the Self, but as its central figure it is only one symbol. Christ is an image of the Self, which is the central symbol of the Imprinter in Christianity, not Judaism or Islam.

For Jung, a mistaken reading of religion was confounding the local God-images of world culture with the Imprinter. The Imprinter is what leaves an *impression*, or *imprint*, on various cultures, tribes, or nations. Insofar as this Imprinter is a universal archetype in the human psyche, however, it is universally valid across all religions, races, and nations. Thus, to get beyond the local references to a particular God-image, as represented by founders of religions, was to leave the God-images for the Imprinter, or God for the Self, emanating in each individual soul from the Ground of the soul. By positing a God beyond all God-images in the divine ground of the Godhead, Eckhart made the bridge between theology and psychology possible before Jung.

Such a shift in focus from absolutism in any one faith to religious *relativity*[548] allowed Jung to *see* through the teachings of religious reformers' manifestations of various *typos* of particular God-symbols, to the Imprinter in the psyche patterning all religious cultures. This Imprinter was synonymous with God, the Self, Mary Mother of God, or the Paraclete in Eckhart's works.[549] This was not "psychologism," for the same truth could be found in Eckhart's theology of the Word. In his psychological "Commentary on 'The Secret of the Golden Flower,'" a Chinese alchemical text, Jung used Eckhart in his own self-defense, when he asserted: "Should Meister Eckhart be accused of 'psychologism' when he says, 'God must be born in the soul again and again?'"[550] Jung's defense leads me to another principle present in Jung's teachings on Eckhart: God's continuing incarnation in the soul of collective humanity is synonymous with the psychological process of individuation on a relative plane, *giving continuous birth to the vocation of the Self, or the Paraclete within*. What this means is a union or inner marriage of Christ with the Spiritual Self.

Jung quoted Eckhart again in *Aion*. This time he cited him in a footnote on the capacity of discernment: "And therefore the highest power, seeing her stability in God, communicates it to the lowest, that they may discern good and evil."[551] Eckhart's meditations on discernment may have helped to form a paradigm for Jung's writings on ethics and conscience, which leads me to another complementary principle in Eckhart's and Jung's teachings.

In Eckhart's oeuvre, the highest power in the soul is the intellectual faculty, the function of knowing and absolute knowledge, or to be more precise: intellectual-intuition. This highest power of discrimination above the opposites discerns the contraries of good and evil *between* the highest and lowest powers in the soul. It was by virtue of the soul's integrative powers to judge from the highest Light of God (or what Jung called in 1958 a *superstructure in conscience*) that the Word can be heard as a moral imperative in the just person through justice and mercy or love, which is known in theological language as the *Vox Dei*. This was, in its spiritual essence, considered to be a purified voice of unity and being, not contaminated by division, evil, nonbeing, or Nothingness, *not*. Existence and intellect, life and intuition, Unity and bliss are in this sense Absolute in the Imprinter.

In Eckhart's theology evils are nonbeing, *not* God, because God does not cause evil. The "final cause of creation is the whole universe,"[552] which includes God's creation of the opposites of good and evil in human nature. But from the point of view of God-consciousness, the human shadow is an infinitesimal part of the transhuman magnificence of the Cosmos, which God is. The shadow is so small in fact that it cannot be counted in relation to the One in which He-She only sees infinity—infinity being a universal multiplicity of ones that all add up to One, or One in Many when human negation and privation are subtracted. God does not exist in evil things equally with the good since, as privation, evil does not equal One. Evil is pure negation. Evil is not a part of the divine equality of God because it is a negative number $-1 =$ Nothing. A privation from the One is a fall from Wisdom, as it is not wise to do evil out of relationship to the whole.[553]

CHAPTER 25

JUNG'S RESEARCHES INTO THE SELF AND NO-SELF

Jung wrote in *Aion*: "Meister Eckhart's theology knows a 'Godhead' of which no qualities, except unity and being, can be predicated."[554] He continued with another astute statement about Eckhart:

> The world-embracing spirit of Meister Eckhart knew, without discursive knowledge, the primordial mystical experience of India as well as of the Gnostics, and was itself the finest flower of the "Free Spirit" that flourished at the beginning of the eleventh century. Well might the writings of this Master lie buried for six hundred years, for "his time was not yet come." Only in the nineteenth century did he find a public at all capable of appreciating the grandeur of his mind.[555]

I'm not sure why Jung quoted Eckhart for two pages in his chapter "Gnostic Symbols for the Self." Eckhart was certainly no Gnostic. Jung seems to have confused the symbolism of the universal "Ground" with the "Deity itself."[556] Jung was searching for the right metaphor to describe the difference in Eckhart's theology between God and the bottomless Ground. When Jung was asked, moreover, to write a "Foreword to Suzuki's 'Introduction to Zen Buddhism,'" he turned, not surprisingly once again to Eckhart to describe the meaning of the experience of *satori*, or *enlightenment*, as evidenced in the well-known story Jung was fond of retelling when Eckhart *saw* a vision of a "little naked boy."[557] Jung equated this vision with the appearance of the Self. While continuing his comparisons with the Buddhist experience of satori, Jung turned to the "characteristically Eckhartian assertion: 'God is Nothingness'"[558]

Moreover, Jung wrote on the similarity between Zen and Eckhart: "The occurrence of satori is interpreted and formulated as a *breakthrough*, by a consciousness limited to the ego-form, into the non-ego-like self. This view is in accord not only with the essence of Zen, but also with the mysticism of Meister Eckhart."[559] It is important to point out that he said the *mysticism*, not theology of Eckhart. Why did Jung and other interpreters of Eckhart in modernity always have to use the terms *mystic, mystical*, or *mysticism*, when referring to Eckhart? And why did Jung put Eckhart's theology of the Ground into his chapter on Gnosticism? I don't think that Eckhart in his unmarked grave would appreciate this.

Eckhart's God-images were all steeped in Christian symbolism and natural science. Alchemy was familiar to him through Albert. But his God-concepts were as close to perfection as Christ's were, or any of the saints. He was Catholic through and through and trans-dualistic, both relativistic and Absolute.

In a letter written in 1960 to Herbert Read, Jung wrote another fascinating statement about Eckhart:

> Your blessed words are the rays of a new sun over a
> dark sluggish swamp in which I felt buried. I often
> thought of Meister Eckhart who was entombed for 600
> years. I asked myself time and again why there are no

men in our epoch who could see at least what I was wrestling with. I think it is not mere vanity and desire for recognition on my part, but a genuine concern for my fellow-beings. It is presumably the ancient functional relationship of the medicine-man to his tribe, the *participation mystique* and the essence of the physician's ethos.[560]

This final nod to Eckhart was perhaps Jung's most interesting statement about how he and Eckhart were spiritually connected, ever since his dream of the Crusader emerged while he was struggling to jump out of the shadow of psychoanalysis and its stultifying views. By the time Jung penned this letter, he had done his job and done it magnificently. He could let go of his radical empiricism, in his final approach toward death, and remember the hero who had helped him formulate his arguments against his father about God not being good enough and needing *us* to become better.

Jung had been led by Eckhart as an ancestral spirit and wise inner teacher during his hour of greatest need—his so-called "fallow period" between 1913–1917—to find inner peace in his soul through a process of letting go (*gelâzenheit*) through sacrifice or crucifixion, spiritual motherhood, and detachment, and thus, he gave birth to analytical psychology. The dark sluggish swamp in which he *felt* buried a year before he died came from the misunderstandings that had arisen by psychologists and theologians alike over what he meant by the Self, God, and the archetypes in the collective soul of humanity. He said he *often thought of Meister Eckhart* and asked himself time and again, why there were no men in his epoch who could see what he was *wrestling* with. Eckhart was a God-wrestler, a second Jacob, like Jung was, but his wrestling with God was with the shadow of Nothingness in us as a human species and with a collective institution that tried to reduce him to *not*.

255

As I've said repeatedly, Eckhart lived in Jung's soul as a *Self-figure.* Jung may not have understood Eckhart theologically as I have attempted to do in Part II, but there is no doubt that Eckhart helped to transform him, as he has also assisted me and so many others in modernity and postmodernity who are coming to him for consolation in times of dire need.

CHAPTER 26

ECKHART'S SELF-NOTION

In the West, Eckhart was the first in whom the Self-notion was clearly articulated as a process of continuous birthing from the Ground of the soul. From the beginning of Jung's career in Switzerland, and as the founder of the Zürich school of analytical psychology, Jung has been misunderstood by more than a few of his most avid readers and peers, and as I mentioned, he felt chagrined at the end of his life that some theologians misunderstood him too. He often thought during times of personal travail of Eckhart, and now Eckhart is experiencing a remarkable revival and we may all be glad and grateful for it.

As just quoted in the previous chapter, Jung asked himself time and again why there were so few people in his epoch who could see at least what he was wrestling with. Whatever the mystery of Jung's vocation was, Eckhart was, in my view, at the center of it as a transformative *Self-figure*, an inner relation, or Christian relative and ancestor who transmitted what Christ really taught him about the birth of the Holy Spirit in humanity over the past two thousand years.[561] We have now entered the Age of Aquarius, where anthropogenesis is the new myth we all walk in, and we must take responsibility for *being* birthers and mothers and fathers of the Self that wants to emerge though our respective vocations.

As a medical doctor, writer, renowned lecturer, and world-respected psychiatrist, Jung's aim had always been to express a genuine concern for his fellow-beings. I think Jung's love for Eckhart went much deeper than anything he said in print. I think he loved Eckhart with great admiration and devotion. This chapter will give the hungry reader a foretaste of Eckhart's *super-substantial bread*. There is so much more to feast on as I am editing this chapter on Easter Day, 2024. We are all hungering for the goodness of God that Eckhart preached, from Erfurt to his last breath in Avignon.

What can we learn from Eckhart about healing from sufferings that coincides with the *essence of our physician's ethos, whether as psychotherapists or pastoral counselors or readers searching for spiritual treatment*? It was presumably the ancient functional relationship of the shaman to his tribe, Jung said, which means to me presumably all human tribes that are individuating. We don't know how Eckhart felt at the end of his life. Like Jung, I have often thought of Eckhart in my life, too, as I am now sixty-eight and aging by the day. He is to me today, in the field of Christian theology, what James and Jung were and are to me in the field of empirical analytic psychology: an inner transformative *Self-figure*. "The light God bestrides the bridge—Man—from the dayside; God's shadow, from the night side," said Jung. What is God's worst shadow? For Eckhart, it was the "shadow of nothingness."[562] This was the worst evil known to Eckhart, evil Absolute. We are standing on the edge of the abyss as a human species. A third world war or climate change could reduce our species to Nothing. God's shadow may be the violence in God that we cannot control, because of human beings, not God.

For now, I want to leave the reader with a few propositions that I've found in Eckhart's theology that may be helpful in anticipating what awaits us as spiritual nourishment in what lies ahead:

1) *The birth of the Word is taking place in the Ground of the soul at all times.*
2) *True detachment is equivalent to an annihilation of the self.*

3) *The soul must be completely empty to receive God's grace, or the Self's, in Her or His fullness, through the Paraclete.*

4) *When the soul is completely annihilated in the Ground of the Godhead, they (there is no gender in Eckhart's use of the word soul) simply act virtuously according to God's, or the Self's will, which is pure Goodness at the level of the Higher Self.*

A few questions to ponder: Should we limit analytical psychology to relativism and leave all metaphysical considerations out? Should we limit Eckhart's theology to Christian mysticism? Where is the uniting Ground, the bridge between these opposites?

CHAPTER 27

INCARNATION IN THE WORKS OF ECKHART AND JUNG

Eckhart's myth of the Paraclete as the Prince of Peace (Is 9:6), or as Peacemakers who are called the blessed children of God (Mt 5:9), has long since been superseded by a more complete psychological God-image in human history, beginning with the theology of Jakob Böhme's *unio oppositorum*, followed by Jung's *principium individuationis*, and William James's Transcendental Self.

Eckhart's theology was closer to Buddhism than it was to the theology of Augustine, Albert, or Aquinas, however. It was a unique theology of trans-dualism. In the documents of his "Defense," the theologian does not engage an active imagination. Instead we hear the serpent of his *anger*, one of the seven deadly sins. He was momentarily poisoned by it, so much that the Church would have to struggle to find a panacea. As I see it, this poison has the potential to become a medicine for the Church, if it can integrate the shadow. This poison has been metabolizing, slowly, over the past seven hundred years since Eckhart first took up residency in Cologne.

There has not been an apology from the Vatican yet. Yet Eve and the Serpent were united in the wisdom-body of the preacher at the midpoint on the crossbeams. The paradox of supreme opposites in his life as a theologian was transcended in a crucifying stroke; he was crucified at the pivotal moment of his life on the cross he had held up high, not Christ's cross, but his own, as a light for the nations of European Christendom to contemplate. Eckhart became thereby not only what Jung called a "second Christ" but a new Israel, a second Jacob. His body and psyche were united through his techniques of prayer and bliss, and the synthesizing powers, where the superior and inferior powers of his soul touched, were kissed by the mouth of his beloved Christ in his moments of pain.

Eckhart fought a good fight, but it made him sick in the end, and he died in poverty and humility and anonymity in Avignon. The fight with the shadow and evil, which Jung never tired of teaching us to wrestle with, has to do with blood; according to Eckhart, it was his own *blut*: "The noblest thing in man is blood, when it wills good. But the most evil thing in man is blood, when it wills evil."[563] I believe Eckhart's blood is the blood that could redeem Christianity from its own worst evils. The true churches of Europe or the Americas are ones that are no longer specifically Christ-centric; they are now, after Eckhart, James, and Jung, Self-centric. The new theologies or psychologies that preach or teach the way of individuation, as the way of the present and the future, are founded on the rock of totality, not Christ as a myth of perfection, but wholeness.

Resistance against the organized Mass means holding one's own against all evil institutions, perhaps especially the churches and dualistic dead theologies of Europe and the United States. Eckhart and Jung gave us ways to create our own personal myths, our own theories of truth, and to follow our own spiritual paths to Self-awakening and Oneness.

This is why I feel we need Eckhart's theology today as a complement to Jung's psychology: to free us up to follow the path that we feel most called to walk upon, toward our own spiritual Liberty. This is where Eckhart and Jung agreed in principle. Toward the end of Jung's life, he stated to a small group of theologians that "Christ within us" is nothing other than "God in us," and the will of God not only wants to enter into us as empirical human beings, but to burden us with his paradoxical "good-bad essence," for "God and his works appear to be ambivalent, and this ambivalence burdens us."[564] As discussed in Part II, Eckhart exposed the "good-bad essence" of the Catholic Church as an inescapable fact of its illness.

For theologians, the problem with Jung's essay "The Transcendent Function" is this opening sentence: "There is nothing mysterious or metaphysical about the term 'transcendent function.'"[565] Why did Jung, the natural scientist, take the mystery and the metaphysics out of his psychology from its inception in 1916? Later in 1921, Jung said further about Eckhart's God-concept that the Dominican did not conceive of God as "absolute," yet at the same time he added that the "God-function" is nevertheless characterized by its "absolute ascendency over the will of the subject" and it "transcends conscious understanding in acts."[566]

To those who read Jung's work closely, it may be clear that by the term "God-complex" Jung was actually analyzing a split in what he called the *ambivalent God*. This idea of two wills in God does not fit in entirely with what Eckhart actually taught and preached about God. For the birth of God, Christ, or the Paraclete was for Eckhart transcendent of all the complexes in the human psyche and was, therefore, in Eckhart's definitions of incarnation *Existence Absolutum*, beyond any specific culture including the churches of Europe he was addressing.

Therefore, to expand Jung's essay "The Transcendent Function" into theological territory, one would have to postulate first, a God-function that is relative and *also* Absolute, located in and outside of all human cultures; second, a dependency between God and human that places its greatest accent on the realization that God needs each person, each single individual, to wake up their God, or Goddess Nature; third, a Word that is in each of us that is not always ambivalent but essentially unitary, One, not two, and yet plural and singular at the same time because it is pure Oneness; and fourth, that each of us is a vehicle for incarnation not only of Jung's ambivalent God-image, but also of the Christ-image, Buddha-image, or Great Spirit–image, or whatever God-image you might prefer.

Eckhart came into his own after the Last Crusade had failed in Jerusalem. The so-called opposites in the God-images portrayed in Judaism and Christianity and their apocalyptic predictions that Jung warned us about do not appear much at all in Eckhart's works. For Eckhart, God was always higher, superior, and deeper than any complex in the human soul, or psyche. The Ground as the fourth continuum of a God beyond God, beyond all names, all images, and ideas of Divinity was an experience of *Esse Absolutum,* above all categories of thought.

God, to Eckhart, was present in the world before humanity came into being as a species, and he opened himself up to this God-principle as a human God, and identified himself totally with it, with a singleness of Eye and God-consciousness. God's Eye and Eckhart's Eye were one Eye, one seeing, one knowing, one Love. Everywhere Eckhart looked he beheld the beauty of God because he was first and foremost a naturalist and a pantheist. He worshiped God in a caterpillar as he also did in Lord Jesus.

Eckhart's solution to the problem of sins and human evils, since God was not evil, was to lead his listeners above the will into the world of pure intuitive seeing and perpetual running into Peace through a vocation to live by. The image or symbol that was born in him of a child of Nothing happened in a detached wakeful state, in an imaginative mind, achieved through meditations on Nothingness. He was in this sense our Buddha to the West. Eckhart's new God-image was empty and nearly equivalent to zero because he arrived at the place from which all God-images emanate out of and in the primal Ground.

As an image of Nothing, the child he became pregnant with, as a fatherly and motherly monk, emerged from a groundless Ground of Nothingness, beyond even God and the soul and for which Sophia was the transmitter of a higher Wisdom and Light. Eckhart's God-concept was simple in its complexity and complex in its simplicity, yet its paradoxical unity enlarged the theological vision of Catholicism that focused obsessively on Jesus. A Jew like Martin Buber felt at home in Eckhart's Church, so much so that he wrote part of his dissertation on him.

Eckhart served a Father and Mother function for the Church during his pregnancy and birth-giving as a monk that was unprecedented. He showed how a Dominican monk could himself become a mother of God and father of God by lying in the maternity bed with a new image of God, in the Ground and highest temple of his soul, as Wisdom.

To the interested reader I recommend staying conscious of the theological and psychological differences in Eckhart and Jung. Jung's God-notion and Eckhart's Self Absolute were not the same; in Eckhart's Higher Self, evil was close to nothing, whereas in Jung, it was so central an aspect of the God-image that he assigned it an equal coexistence in God, which is nowhere to be found in Eckhart.

Jung's analysis of Eckhart, as interesting as it is, does not provide us with a theological understanding of what God truly connotes for contemporary society. I have been in quest for over four decades for a more synthetic bridge between psychology and theology, or a marriage between Christian thought and analytical theory and practice, a footbridge that might help to take us forward as a field toward a better understanding of God, for ourselves and our patients, one that can give equal consideration to the relative and Absolute.

Eckhart gave Jung a key that opened the door to the way that Jung called analytical psychology and psychological relativity. Yet, Jung's practice of the psychological transcendent function, which Jung prescribed to patients in modernity, as a solution to perplexity in world affairs, was problematic if one gets stuck on Jung's sometimes dogmatic statements about God's ambivalent nature. To be sure, there is an ambivalence in the Self that needs integration. Jung's method of giving birth to Christ within, however, was his way of birthing something more than what is relative—what Eckhart called the Absolute, for about God he taught: "He is absolutely the Absolute."[567]

To properly provide a model of the soul that is not only *esse in anima,* but also *Esse in Anima,* with a capital *E,* we would be wiser to create a bridge between the relative and the Absolute that Jung neglected to construct because that was not his calling. Jung's vocation to the natural sciences was always a calling to point out the contradictions and ambivalence in the Western God-image. Eckhart's primary callings were to theology and preaching the Word of God.

What Eckhart said humans need most is to receive an impulse from the primordial eruption, which can carry us above the angels and even God into the Nothingness that gave birth to us all in an infinite Universe of Absolute Existence that wants to incarnate itself as an archetype of mercy and peace. We are destined to become peacemakers who are the children of God and instruments of the God's Peace, which is forever with us and within us, and can impregnate us with Love. God is not only relative, but He or She (Sophia) must also be Absolute in the soul when it becomes a birthing place in the Ground, connecting Cosmos and psyche. This Ground can be accessed only by becoming Nothing, through a death on the cross, where Self, Savior, or Messiah knows how to discriminate between good and evil and say "Away!" to the Antichrist.

PART IV

MEISTER ECKHART AS A DISPENSER OF SACRED MEDICINE

CHAPTER 28

THE TRANSFERENCE OF CREATIVITY

To be sure the transference is the primary thing in any analysis. However, not enough focus was devoted to the transference of creativity in early life onto great personages in history who embody the highest potential realizations of spiritual Wisdom that can lift a young person out of the morass of infantile depressions, dependencies, and neurosis into God-consciousness. I find nothing of this in psychoanalysis, but in Jung the tracks of Eckhart's self-concept are virtually everywhere, if one takes the time to follow all of the threads that have been mostly missed by his biographers—with the exception of Sonu Shamdasani, to whom I am greatly indebted.

This kind of imprinting, by identification with truly transformative Self-figures can occur very early on in life, and may even leave a lasting imprint on the soul of an individual. Such an imprint of early experience may convert into a spiritual *archetype of destiny,* or a beacon of great Inner Light.

Withdrawing the projections of the archetype of the great man or great woman onto creative persons is necessary. Jung taught patients in analysis, who at first idealized him as an analyst, to instead *awaken* the voice of the Self, or "Christ within." He also spoke about an affinity that may radiate energy like a *magnet* and draw an analyst and analysand together into a closer union in the spacious Self field between them.

When *affinity*[568] is lacking, no synthesis of the personality through an inner marriage of souls may be co-created by an analytic couple. *Vocation plays a key role in this process.*

If there is no *spiritual attunement to the calling* in a patient by their analyst, a dialogue with the soul cannot bear vocational fruits.[569] *Affinity* is primary in analytic relationships according to Jung. But too much affinity can also lead to relational problems. The projections of infantile complexes onto a friend, mentor, or an analyst are attempts on the part of a young person's psyche to repair damage that was done in infancy, childhood, or latency to the ego-Self axis, whether by parents, relatives, or teachers.

That is why I believe Eckhart was so important to Jung and why he is so vital to me. He helped Jung learn how to let go of himself and to sink into his own Ground of being and becoming. Goethe and Nietzsche were also vital to Jung's nascent development. Jung, however, was highly critical of Nietzsche, whereas he never once uttered a critical word in print about Eckhart, although he quoted him frequently. Why was this? Jung always referred to Eckhart with high admiration for his native Germanic genius and looked to him for theological understanding when his empiricism fell short of hitting the mark.

Eckhart therefore represented a very high ideal in Jung's psyche, a Self-figure he looked up to and respected later as his *equal*. I find the affinity Jung spoke of in a few of his references to Eckhart in his essay on the transference: an *affinity with the Self within*. This essential teaching came through clearly in the following beautiful line in Jung's 1921 essay: "Strangely appealing is Eckhart's sense of an inner affinity with God, when contrasted with the Christian sense of sin."[570] I think Jung had a deep inner affinity with Eckhart's ideas on repentance and forgiveness of sins.

This affinity that many of us transfer onto Eckhart is one of the reasons he has become so popular over the past century. Jung's transference onto Eckhart helped him accept his sinfulness without the terrible torture, hell and damnation, fire and brimstone theology that only frightens and traumatizes young Christian children, as I know only too well from my analytic practice. This is why Eckhart is so deeply refreshing to read! He does not say the soul is filled with sin and evil; he says *your soul is the birthplace of God, and God is dependent* on your giving birth to Holy Spirit or the Self within you. "Eckhart states bluntly that God is dependent on the soul, and at the same time, that the soul is the birthplace of God."[571]

What is this birthplace, if not a place of Love? Indeed. A primary goal of any analytical relationship of the mature type is *love* on the part of an analyst for the sake of a patient's vocation, through an inner union or *spiritual marriage* in the patient and psychotherapist. This spiritual wedding ultimately can lead to the emergence of a successful career, happy partnership, marriage, and enduring friendships.[572]

We know that Jung drew his ideas from a plethora of different sources, and it might at first sound exaggerated to hail Eckhart as Jung's most transformative inner teacher on spiritual matters, especially when reading his *Black Books*, or *The Red Book*, but we can indeed hear echoes from Jung's readings of Eckhart in many of his best formulations.

Archetypes operate in this way: as congenital imprints of experience they are later filled in by historical details in a person's life. Jung was not only born into a religious family; he was born naturally religious and was, I believe, predestined to transform the very way we understand world religion, from the ground up, as systems of healing. What Jung was essentially postulating in *The Psychology of the Transference* in 1946 (a prelude to his masterpiece on alchemy, *Mysterium Coniunctionis*) is that analysis is preferable when the dialogue with the Self is between an analyst and analysand in a *continuum* or field between the couple. Moreover, it is particularly fertile when the analytic relationship nurtures a connection to the inner voice within a patient, which can sometimes be heard as a Word of God.

CHAPTER 29

ECKHART AS A PEACEMAKER

Eckhart followed a path to wholeness with four consecutive steps into God-consciousness, or spiritual awakening. His frequent metaphor of the soul's evolution in four stages or strides was captured in the following parable:

> The soul strides into God with four steps. The first stride is when fear, hope, and desire grow in it. It strides further when fear, hope, and desire are brought to an end. Thirdly, it comes to a state of forgetting all temporal things. Fourthly, the soul strides into God where it will remain forever, reigning with God in eternity; and then it never thinks of temporal things or itself. Rather it is completely dissolved in God and God in it. What it does then, it does in God.[573]

The four *strides* suggest a transport to higher stages of understanding, in which Eckhart's soul became identical with Wisdom, or God's Word. Eckhart's experience of *striding* across long distances is evident in his metaphor here; and given his many journeys between France and Germany as a monk, preacher, and traveling scholar, he walked many steps. Four strides create a four-tiered paradigm for the process of moving progressively toward God-consciousness in successive acts of awakening or *arising*. One of my favorite Eckhart sermons begins with a meditation on the words *puella surge* (Luke 8:54): *soul arise!* Eckhart preached: "Our Lord said to the girl: 'Arise!' With this simple word our Lord Jesus Christ teaches us how the soul should rise up from material things."[574]

The girl was Eckhart's anima, the soul that was transformed from lower levels of Eros to the highest levels of Eros, symbolized by Mary, the sister of Martha; the Virgin Mary; and Sophia. This led him to stride perpetually into peace. As Jesus said in John 16:23: "These things I have spoken unto you, that in me ye might have peace." Eckhart then added: "He to whom God is present in all things, who is in full control of his reason and uses it, he alone knows true peace."[575]

The archetype of the peacemaker is a universal image of harmony among various tribes and diverse cultures of the world. Eckhart, like Christ, was a peacemaker. So was C. G. Jung. Jung's vision of Eckhart's theology was purely psychological. Nevertheless, he admitted that what he had to say was his own subjective bias. Jung was a peacemaker who fought all of his life to make the dark side of the God-image conscious in himself, his patients, and collective humanity through his *Collected Works* and many public lectures. The word *peace* appears frequently in the Old and New Testaments (Is 9:6; Mt 5:9).

In Eckhart's sermon a person who is *striding* in perpetual peace is a heavenly person. Such a person has experienced a death to the soul and a transfiguration of consciousness into the Higher Self that is *equivalent* with God. Eckhart was describing a unitive experience in which his soul became completely dissolved in God-consciousness and God in it. What the soul did then, she did in God because she had become One with Wisdom, Sophia, and this brought her peace.

Peace exists as a state of mind, a state of rest[576] that we can return to, to be *perennially peaceful,* not permanently but impermanently. It's a *unifying condition* where war and strife have been temporarily canceled. The transcendent state of being can be so perplexing psychologically unless you have experienced it, for in the highest states of mind the opposites are dissolved into unity, where "the *idea* of evil is good, and the idea of good and evil is one and the same."[577] The trans-dual nature of this *fourth state of Self-realization* in the Absolute is superconscious visioning beyond any imaging.

Jung's Self-concept has created some confusions in the theory and practice of analytical psychology. In this chapter, I will invoke Eckhart's help to try to clear up some of the misunderstandings. Eckhart preached from the place of Wisdom within. He was living on a plane of reality that is higher than most of us can live with very much consistency. At times we may attain it. But Eckhart gives the impression he existed for long periods of time *above* the opposites. In the chapter "The Self," in *Psychology: A Briefer Course,* William James spoke of the Transcendental I as "the *Thinker*; and the question immediately comes up, what is the thinker?"[578] Later, he drew a line of distinction between the I and the Me. The problem of who the transcendental *Knower* is, James said, "is a "metaphysical problem," and psychology as a natural science need take no account of its source and origin.[579] This view changed over time, as James's soul evolved and extended deeper and deeper into the *trans-marginal fields.* Later James wrote: "I will now confess my own utopia, I devoutly believe in the reign of peace."[580]

There's a lot of bad theology in Catholicism and Protestantism that Jung helped us illuminate. What Jung provided was a *medicine, a remedy, a therapy, for bad theology that was mostly dualistic.* He did not stride, like Eckhart did, to forget all temporal things and dissolve his soul completely into God the Absolute. That was not Jung's vocation. Jung's calling was to stay grounded in his soul, to dialogue with it. So, we have to keep such differences in mind when we examine their complementary paths into God, or the Self.

Following on the heels of an insight I received from my Jungian colleague Charles Asher into the Zwinglian background of Jung and his family of origin, I began to put forth some tentative hypotheses to clarify a few of the main differences between Eckhart's and Jung's paths:

1) Jung's personal equation that God is good and evil was influenced by religious traumas in his early childhood. His vision of the Hebrew-Christian God-image was religiously sourced in terrifying stories and sights of a boy accosted by a violent imagination of God's omnipotence.

2) Jung's God of violence was sometimes confused with evil when he debated theologians; however, evil is a moral quality that cannot be attributed to the Trinity or the fourth state of detachment above the opposites. Making the shadow, evil, matter, and the feminine face of Divinity into the missing "fourth" is certainly problematic theologically. This model of the Self emerged as a post-traumatic phenomenon, accompanying Jung's religious fantasy of a dualistic God that his psychology was called to *heal*.

3) Jung's fight with the shadow of God was Jung's fight with his traumatic God-complex, as I have seen in my own analytic practice with children who were raised Protestant or Catholic and subject to abuse in relation to erroneous Church teachings or teachers. Perhaps Jung's ambivalent God-image relates to the experiences of some Christians who are raised in abusive religious households, but it was not my personal experience and his quaternary view of the Self is not necessarily my God, or Eckhart's.

4) We Jungians need a new narrative of the Self that is a natural outgrowth of the psyche, and for this we might turn to Eckhart for a healthier and more unitary view of God.

5) All four of the dimensions of the Self included in a world of pure experience and our individual theories of truth in psychology emerge out of our experiences. This means that we cannot rely on Jung to give us an answer to the question

of what God is in our own experience. Eckhart postulates that God is *absolutely Absolute, Ultimate Reality*—absolute existence, intelligence, goodness, and peace, which suggests we would be wise to include the Transcendental Self in our empirical calculations.

6) A dualistic God-image composed of equally Good and equally Evil aspects cannot safely serve us as Jungian analysts in our practical clinical work with patients; on the other hand, dualistic theologies by Augustinian or Dominican or Protestant theologians cannot help us either. To solve the problem of dualism between the relative and the Absolute, we would be wise to consult Eckhart.

7) A spiritually democratic Self as relativistic and empirically factual, and as Ultimate Reality, is essentially *trans-dual*, free from the emotional aftereffects of trauma that accompany a split God-image catechism. Such a Self-notion patterned upon goodness, knowledge, and experience of the entire Universe heals traumatic beliefs.

In a Christian spiritual sense, carrying our own cross connotes a temporary dissolution of our limited ego consciousness, or soul, so that the Supreme Self may emerge victorious over the inferior person. Then peace may preponderate as a higher consciousness where the body and sex are not excluded from Divinity. The Counselor spoken about in the Hebrew Bible was the "Prince of Peace." This was and is the Counselor or peacemaker inside each of us (Isa. 9:6). God or the Divine Being as a peacemaker is *intimately responsive* to world events, so that the Self can evolve and change as consciousness evolves.[581] God is affected by everything that occurs and gives back to the world new possibilities of being. *We are being given the next best possibility at each moment when we are stepping or striding or running spiritually into peace.*

Jungian psychology has not made the most out of the best theological thinking, especially the thinking of Eckhart, who Jung understood psychologically, but not so well theologically. This book is an attempt to elucidate this point and correct for some of Jung's theological miscalculations.

Our choices contribute to what is possible in each and every *now.* When we choose peace over war, good over bad, love over violence, Eros over Thanatos, evil is being continuously worked with and changed by Divine Goodness through us. This image of the Self is more healing than Jung's Self-concept, to my mind. Eckhart's theology promotes a more supportive and positive responsiveness of the Self's primary principles of democratic freedom and liberty worldwide. When Jungian analysts hold a dualistic Self-image rather than a *trans-dual Self-notion,* we can be too accepting of destructiveness in analytic interactions and practice.

What brings healing and unity to the personality more than peace? To allow psychic processes to grow in peace, as Eckhart and Jung modeled for us, is no easy task in today's world. Nobody living today can exist consistently at the level of Eckhart's teachings. He represents an archetypal ideal of peacemaking to be striven toward, like Buddha.

The world is forever distracting us with endless noises and evils of modern civilization. The vocation of the Higher Self promotes a pathway to global peace. What we need is more detachment, not more attachments. Attachments are an endless source of misery. They may bring temporary joy in a relative sense, but the soul that has died to the world and become detached from worldly things, experiences peace beyond measure. Eckhart knew this to be true experientially and theoretically. He ran and strode continuously into peace, even on his deathbed in Avignon.

To internationalize peace in the spirit of democracy, we must establish stillness and silence within ourselves first. To experience the One, we need the Holy Spirit of Infinite Mercy. "No one can receive the Holy Spirit," said Eckhart, "unless he [she] lives above time in eternity."[582] Eckhart's soul lived, for the most part, high in the superconscious. Even while he was working, he was striding and dissolving in peace. When we are in our right vocation, we are living in peace. As Jung said: "That gives peace, when people feel they are living the symbolic life, that they are actors in the divine drama."[583]

In 1949, the Jesuit theologian Teilhard de Chardin said in "Faith in Peace" that "[Human]kind is not only capable of living in peace but by its very structure *cannot fail eventually to achieve peace*."[584] Why is peacemaking so important for the practice of analysis today? Because the right kind of symbolic life can infuse the right kind of *healing* energies into the soul of the world. Peace brings healing, and healing brings peace. There is a reciprocal relationship here. The peacemaker archetype promotes an approach to peaceful existence. God is always absorbing new possibilities in humanity, transforming what could be and, hence, guiding darkness and chaotic affects, or turbulent emotions, upward toward the apex of Light. This is basic Dominican, Jesuit, and Franciscan theology. In 1219, horrified by the atrocities committed against Muslims and Jews, St. Francis met with Sultan Malek al-Kamal in Egypt during the fifth Crusade and attempted to convert the Sultan to Christ in an attempt to put an end to the conflict of the Crusades. Francis was a peacemaker like Eckhart was.

I wrote my thesis on Eckhart under the spiritual direction of William Everson who embodied the archetype of the peacemaker when he wisely stepped in to mediate between my thesis chair and me. I'm eternally grateful to him for his wise counsel and help. During this time, he described the issue between the two bridge-builders of Dominican theology and Jungian psychology (White and Jung) as having been abruptly halted over "the doctrine of the non-essentiality of evil as seen in the abiding tradition of the Church since Augustine, which Jung opposed."[585]

In the aftermath of the atrocities of WWII, Jung thought evil was too substantial a reality in the world and psyche to be explained by the doctrine of the *privatio boni*. In other words, evil was essential to Jung, and thus an equal part of the God-image that must not be diminished by abstract theories. While in the midst of believing that he was challenging Jung's right to task God with unconsciousness over his own evil, Victor White was also spiritual counselor to Everson at St. Albert's in Oakland. At this time, Everson, still himself a monk, or lay brother, was going through a bout of personal depression, a profound period of spiritual aridity, a dark night of the soul.

White was perhaps the right man to understand Everson's vocational dilemma, since he too was suffering from the recent loss of his personal friendship with Jung whom he had dearly loved. Also, he was in agony over the recent loss of his theological career as professor of dogmatics at Blackfriars. The Vatican had been breathing down White's neck for championing Jung's writings, and White was in a vocational crisis over the sacrifice of his career as a respected teacher. He was also in suspended ambiguity about his possible future as a Jungian "analyst." White's spiritual calling as a counselor and self-appointed "analyst" was in serious jeopardy by the time he arrived in California. Jung had personally asked him to be on the list of founding members of the C. G. Jung Institute of Analytical Psychology in Zürich. His whole creative theological and psychological future was suddenly thrown into uncertainty. White's name had been coveted by Jung to provide *moral* authority to his movement. But after White attacked Jung publicly in print, he was considered a threat to Jung's psychological project.

Everson was a vocational counselor, a spiritual guide, and Jungian teacher at heart.[586] He distinguished between vocation and career in the following way: *vocation is where your motivation is; career is the impact of your vocation on the world.* Vocation is where your deepest source of motivation is, and it comes from the Supreme Self, with a capital *S*.

When Everson spoke about the vocational archetype and its impact on individuals and the world, he was speaking about that innate expansive potential in each human being to manifest their goodness over the exigencies of their negative potential. Career has to do with one's relationship to collectivity, group consciousness, culture, or the nation in which one lives; it is the impact of one's work on the outside. It is not an occupation or day job. An occupation is what one does to earn a living. A career may not coincide exactly with vocation; it may simply be how one makes money and helps a person forge a public identity or persona, which can undergo changes at different life stages. Vocation, on the other hand, relates to the notion of psychological and spiritual transformation, being and becoming. This is what vocational dreams can do for us: they may transform consciousness by *illuminating* us! They do awaken us. They motivate us to arise! *They awaken us to our destiny and creative freedom.*

Sometimes, if our soul is spiritualized and dies momentarily to the world to undergo total transformation, she can inspire us to utter the Word of God, whether we are in a secular or sacred profession, whether religious, agnostic, atheist, aesthetic, or scientific. Not only theologians can speak God's Word; God exists in each person. Our vocation is what is universally and eternally true in us. It is what the Higher Self would like us to do freely with our freedom *sub specie boni.*

Everson's work in *Birth of a Poet* became his laboratory for an investigation into the nature of vocational archetypes. His research led him to make some leading discoveries, particularly in the area of spiritual calling. Looking back at his life, I would venture to say that he was one of the most electrifying poets America has produced. By recourse to the dream life and by listening, in silence, to the sequence of his meditations on the Santa Cruz campus overlooking the Monterey Bay, beneath towering redwood trees and the open sky, students were open to direct experiences of Absolute Intelligence and goodness at work all around us, within and without, in the Cosmos and psyche. What gave Everson power to transmit his notion of vocation as a direct way to *experience* God was the aliveness of the West Coast as a spiritually vibrant literary region and his eighteen years as a Catholic poet in the Dominican tradition.

As we've seen, in Eckhart's theology God does not cause evil; God permits evil, but God does not see evil when it is happening on earth because evil is Nothingness in the light of God-consciousness. "God is in the soul with His nature, with His being, and with His Godhead, and yet He is not the soul."[587] "His being and His Godhead depend upon His working in the soul. God be praised, God be praised!"[588] God's work and God's praise in His Godhead cannot be mirrored in the soul by the blood of war. God's being and the Godhead are *dependent* on God's working in our souls as peace, not war, in us.

CHAPTER 30

MEISTER ECKHART: DISPENSER OF SACRED MEDICINE

Eckhart, like Christ, was a healer, a shaman. Shamans, or medicine men and women, have been given curative powers to overcome contaminations from affective toxins and their harmful projectiles that are shot at them by devilish or spiteful people. This was true in Eckhart's life. He immunized himself against violence and evil by accepting the inner *violence of the two crosses,* and then he arose out of his self-sacrifice as a true healer of his Dominican tribe.

Experiences of Self may come from reading Eckhart, by dreaming or meditating with him. In my experience he has led me to a metanoia of consciousness, where changes in personality may become permanent. I may have forgotten my calling at times, but research into my calling dreams reawakens me in an instant. Eckhart taught me to open my *inner eye of intuitive insight,* to recollect the Self from external projections, and awaken "little sparks" in the soul that shine like precious jewels. To comprehend what he meant by *total transformation,* I recommend you discard everything you may have previously learned about God from dusty theology books. *Then you must experience the Word of Wisdom (Sophia) as a living empirical-metaphysical reality within you.*

The vocation of the Self in Eckhart's and Jung's writings aims at world peace: "God is a Word, an unspoken Word."[589] Eckhart preached, for "All creatures wish to speak God in all of their works; they all speak as well as they can, but they cannot speak Him. Willy-nilly, whether they like it or not, they all want to speak God and yet He remains unspoken."[590]

The unspoken Word is the *apophatic* dimension of Divinity, in contrast to the *cataphatic*. *Apophatic* is the dimension of the Divine that can never be named because it is essentially endless, like an infinite Abyss or bottomless Ground; whereas *cataphatic* is the aspect of God or the Mother Goddess that can be named, such as Elohim, Sophia, Immanuel, and the Virgin Mary. Eckhart served in the archetypal role of a shaman to his Catholic tribe by opening our minds to the bottomless abyss. One cannot understand Eckhart without an inner *experience of the Ground that is Groundless*. One has to awaken Eckhart's spiritual presence within one's own psyche to experience what he meant by the birth of the Word in the highest temple of the soul, by equality, and by *your way to God, as the best way of the present and the future*. I believe we must dream with Eckhart to re-awaken his archetype, his exemplar, if we are to truly know what he was talking about, such as when he said to his disciples, for instance, that he would be delighted if they "could find God and enjoy Him in *any* way and in *all* things."[591] This was his final teaching before he left Cologne to answer charges of heresy leveled against him by a corrupt curia in Avignon. For me, Eckhart has become a *transformative Self-figure*[592] in the collective soul of humanity; he is no longer merely a historical personage who walked the earth. His steps are still around. We need only to stride backward in time with him into the Light through the grace vouchsafed to us by our vocations, to know the truth in God and speak it in our own ways. It is not enough to experience inner images in passivity alone; *one must also act upon them vocationally*.

Jung taught us that the inner voice could be interpreted and worked with through analytical techniques. Eckhart wrote of the Word in a theological sense, much in the same way that Jung wrote of the inner voice in a psychological one. There are, as we've seen, important differences between them. To be sure, it is on the topic of vocation that Eckhart and Jung arrived at a point of general understanding and mutual agreement in soul and spirit. *The Word can be made flesh through the channel of your vocation.* Vocational actions are born out of the Universal Ground from which any human soul may become open to an equality with everything in the present fertile moment in space-time where synchronicities are happening. God's image and non-image are everywhere in the Universe.

Eckhart taught his listeners to *stay true to their vocation, their ways to God, and not be thrown off by Church officials pretending to be God's "authorities."* He provided a paradigm for individuation that every nation could corroborate as true because he was speaking the transnational language of the vocation of the Self, the vernacular of modern analytic psychology, inaugurated by James and Jung on two sides of the Atlantic. Eckhart's nonconformist way of preaching the Word with justice and mercy is desperately needed today in the field of Christian theology—and also in society globally and generally during a time when economic and political mentality and lies threaten the whole world with ruin. There are so many mass movements with toxic opinions attempting to drown out the voice of democratic citizens. We would be wise to give Eckhart's theology a full hearing, so as not to perpetuate the same old mistakes of the Church by splitting the opposites and promoting so-called just wars.

In this respect, Eckhart and Jung were on the same page: they each taught us in their separate and unique ways to dialogue with the child archetype within, with the four levels of the anima or soul, with the four functions of consciousness, with the Serpent and Eve, Mary and Martha, God and Sophia, and to chase out the merchants from the temple of Wisdom, by undergoing a symbolic death and a second resurrection. They taught us the *ways of the Cross,* two of them, and how we might integrate the darkness of God to avoid our own species' annihilation.

Eckhart's language was the universal language of the human heart. This unitary language was intended to unite the whole human race. It could lead us all potentially through *equality between everyone* to an ideal of world peace. If the world is suffering, God is suffering, Eckhart asserted. Eckhart was, then and now, a dispenser of sacred medicine because he is still with us in the Now. He is operating today in the sacred lineage of shamans as an archetype within, which seeks to dissolve the barrier between the sacred and the profane through the primacy of the Word. Eckhart often talked of being in the "right state" of mind to maintain our close connections to the earth; taking God *equally* in all things and with an "equal mind" can lead us to experience that those "to whom God is thus present in all things ... [know] true peace."[593]

How do we bring the mind into peace by praying to God to free us of God? By becoming Nothing. Eckhart's instructions about how to meditate were stated succinctly: "he should not let himself be caught up by his *internal* imagery, whether it be in the form of pictures or lofty thoughts, or inward impressions or whatever is present to his mind."[594] Eckhart's words parallel Buddhism here, because like Zen, the mental states he entered into were beyond the panoply of God-images: "For our whole being depends on nothing but a becoming-nothing."[595]

Some old-fashioned Westerners seem to have an inborn fear of Nothingness. Yet all beings, in Eckhart's view, smack of Nothingness. The important thing is the birth of God out of Nothing through your calling. Eckhart said further: "If anything is in God, it has peace; as much as in God, so much at peace."[596] "In short," Eckhart observed, "it means that one should be at peace and well established," and therefore he prayed that we may all be "established in this peace."[597]

The way to peace does not begin with creation, but rather with the "destruction of the self."[598] This may sound excessive, which it is. Without excess, however, there is no birth, no passion. Total destruction is followed by total creation, without which the Preacher could not have spoken God's Word. By destruction, Eckhart meant pure detachment, *abegeschiedenheit*: "pure detachment rests on the highest, and he is at the highest, in whom God can work all His will."[599] "That is why detachment is best," Eckhart concluded, "for it purifies the soul, purges the conscience, kindles the heart, awakens the spirit, quickens the desire, and makes us know God, and, cutting off creatures, unites us with God."[600]

He meant that we would be wise to unite with an "essence that embraces all essence"[601]—or an *equality with everything that is*. This is equivalent to what Buddhists call not-knowing. In 1308, after he became Meister Eckhart, he wrote *The Book of Divine Comfort* for Agnes, Queen of Hungary. To be sure, Agnes was suffering terribly from anguish, grief, melancholy, horror, and outrage over the unimaginably traumatic murder of her father. In this book, Eckhart covered all kinds of situations in which persons might find themselves suffering. He was both practical and specific about how we might find peace during such times of travail and emotional turmoil. Take, for example, a person you may know, one who has been recently fired from a job, or has lost a large sum of money or personal possessions, or suffered the death of a loved one. Eckhart had an answer for these blows of fate. He said, "Suppose a man has had honor and comfort for many years, and now loses this by God's decree. That man should reflect wisely and thank God."[602]

This may be a difficult pill to swallow. Why should we thank God for misfortune? Here, Eckhart was right psychologically: it is better to love one's fate than to rebel against it. Such *divine consolation* (consolation through Grace, *Gnade*) can relieve a person of tremendous hurt to the heart, career, or pocketbook! God forbid it should happen to any of us. But it sadly does. When it happens, we may be motivated to look inward, instead of outward, for answers to problems of fate. We may be led to reflect more wisely on questions concerning our callings in life.

Eckhart was essentially saying that to struggle against fate is to struggle against God. For, if God is fate, what does one have to worry about? God is suffering too, not only with the afflicted person, but also

God *Is* suffering in you. You are the cause of God's existence. Why, therefore, should you be sad, anxious, or angry about loss of honor or persons or creature comforts? I know this sounds radical and it is! But "God wants suffering,"[603] Eckhart preached. It is better to know that God is carrying the cross of suffering through His mercy in you and that you too have your own heavy cross to bear. Two of them, in fact. "I also declare of a surety," he asserted further, "that God is so fond of suffering with us and for us if *we* suffer purely for God's sake, that he suffers without suffering."[604] How can God suffer without suffering? This is a parabolical statement. Eckhart declared further: "To suffer is such a joy to Him that suffering for Him is no suffering."[605]

Why does God *permit* evil at times in our lives without intervening in our tragic fates? In order to metabolize this truth emotionally, we must be in the right state, reduced to Nothing, to find an *antidote*. "And so," Eckhart continued, "if we are in a right state, our suffering would be no suffering but a joy and a comfort."[606] Divine comfort, in other words, is always found through a spiritual retreat into our own Ground of empirical experience, into the very source of our existence, Nothing. Blaming God or our enemies for our outer misfortunes is not the answer. The answer is to develop better armor: the protective light or shield of God-consciousness.

We psychotherapists look for ways to bring consolation to our patients to help relieve them from suffering every day. That is our primary work. Truly, there are conditions that are horrific in our patients' lives (and in our own lives as well!) where someone is mistreated by someone they trusted, someone is betrayed or emotionally or psychologically or mentally injured, like Eckhart was by a violent institution. Whether by family, group, Church organization, or a friend, out of some kind of unconsciousness, injustice, envy, or hatred, shit happens. Evil is a reality, and it is here to stay. Yet, as Eckhart prescribed, "Whatever a good man suffers for God's sake, he suffers in God, and God is with him in his suffering."[607] He strode even further into Wisdom: "If my suffering is in God and God suffers with me, how then can my suffering be painful when suffering loses its pain, and my pain is in God and my pain *is* God."[608]

Eckhart's sense of equality goes far. Not only is God's Ground your Ground, but your suffering is God's suffering and your pain *is* God's pain. "Suffer therefore, in this fashion for God's sake, since it brings such great profit and blessing." And he continued:

> Our Lord says, "Blessed are they that suffer for righteousness' sake" (Mt 5:10) ... Now take note, all who have good sense! The swiftest steed to bear you to His perfection is suffering, for none will enjoy greater eternal bliss than those who stand with Christ in the greatest bitterness. Nothing is more gall-bitter than suffering, nothing more honey-sweet than having suffered.[609]

The question for us today is not whether the tales Eckhart preached were scientifically true, but how, upon reading Eckhart in a time of turmoil in our world, can his teachings become *sacred medicine* for people who are searching for answers to social problems, for the earth's suffering from climate change? How can we tap into the power of the Word to make social changes happen?

As well as being a Jungian analyst, I am also a Western writer, and the archetype of the healer calls me to teach and write. It all began with my thesis on Eckhart at UCSC in the redwood forests of the West Coast. That is when I began to learn what it means to live in the Christian mythos in good relationship to trees, like Eckhart did in the Thuringian forests as a boy. Before that I was searching for my destiny. Finding Eckhart was like hearing the Word of God for the first time, in all of its immense theological power and splendor. He captivated me, drew me in, pulled me out of the world of my ego into the power and grace of my vocation.

Today I often read Eckhart for personal meaning when I need *spiritual comfort*. That was his calling as a Counselor (Matthew 3:11) and preacher. Just as I turn to Jung for psychological comfort, I've turned to Eckhart for theological instructions on how to find healing from psychic infections, through contemplation, journaling, and prayer. He has become an inner guide in my soul and has remained my greatest spiritual teacher. Most of my writings on Eckhart remained unpublished in my youth, as it was mostly intellectual, not experiential enough, by which I mean, I was not in touch with own personal *feelings about what I read in his German sermons*. My soul had not become the world at UCSC. It was still too small. I was an undergraduate, as Eckhart was when he was studying under Albert in Cologne. Only Everson was my Albert.

We are at a major turning point in our conceptions of the world's religions, and the question is what the new myth might be for postmodern people still in the waiting room. What can a thirteenth/ fourteenth-century theologian have to teach us today about the Universe and our small place within it? Has not the history of a science of religions proven that the archaic beliefs of our ancestors have long since been surpassed by philosophy, theology, and now, by analytical psychology? Not so fast.

I agree with Jung on many matters pertaining to the importance of dreams and the imagination, in helping to give shape to a science and art of contemporary Jungian analysis, and mythmaking or "mythologizing," and in Jung's "Relativity" essay, Eckhart is quoted as having said specifically about those who possess God, Christ, or the Holy Spirit within, and those who don't:

> Whereas he who has not God as such an inner possession, but with every means must fetch him from without, in this thing or in that, where he is there sought for in vain, in all manner of works, people, or places; verily such a man has him not, and easily

something comes to trouble him. And it is not only evil
company that troubles him, but also the good, not only
the street but also the church ... For the hinderance lies
within himself, because in him God has not yet become
the world.[610]

About these passages Jung wrote interestingly: "'Fetching God
from without' is the equivalent of the primitive view that *tondi* can be
got from outside."[611] *Tondi* was defined by Jung as "the magic force
around which everything turns."[612]

Detachment is the highest virtue in Advaita Vedanta (non-
attachment in the Bhagavad Gita) and in Buddhism (in the Pali
Cannon). Why is detachment so important in Eckhart's theology?
Whatever your particular God-image may be, Eckhart said, "In your
acts you should have an equal mind and equal love for your God, and
equal seriousness."[613] And "The deeper the well, the higher it is; height
and depth are one ... For our whole being depends on nothing but a
becoming-nothing."[614]

Eckhart's focus on becoming Nothing really interests me. What
did he mean by this? To be in *right conscience* means giving birth
not only to a symbolic life, which can be productive of good or evil,
but also a "vision of peace." Peace cannot exist without Nothingness.
When we cling to our God-images we are not at peace. For by clinging
to the image, we lose God. What was Eckhart's solution? "So, leave
all images," Eckhart preached, "and unite with the formless essence,"
for "no man [woman] is happier than he [she] who has the greatest
detachment."[615] Detachment, therefore, was the key.

More detachment would go a long way toward helping to heal the
earth and the world's people today. Pure detachment is the way to
true peace and happiness: "I find, as well as my reason can testify or
perceive, that only pure detachment surpasses all things."[616] Eckhart
taught that in a *bare mind* we can experience the "essence that embraces

all essence."[617] He said further about his technique of prayer in the *Talks of Instruction*:

> We should pray so intently, as if we would have all members and all powers turned to it—eyes, ears, mouth, heart, and all the senses; and we should never stop until we find ourselves about to be united with Him whom we have in mind and are praying to: that is—God.[618]

Later, he said that the only prayer worth praying for is *becoming rid of all images of God*:

> Therefore I pray God to make me free of God, for my essential being is above God, taking God as the origin of all creatures... But in my breaking-through, where I stand free of my own will, of God's will, of all his works, and of God himself, *then* I am above all creatures and am neither God nor creature, but I am that which I was and shall remain evermore. There I shall receive an imprint that will raise me above the angels. By this imprint I shall gain such wealth that I shall not be content with God inasmuch as He is God, or with all his divine works: for this breaking-through guarantees to me that I and God are one.[619]

CHAPTER 31

ECKHART AS A SHAMAN FOR OUR TIMES

Eckhart understood long ago that there are *healing powers* in nature and the soul that can be cultivated through deep inward concentration. Like certain medicines, words contain curative remedies for human suffering, as we know from the art of psychotherapy and confession. Theology and analysis are both pathways to healing. In this chapter I will unpack some of Eckhart's metaphors that provide evidence that he was a dispenser of sacred medicine.

There is a passage in one of Eckhart's sermons that caught my eye because of its remarkable wisdom and curious use of symbolism. In it he seems to make a connection between the knowledge of instinct, inborn in animals, the power of stones, and the power in words to convey a portrait of an analogous power that we can get in touch with through attending to the Word within and without, for the Dominican's faith was that all things contain Wisdom.

> Herbs have great power. I heard how a snake and a weasel were fighting. Then the weasel ran away and fetched an herb and wrapped something round it and threw the herb at the snake, and it burst asunder and fell dead. What gave the weasel this wisdom to know

the power of the herb? Great wisdom resides in this. Words too have great power: we could work wonders with words. All words have their power from the first Word. Stones too have great power through the likeness wrought in them by stars and the might of heaven.[620]

I have no idea where he heard this story. Obviously, it is factually false because weasels have never behaved in this way. Although weasels do in fact hunt and eat snakes, there is no evidence in the natural sciences that a weasel ever wrapped up an herb and blew up a snake to kill it. Eckhart was giving us a theological parable! What did he mean by it? Herbs do have medicinal powers. For me, the main take away from the story is that we could work wonders with words if only we could find ways to tap into *the power of the first Word*, the archetype of Wisdom within and without. Snakes are Words of God and so too are weasels. But the power in a weasel to explode a snake with an herb certainly rings true, if we understand it metaphorically: the place of the primal eruption exists in all creatures and all human cultures. I believe Eckhart tapped into the wisdom of the shamanic archetype in the World Soul.

Jung talked about Eckhart's idea of *becoming the world*.[621] This notion was later taken forward in Jung's essay on "The Psychology of the Child Archetype," where he wrote: "Hence, 'at bottom' the psyche is simply the 'world.'"[622] Eckhart's conceptions of God and the Godhead were intrapsychic and extrapsychic, in a word *transpsychic*—known and unknown, nothing and everything, in a divine play of being and nonbeing in communion with all creatures. Over the years I've come to see Eckhart as a great *medicine man* with a remedy for our common human woes and afflictions.

Fate ails everyone, and overcoming blows of fate is no easy matter. Eckhart opened doorways to my Self-path inside and outside of the Church. Eckhart was a door, just like Christ was and shamans are: "Christ says, 'I am a door' (John 10:9) ... I said one day that the door was the Holy Ghost: there He is poured out in goodness into all creatures."[623] The door of the Holy Ghost was poured out in the weasel and the snake and in all creatures. This shows us how pantheistic Eckhart's theology really was. The Paraclete can become a doorway to the Self in humans. It opens up through our various fields of vocation.

As I've previously mentioned, Eckhart gave special significance to the symbol of the gateway. He began by quoting Jeremiah 7:2. "Stand in the gate of God's house and preach the word, declare the word!" Transformation, according to Eckhart, is a state of being *trans-imaged* (*überbildet*) in the Absolute Intellect.[624] How to get *überbildet* is the aim of this book: how to rise above all God-images. Eckhart showed us how to make it possible: "You should be firm and steadfast; that is, you should be the same in weal and woe, in fortune and misfortune, having the noble nature of precious stones."[625] To see the divine sparks shining like glistening jewels within, like shamans do while journeying, dreaming, and visioning, contemplation or quiet prayer is needed.

Equality happens when there is less attachment. I was originally drawn to Eckhart in the late seventies by his idea of spiritual freedom to pursue a path to liberty with equal rights for all. Reading Eckhart is like taking *a breath of fresh air.* My nervous system begins to calm down and breathing comes much more easily. He calms my soul. Everything begins to slow down to Zero. Eckhart's ability to free us from suffering with a spiritual *medicament* of a rarified wisdom for what's good in nature has been a solace.

Eckhart teaches readers to stay close to the Ground (*Grund*). This closeness to the Ground can keep us humble and dependent on God, just as God depends on us for our very survival: "I said the day before yesterday that heaven can only work in the ground of the earth ... The more a man is sunk in the ground of true humility, the more he is sunk in the ground of divine being."[626]

Humility was Eckhart's medicine for the infections of society. The seven virtues—1) humility, 2) charity, 3) chastity, 4) gratitude, 5) temperance, 6) patience, and 7) diligence—are an *alexipharmic*, or antidote, for the seven sins, and they are all interrelated: "Though a person may incline to the practice of one virtue rather than the others, yet they are all interconnected."[627]

Eckhart is beginning to reach a wide international audience through scholars such as Bernard McGinn. Even more widely known are books by Eckhart Tolle, a popular "guru" whose thoughts bring together the medieval preacher's teachings with a lot of nomenclature that is not truly Eckhart's. He even took his first name from Eckhart. Such authors, to name only two, are helping spread Eckhart's teachings globally to those who are hungry for the *medicine* of Wisdom, which ultimately would bring peace and harmony in alignment with "Nature's God" if we could be more *virtuous* and less attached to material possessions, oil, and cars. By *God's medicine,* I mean the spiritual medicine of the earth and sky, a grounded life in Nature, where all our virtues are *interconnected.*

One notion that has been mostly overlooked in Eckhart scholarship is that Eckhart was part of a long lineage of healers known in all cultures as holy people, healers, medicine men/women, or shamans. This is something I discussed with Everson in our coauthored book *The Shaman's Call.*[628] Now I'll develop that idea a bit further.

In *Rede der Unterscheidunge* (1295–1298), when Eckhart was between the ages of thirty-five and thirty-eight, he made his *shamanic vocation* known at inception as a preacher and counselor of the Word. This was a trans-dual vocation he served with humility and devotion for the rest of his life. He did this in an equalizing way, maintaining a balanced mind between his outer life and inner life, career and calling, preaching and counseling. This shamanic calling remained his central Self-path until his death. It was a way that was and is open to all people: a spiritual path to healing via direct unmediated transport to Wisdom in the eternal Now. Eckhart was a Word-shaman, a speaker of Truth from the primal eruption.

Eckhart wrote *Talks of Instruction* when he was prior of his Dominican Order in Erfurt. It is, indeed, *medicine* for the soul. In it he reveals himself as a dispenser of the prayer of "penance in which one improves greatly in the highest degree ... This penance is truly a state of mind lifted into God away from all things."[629] This practice remained central from the beginning to the end of his career as a form of praying for Nothing.

Penance is a practice of *inward detachment* or *letting go* (*abegescheidenheit, gelâzenheit*) in a high state of contemplation in Sophia, an inward meditation that is *überbildet* (*trans-imaged*). It consists of a process of emptying the mind completely of all imagery and arriving at a state of exquisite peace. Eckhart called it an inner-oriented "right state" of mind.[630] God-consciousness (awareness, being, and bliss) is possible for anyone in the present, he said, for "God is a God of the present" (*"Gott ist ein Gott der Gegenwart"*).[631]

Eckhart was in quest of a unitary theology of the Christian faith, coupled with a stable grounding in natural sciences, astronomy, and practical life. He was in search of a new theory of the inner and outer Universe, which could answer Aquinas's opening query in the *Summa Theologica* about whether sacred theology could be properly considered a science or not. In his Latin *Commentaries on Genesis,* Eckhart quoted Maimonides and echoed that the entire Old Testament is either "natural science" or "spiritual wisdom."[632] He believed the Old and New Testaments were equally *trans-dual.* His sermons were not so much about salvation as about thanksgiving and praise. Eckhart was mostly interested in the notion of creation of an individual form from a universal pattern or prototype (God's Word) out of the unformed Godhead, or Ground (*Grund*).

Given his modest beginnings, it's a miracle Eckhart achieved what he did. If my hypothesis is correct, one of the central reasons for his profound spiritual transformation into a shaman for our times was that he benefitted greatly from a series of transformative relationships, as did Jung and as have I. One relationship in particular cannot be overlooked in the search for an answer to Eckhart's miraculous change of character, heart, and consciousness—his personal friendship with his mentor in the order, Dietrich of Freiberg (1250–1319). His role as a transformer was crucial.

Eckhart's study and friendship with Dietrich is one of the lesser-known keynotes in most Eckhart biographies. Dietrich, however, was a major rather than a minor figure in his spiritual metamorphosis. In *Dangerous Mystic: Meister Eckhart's Path to the God Within,* Joel F. Harrington filled in some of the missing historical facts concerning the relationship between these two luminaries. Discovering the connections requires an eye and an ear for *psychobiography,* a Jungian analyst's comprehension of the subtle, internal complexities of the Self-structures and shamanistic structures that helped to shape Eckhart's character and led to his transmutation as a *dispenser of sacred medicine.*

Dietrich had political clout to promote Eckhart's career as a scholar and academic. He was interested in helping him follow his *Self-path* as a Dominican, not somebody else's. Having a mentor in the order who had influence like Dietrich enabled Eckhart to acquire intellectual knowledge and administrative skills and modeling in relationship to an intellectual man of theological courage. Dietrich taught the novice to awaken the divine spark (German *vünkelîn*; Latin *synderesis*) in the soul within him, while at the same time remaining true to his busy clerical duties.

To my mind, it was Eckhart's vocation to theology and spiritual healing that transformed him, and these two callings were present also in his mentor. Dietrich transmitted to Eckhart some healthy skepticism toward theological postulates contained in some of Augustine's masterworks and demonstrated for the younger pupil a critical and fearless approach toward learning. Such a friend, once internalized as a living inner Self-presence, enabled Eckhart to stride forward with an open mind into new post-Christian territory that was forbidden by the Church as a collective organization. Albert and Aquinas had formidable minds, with soaring intellects, no doubt, but they were not as attuned as Eckhart was to the reality of the psyche and its feminine Ground of being and nonbeing.

Dietrich was a theologian who stood on the shoulders of saints, yet he helped Eckhart learn how to transcend *all* his previous masters, including Augustine and Aquinas. Dietrich's quest for a unifying theory of the material and spiritual worlds became the starting point for Eckhart's postulate of the Ground. In Dietrich's theology, the emanations of light encompassing all material and spiritual realities opened gates of understanding in Eckhart's mind. Dietrich devoted much attention to the study of optics, including a famous treatise on rainbows.[633] His focus on light helped elevate Eckhart's soul, or anima, into supernatural spheres of pure *seeing*. Eckhart took his thoughts about the origins of light forward toward a more subjective experience of God as a Lightning Bolt (*Blitz*) within and without. Eckhart placed experience of undifferentiated unity with God at the highest pinnacle of human understanding.

Eckhart opened the doorway to the age of the Paraclete through the channel of his *shamanic vocation*. He dispensed his teachings as a blessing to his entire Dominican Order—a universal medicine of *equality with God*. By medicine, I mean the medicament of being born out of Nothingness in his own original Dispensation. Nothingness leads to an experience of equality with Nature through the prayer of quiet, or emptiness. Then the joyous birth of the inner child arises through our vocations in the world. This outflowing from God into the world makes all creatures equal, not only humans. Nothing opens us to receive all that God is better than Nature does. Nature is the ultimate Church. Nature can heal us today, if we can accept our humility before God as the Universal Reality. Such a remedy was transmitted to many of Eckhart's devoted followers, such as Henry Suso and John Tauler. Eckhart's remarkable egalitarianism, his democratic equality with women, was the most controversial among his teachings.

After he left Dietrich behind, Eckhart resided at St. Jacques Priory between the ages of forty-two and forty-five. This was a major turning point in his life, a life-stage when the creation of an individual *nucleus* out of a Universal principle or prototype of the Divine, a heavenly type, was most ready to incarnate itself as a factor of his individuation. Eckhart's frequent expressions of *awe* at the beauty of the Universal Deity in everything reveals his amazement at the miracle of *equality inherent in the entire order of things.*

In Sermon 24, for instance, Eckhart made it clear that the shell must be broken open for the goodness of the kernel to burst forth.[634] This metaphor of breaking the kernel suggests rupturing, opening, or cracking the cosmic shell of our limited, human ego consciousness to bring out the Self's full virtues, ethics of justice and love and peace, as individuating factors. Moreover, Eckhart's views on suffering were uniquely monotheistic and shamanistic, a synthesis of the three monotheisms *plus* Greek philosophy and science and a pantheistic/panentheistic sweep enabling us to see the beauty in all things.

The Christian who carries their cross in life, in Eckhart's view, does not only transcend suffering, but they also bear suffering gladly, and willingly, by allowing God to carry their pain internally. By picking up and carrying their own cross, they *accept the agony of crucifixion by welcoming it!* This focus on dismemberment of the ego is very shamanistic. "For truly, if anyone had denied himself and wholly forsaken himself, nothing could be for him a cross or sorrow or suffering; it would all be a delight to him, a happiness, a joy to his heart."[635]

Humans in quiet prayer, penitence, and peace, compel God to come forth through their acceptance of pain, and this reception becomes the *cure.* Moreover, if one has repose in the soul's apex, Eckhart said, God must be born in that person. He insisted that we should not only be like grace and justice, but also *be grace and Wisdom's mother.*

Eckhart was strongly influenced by Maimonides and Avicenna. According to Maimonides, the Holy Bible is a book of spiritual wisdom (*Sapientia*) whose inner meanings are hidden beneath the shell.[636] So not everything Eckhart said was novel. Eckhart's methods of exposition were not only Jewish and Christian, but also post-Islamic.

Christ and the Self were to Eckhart one in a democratizing

shamanistic sense, no matter what name we may wish to assign to God, whether the four-letter name *YHWH* (the *Tetragrammaton*), *Adonai,* or *Shaddai.*[637] Whatever the names of God, *experience* was always paramount, and even the holy name *Christ* was insufficient. "All distinction is repugnant to the infinite. But God is infinite."[638]

What Eckhart aimed for, as an archer and shaman, was an extension of the Two Testaments in a *Word-medicine* that could be imbibed by anyone, regardless of creed. He promoted a universal metaphysics of Christian morality and a science of ethics, based on fourteens pairs of conceptual opposites, the seven virtues and seven sins, comprising the essential wholeness of human beings.[639] God in Eckhart's understanding was pure *isness* (*istigkeit*), *oneness, existence*: the highest Love and Light.

Eckhart was reassigned at age of forty-five to Strasbourg, where he began to preach to Dominican nuns and Beguines, women who were seeking a more sensually embodied experience of God than what they had read about in dry Christian theology books. They sought words that rang truer to their own spiritual experiences, rather than cold type on a page. In Eckhart the Paraclete was a living reality, and they *felt* it by God when listening to him.

Part of the price he paid for being at the center of support for the Beguine movement was the violent onslaught of patriarchal suppression by the Church. The sudden shift in focus from Parisian scholasticism in Latin, to preaching in vernacular in Strasbourg and then Cologne, changed Eckhart's outlooks. He became increasingly spiritually democratic, and his philosophically trained Neoplatonic thinking began to become more nuanced toward *equality* between himself and his growing female audiences. His focus on the feminine principle of the Godhead, Wisdom, becoming mothers of God, and the divine birth within, all became pivotal to his surprising success throughout much of Europe.

Eckhart was called to *cura monialium*: pastoral care of nuns.[640] Although he had counseled nuns in Erfurt, prior to his stay in

Strasbourg, it was only at this turning point or *transitus,* a transit from scholastic to priest, then to *shaman-preacher,* that the archetype of the healer of Christian souls was suddenly *awakened* in him in a profoundly egalitarian way. This abrupt switch from being a privileged university professor with overreaching plans, to a humble pastoral *physician of his priory* (while standing at the head of administrative affairs), activated the archetype of the wounded-healer in such a way that he became a great *spiritual Counselor of his whole Dominican tribe and potentially all Churches in Christendom.*

I see the archetype of the shaman especially at play in the *Book of Divine Comfort,* written around 1308, a volume composed at the same time the archetype of pastoral counselor of women and men was awakened in him more fully. In this excellent treatise, Eckhart applies his theological principles as a scholastic to his central calling as a *physician of souls.* The *way* of the Counselor and preacher of the Word of God was for him a more direct way to the Self within, his own unique Self-path.

Such a path of experiencing God within was and is open to all people through the doorway of their heart. It's not limited to an enlightened few, primarily male Catholic theologians in Church organizations; divinization is open to anyone in whom the vocation of the Paraclete, or Self, may be revealed and be made manifest by means of the central archetype of wholeness: the vocation of the Self in humans. This is what makes all humans *equal.*

In Strasbourg, Eckhart found his voice as a spiritual Counselor, shaman, or comforter. His aim there was to lead friars, religious women, and laypeople alike, to experience grace, fullness, and joy in life. In one sermon, he even assured his audiences that before they left the Church that day, they could find divine joy within themselves, such as he had himself through the simple prayer of humility and a quiet mind.[641]

Eckhart was a shamanic Seer, a seeker of visions, as Jung also was. At this juncture in his spiritual life, Eckhart became a *Word-shaman,* a master theologian who administered the curative power of the Spirit that his congregation was thirsting for. By letting go of his university career as a top-notch teacher, he traced language back to the shamanic archetype and from there received his medicine-powers, as a preacher and healer through God's Word. He told audiences wherever he went that by a simple prayer, the prayer of quiet, they could experience happiness that has the capacity to heal human ailments, and that his congregation could receive this blessing of grace before leaving the Church *that very day*. He offered a sorely needed transmuting medicine[642] long before the advent of analysis.

Eckhart lived equally in the upper, lower, and middle worlds. Eckhart mentioned the word *Ground* more than 140 times in his sermons. This metaphor cannot be found anywhere else as often as they are in Eckhart's writings. The *Grund* and metaphors like the birthing of God are uniquely Eckhart's.[643]

Eckhart declared, in all humility, that if he did not submit to his calling to preach the Word of God and to counsel those who were ill or suffering, "God would not be."[644] His Word was a spiritual medicine. Preaching, his first vocation, was what he called "being-at-home."[645] Being-at-home is not really a "way" or a means, Eckhart added, but a *place* within and without where one is united in "joyous eternity!"[646] Moreover, as a shaman who was always close to the Ground, he taught and preached that the seven virtues are principles of an ethical science.[647] *The highest virtue above all for him was the science of detachment.* "You need not seek Him here or there, He is no further than the door of your heart."[648]

The *sacred medicine* Eckhart had to dispense was the secret serum of your vocation—your calling to give voice or form to the divine in you. In the final paragraph of Part III of *The Book of Divine Comfort*, Eckhart said, "'Those who are well,' says our Lord, 'have no need of medicine' (Luke 5:31). The physician is there to heal the sick."[649] Thus, the function of healing was as evident in theology as it is today in depth-psychology: clergy and psychotherapists, pastoral counseling and depth analysis, are all rooted in the Ground of the shamanic archetype.

We are in dire need of Eckhart's medicine today. I see Eckhart during his time in Strasbourg and Cologne as returning to the humble role that he had originally assumed during his inception at Erfurt in the Order of Preachers. Assuming the mantle of a *preacher-shaman*, a physician of souls, he offers us the superessential bread and wine of the Holy Spirit that we need as daily food in the Age of Aquarius.

In sum, Eckhart was a physician of Christian and non-Christian souls. He provided a cure for an illness in the Catholic Church, which is still ailing terribly. As an administrator of his Dominican Order, he *administered an antidote* to an overly patriarchal view of scripture and opened a doorway for women and men to embrace their humility as human beings who are *all created equally in God's Light.*

Bill Everson defended my thesis with the watchdogging eyes of a true Dominican. I am happy to say that I was given honors for my thesis on June 4, 1982, for which I am forever grateful. After Bill's death on June 2, 1994, I helped to carry his coffin at St. Dominic's Cemetery in Benicia, California. Next to Everson, Eckhart has been my only Christian teacher, other than Chardin. Like Jung, I couldn't read Aquinas. I found him to be far too dry, except for a few sections in his *Summa Theologica* that I found to be brilliant.

No Christian theologian has spoken to the needs of my soul as directly and consistently as Eckhart has, other than Jung's comments on him. *He is a medicine of science and democratic spirituality whose words should be read by as many people as possible to help transform the world.* In a way I cannot fully explain, he has become a living part of me, as he was also in Jung. "You see," Jung said, "from the beginning, our individual consciousness only lives by a continuous series of pregnancies and births, a continuous series of transformations."[650] This is essential wisdom complementary to Eckhart's, for as the shaman-preacher rightly said: "Means are twofold. One, without which I cannot get into God, is work, vocation or calling in time, which interferes not one whit with eternal salvation."[651]

CHAPTER 32

IMAGELESS MEDITATION ON THE INFINITE GROUND

Whatever our calling may be, we are instructed by Eckhart to work without a why:

> Out of this innermost ground, all of your works should be wrought without Why. I say, truly, as long as you do works for the sake of heaven or God or eternal bliss, from without, you are at fault ... life lives from its own ground, and gushes forth as its own. Therefore it lives without *Why*, because it lives for itself.[652]

Not all Christocentric Christians would agree with Eckhart and Jung that the Paraclete represents a further stage of transformation in the Christian mystery. Yet God needs us and cannot know himself without you and me:

> The Father cannot know himself without me, seeing that I stand in the ground of the eternal deity wherein his whole incomprehensible work is wrought with me and what is comprehended that I am. By which I mean

the light of the Sun, the universal life-giver, therefore I see that God cannot know himself without me.[653]

What kind of a man was Eckhart? Who was he, really? All I knew is that when I read him, something within me was *healed*. I felt whole. *Cured* from my neurotic suffering. It was temporary, of course, but perhaps Eckhart had enabled me to tap into some deep ancestral memories. Not having been raised religiously Christian, I received the highest medicine the Church could possibly offer me, and this is what Jung rightly called the *relativity of God*: God's dependence upon humans and humans' ultimate dependence upon the Creator. It helped me to know that I was not alone in the universe of thought, that we are all in this evolving panorama of life-transformations together. I knew Jung's central article on the Master well by the time I read him. Yet there was something holy about reading Eckhart's sermons that could not be explained through the lens of empirical depth psychology: a portal that opened into the Beyond, a spiritual *healing that was qualitatively different from my readings in analytical psychology.*

Jung helped me see psychologically from an empirical standpoint that every *typos* requires an *Imprinter*.[654] Yet Eckhart became One with the Imprinter, where truth flowed into him and out of him *supernaturally* through grace:

> If I were not, God would not be either. I am the cause
> of God's being God: if I were not, then God would not
> be God ... Here, God finds no place *in* man, for man by
> his poverty wins for himself what he has eternally been
> and shall eternally remain. Here, God is one with the
> spirit, and that is the strictest poverty one can find.[655]

Eckhart not only became one with the imprint, the *typos* of God; he became One with *the Imprinter behind the imprint*: the Godhead. He became *equal* with the Paraclete as the God of Love and was, therefore, the creator of his own destiny. This went beyond conventional Christianity into the incarnation, not of God or Christ, but of the Spirit. *Eckhart's theology was an art and a therapy of giving birth to the divine Word in the eternal Now, speaking the Word of God or the Self—whatever term one may prefer to describe the experience of the sacred—via a vocation to live by in a simple and immediate way.*

Eckhart wrote that "the whole universe as one totality (as the name implies, because universe means 'one') comes from the Simple One, one from the One in a primal and immediate way."[656] *Totality* is a frequently used as a synonym for individuation in Jung's works; totality is becoming the unique and singular individual you are destined to be. Yet "one totality" means something different from what Jung meant by individuation. Listen again to Eckhart: "If God is to make anything in you or with you, you must first be reduced to nothing. Therefore enter into your own ground and work *there*; the works that you perform *there* are all living."[657]

As we have seen, for the Dominican, the divine birth of his vocation as a preacher, theologian, and shaman, was born through a *calling dream*. This dream, this vision of God, became a *universal medicine* for all creeds of the Church, a holy Sacrament, a *call to sacred action through nonaction*. Dreams like the one that came to Eckhart, the naked child born of Nothing, are rare.

"It is generally true that the parts of any whole whatsoever do not confer existence on the whole, but rather receive existence from, through, and in the whole."[658] Wholeness in this transcendental sense was *equivalent* to Oneness in the Universe, or Universal Totality. "Existence is God": (*Esse Deus est*). We have to experience our own calling dreams to know what the "citadel," "spark," or "castle" transcending everything in space and time essentially is.

We each, in our own ways, have to converse with our own Eckhart, make use of him in whatever way we might, for our own spiritual betterment. In Eckhart's words: "God's chief aim is giving birth. He is never content till he begets His Son in us. And the soul, too, is in no way content until the Son of God is born in her. And from there springs forth grace. Grace is thereby infused."[659] Eckhart's *medicine was linguistic and can be administered transnationally because his language was the universal language of the heart and intellect.*

Jung called the Paraclete a "very important step beyond Christocentrism."[660] The conventional organization of the Church is still living in a Christocentric mythos. This is a problem most books on Eckhart fail to address with lucidity. When seen through the lens of the Church organization, most contemporary writers fail to see *why* Jung's challenges and contributions to Christianity were so much in line with Eckhart's. They were both individuals in post-Christian history who accepted their callings from the Self. They both followed the paradigm of the Paraclete. They each carried a heavy cross, but Eckhart carried two to his grave in Avignon.

Recently, after I heard a thousand people had shown up to learn mindfulness meditation at a continuing education course for psychotherapists, I asked a friend: "Why is so little attention being given to the West's greatest spiritual teacher?" My friend asked to my complete astonishment: "Who was Meister Eckhart?" I was completely dumbfounded. Moreover, when I reread (at a Tibetan Buddhist retreat center, Ratna Ling, in Northern California) Eckhart's treatise *On Detachment,* I thought I was reading the Pali Cannon. Why have so few Californians read him? This was a puzzle to me.

Eckhart's trial by Pope John XXII, a Franciscan, was a historical tragedy that pointed me back to the fierce turf wars between Dominican and Franciscan rivals at a much earlier date than the Reformation. Returning to Eckhart during the five-hundredth anniversary of that historic event, led me to ponder how the inquisition's subjective scrutiny of Eckhart's sermons was probably patterned by a bipolar split in the Christian national complex, between France and Germany, that was rife with bitter envy and enmity in the Church itself.

In a dream (dreamt on March 28, 2016) a thirty-seven-year-old German woman suddenly appeared out of the past, speaking to me about a German relative of mine who had been influenced from a far distant ancestor from five hundred years ago, who'd been directly inspired by Meister Eckhart's teachings. That would place this ancestor right around the time of Luther, I reflected in the dream state. I desired to know in my dream what she could tell me about this early German ancestor, so I engaged with her in an active dialogue: "What did your distant ancestor know about Meister Eckhart's teachings?" I asked. She replied: "My relative told me about the distinction his ancestor had made between God as the Trinity and the fourth principle of the Godhead, the Ground of the soul, how he was taught to leave God for God, and how this basic teaching of leaving God for God had formed the basis for the Master's teachings, which inspired Luther and the Reformation."

That morning, after I awoke, I drove to the Buddhist retreat center where I attended an annual retreat with a Jungian shamanic drumming and visioning group I had been a part of for eleven years. I drove along the Pacific coast, passing through Bodega Bay and Jenner, and made my way up to the redwoods below Ranta Ling. It was dark by the time I parked my car.

All the way up the coast, I had been listening to Bach's Mass in B Minor and thinking about Eckhart. He was the Master, to my mind, who established a bridge in medieval Christian society to states of satori in Zen Buddhism, without knowing anything about the philosophies of the East. Sometimes, in one's youth, one hears a calling from the Self to Awake, to take a particular course of action, as I had at UCSC, and arrive at moments of "breakthrough." Only afterward (in my case three decades later) does one come to understand what bitter conflicts were being worked out in one's distant family of origin that might have led to a particular course of activity.

My revised book on Eckhart, which began to take shape three decades later, eleven years ago today on Easter, was being written out of the suffering of the Catholic-Protestant split in the European psyche, a split in the cultural psyche of Germany and France, which led to the horrible devastation of the Thirty Years' War. This horror within Holy Roman Empire history was fought between 1618 and 1648. The quarrel reached its inception point by 1513 (521 years ago), when Luther gave birth to the Reformation. The Thirty Years' War was one of the most destructive wars of all battles in European history. Between five and eight million lives were said to have been lost. Some areas of Germany, in fact, lost half of their population.

I was called to write about spiritual democracy in the multicultural and multireligious West for the next several years, after I had returned to Eckhart's work and put it down again after writing a hundred pages or so. Through journaling I began to see that this initial effort to chart out my own personal story of individuation, my theory of truth, as a Californian, began with my thesis on Eckhart, who was quite democratic in his spiritual outlook as a Catholic.

My question at that time was whether Eckhart's idea of "breakthrough" out of his traditional images of God for the ineffable and unknown Ground of all empirical being might be a basis for a broader understanding of the Divine than most other previous God-notions had made room for in Christocentric Christendom.

A Chance Encounter with a Friend

My wife, Lori, and I had a friend join the two of us for a walk into the redwoods behind our home at about this time. As it turned out (and I did not know this prior to our stroll), she had received her doctorate from Tuft's University with a major in German languages. She had taken courses in Middle High German, and although she was a bit rusty in the vernacular, she spoke *Hoch Deutsch*, or High

German, rather fluently. She was also a translator and had translated some of Rilke's poetry for a book while studying Jung in Zürich. I was surprised and delighted by the coincidence between my appearance of the dream anima, or German soul, and this outer chance meeting with our German-speaking friend.

I had been sitting for a few days with Eckhart's German Sermon 72 in Walsche's translation, where Eckhart began: "The prophet says, 'Lord, have mercy on the people that are in thee.' Our Lord replied, 'All that are sick I shall heal, and willingly love them.'"[661] It's a magnificent sermon. I was at that same time drawn particularly to Jesus's lines: *"All that are sick I shall heal."* Healing, after all, is the shaman's tradecraft or calling, and I had been particularly interested in this aspect of Eckhart's work as a preacher of God's Word. How can the Word of God heal us? I had been wondering for many years how I could build a bridge between psychology and theology.

During the walk in the redwoods, amid the great rings of once-giant ancestral Sequoias, I told our friend about this beautiful sermon by the Dominican. I also mentioned that I had *Meister Eckhart: Deutsche Predigten und Traktate Herausgaben und Ubersetzt von Joseph Quint* at home on my bookshelf, and asked if she would be so kind as to take a look at it with me.

When we got back to our house, she asked to take a look at the passage that interested me most. My main question to her as a translator was about the meaning of the German word *Barmhertzigkeit,* which is repeated several times in the sermon. She was very moved by Eckhart's language. She told me it was a *gehobene sprache,* elevated speech. The Word *Barmhertzigkeit* is *ein gehobenes Wort,* a high Word, she said. I loved this!

Meditating on the meaning of poverty of spirit, Eckhart had said in the sermon: "a poor man is one who wants nothing, knows nothing, and has nothing."[662] This all sounded very Buddhist to me after returning from sitting in silence in the redwoods and doing some shamanic drumming at Ranta Ling. We then looked up the word *Barmhertizkeit* in *The Oxford Duden* and *Cassell's* German Dictionaries and compared the two translations of the word side by side. Everything began to make sense: Oxford translated the word *Barmhertizkeit* as mercy first, compassion second; Cassell's translated the word as compassion first, mercy second. This comparison was highly significant!

At first glance, the inflections on a single word in that beautiful sermon and its two translations led me to see that they might be used synonymously. But were they really the same in Eckhart's mind in Middle High German? What came up repeatedly in our readings of the sermon in Joseph Quint's High German translation from the Old German vernacular were the words *erbarme* and *erbarmen*, which mean "compassion for, or with," or to feel *mitleid* with someone, namely suffering with or mercy! Another word that kept coming up in the sermon is *Gnade,* or Grace.

We wondered out loud together whether Eckhart meant mercy or compassion. This interesting linguistic test, arranged by a fortuitous synchronicity, confirmed my intuition: Theologians with the broadest grasp of Eckhart's entire works, in German and Latin, are typically the ones who have an advantage in terms of giving us Eckhart's precise meanings. This is important today when there is so much focus on environmental justice and my love and mercy for redwood trees!

What I took away from my discussions with my anima and my friend was the fact that Eckhart's medicine as a shaman for his times and ours was dispensed via his ability to *suffer with us, to carry Christ's Cross and his own Cross, aloft with joy, and to celebrate and administer bliss to us on our journey through life toward an ocean of peace through super-substantial Grace.* Sermon 72 is a great summation of Eckhart's entire teachings. I wholeheartedly recommend it to readers. But these minute subtleties in translation do not compare with the more pressing issues in theology, which is how to interpret Eckhart psychologically, which was Jung's greatest gift. And as I have argued in this book as a post-Jungian also theologically!

The Need for Self-Criticism

Jung wrote in *Mysterium Coniunctionis*, "Every theologian speaks simply of 'God,' by which he intends it to be understood that his 'god' is *the* God. But one speaks of the paradoxical God of the Old Testament, another of the incarnate God of Love, a third of the God who has a heavenly bride, and so on, and each criticizes the other but never himself."[663] Such self-criticism is at the heart of Jung's method of analysis and spiritual practice. Today, no one can claim to have discovered *the* truth in Eckhart scholarship, only a partial "truth" to a universal mystery of the Self, which exists as a spiritual reality inside each of us through the miracle of the Paraclete.

The goal of analytical psychology is to reunite the mind with what Jung called the "eternal Ground of all empirical being."[664] What is the Ground of all empirical existence and how can we experience it? The divine Ground can be accessed by anyone through traditional methods of meditation that are offered by any one of the world's religions. Any techniques of inward meditation may be used by an individual or group who comes to "know beyond all doubt, that empirical reality has a transcendental background."[665] Jung's focus in analysis was on empirical reality, getting to know the empirical God-image in his patients dreams and visionary experiences, not to expound on the *transcendental Ground of all being itself.*

The Godhead is always wider and higher or lower in-depth than God or Christ, YHWE or Mary. In my authoritative Kohlhammer volume by Joseph Quint, I read in High German: *"Darum bitte ich Gott, das der mich Gottes quitt mache"* ("Therefore, I pray to God to rid me of God.")[666] We must take Eckhart at his Word: he means what he says about God and the Godhead's fathomless depth and height. No theology can touch it. It is that sacred.

Eckhart's vocation was to tell us what God and the Godhead are in their Ground; this was his spiritual calling. He was always leaving his empirical experiences of God for the Absolute: "For man must always do one thing," he proclaimed, "he cannot do them all. He must always be one thing and in that one find all."[667] Eckhart stressed the importance of giving birth to the Word of God in the eternal Now of creation through the technique of *Gelassenheit,* or "letting go." This simple meditation technique was a way to connect with the inner Christ, Paraclete, or the *primal shaman* below and above all empirical beings.

This type of prayer leads to the practice of *abegeschiedenheit,* or letting be, a prayer of becoming still in a bare mind, restful, and unworried by anything, in peace. As I view it, this is a practice that can be of great benefit to the practice of psychotherapy generally as well as being a practice of study and experimental research in the annals of theology and religion worldwide.

Eckhart did not confuse God with the *imago Dei.* On the contrary, his view was that the "God" we can know by supernatural grace, inspiration, or transcendental knowledge is God the Trinity (Father, Son, and Holy Spirit) yet, beyond this representation of the Three Persons, is an unknowable and unfathomable Ground, *die Gotheit,* a fourth feminine dimension above and below being, a Nothingness that gave birth to the entire Universe. Trinity and quaternary, God and the Godhead, were, for Eckhart, as different as heaven and earth in their distinctness. Eckhart said when the soul reaches the essence of the Ground itself, it sinks ever deeper into the abyss of the Godhead, so that it never reaches the bottom. Eckhart spoke of humanities' essential *equality* with God, Sophia, and with Mary. "What good would it do me for Mary to be full of grace if I were not also full of grace?"[668]

Eckhart was seven hundred years ahead of his times. His practical technique for becoming free of worry and standing in the stillness and silence of a bare mind is a powerful *medicine* for readers and listeners of his sermons today. He speaks out for women and men, for our planet, for the Divine Feminine and the earth, out of a state of emptiness that is the precondition for all compassionate thought and being. This may be why he is so well liked by people of all faiths. Eckhart's highest prayer is a *medicine* that needs to be widely administered.

To do justice to Eckhart, to show how his work is a trans-dual bridge between Eastern and Western religions, reflective of both the relative and the Absolute, the reader will have to grasp Eckhart's most comprehensive thoughts on the nature of the soul (*anima*), God, the Trinity, the Godhead, and Ground (*Grund*). As McGinn noted, "We must grasp the interaction between the *Lesemeister* (master of the schools) and *Lebenmeister* (master of preaching and living) if we wish to understand Eckhart whole."[669]

As Eckhart put it in Sermon 15 of his German works: "Truly you are the hidden God (Is 15), in the ground of the soul, where God's ground and the soul's ground are one ground."[670] Similarly, God's *esse* and the soul's *esse* are one Absolute or *Esse Absolutum* at the highest level of the soul's powers in Wisdom. Detachment leads us to the simple "'One,' separated from all duality."[671] When the soul has become truly void of all symbols, Eckhart declared: "Here God's ground is my ground and my ground is God's ground."[672] This is the shamanistic Ground of the human psyche from which all religions have come. I'll now end this chapter with one of Eckhart's most challenging definitions of God: "I am good, God is not good ... if I say God is a being, that is not true: he is a transcendent being, and a superessential nothingness."[673]

Try as one might to fit Eckhart's teaching and preaching into a neat theological formula, his metaphor of the ground can only be understood through experience. Jung said specifically, after quoting Eckhart for an astounding fifteen pages straight, during his ETH Seminar *Psychology of Yoga and Meditation* (and which I encourage my readers to study):

> Until now there has only been the Pfeifferian manuscript
> in Middle High German and Latin. A new edition is
> coming out. We have the good fortune and honor to

possess a manuscript of Eckhart's in Switzerland, namely in Basle... We are beginning to understand him a little, not least because in the mean time we have incorporated within us the spiritual treasuries of the East. There is an extraordinary relationship between Eastern ideas and the ideas of Meister Eckhart, which is yet to be fathomed.[674]

This is a masterwork for a future post-Jungian who can make the bridge clear. I have provided some helpful hints of how this might be done in my 2022 book on Western Yoga.

It was Eckhart's belief that a person who lives by the Word is *equal* with God. He said so in his "Defense," where he claimed that he'd never been accused by anyone of heresy "as my whole life and teaching testify, and as the esteem of the brethren of the whole order and men and women of the entire kingdom and of every nation corroborates."[675] This was a remarkable statement. What did he mean by it? The esteem of the brethren of the whole order? I think he meant all of the orders of *men and women of the entire kingdom and queendom of God upon the earth*. I believe this to be true in my bones, in my DNA.

CHAPTER 33

EIGHT DEAMS ABOUT MY THESIS ON ECKHART

In what follows, I'm going to provide readers with an overview of eight dreams I had between January 8, 1980, and June 17, 1999, beginning when I was writing my thesis on Eckhart and Jung at UCSC. Afterward, this major work of scholarship continued to live in my psyche to remind me of my Self-path. These dreams are all out of the ordinary and were accompanied by affective experiences of the *numinous*. They are personal, transpersonal, and archetypal in nature. Because of the fact that my Christian cultural roots are in Europe, I was able to tap into a transpersonal level of my psyche in Germany. Ancestral memories, that is, from the distant past, were still alive in me and were unearthed from my inherited Ground. Although it is true that I was living in California when I had all eight dreams, the locale of three dreams took place in Europe (#1, 3, 4).

These eight dreams offer empirical evidence that verifies Jung's hypothesis that there is a national level of the psyche and archetypes of specific regions in the world that are changeless and central to our individuation. For myself, this meant that below my identity as a Californian, there was a spiritual dimension of my psyche that was ancient, Judeo-Christian, and Lutheran-Catholic, and about which I knew very little other than the fact that my paternal grandparents and my ancestors were from Plauen, about sixty miles north of Erfurt. The locale of the remaining five dreams was either Santa Cruz, or Orinda, California. What they point to is the probability that our ancestors are still alive in us and are guiding us in a teleological way toward the pursuit of our vocations.

I owe a great deal to my paternal grandmother, who traveled from Germany to help raise me at six months old in Pacific Grove and then returned to Germany when I was three-and-a-half. She later sent me my first copies of Eckhart's sermons in Middle and in High German in my early twenties. She encouraged me to pursue my calling at UCSC, yet I know very little about our family history. I had been to Germany to visit her on four occasions in the summer months during my high school years, so I had a *feel* for Germany and I felt at home there.

This much I do know, however: She was a deeply religious person and had sung for a period of time in the Lutheran Church. She prayed every day and conveyed to me at a very early age, before I could talk, a Lutheran faith and a passion for her calling as a mother, grandmother, baker, and former Church vocalist. In her youth she sang hymns. Classical music was present in our home from the earliest days of my infancy, so the Christian spirit was certainly alive in the home, even though we never went to Church. Moreover, my grandmother's voice was very resonant and soothing. She sang to me quietly before bedtime, leaving an imprint in my mind of her sonorous German *voice*. She loved me unconditionally and conveyed to me something of the spirit of my descendants. My mother, whose home area was bombed by the Germans in France, was a recovering Catholic. She had an ambivalent relationship to the Church for most of my early lifetime. As a result, my three siblings and I were mostly skeptical toward Christianity. Only in France did we marvel at the magnificence of the glorious medieval Cathedrals.

I wouldn't describe my experience of discovering Eckhart as a "conversion" to Christianity; my psyche was already Christian even though I didn't really know it. My being captivated by the charismatic theologian and preacher from Erfurt was much more organic and seemed to arise naturally from my native soil influences in California after meeting Everson. Nevertheless, in four of the eight dreams, I traveled backward in time to the medieval period, when Eckhart walked the earth. Two of the dreams have, as the reader will see, a distinct *feeling* of my having been in Erfurt before.

When I look back at my dream journals, I'm amazed at the sense of timelessness that exists in the historical unconscious. Jung spoke in his *Collected Works* about prospective dreams that contain portraits of the ways in which future actions will later be taken up as works in the world in a meaningfully *symbolic* pattern that provides hints of our destiny. Therefore, I hold all these dreams to be sacred. I have always protected them, owing to their personal quality, yet they may be of objective value as *imprints* of experience to support my hypotheses about the trans-dual nature of the human psyche and the centrality of vocational archetypes. We simply cannot know where our calling will lead us to when we are young, what impact our vocations might have upon the career world, but it is our ethical responsibility to work with such images and be true to them, as best we can—first, by remembering them, and second, by living out their general structural designs as an architect might construct a house from a blueprint. Calling dreams are data for verification and development of theoretical structures. Therefore, as an analyst, I have to show my feelings as well as express my ideas in order to arrive at an overall theory of vocation during the process of authoring this book.

A Synchronicity

Before I report my first dream, I will share an experience that occurred before I decided to write my thesis about Eckhart. I was sitting outside, near the provost's office at Cowell College on the

UCSC campus, contemplating whether or not to leave the experimental psychology department and write my own individual major in "Depth Psychology and Religion." I was in vocational perplexity at the time and was hoping Jack Engler, the dean, might be able to help me make up my mind about what to do since I needed his stamp of approval to chart my own academic course.

As I was relaxing in the sun on a beautiful fall morning in the Santa Cruz mountains, next to a large coastal redwood tree, a young woman suddenly stopped by to chat. She said, "hallo." I immediately noticed her German accent. I was drawn to her and replied "hello." We quickly sparked up a conversation in German for about ten minutes before Jack arrived. She told me she was living in Carmel-by-the-Sea across the water from where we were chatting. I was sitting on the bench and looking up into her eyes; the sun shone above her head. She added she was commuting daily to the campus, and her name was "Gabrielle Eckhart"!

Well, that solved my problem on the spot. I was flabbergasted. Even before I stepped foot in the provost's office to consult with Jack about my quandary, there was Ms. Eckhart in the flesh! This was an unmistakable synchronicity that filled me with a deep sense of wonder. Looking back at the event, it seems like she was sent to me from the unconscious to confirm my choice of following my calling in my own creatively independent way.

This was one of those irrationally improbable mind-matter correlations that was simply, as Jung said about synchronicity experiences, "just so." Although I had to ask myself later what the probability was that such a fortuitous event could have happened, it seemed to be much more significant than mere chance. It felt *destined*.

I do not know how many students had the last name of Eckhart at that time at the university, but to have crossed paths with her at that precise moment and for her to suddenly begin speaking to me in German, then to hear that she was commuting from Carmel-by-the-Sea, where I was born, across the Monterey Bay, was a meaningful chance beyond statistical odds. It was too meaningful to be merely random. It was truly "miraculous."

I'm not a mathematician, yet someone with a calling to math could conceivably calculate the statistical chances of such an acausal encounter happening from a quantitative angle. Yet, qualitatively, it was an experience that filled me with *joi de vivre*. I'm sure the probability would *not* fit neatly on any bell curve! It convinced me without a shadow of a doubt that there is an ordering principle in the Universe that is patterned upon an archetype of destiny. In my case it has led me to attempt to bridge a gap between Eckhart's theology and Jung's empirical psychology, which, given the forty-four years it has taken to complete this book, was no easy task. Publishing my thesis as I wrote it at twenty-five would have been far too premature.

This *fortuitous* meeting with this young woman meant that I had a definite calling to proceed with writing my thesis on the great Dominican. But publishing a work on the Master was a whole other challenge, one that would require much further study and maturity. What it suggested to me, moreover, is that there is work to be done according to ancestral natural laws. The ancients want something from us and we have to respond; there's unfinished business in one's ancestry, based on a fundamental *numerical rhythm,* a natural harmony, a symmetry of existence in human interrelationships, societal processes, and chance happenings that require our devotion and attention to details of meaning and transcausal order. It confirmed that we all owe something to the dead.

Seven is one of my favorite numbers, and here she was (an attractive hook for my anima projection!) on the *seventh* day of November! As you'll see in dream #5, the number seven later showed up in my dreams about Eckhart. To be sure, in this instance the soul-image I projected upon Miss Eckhart was German-Christian. She was Deutsch, perhaps Lutheran given her ancestry, although I didn't ask. This is the way spiritualized soul-projections work. They come completely out of the blue spectrums of the colorful unconscious. After our brief encounter and my momentary illumination through grace, I never saw her again on campus. She simply vanished, almost as if she might have been a dream-woman sent to me with a message about my future from the hand of God.

Dream #1

The first dream came to me on January 8, 1980, while I was preparing for my teaching assistantship for William Everson's course.

> *The first part of the dream centered on the building of a large wooden Cross. My brother and I were building the Cross on the top of a high mountain for my older sister. My brother carved some very loving statements into the wood of the Cross for my sister to behold. Then, we elevated it by her window so that she could crouch to see the Cross from where she was sitting in a room of a fortress that looked out at the hill. She came out of her room in a ballerina's outfit with some little black ballet shoes. She then began dancing and twirling around like I'd never seen her spin and dance before. She looked marvelous, up on her toes, moving like a ballerina and spinning around the Cross in her excitement with profound joy. After her whirling ballet, the scene changed.*
>
> *Then I traveled with my dream-sister down the other side of the mountainside, leaving the castle she'd been residing in to my brother's care. The Cross was constructed to guide travelers to a retreat down the hill in a verdant forest. We descended there on foot and there was no longer a road to travel on. We walked on and came across a group of monks from the village in*

321

the forest community below. They said the Christians there all ate at 4 o'clock once daily and meditated continuously the rest of the time in the monasteries.

We (me and my soul-sister) then came to a little trail on the descending hillside, where we meet two friars who were dressed in long black robes. The friars set us up onto two brown horses and led us together into the innermost part of the city at the center of the forest, while riding on their two horses next to us. There were now four horses in all: two for me and my sister, two for the friars. We passed through the city's main streets on horseback, moving at a steady gait toward the city center. We left the four horses behind on a hillock to pasture and then began walking farther together as a foursome. I suddenly looked behind me at the hillside and saw the beautifully verdant knolls in radiant golden-green light, shimmering in luminescent hues beneath the beaming golden sun. We then traveled in a car together the rest of the way, toward the very center of the city. Every building we saw along our path was a monastery, a sacred sanctuary, a church, or a cathedral, formed around a little landmass at the center. The city was completely Christian; every type of church and cathedral one could possibly visualize was there. When I looked up, I saw spires, domes, square buildings, round buildings, many different types of basilica architecture; as many medieval religious structures as could be imagined were there! We traveled down a long aisle, past many churches and places of worship, to the very epicenter of the city.

We then climbed out of the car and entered a round building, with seats that spiraled inward toward a midpoint, where a golden altar stood upright, with a *religious man, who was very energetic and who had a powerfully magnetic personality and resonant voice, speaking God's Word. He was delivering an unbelievably electrifying and beautiful Sermon. He gave me a distinct feeling for what Eckhart might have been like. A lovely Mass played over a stereo system (a modern one), and a chorus of chanters sang along with the classical music. It was all very beautiful and holy. As I listened to the preacher and the music, I thought of my senior thesis, which I was just then beginning to write on Eckhart and Jung. Upon awakening, I realized suddenly I should get my privacy and begin some serious writing.*

Now, this dream about the cross clearly represents a correlation that exists in the human psyche between a vocational symbol—the cross high on the hill—and the speaker of God's Word at the *nuclear* point of his sermon delivery in the city below. There seems to be a union between the more familial and introverted activity on the hill, with my brother and sister, and the bustling extroverted activity life in the city and multitude of European churches and cathedrals. What did this mean to me at the time? Why so many dreams about the cross (this was the sixth dream about a cross since my senior year of high school)?

I had no previous conscious relationship to it as a religious symbol prior to my keeping a dream journal. I had no relationship of any kind to the Church, nor did my family. My grandmother never took me to church services during my summer visits to Hof, Germany. As a family we had no positive relationship to Christianity, in any religious sense, except at Christmas and Easter. In fact, it is curious why both the Catholics and Lutherans on my French and German sides had almost completely abandoned Christianity. The only exception was the little Lutheran prayer my grandmother had given me to recite at the age of four, a prayer I recited to myself in quiet along with the Prayer of St. Francis I'd been saying daily since I met my first Jungian analyst at age twenty. My analyst gave me a copy of the prayer on a little laminated yellow card with a picture of the Saint on it on one side and his prayer on the other. I repeated it every day and night while I was having these eight dreams. Here was a fantastic dream of the cross that came to me while I was beginning to write my thesis at UCSC. It heralded something imminent and momentous I could not yet see, but only divine in a prospective way.

In *Jung and the Problem of Evil*, published in 1958, the author H. L. Phillip published a long correspondence between himself and Jung in the form of some specific questions and answers. Jung's views on the meaning of the cross were made explicit in that exchange. He said as follows about it:

> Christ has shown how everyone will be crucified upon his destiny, i.e., upon his self, as he was. He did not carry his cross and suffer crucifixion so that we could escape … Christ is the model for human answers and his symbol is the *cross*, the union of opposites. This will be the fate of man, and this he must understand if he is to survive at all. We are threatened with universal genocide if we cannot work out the way of salvation by a symbolic death.[676]

Jung was probably thinking of a possible third world war here. Today, the universal genocide we are facing is also from the threat of climate change. To believe in Christ and his death on the cross is one thing, yet to carry the burden of one's own cross, to suffer the fate of symbolic death, outstretched on the crossbeams, the agony of crucifixion, requires a sacrificial act of suffering—one that is excruciatingly real if we are to reach a hopeful resolution during the times we are living in. Not all of us are aware of the looming dangers, but the accumulating disasters are more numerous than we have hitherto imagined. The human ego must paradoxically suffer the fate of the cross in an agonizing process of crucifixion, if we are to be saved as a species. The cross may well be our symbol for what is just over the horizon. As I've discussed, Eckhart said we must actually carry two crosses: Christ's cross and our own.

The joyful spinning of my sister, a well-grounded, athletic, spiritual soul, twirling ecstatically around the cross, suggests a path of embodied consciousness in California in 1980. At the time, I was practicing Iyengar Yoga and in good shape physically as well as spiritually. My mother, as I mentioned, was a gymnastics teacher and a track and field athlete and so was I. Yet no one in my family practiced ballet. So this was an archetypal scene. The place of the dream appeared to be medieval Europe, probably Germany.

She—my anima—was happy beyond belief at having been given the green light to go ahead with my plans to become self-reliant and write my thesis on Eckhart. My soul was ecstatic. Her spinning around the cross revealed her joy in twirling and dancing. Moreover, the spiraling movements toward the center of the Christian city paralleled my soul's whirling over my rediscovering of my Christian roots. My family soul was delighting in my adhesion to Christianity, with the cross as its central symbol of death and resurrection. The crux was carved by my dream-brother, a companion figure who was not my outer brother but a wood-carver like me. I love to whittle.

My dream-sister danced and spun like a dervish in her excitement. She was not in a mystical or trance state; she was a stylized artist, a ballerina, and imitating the steps of a Sufi artisan. It was with her that my dream-ego traveled, down the hillside toward the forested area, where we met the group of monks and two friars dressed in flowing black robes. Were they probably *Blackfriars*, a common name for Dominicans and pre-Lutherans? I found it curious that they approached me with four horses. Why four? Four horses are symbols of tremendous physical power and energy. They were relied upon heavily in Eckhart's day, but Eckhart walked most everywhere by foot and he didn't ride, although he loved to watch horses as a boy, in the town of Tambach, and was trained before he became a monk at fifteen in "horseback riding and hunting with hawks and hounds"![677]

As mentioned, Eckhart was probably raised in Tambach, or perhaps nearby Gotha in Thuringia. Four decades ago, I had no idea about any of his history as there were no good biographies on Eckhart. Yet my inner architect or dream-designer seems to have accented the forested area in particular, where the monastery was located and the horses grazed. As we neared the innermost part of the city, *I looked behind me at the mountainside and saw the beautifully verdant hills in radiant golden-green light, shimmering beneath golden beams of the sun.* The accent on the forest, trees, and light is also highly significant because God is sunshine magnified across billions of galaxies against an abyss of infinite darkness.

Moreover, the *four horses* are suggestive of wholeness. The shift in scenes from the hill to the two guides, friars or monks, and the horses and the medieval monastery scenes to the car ride to the city suggests a transit in time from the medieval period to the postmodern. Also, the fact that the monks in the monastery all ate once a day at *four o'clock* again suggests organic wholeness and wholesome living through contemplation and fasting and then feasting on the food of God in Nature.

Nearing the city's epicenter, we exited the car and traveled on foot together to the round building to see the man who was speaking so eloquently and brilliantly. He gave me a distinct impression of what Eckhart might have been like, a charismatic preacher of the Word. Some further background on my first experiences of Eckhart might help to clarify my inner relationship to him in the context of my calling as a Jungian analyst.

The first time I saw a book by Eckhart was when I was sitting across from my first Jungian psychotherapist, Kathrine Whiteside Taylor, during a psychotherapy session. I was twenty years old then, and she was close to eighty. She had gone to the kitchen to make us some Earl Grey tea, her favorite English teatime beverage that always stimulated us into intellectual discussion. She was an exceptional teacher of Jung and was widely known in the Bay Area. As I glanced at her bookshelf while the tea was steeping, a little red-and-white book by Meister Eckhart jumped out at me. I inquisitively picked it up and began dreamily leafing through its pages. It was a book by Raymond Blakeney. I recalled reading about Eckhart in Jung's works, in volume 13 of the *Collected Works,* and I knew he had been important to Jung, yet the book seemed to have leapt off the bookshelf, as if it were meant solely for me.

Kathrine lent the book to me. I took it home to read it. Then I purchased a copy of my own at Cody's Bookstore in Berkeley. It was so precious to me, a sacrament, really. I savored every page I read. I no longer have that book because I read it so many times the pages all fell out of it, and I could no longer keep them in any coherent order.

It was during office hours with Bill Everson that I first had an intellectual discussion about Eckhart. I had internalized the words of the Master by then from many other scholars, and I began to make them my own. Everson was quite knowledgeable about the Dominican. He spoke extremely highly of him, quoting from his works by memory. One of his favorite sermons was "Blessed are the Poor in Spirit." He read a passage to me from a volume of Miss Evans's translation of Franz Pfeiffer that I'd checked out from the main UCSC library.

The fact that my brother and sister appeared in my first recorded dream about Eckhart suggests that they were both parts of my inner brother and sister complexes when they were both grounded and somewhat idealized; they were in the process of being *transformed* as internal structures within my psyche while I was at UCSC. My inner soul-siblings began to gradually undergo a structural change in their spiritual characteristics as I was reading Eckhart and meditating on his words constantly along with reciting the St. Francis Prayer. My dream-sister, dancing and twirling around the cross, was a developing part of my spiritualized anima, who had been activated through my studies and my ongoing conversations with Everson. As Eckhart said: "And I

327

say that in this light [the Light of the Cross] all the powers of the soul lift themselves aloft. The senses leap into thoughts."[678]

Although my anima was *leaping* and twirling, she was completely silent. So too was I. The friars and monks who all ate once a day at four o'clock were also suggestive of contemplators of the Word. They reminded me of my years as the head cook of the "Refectory" in Walnut Creek. I had no idea what a refectory was back then. Yet symbols of the Self often appear in dreams and alchemical and religious symbolisms as quaternary motifs, and spiraling around a central point, or circling toward an epicenter, suggests *circumambulation.* So too during our journey to the city center. Our spiraling movement suggests we were moving toward an *archetypal nucleus, and that nuclear center of energy that had the power to unite all of the cathedrals and churches of Europe had been embodied by the most spiritually democratic of all Catholic preachers in Germany and France.*

Moreover, every type of Christian church imaginable appeared on the road to the city. suggesting the preacher was the *nuclear symbol* in me who had the potential to bring the diverse elements of the dream's thoughts together through the Word into a scintillating synthesis. The Christian structures spun inward toward the inner spiritual man, the higher man, the aristocrat, the holy man, the speaker of God's Wisdom and Mercy.[679] He had the magnetic power to unite the plurality of the Catholic and Lutheran churches, despite the many schisms and the diversity of denominations that led to terrible bloodshed during the Thirty Years' War.

This, of course, was a very grand dream, one that I certainly could not live out through a spiritual calling as a preacher myself—that was not my vocation. But as a Jungian analyst, I understand it now as my calling to at least write about what I saw there in my inward vision. The immovable point around which everything else turned contained the very essence of the total history of Christendom wisdom: 1) the cross on the high hill (not Golgotha, but somewhere in the forests of Germany); 2) the spiritualized anima who dwelled in an inner castle on the high hill; 3) the personal brother; 4) the Brothers in the monastery, who ate at four; 5) the two Blackfriars who became our spiritual guides; 6) the four stout horses; 7) the cathedrals, churches, and religious structures of various types; and 8) Christianity's core teachings that were being spoken from the mouth and tongue of the charismatic preacher at the nuclear center and whose mind was on fire.

All eight themes were condensed into One essential principle: the Word of God from the Book of John and the sermon being delivered by a man who reminded me of the greatest Dominican preacher who ever walked the earth: Meister Eckhart. It was a numinous experience to witness him in dreamtime and to partake of his blessings and his supernatural intellect and receive his grace.

I mentioned the recurrence of the cross in my dreams. *In an earlier dream an old German man came to greet me at a Pacific seaport, and he gave me a neckless with golden crosses on it.* The first Dominicans arrived in Monterey in 1850. I had no knowledge of this until recently when I visited a little church in Benicia before having lunch with a friend.[680] The Christian man in my Monterey dream was, I thought at first, a part of my Lutheran ancestry, an archetypal figure from my father's side of the family. But the man bore a neckless with golden crosses in his outstretched hands, and he could certainly have been Catholic. Moreover, seventeen days later, *I dreamt of Brother Antoninus (not Bill Everson but "Antoninus" in his Dominican robes), who instructed me to build my own cross out of a dried-up oak tree, which I referred to in the dream as my "Tree of Life."*

Returning to my dream journals helped me grasp the emotional significance of carrying of the cross and what that really meant to a medieval Christian, to Eckhart, and me. This instinctive knowledge was stored up in the unconscious in my ancestral soul and my dream-sister danced it. She didn't speak the Word intellectually; she danced. *She knew* what my dream-ego did not know at the time about the meaning of the cross as a living symbol. In Latin Sermon XLV, which I hadn't read until 2021, Eckhart went even further:

This is why it says in Matthew 16: "If anyone wishes to come after me, let him deny himself, take up his cross and follow me" (Mt 16:24). "If anyone"—see, with no exceptions. In this everyone is on the same footing, servant and lord, poor and rich, noble and base ... a human being ought to raise and exalt his cross freely ... so every contrary and every hostile thing loses its evil and ill-nature in the soul that has been clothed in the armor of light, so that the soul no longer feels it, but rejoices and delights in suffering for the love of Christ.[681]

How can we understand this profound statement psychologically? *What does it mean to be clothed in the armor of light, so that the soul no longer feels suffering in her lower nature, but rejoices and delights in suffering in her higher nature?* My anima was light on her feet and her reward was measureless joy. It was this happiness in my sensual-spiritual anima that I brought to my thesis on Eckhart because Eckhart had awakened the archetype of Christ within me. Yet this bliss was not to be found in any church. My Christian anima has always kept her faith secret, as it was unclear, as a Jungian if I was really living in a Christian myth. Whatever my myth was, it came *after* Christ. Christ within was different from Christ without; it was always a verbal path, linguistic, emotional, spiritual, a quest for the unspoken Word inside of me in the quiet of my study. I said the prayer of St. Francis in secret constantly. Nobody knew about it.

Throughout high school, I worked my way up to become the head cook at the Refectory. The *Refectory*! The common definition of a refectory is a dining hall in a religious institution, where monks eat together. This was another one of those mysterious mind-matter correlations in my youth before I met Bill Everson. I presume the friars and monks in my dream ate at their medieval refectory. Moreover, my shift at the Refectory restaurant often began at four o'clock! So many moments of synchronicity have occurred around Eckhart that I am often baffled. It seems to me, in retrospect, that I was destined to travel with Eckhart on my own Self-path, to find my own inner relationship to Christ within as a Jungian.

I see this dream as one of the culminating events of my inner life while I was practicing and teaching and writing at UCSC under Everson's guidance and while I was practicing yoga daily. This jewel of a dream supplied rich empirical grounding in the psychology of vocational dream analysis.

One more amplification is necessary here: the verdant golden-green hills that I saw when I turned around to gaze at the peak on which the cross had been erected. Green symbolizes the Paraclete. It is the hue that symbolizes the *future works* of humanity, the continuing incarnation of the Self in everyone. Jung seemed to have thought the Paraclete was the central Christian symbol, not Christ but what comes after Him. For myself and for Jung what came after Christ was the Self, and Eckhart was the first figure in Europe in whom the Self was incarnated as the idea of the relativity of God.

Furthermore, all of the scenes in this dream seemed to take place on one half of my ancestral ground in Germany. The other half of my DNA is French, and that ancestry was probably Franciscan. Also, the church music that was playing from the modern stereo equipment in the second part of the dream was emblematic of my listening to Bach's majestic cantatas and Masses at that time, particularly the Mass in B Minor, which I'd often sung. The rapture in my anima had to do with the fact that I was listening to and singing with my records at UCSC, and this habit, which was inspired by my younger sister who is a vocalist and who was living in Santa Cruz at the time, often led my soul into numinous experiences of ecstasy over Bach's genius in depicting the Passion, such as during the majestic *Crucifixus* and *Et Resurrexit*.

Abiding in the *God-function* is abiding in the vine: "I AM the true vine, and my Father is the husbandman ... I am the vine, ye are the branches: he that abideth in me, and I in him, the same bringeth forth much fruit: for without me ye can do nothing" (John 15:1, 5).

How can we abide in the Self without being cut off from the vine of truth? Eckhart showed us how: through the prayer of quiet. Prayer is a form of active imagination, when nothing is asked for and nothing is expected from the Self in return. It is a simple appeal for a conversation with numinous experiences of great significance that cross our paths at decisive turning points in our lives. These inner dialogues with the Self are what I consider to be prayer in an analytical-psychological context. Petitions in prayerful silence may lead a patient in analysis to become pregnant with prospective purpose and meaning in any moment in time.

One thing I can attest about vocational dreams before proceeding further is that Absolute knowledge has a spark, a lightning bolt, or a *blitz* of Divinity in it. This is why it is Absolute: its existence, as Jung says, "can only be transcendental, since, as the knowledge of future or spatially distant events shows, it is contained in a psychically relative space and time, in an irrepresentable space-time continuum."[682] The important thing to note here is the power of the numinosity that came with successive nods that I was receiving from Everson and Katherine, who was now my mentor, about the rightness of my vocation to become a Jungian analyst at the time.

In ancient times, synchronistic events were typically interpreted as signs from the gods— *numens*. The word *numinosum* comes from the verb *nuere*, which means to "nod" or to "give a sign." When a Self-figure, such as Everson, nodded to me, either externally or in a dream state, the numinosity was sometimes overwhelming. As I began reading Eckhart deeply, the lightning began to break and strike again and again.

Lightning is often symbolic of the Holy Spirit. In Eckhart's theology of the Word, metaphors like fire, lightning, or the eagle of the Evangelist John were all symbols for the Paraclete.[683] Our likeness to God was captured by Eckhart's striking metaphor of our likeness to a flash of lightning: *"ein Gleichnes am Blitz finden."*[684] Jakob Böhme (1575–1624) who read Eckhart, wrote, "The *Liberty shines forth as a*

Flash," or the *"Birth of light."*[685] And as Jung wrote, in a letter in 1952: "What can, but need not, happen then is the spontaneous action from the unconscious, an action which is symbolized by the alchemists, Paracelsus, Boehme and the modern unconscious as *lightning.*"[686]

In the process of divinization, Jung wrote we all suffer, so to speak, from the "violence done to" *us* "by the Self."[687] The blitz from the God-function is also equivalent with the little "spark in the soul," or *das fünklein.*

Dream #2

On February 19, 1980, about a month after my last reported big dream, I dreamt again while reading and writing about Eckhart:

> *I find myself in a house somewhere getting up out of a deep dream state. Suddenly an overwhelming power comes pouring out of the innermost depths of my being. I see in a visual image an all-embracing sphere with an inner center, or cone; I know in the dream that this center and circumference is the soul, and its deepest archetypal core is Light. Suddenly loud thunder crashes all around me from outside and from within, and from the point of the innermost recesses of my soul, a flash of light suddenly shines forth like a bolt of lightning, from a Universe within.*

I awoke from the dream with a startling realization of the Holy Spirit's presence. I was jolted out of my sleep and left with an overwhelming sense of numinosity, a miraculous light presence, to which I bowed down with reverence. The mandala image I had just painted previous to this dream had left an indelible imprint on my vision, an after-image, or memory imprint, so that when I awoke, it was as if the dream symbolism and mandala image formed a kind of double vision. I had this dream while I was reading Eckhart's sermons, as I said, and the experience of being struck by lightning had much to do with the sense of inner enlightenment I felt at the time. Whether such dreams can be studied empirically as facts of science, or whether they will forever remain outside the field of vocational dream research is a question that cannot be answered here without stripping away the sense of mystery that is, without any question in my mind, metaphysical. To be sure, the answer must be both relative and transcendental to my dream researcher's mind, or trans-dual. The power of the thunderbolt was unmistakably violent, and it struck me with a great deal of inner force, hardly an experience of the meek and mild Jesus.

In order to understand why Eckhart is so vitally important to the evolution of the Christian myth in postmodernity, we have to unpack Jung's careful exegesis about the meaning of the Paraclete as a progressive idea of the Self a bit further. The Self, according to Jung, corresponds to the Holy Ghost, the final revelation of the Christian conception of God, but *after* Christ comes the fourth efflorescence of the feminine principle in human psychology: the *Assumption of the Virgin Mother.* Jung wrote: "The quaternity as union of the Three seems to be aimed at by the *Assumption of Mary.* The dogma adds the feminine element to the Masculine trinity, the terrestrial element (*virgo terra!*) to the spiritual, and thus sinful man to the Godhead ... Protestant critics have completely overlooked the symbolic aspect of the new dogma and its emotional value, which is a capital fault."[688]

The Paraclete manifests itself primarily through *numinous* experiences that are revealed to us through dreams, thoughts, intuitions, vigorous exercise, yoga, walks in nature, and active imaginations. Experiences of *numinosity* emanate from the Self, and they must not be forgotten; they should be recalled regularly, so that the reality of the psyche may reveal its mysteries. Such experiences can provide us with evidence to verify the *hypothesis* concerning the continuing incarnation of God or the Self, a terrestrial process of being grounded in the roots of vocational archetypes that form the *nuclei* of the personality at the innermost center.

The three main qualities attributed to the Paraclete, according to Jung, are *procreative, fructifying, and inseminating* potentials that aim toward bringing forth "works of divine parentage."[689] *We are all destined to bring forth works through our divine parentage, by virtue of the goodness of our vocations.* This means if we are to receive the Holy Spirit into our psyches, we have to accept our own individual life-patterns, by which I mean our calling archetypes, as Christ accepted his. Moreover, the Paraclete "is the *identical breath* of God and His Son in a new incarnation."[690] Jung wrote further: "Thus, Mother of God can, therefore, be regarded as a symbol of mankind's essential participation in the Trinity."[691] We have seen how much Jung was influenced by Eckhart, and I am attempting here as an analyst and Jungian dream researcher to provide verification for not only his ideas about God, Christ, or the Self, but Eckhart's and mine as well. Many of my most original thoughts have arisen from my dreams and only after sitting with them for many years am I attempting to interpret them in theoretical terms so that the reader can see for herself why Eckhart is so very important to the evolution of Christianity.

Dream #3

In the third dream from July 24, 1981, I entered some strangely familiar ancestral ground.

I find myself traveling down an ancient medieval street in Germany. Someone tells me that the church bell that we were passing and that was being rung belonged to Meister Eckhart. It made a beautiful ringing sound, and I saw that it was inlaid in beautifully preserved wood, to which the metal bell was attached. Then, I travel to an archaeological site and joined a group of people who are all familiar to me from my past. I knew that I was going on an archaeological dig that my father had once made at a later part of his life before his early death. I see many beautiful relics from very far back in German history.

My dream-father is not my real father, however, but an ancestral father, from the dim Middle Ages in Germany when Eckhart had walked the earth. I go to him (the ancestor-father), and we spark up a warm conversation. He is very happy that I've returned to Germany from the United States. He shows me precisely where to dig in the soil. I unearth some very beautiful stone carvings and inlaid metal Crosses, with precious jewels from the rich humus. The stone artifacts are more archaic than the Crosses, however, and they seem to go back even further to the time of early Germanic peoples, prior to the Middle Ages. This all makes sense to me, because they are found at a deeper level of stratification, at a site farther down the river.

I feel that I'm a long-lost son of this ancestor-father, a son who had gone to a new land (Carmel-by-the-Sea,

California), and who had just returned to the place of his Nativity. I work diligently in the excavation site, and my dream-father is very pleased with my return, as are, not incidentally, my mother and three siblings, who also work diligently on the same site. We all unearth some old Christian relics from the archaic Ground.

Emotional passion suddenly rushes up into my eyes and vibrating waves of pulsating energies enter my head. I'm spellbound by their (my family's) gaze as they look at me; their compassionate look, which speaks directly to my heart as gratitude enters me as our eyes meet. They appear to be thanking me in silence with their knowing looks.

Then, I am off down the road, enroute to a university; presumably the scene has changed now to UCSC. When I arrive, I speak to a professor, and I think of the joy that the university brings me, when I am truly given a place as a teacher (in Everson's course "Birth of a Poet"). Suddenly, a ray of deific light penetrates my scalp, from the sun's penetrating rays overhead, and I'm filled with a divine enthusiasm, illuminated by light waves, beams of radiating warmth and energy. I enter into an ecstatic state, and I know that the university is a place through which my teachings on vocation will eventually be brought forth to full fruition in the world.

A young student from "Birth of a Poet" comes close to me and asks me about my work on my senior thesis on Eckhart and Jung. I respond from deep centers of the Self, letting the Word of God pour forth deeply from my innermost being (recalling my first Eckhart dream of the Preacher). I say that the miracle about Jesus's life is that he no longer stands outside of divine knowledge, but he is now implanted directly in divine knowledge, and this is what makes him such a profound Poet. I teach this young man and a fellow friend that this is the true meaning of the vocation of humanity: that one attains a deep adhesion to the Self, so that whatever one articulates through the call, is capable of becoming the Word of God itself.

Now this dream contains several motifs that I will comment upon in sequential order. The ancient medieval street in Germany was possibly Erfurt in Thüringen, where Eckhart preached. The church bell belonged not to a creed; it belonged *personally* to Eckhart, which is to say it was really his bell. This means that I was traveling back in time to see and hear Eckhart's bell in the medieval period when he walked the earth and to learn from its sound how to be a true Christian.

Bells are often used in meditation services, whatever one's religion. They put us in tune with God's timeless rhythms. I had purchased a set of Tibetan bells that I used to ring while I meditated and before practicing Iyengar Yoga every morning at UCSC. I gave these bells away to a woman friend of my ex-wife's who generously typed up my thesis; I gave them gladly as a gift for her fiancé who was a musician because I had little money.

Here, in this dream, the meditation device is a Church bell, which means that the notes it intonated were uniquely Eckhartian sounds, still ringing in the historical psyche of Europe and within me. The ancestral father figure from the Middle Ages in Germany appears to have been a Self-figure along my paternal line, which goes back to Plauen, Germany, about 90 kilometers east of Erfurt and where my relatives were living before World War II. The artifacts I unearthed in the ground near Eckhart's bell were crosses with precious jewels and older stone carvings. This was the *seventh* vocational dream I had by this time with the symbol of the cross in it. I mentioned three of them previously.

Again, a transformation has taken place in my parental and sibling complexes, as they were all happy, joyous, and ecstatic that I'd found these religious relics, artifacts, and they all enthusiastically helped with the excavations. My inner mother too was quite mirthful. The ray of light that penetrated my scalp from the sun and filled my dream-ego with divine enthusiasm was an emotional emanation from the universal center of the Self, a light of Christ, and the vocation to teach Eckhart and Jung at a university. This was a calling dream I had not yet fulfilled, and I only completed that task when I taught Eckhart at the Unitarian-Universalist Church of Berkeley.

I then instructed a young student from "Birth of a Poet." I demonstrated through affective and instinctive-spiritual actions how I respond from deep centers of the Self by letting the Word pour deeply out of my innermost being while dreaming on autochthonous ground as a Californian. This is a technique I learned from Everson, who received it from the Dominicans and Eckhart. Everson also wore bells on his ankles at UCSC in class, so his steps would often make a soft ringing sound.

My comment in the dream concerning the miracle about Jesus's life no longer standing outside of divine knowledge suggested a change had now happened in human evolution as well as in myself. The archetype of Christ was now imprinted in collective consciousness within every living being through our ability to speak God's Word, that is, in you and me. This is what made Eckhart such a profound archetypal poet and a shaman-preacher and he lives as an archetype in all of us. He is now an archetype in the World Soul. I taught the young man and a fellow friend of his that this was the true meaning of the vocation the Self in humanity: one articulates the Self as a Word of God via a vocation to live by.

What was transmitted to me in this dream was what Eckhart called Absolute or supernatural knowledge about the vocation of the Self, or the Paraclete, in collective humanity. The Self in Jung, or Word of God in Eckhart, are essentially One in the dream. As Eckhart said in a vernacular sermon: "Got und ich, wir sind *eins*" ("God and I, we are *one*").[692]

The archeological dig into early historical deposits of Germany and its first Christian churches in the lower part of the river was also significant, as archeology was one of my first motivations as well as anthropology. My brother happens to be an archeologist in San Diego County. Also, during my journey to Erfurt, in June 2019, I was speaking to theologians, preachers, and ministers in Eckhart's Church about the significance of digging into the ancestral ground as an archeological motif in dreams, an act of digging in the soil or humus of the human psyche. To my great surprise, on my way home back to California, I met a young man at the airport who was studying archaeology at the University of Tübingen in southern Germany. He told me he was working on some ancient religious sites going back to the same medieval period (1260–1328) when Eckhart lived; he and his colleagues were currently unearthing even older religious sites, churches and monasteries throughout south and central Germany along the Rheine. This was another synchronicity surrounding my fascination with Eckhart that awakened my mind.

Dream #4

On August 14, 1981, I had another dream about Eckhart that shows how deeply my interest had gone by the time I was getting ready to finish my last four quarters at UCSC.

> *I find myself in a countryside working on a beautiful painting, which I'm reproducing after the likeness of a portrait that was apparently painted in the thirteenth century by Meister Eckhart. I paint in trees, grass, and earth by blending colors that reflects their natural hues in the portrait, while adding some of the attributes that reflect their accompanying forms of superabundant light. I notice that I've omitted some of the characteristics of*

*the sky, so I blend in some Mediterranean blue as I fill
in the firmament. As I stare at the Eckhart portrait from
which I am working in my reproduction, I'm amazed
at Eckhart's ability in centuries past to represent the
pantheistic God in his sermons.*

In amplifying the meaning of the dream it is important to note that
Everson had given me a copy of Ananda K. Coomaraswamy's book *The
Transformation of Nature in Art,* which contains an important chapter
on "Meister Eckhart's View of Art."

So, I dreamt that I was painting a reproduction of that beautiful
landscape portrait by Eckhart, which suggests that Eckhart's sermons
were a true transformation of nature through art. As a Jungian, this
means a portrait of instinct, the instinct-image of the preacher and
theologian who stays true to the truths that arise from their own
autochthonous ground. Eckhart was not an imitation of Albert or
Aquinas; he went beyond his masters into a field of unmistakable
originality.

I knew at the time of the dream that Eckhart could help me
understand the problem of theology from an aesthetic point of view,
and that's why I was painting a reproduction of his landscape portrait.
In a way that seemed to be mysteriously predestined, my three decades
of wrestling with the problem of how to write a book on Eckhart
from a Jungian point of view that could speak to contemporary
people would be worked out in time through many friendships. All
of these developments were mysteriously foreseen in advance by my
unconscious.[693]

Intellectual friendships reflecting natural processes in the world
and psyche may arise from specific archetypes within the various
vocational fields when they are viewed from within and without. The
particular archetype I had been called to work in at UCSC was the
ongoing dialogical field between psychology and religion. Jung, who
had turned Everson on to Eckhart while he was in the Dominican

Order in 1955, referred to such synchronicities as "sporadic." The Eckhart dream-portrait revealed the importance of adding in some deep Mediterranean blue, which represents the ultraviolet spectrum of the collective psyche, or the superconscious. This is the level of the psyche from which Eckhart preached in Strasbourg and Cologne. The scene took place somewhere in Germany, not France.

In the writing of this book, I have relied on several translations of Eckhart to follow my own inner guidance toward the true Eckhart I have been inspired to paint for you. I feel this is the best way to provide you with a poet's view of what Eckhart means to me, as an artist and natural scientist, for postmodernity. Therefore, I have had to hold my own on such issues of pantheism and panentheism so as not to make Christ the center of everything. Eckhart and Jung both stressed the third person of the blessed Trinity over Jesus, and this advance makes room for the reader to find her own Self-path and not have to make Christ the center of her spirituality. Rather, my hope is that she will paint in the artistic lines in Eckhart's sermons that speak to her most and spark her vocational interests. We all have an Eckhart within us because he is an archetype in the collective psyche now that speaks to artists and scientists and Christians alike. The future of Christianity is, according to Eckhart and Jung, beyond the teachings of Jesus. It is not imitation, but approximation to his archetype that matters most, and we each have our own Self-path to follow.

My calling has been to write a Jungian interpretation of what Eckhart meant to Jung, what he means to me, and what his theology of the Self and God means to the world, and to the hopeful evolution of Christianity, beyond its current state of patriarchic bias. The most important take away from my dream is that it can hopefully help the reader become more trans-dual in her thinking. Sometimes I don't understand theologians and I have read many of the best books on Eckhart. Every time I get confused, I return to the Meister, and I feel free and liberated and at peace again. *I am an Eckhartian in mind and heart.* I have never known any other Christian teacher, except Everson, who spoke to me with such depth of feeling and with such power to evoke the numinous in me. Even the New Testament did not awaken me in the same way Eckhart has, and for this, I am eternally grateful to him. To Matthew Fox also, of course, since he helped me in my career as writer and celebrated Everson at his centennial at UCSC and invited me to join him for a teach-in at our beloved Preacher's Church in Erfurt.

What theologians typically do not understand so well is the reality of dreams. *Christ left us the Paraclete so that we can become who we are,* not imitations of Jesus, but imitations of the Self, the basic blueprint out of which we are resurrected into an entirely new life in our own way. Analysis is not a replacement for the Church because there is an *inner Church, or Mosque, or Synagogue,* inside each person, and it has no denominations. It needs no council in Rome. This is Spiritual Democracy American style. There is no God-image at its center other than "Nature's God." That was the portrait of Eckhart that I was painting.

Vocational dreams can appear when a person is undergoing the process of individuation. They can appear in the form of daydreams, such as happened to Eckhart, or through visions that confirm through their teleological intentions a future career in the world that they may not be able to see clearly at the time. We need patience to allow dreams to work their magic on us in the unconscious. My point is that we are meant to serve our specific vocations, and in so doing, we are in service not only to God, but to a Nature that is transhuman and primordial. Everything in Eckhart's sermons revolve around the present moment in time when we are capable of rising above our suffering through inward meditations and responding to our calling in the Now. Here is Eckhart speaking:

> God is in this power in the eternal Now. If a man's spirit were always united with God in this power, he would not age. For the Now in which God made the first man

343

and the Now in which the last man shall cease to be,
and the Now I speak in, all are the same in God and
there is but one Now... Therefore nothing new comes to
him from future things nor any accident, for he dwells
in the Now, ever new and without intermission ... all
the future and the past are there in one Now. That we
may attain to this Now, so help us God. Amen.[694]

What might such a prayer in the Now lead to psychologically and
spiritually in the human soul, if the Divine were to answer problems of
our sufferings today? What kind of an experience might this kind of
silent prayer lead to? My hope is that this book will spark a vocational
dream to give your life greater significance.

I define a calling dream as a *dream of vocation*, a dream, whether
fantasy thinking, vision, a nocturnal dream, or active imagination that
comes naturally or supernaturally from the very core and heart of one's
humanness, as a *call to sacred action*. We all have the potential to give
birth to vocation, whether in mathematics, computer science, music,
psychology, or art. Dreams like the one that came to Eckhart of the
little naked boy who was a King can lead the way to the fulfillment of
your destiny-pattern, if you can be quiet enough to listen to what the
Self wants from you in any given moment. In the *Now*, everything is
pregnant with meaning and possibility, and everything is contained in a
secret order, in one space-time continuum where unity resides. Eckhart's
method for healing was and continues to be to teach us *how* to give birth.
In Sermon 72, Eckhart opened by quoting Hosea 14:5: "All that are sick
I shall heal, and willingly love them."[695] This was the essential message
of Eckhart as a shaman-teacher, a preacher of the Word.

All vocations that come from the Word are sacred, according to
Eckhart. He tells us that we have only to listen to the Word in the
highest powers of the soul (will and intellect) to discover the vocation
to which we are each most strongly called by God. We are each given
a vocation with which to respond to the fullest innermost call of life,

each path leading to the same goal, namely Self-realization. Unlike Christian mystics who were wedded to passive contemplation as the gateway to God, Eckhart stressed a much more active role for the aspiring spiritual seeker—through our creative encounter with the world, God becomes recollected vocationally. In other words, the inner images and Word awakened in contemplation point to God's continual birthing through human actions from the divine Nothing, out of which the whole Universe came into being. It is not enough to experience inner images in passivity alone; *one must also act upon them vocationally.*

God's image is everywhere in the Universe. This was Eckhart's main point. We have a dependency on Nature's God. Eckhart taught us all to become Mothers of God and give birth to Wisdom: "If you would find the newborn king, you must outstrip and abandon all else that you might find. That we may outstrip and cast behind us all things unpleasing to the newborn king, may he help us who became a human child in order that we might become the children of God."[696]

Dream #5

I had another dream about Eckhart on October 18, 1981, that provided a prototype for the way this current book has taken shape over the years.

> *I find myself with Bill Everson outside the entrance of a large library. He is holding seven bound volumes of contemporary writings on Eckhart, which have all been written from a Jungian perspective. Bill is overwhelmed by the significance of what he has created, and he knows of its inherent value for the world. I look closely at the seventh volume, which is bound in pigskin (presumably bound by hand by Everson himself, who was a master*

> *craftsman, a printer, and a pantheist). On the front page*
> *of volume seven, I see a painting of a Cross with five*
> *different symbols that are painted on the vertical pillar.*
> *The central symbol on the vertical axis is a painting of*
> *the Feminine in the very center of the cross arms.*

In his monograph on *Synchronicity,* Jung wrote that "number" is "the predestined instrument for creating order, or for apprehending an already existing, but still unknown, regular arrangement or 'orderedness.' It may well be the most primitive element of order in the human mind."[697] Moreover, Eckhart wrote: "A natural order is one in which the highest point of what is inferior touches the lowest point of its superior."[698]

In this fifth dream, the seven volumes of contemporary Jungian writings on Eckhart were all lined in animal skin (pigskin[699] to be precise). The seven volumes represent many volumes I would have to write before I could edit it down to a more readable size that my collogues might want to read. Originally, it was an 800-page opus magnum. Thanks to my editor's gentle and wise suggestion, I shortened it.

The cross at the center of the portrait on volume seven was the primary symbol, and it was not Christ at the nuclear point where the vertical and horizontal crossbeams touched and kissed but the *feminine.* It was not Mary, the Blessed Virgin Mother, but my intuition tells me it was Sophia. This is significant because it suggests that the last volume contains the mystery of the evolution of Christianity to the point where we are now, and it was my inner Everson who wrote it, not my dream-ego. The future of Christianity will be focused on the incarnation of the feminine into the soul of collective humanity, and the seventh volume of a Jungian work on Eckhart will provide an important answer to the problems of the church and its theologies that have been out of touch Nature's God, and "God's nature," to quote Eckhart again.

Dream # 6

I had the following dream on April 17, 1999:

I find myself with a large group of people. We are standing by a large river that runs along a big moat. The ocean is nearby, and it raises up the mouth of the river at high tide. I am with a woman in particular who I seem to be partnered with. She is a dark-haired woman with an olive complexion. As we are standing together, on the side of the river mouth, the sea starts to swell with running water that rushes up the tributary, so that the road is suddenly flooded, and the people are all driven up the riverbank to seek out the higher ground. I am among a crowd of people who make for safety, while some others are endangered by the onrushing flood ...

All disaster breaks loose and I find myself in a line with many other people, who are getting food for themselves. They are prepared for the long journey home to where they live. Our cars have all been stranded ... Then, I walk alone with my female partner ... I take her on a long journey, which leads us through the mud. We end up all covered with black-earth, which soils our clothing. I hear the inner voice tell me that I need to "listen and follow the Feminine." We end up taking a cable car through Highlands. We are hungry and dirty and tired, but we climb on board with some people and head off to a nearby city.

When we get out, we are greeted by a man who escorts us to a grassy-green meadow. The man tells me he is going to introduce me to my Brother (not my personal brother but my transpersonal "Brother" in a Dominican sense). A man approaches us wearing old

347

European garb with a long, oval-shaped stone in his hand that is shining with emerald-green hues. He looks a little like a leprechaun, but stands a bit taller, and has an earth-red beard and a hat that matches his brown earth-toned trousers. I suddenly feel a numinous rush come over me, as I look at the Greenstone, which he points at my woman partner. He flashes it suddenly with a beam of green light that emanates brightness and illuminates her. I am stunned to see the black dirt fall miraculously from her body and her shoes and clothes and her hair. She is left immaculate as a Spring morning. Then, he points the stone at me and he says, "I bless you in in the name of the Holy Ghost." I believe he says the Father and the Son too: "I bless you in the name of Christ." When the emerald-green light of the oval stone hits me with its beams of green glory, I'm left stunned with ecstasy, and I look at my clothes to see that they too have all been purged of the awful blackness. Tears began to well up from my eyes. He leaves us with some ancient oriental Japanese cooking irons, which have some Japanese writing on them and Japanese designs. We are blessed with some wonderful food, which has been cooked for us and which we gladly eat. I am nourished by the food and I savor it. Then I take the cooking irons with us to her home. I look again into her eyes, as I know that I am to marry her. I anticipate meeting her parents. Then I am awakened by a numinous feeling coming over me from the clean clear light of the translucent green stone. Upon awakening the feeling is still with me, as are the uprush of tears to soothe my ailing sinus and aching lungs.

"'Those who are well,' says our Lord, 'have no need of medicine' (Luke 5:31). The physician is there to heal the sick."[700] Whoever the inner Brother was, he reminded me of Eckhart. I felt healed by him. My bronchitis soon dissolved after this dream. I felt like I had been transmitted a medicine that was far better than anything Western medicine could have offered me: a direct infusion of the Holy Spirit. These kinds of things have happened to me more often than I can count. What these dreams show in the simplest of terms is the way in which Eckhart's healing influence continued to live inside of me over the course of several decades. The green stone is a symbol for the awakening of the Holy Spirit. As Jung wrote in a letter shortly after his illness in 1945:

> It always seemed to me as if the real milestones were certain symbolic events characterized by a strong emotional tone. You are quite right, the main interest in my work is not concerned with the treatment of neuroses but rather with the approach to the numinous. But the fact is that the approach to the numinous is the real therapy and inasmuch as you attain to the numinous experiences you are released from the curse of pathology. Even the very disease takes on a numinous character.[701]

Three months later the healing continued, and I had another dream.

Dream # 7

June 17, 1999

I find myself in a spacious park of some kind. I will be camping outside, with Danielle and Immanuel. We want to move from the part of the park we are now in to another part where houses are for sale, and I want to buy one of them. We move our car to another area near the center of the park. There is a beautiful peacock calling loudly in the center of the park, like the ones up the hill from where I live in Orinda, above Grizzly Stables. They make splendid calling sounds. I am concerned that it will keep me up at night, but I go toward the center anyway.

In the epicenter I see Barbara Williams from Rainbow Psychotherapy Associates. She is standing around the fountain, telling a group of people that she is collecting donations for the cake and supplies she has purchased for the celebration party. Many people from around the world have come to this sacred cistern where swamis and religious followers are dipping their hands into the holy fountain and where the waters of Christ are flowing into everlasting life (John 4:14). I kneel and put my hands in the fountain, up to my arms, and I think suddenly of Meister Eckhart. I cannot take my hands out of the water. It is as if they are fixed in my place of worship. I look at the men from the East, from India, next to me. They too seem to be transfixed by the waters of the Holy Spirit. It is mesmerizing. I know that when I take my arms out of the water, I will be able to use them for healing: the laying on of hands. I will be blessed and be a bestower of blessings on my fellows. I feel humbled by this. This is the water Christ spoke of in the New Testament that is symbolic of the Holy Spirit (John 7:39). I hear the Peacock let out a loud cry at the center of the park near the water-source, and I know that it is the call of Christ. I feel somehow indebted to Barbara, and I think of the property that I wish to buy, on the boarder of this secluded and blessed region in Nature.

As Eckhart said while meditating on this passage in John: "The Holy Ghost wells up in us and flows from us. That is what our lord, God's Son in the Godhead, meant by saying, 'Whoever drinks from the water that I give, in him a fountain of water shall arise, springing up into everlasting life'" (John 4:14). And St. John says he was speaking of the Holy Ghost (John 7:39)."[702]

Or, as Jung wrote, "It is not in the least astonishing that numinous experiences should occur in the course of psychological treatment and that they may even be expected with some regularity."[703] The peacock occupies the highest place in alchemy as a symbol for the *cauda pavonis*, or the Holy Ghost.[704] *I kneel to the ground and put my hands in the fountain, up to my arms, and I think suddenly of Meister Eckhart!*

Dream # 8

I will now reveal why I have been so drawn to Meister Eckhart for these past forty-four years and what set me off on my Self-path as the author of this book at UCSC. I trust that my readers may feel similarly as I do that *experience is our best teacher.* Eleven years after I finished my thesis on Eckhart, I had the following dream on August 27, 1993.

> *I find myself by the kitchen cabinet in my home in Orinda. I put a bottle of green liquor up on the shelf after drinking some. Then, I fall down to the floor and slip into the abyss. My body becomes paralyzed. I cannot move at all. My whole psyche is suddenly filled with the incredible awe of profound darkness while my body is immobile. I then get up and try to make it to my bed, as I know I'm going back through an age regression in time to my first experiences of encounter with the unconscious in childhood at the age of four. It is my*

childhood dream again, the recurring dream of the abyss
I had as a boy, from four to seven years of age.

As I make my way back to my bedroom, I am
suddenly hit by the throng of 1000 voices. A man's voice
comes through clearly out of the throng ... I struggle
to wake myself up in order to write this all down so I
do not lose it. I realize that I have discovered what the
nuclear symbol of my childhood was for me at the age
of four, before I could understand what was happening
to me: the void, the abyss, profound darkness, mystery,
eternal life. The numen (the Latin word for nod or what
Rudolph Otto and Jung called the "numinous") pierces
through my psyche with feelings of tremendous awe.
When I awaken, I realize this is why I wrote my thesis
in 1982 on Eckhart.

The flask of green German liquor in the kitchen cabinet was symbolic of a trance-inducing medicine from my German side of the family, a history I was completely unaware of until I looked the green German liquor up on Google. My father used to drink various types of liquor, and he had a bar built into our old home in Walnut Creek. I remember tasting different liquors, including from the green flask during my early adolescence. I used to sneak into the walk-in bar. There was also a silver Knights helmet inside, with eight shot glasses in a red velvet interior. The unconscious works in mysterious ways. I could not possibly have remembered what the green liquor bottle was until I searched for it online. The memory was deeply lodged in my subconscious. But somehow it had formed an imprint that stayed with me on an intuitive level.

I was flabbergasted to find the bottle on the Internet. It was a flagon of *Jägermeister*. I recognized the liquor bottle immediately, because of the glowing Christian cross between and just above the antlers of the stag on the front label. *Jägermeister* means in German "Master of the hunt." But the word *Meister* jumped out at me immediately. At Santa Cruz, I had written my senior thesis on Eckhart from a Jungian perspective. One of the first things that drew me to study him was his references to the Ground of the Soul, as a bottomless abyss, a "ground that is groundless."[705] A *groundless Ground* or *Grund* and *Abgrund* (abyss). The Dominican's theology came directly to mind. The image of the cross above the stag's antlers was a historical symbol from the visions of two Christian patron saints of the hunt: Saint Hubertus and Saint Eustace. Both converted to Christianity after they saw a vision of a cross above the antlers of a stag.

I am sure I tasted that liquor in my adolescence, probably around the age of fourteen, my freshman year of high school. I was fascinated to find out on Wikipedia that *Jägermeister* has fifty-six herbs and spices in it. They include licorice, anise, poppy seeds, saffron, ginger, juniper berries, and ginseng. *Jägermeister* has a signature green bottle and is 70 US proof. Thus, imbibing some of this medicinal liquor had a trance-inducing effect on my dream-ego, and falling to the floor, I fell into the abyss again and was stupefied. Slipping into the abyss after sipping the liquor was like entering into a state of Nothingness, which I knew from my recurrent dreams as a four-to-seven-year-old boy, and also later from my reading of Eckhart.

The profound darkness of the abyss filled me with incredible awe, a reverential experience of fear and wonder over the immensity of the Infinite that has no bottom and no top. Its vastness is unfathomable. After I returned to my right senses, I then made my way half-consciously back to my bedroom. At that point, I knew was going through an age regression, to my first conscious experiences of the objective psyche in childhood. My father was a subject in post-doc hypnosis experiments at Stanford University, and he would sometimes ask me to count backward and then let him know on a scale of 1–10 how deep I was in a hypnotic trance. I used to tell him 7. But I did that to please him. I was never that deep. I always retained a sense of semiconsciousness in the hypnotic sessions, which occurred perhaps four times or so, on my bed. He used a little flickering light to put me under, but I never lost full control, whereas in my dream, I was completely immobile and truly at a 10.

I was then suddenly hit by a throng of 1000 voices from my unconscious. A man's voice said something out of the multiplicity of voices; he asked me a simple question about my dissertation. I then struggled in the dream to wake myself up to write down my experiences, so I would not lose them because they seemed so significant to the hypothesis I was currently working on at that time, most importantly, my hypothesis of the *nuclear symbol*. In my half-wakeful state, while still dreaming, I realized that I had discovered what the nuclear symbol was for me in my childhood: the void, the abyss, darkness, eternal life. These are all synonyms for the abyss or Ground in Eckhart's works. The numen (or numinous feelings) passed through me again with the one powerful emotion of awe.

When I awoke, in the semiconscious dream state, I knew from the throng of voices arising from the abyss why I was so drawn to Eckhart as my spiritual father and ancestor. I knew that the abyss was equivalent with the Ground, a deeper level of the collective unconscious beyond the archetypes, and it could be accessed by drinking some of the *spiritus* from the German liquor carafe or *Jägermeister*. Thus, this mind-altering symbolic "medicine" was the green German *Spiritus* of Meister Eckhart, the Holy Spirit that had filled me with awe and wonder, over the immensity of the Ground from which all of the voices of vocation sound from the deep.

Thus, at its *psychoid* depth I realized through direct inner experience that the nuclear symbol is simply imageless, formless, without any clear representational names, images, or forms. It is an *experience* of abysmal darkness within darkness, a void, the holy *emotion of awe*. When we are in the abyss we are stunned with wonder, mystery, awesomeness, tremendousness over the miracle of our small existence on the planet, and the universal miracle of existence in an objective sense throughout the entire Cosmos, a trans-dual reality we can only offer prayers to and celebrate for the fact that we are even here, in the Now. In every precious moment we are inhabiting our breathing selves in our human bodies.

An important additional piece of information in my interpretation of this dream is that I never drank liquor at this time in my life, only an occasional glass of red wine, or a glass of Champagne. This dream was, therefore, synchronistic, since the Ground of vocational dreams I had been researching, at UCSC, John F. Kennedy University, and Lincoln Child Center, was something that reveled itself spontaneously to me in a stunning metaphor when the throng of 1000 voices sounded from the infinite abyss. I saw intuitively then that the calling to vocation comes not from a specific archetype of activity in the psyche, but as One Voice chosen out of a plurality of many voices. I believe this Ground upon which I was lying in my dream, rapt in trance, was the shamanistic foundation out of which the best sermons had been preached. I was in California dreaming, of course, but it is the same Universal Ground.

APPENDIX I

Seven Sermons to the Paraclete

I wrote these prose poems while I working as a Jungian psychotherapist and marriage and family therapist at the California Counseling Institute (CCI) of San Francisco in 2000. At the time, I was invited to give a talk on Eckhart at St. James Church, and I secretly wrote these sermons out in my journal as I was waiting to deliver my talk. Some of the patients at CCI were in mixed marriages, such as a Buddhist man married to a Catholic woman, or a Muslim woman to a Quaker man, or Hindu woman to a Jewish woman. It was a very ecumenical mix of people and sexual orientations. Therefore, the seven sermons are in a sense my answer to the problem of Christianity as a creed without any bridge-building from the Holy Spirit to assist us as psychotherapists with the healing of divisions between different religious faiths. The Seven Sermons are my synthesis of Eckhart and Jung's teachings about the Paraclete, but I added an incarnating factor that is not only Christocentric but also Goddess-Centric, East or West, since the Holy Spirit has no gender. The metaphors are all clearly Christian, but they are all meant to speak to many faiths and genders in a trans-dualistic and pluralistic way.

Sermon 1

Let go! Let God act through you. Let the Word be born a second time. There is a calling waiting to become incarnate in the native recesses of your soul. Some call it "right livelihood," some call it "sacred work," others call it "vocation." Let go of your rational will and intellect. Let God act through you. There is no incarnation more divine than Yourself. Let Jesus die in your soul, so that new images of the Self can become incarnate in the eternal Now of the moment. Let go! Let go of Christ's teachings, so that you may become the new spiritual counselors and teachers of women and men. When the foundation of your personality lights up with Divine Energy, you will be filled with a power so fully you will declare God in all of your works.

Sermon 2

When I pick up my pen and write, I become a spiritual man-woman of Wisdom whose identity as *homo religiosis* has become transformational. When I enter my own Ground, I'm blessed with the spirit of enlightenment in the West out of the place of the primal eruption. I become a carrier of the new teachings of the Paraclete. I become a bearer of the message of God. If the Son does not go away, if you do not allow Jesus to die in your soul, then how can the Paraclete come to you? You will remain barren and without child, without the Self. He went away so that God could be born in you, so that God could grow and mature into a new man and new woman, and new images of the Self could flourish and prosper in you. We were each born to be vocalizers of God, not followers of Jesus, or Eckhart, or Jung, but followers of the Self and the Self only.

Sermon 3

Only when Jesus has died in us can the New Religion begin. There is no other way to the Resurrection of the World. (The Resurrection of the World is the incarnation of the Self in all people). Listen again: if Jesus does not go away, if you do not allow Jesus to be crucified and resurrected into God, how can the Paraclete come to you? If God and the Son do not pass into Nothingness, then how can the Self come to you? It was given to each of us to discover the secret of personality as the new way, the new incarnation of God, the new Light; not in Jesus, or Eckhart, or Jung, but in you, reader, in the very ground and foundation of your soul, the place of your Divine Birth.

Only when the images of God you have projected onto the great men and women, the saints, have passed away into the inner kingdom, only when they have died, and been buried in the collective soil of the world's civilizations, can the Paraclete come to us in a new image. The divinization of Jesus was not the final state; the image of the personality, or the Holy Spirit is. The Paraclete is the divinizing principle of the personality in all people. The Paraclete will make itself known to you through what is new. The spirit of the new world will become incarnate in new images of the Self in all people.

Sermon 4

Make yourselves barren and void of all fugitive images, and learn to serve the new image of the personality in all your works. What is foreign is what has come to you from the outside, not from within your foundation. At the foundation of all religions is the emotional-image of Yourself. This is the root of the New Religion. Listen again: Only when Jesus and Eckhart and Jung have died in you, only when they have departed from historical time, to become eternal, can you become bearers of the Self in the eternal now of the moment. It matters most to God that you let go and make room for the Divine Birth of the Paraclete in Yourself. Eckhart was the first thinker in the West to have lain in the childbed with the new image. Jung completed the process, through his incarnation of the Self's divinity. But we are the ones who must lead the way to the incarnation of the Paraclete in the many.

Sermon 5

I lay in the childbed at the center of the world and give birth to the Self. All of my learning, all of my acquired knowledge falls away and a new Wisdom born of experience shines through. We are heading for a new cosmic order of correspondences between the many vocational fields. Something is emerging from the center of them all: a new image of the Self-as-World-Spirit is emerging. Through each center, through each carrier of consciousness, new symbols of the Self are being born. From the center of each person: behold the mystery of the Self! From the spiritual center of all nations: behold the divinization of personhood! Penetrate the secret of your personality and arrive at the New Birth.

I lay in the childbed and give birth to new images of the Divine, new images of the Self in all people. Make room for the Divine Birth. Hasten to that place of poverty and detachment and emptiness in yourself where the Divine Birth can happen in You. If the Birth of the Self does not also take place in you, God cannot know himself.

Sermon 6

What does it mean that Christ left this earth, that he died to his life, that he went away to the Heavenly Kingdom? What did it mean when he said the Paraclete would follow after him? Why did the Church fathers misinterpret his teachings to humanity? Why did Athanasius demand the burning of the "secret books" in Egypt in 367

CE? Because Jesus urged his disciples to go *beyond* him. I do not trust the men in the black robes. I do not believe in the teachings of the Church about the Son of God as an incarnation of Love. I do not have faith in the teachings of Irenaeus, Bishop of Lyons, about the man who died on the Cross and went away in the flesh. For none of this corresponds to my experience of the Paraclete within.

How can I believe in a good God only? How can I have faith in a God of Love and not also *experience* a vision of evil? For God-consciousness to exist, good and evil must stand side by side. Experiences of good and evil alone can lead me to truth. I have achieved a transcendence of the opposites through the writing of this book: God is Good and God is Evil.

My God is not the God they speak of in the churches. I have studied the great religions of the world, Hinduism, Buddhism, Taoism, Judaism, Christianity, Islam, and in all of these religions, I have seen the One. People are all looking for the new ideas, new inspiration, new religion. The more I look into the source of these matters, the more I see: religion is in the methods and techniques by which the teachers of humankind arrived at truth, not in the teachings.

The techniques and methods of the spiritual teachers of humankind have all proclaimed the same essential truth: It is not the goal, but the *way* that offers the most direct route for the people to an experience of the Self. "Tell me your Way to God, and I will tell you mine." That is what the most *democratic* of religions ultimately has to say. Study the methods and techniques, the musings and metaphors of the prophets, and then you have got it. At the root of all religious systems are the methods and techniques of the Sacred.

Sermon 7

The calling to vocation is the way to truth. Follow the calling within and without. Vocations are the ultimate gateways to God. That is what Jesus taught. That is what Eckhart taught. That is what Jung taught: *vocare*. The way to truth rests in one's religious calling, in the spiritual summons from the Divine. If one is true to one's vocation, one embarks upon the way; one prepares the ground for a realization of one's own unique form of devotion to God. Whatever my own particular way to God is, I know I am only a vessel for a new incarnation of the Divine forms, and that when I make myself entirely empty—bare of all egohood—the Self will most certainly shine through.

What I've written here is what the world may want to know for the future. At present, I cannot expect these truths to be accessible to the average person, but I'm certain that in the future, if translators come who can distill my teachings in this book into a method, Eckhart's, Jung's, and my techniques will be of service to others.

Amen.

APPENDIX II

List of Abbreviations Used in Bibliography and Endnotes

AC	Von Franz, Marie-Louise. *Aurora Consurgens.* Ashville, NC: Chiron Publications, 1974.
B	Fox, Matthew. *Breakthrough: Meister Eckhart's Creation Spirituality in New Translation.* New York: Image, 1980.
CW	Jung, C.G. *The Collected Works of C. G. Jung.* 21 vols. Edited by William McGuire. Translated by R. F. C. Hull. Princeton: Princeton University Press, 1953–1984.
DM	Harrington, Joel F. *Dangerous Mystic: Meister Eckhart's Path to the God Within* New York: Penguin, 2018.
EFP	Evans, C. de B. *Meister Eckhart by Franz Pfeiffer.* 2 vols. London: Watkins, 1924, 1931.
EGL	Hick, John. *Evil and the God of Love.* New York: Palgrave McMillan, 1966.
ES	Colledge, Edmund and McGinn, Bernard, trans. *Meister Eckhart: The Essential Sermons, Commentaries, Treatises, and Defense.* Mahwah, NJ: Paulist Press, 1981.
Letters	Jung, C. G., *C. G. Jung Letters.* 2 vols. Edited by Gerhard Adler. Princeton: Princeton University Press.

MDR	Jung, C. G., *Memories, Dreams, Reflections.* Recorded and edited by Aniela Jaffé. Translated by Richard and Clara Winston. New York: Vintage Books, 1961.
PYM	Jung, C. G. *Psychology of Yoga and Meditation.* Princeton: Princeton University Press, 2020.
Q	Quint, Josef. *Deutsche Predigten und Traktate.* München, Germany: Carl Hanser Verlag, 1963.
RB	Jung, C. G. *The Red Book.* Edited with an Introduction by Sonu Shamdasani. New York: W. W. Norton & Co., 2009.
TP	McGinn, B. and Tobin, Frank. *Meister Eckhart: Teacher and Preacher.* Mahwah, NJ: Paulist Press, 1986.
W	Walsche, Maurice O'C. *The Complete Mystical Works of Meister Eckhart.* New York: Herder & Herder, 2009.

BIBLIOGRAPHY

Aquinas, Thomas, St. *Introduction to St. Thomas Aquinas*. New York: Random House, 1945.

Bair, Deidre. *Jung: A Biography*. New York: Little, Brown and Company, 2003.

Bartlett, Lee. *William Everson: The Life of Brother Antoninus*. New York: New Directions, 1988.

Blakney, Raymond B. *Meister Eckhart: A Modern Translation*. New York: Harper and Row, 1941.

Buber, Martin. *Eclipse of God: Studies in the Relation Between Religion and Philosophy*. Atlantic Highlands, NJ: Humanities Press International, 1988.

————. "Hope for this Hour." In *Pointing the Way: Collected Essays*. London: Routledge, 1957.

————. *I and Thou*. New Translation by Walter Kaufmann. Edinburgh: T & T Clark. First published in German, 1923, 1970.

————. "The Question to the Single One." In *Between Man and Man*, 40–82. Boston Beacon Press, 1955.

————. "Plato and Isaiah." In *Israel and the World. Essays in a Time of Crisis*. New York: Schocken Books, 1963.

Buber, M. "Uber Jakob Böhme." *Wiener Rundschau* V, no. 12 (June 15, 1901), 251–253.

Capps, Walter. *Silent Fire: An Invitation to Western Mysticism*. New York: Harper Collins, 1978.

Chardin, Teilhard de. *The Hymn of the Universe*. New York: Harper & Row, 1965.

Clark, James M. *Meister Eckhart: An Introduction to the Study of His Works with an Anthology of His Sermons*. Edinburgh: Nelson, 1957.

Clark, James, and John Skinner. *Meister Eckhart: Selected Treatises and Sermons: Translated from German and Latin, with an Introduction and Notes*. London: Farber & Farber, Ltd, 1953.

Colledge, Edmund, and Bernard McGinn. *Meister Eckhart: The Essential Sermons, Commentaries, Treatises, and Defense*. Mahwah, NJ: Paulist Press, 1981.

Corbett, Lionel. *The Religious Function of the Psyche*. London: Brunner-Routledge, 2004.

Dourley, John. *On Behalf of the Mystical Fool: Jung on the Religious Situation*. London: Routledge, 2010.

———. *A Strategy for a Loss of Faith: Jung's Proposal*. Toronto, Canada: Inner City Books, 1992.

Edinger, Edward. *The Creation of Consciousness: Jung's Myth for Modern Man*. Toronto, Canada: Inner City Books, 1984.

———. *Ego and Archetype: Individuation and the Religious Function of the Psyche*. New York: Penguin, 1972.

———. *The Creation of Consciousness: Jung's Myth for Modern Man*. Toronto, Canada: Inner City Books, 1984,

Evans, C. de B, trans. *Meister Eckhart by Franz Pfeiffer*. 2 vols. London: Watkins, 1924, 1931.

Everson, William. *Birth of a Poet: The Santa Cruz Meditations*. Santa Barbara: Black Sparrow, 1982.

———. *The Veritable Years: 1949-1966.* In Volume 2 of *The Collected Poems.* Santa Rosa: Black Sparrow Press, 1998.

Fox, Matthew. *Breakthrough: Meister Eckhart's Creation Spirituality in New Translation.* New York: Image, 1980.

———. *The Coming of the Cosmic Christ.* San Francisco: Harper & Row, 1988.

———. *Meister Eckhart: A Mystic-Warrior for our Times.* Novato, California: New World Library, 2014.

———. "Meister Eckhart's Spiritual Journey." In *Western Spirituality,* edited by Matthew Fox (217–218). Notre Dame, IN: Fides/ Claretian, 1979.

———. "William Everson: Nature Mystic and Poet Prophet." *Creation* 5, no.3 (1989): 10–14.

Friedman, Maurice S. *Martin Buber: The Life of Dialogue.* London: Routledge, 2003.

Hammarskjöld, Dag. *Markings.* New York: Alfred A. Knopf, 1974.

Harrington, Joel F. *Dangerous Mystic: Meister Eckhart's Path to the God Within.* New York: Penguin, 2018.

Henderson, Joseph, and Maude Oakes. *The Wisdom of the Serpent: The Myths of Death, Rebirth, and Resurrection.* Princeton, NJ: Princeton University Press, 1990.

Herrmann, Steven. "C. G. Jung and Teilhard de Chardin: Peacemakers in an Age of Spiritual Democracy." In *Pierre Teilhard de Chardin and Carl Gustav Jung Side by Side,* edited by Fred Gustafson. Cheyenne: Fisher King Press, 2015.

———. "Colloquy with the Inner Friend: Jung's Religious Feeling for Islam." *Jung Journal: Culture & Psyche* 3, no. 4 (2009): 123–132.

———. "Donald Kalsched: The Inner World of Trauma." *The San Francisco Jung Institute Library Journal* 19, no. 2 (2000): 51–71.

———. "Donald Sandner: The Shamanic Archetype." *The San Francisco Jung Institute Library Journal* 21, no. 2 (2002): 23–42.

———. *Emily Dickinson: A Medicine Woman for Our Times.* Cheyenne: Fisher King Press, 2018.

———. "The Hypothesis of Psychic Antibodies: The Fight of the Kingsnake and the Rattlesnake." *Jung Journal: Culture & Psyche* 14, no. 4 (2020): 1–15.

———. *Meister Eckhart on the Recollection of the Self: A Jungian Perspective.* PhD diss. University of California at Santa Cruz (UCSC), 1982.

———. "Murray Stein: The Transformative Image." *The San Francisco Jung Institute Library Journal* 17, no. 1 (1998): 17–39.

———. *Swami Vivekananda and C. G. Jung: Yoga in the West.* USA and Singapore: Strategic Books, 2022.

———. *Spiritual Democracy: The Wisdom of Early American Visionaries for the Journey Forward.* Foreword by John Beebe. Berkeley: North Atlantic Books, 2014.

———. "Teilhard de Chardin: Cosmic Christ." In *Encyclopedia of Psychology and Religion,* edited by David A. Leeming and Stanton Marlan. Boston, MA: Springer Publications, 2014. https://doi.org/10.1007/978-1-4614-6086-2_9128.

———. "Transpersonal Psychology and the Self-Field: An Overview of the Works of Jungian Analyst Erich Neumann." *Integral Transpersonal Journal* 11, no. 11 (September 2018): 57–77.

———. *Vocational Development in Childhood: A Four-Subject Case Study with SED Type Children.* Richmond, CA: Argosy University, 1994.

———. *Vocational Dreams and the Nuclear Self.* Master's thesis. John F. Kennedy University (JFKU), 1986.

———. *Walt Whitman: Shamanism, Spiritual Democracy, and the World Soul*. Durham: Eloquent Books, 2010.

———. *William Everson: The Shaman's Call, Expanded Edition*. New York: Eloquent Book, 2016.

———. *William James and C. G. Jung: Doorways to the Self*. Oberlin, OH: Analytical Psychology Press, 2020.

Hodes, Aubrey. *Encounter with Martin Buber*. London: Penguin Press, 1972.

Jaffé, Aniela. *From the Life and Work of C. G. Jung*. Einsiedeln, Switzerland: Daimon Verlag, 1989.

———. *Reflections on the Life and Dreams of C. G. Jung*. Einsiedeln, Switzerland: Daimon Verlag, 2023.

Jaffe, L. *Liberating the Heart: Spirituality and Jungian Psychology*. Toronto, Canada: Inner City Books, 1994.

James, Bruno. *The Letters of St. Bernard of Clairvaux*. London: Burns Oates, 1953.

James, William. *Writings 1902–1910*. New York: Library of America, 1988.

Jung, C. G. *C. G. Jung: Analytical Psychology. Notes of the Seminar Given in 1929*. Edited by William McGuire. Princeton: Princeton University Press, 1989.

———. *C. G. Jung Letters*. 2 vols. Edited by Gerhard Adler. Princeton: Princeton University Press, 1973, 1976.

———. *C. G. Jung Speaking: Interviews and Encounters*. Edited by William McGuire and R. F. C. Hull. Princeton: Princeton University Press, 1977.

———. *Children's Dreams: Notes from the Seminar Given in 1936–1940 by C. G. Jung*. Philemon Series. Princeton: Princeton University Press, 2008.

————. *The Collected Works of C. G. Jung.* 21 vols. Edited by William McGuire. Translated by R. F. C. Hull. Princeton: Princeton University Press, 1953–1984.

————. *Dream Analysis: Notes of the Seminar Given in 1928–1930 by C. G. Jung.* Edited by William McGuire. Princeton: Princeton University Press, 1984.

————. *The Freud / Jung Letters.* Princeton: Princeton University Press, 1974.

————. *Lectures Delivered at the ETH Zurich October 1938 to June 1939 and November 1940.* Vol. 6, *Psychology of Yoga and Meditation.* Edited and introduced by Martin Liebscher. Philemon Series. Princeton: Princeton University Press, 2020.

————. *Memories, Dreams, Reflections.* Recorded and edited by Aniela Jaffé. Translated by Richard and Clara Winston. New York: Vintage Books, 1961.

————. *Nietzsche's Zarathustra: Notes of the Seminar Given in 1934–1939 by C. G. Jung.* Edited by James L. Jarrett. 2 vols. Princeton: Princeton University Press, 1984.

————. *Psychological Commentary on Kundalini Yoga. Lectures One and Two—1932.* New York: Spring Publications, 1975.

————. *Psychological Commentary on Kundalini Yoga. Lectures Three and Four—1932.* New York: Spring Publications, 1976.

————. *The Red Book.* Edited with an introduction by Sonu Shamdasani. New York: W. W. Norton & Co., 2009.

————. *The Visions Seminars.* 2 vols. Zurich: Spring Publications, 1976.

Jung, C. G., and Wolfgang Pauli. *Atom and Archetype: The Pauli/Jung Letters, 1932–1958.* Edited by C. A. Meier. Princeton: Princeton University Press, 2001.

Kaplan, Aryeh. *Meditation and Kabbalah.* York Beach, ME: Samuel Weiser, 1989.

Kelly, C. *Meister Eckhart on Divine Knowledge.* New Haven, CT: Yale University Press, 1977.

Lammers, Ann C. *In God's Shadow: The Collaboration of Victor White and C. G. Jung.* Mahwah, NJ: Paulist Press, 1994.

Marin, L. "Can We Save True Dialogue in an Age of Mistrust? The Encounter of Dag Hammarkskjöld and Martin Buber." *Critical Currents,* no. 8. Uppsala: Dag Hammarkskjöld Foundation, 2010.

McGinn, B. and Frank Tobin. *Meister Eckhart: Teacher and Preacher.* Mahwah, NJ: Paulist Press, 1986.

Neumann, E. "Peace as the Symbol of life." In *The Essays of Erich Neumann.* Vol. 3, *The Place of Creation,* 264–319. Princeton: Princeton University Press, 1989.

Progoff, Ira. *Jung, Synchronicity, and Human Destiny.* New York: A Delta Book, 1973.

Quint, Josef. *Deutsche Predigten und Traktate.* München, Germany: Carl Hanser Verlag, 1963.

Rohr, Richard. *The Universal Christ.* New York: Convergent Books, 2019.

Rudin, Josef. "A Catholic View of Conscience." In *Conscience: Theological and Psychological Perspectives,* edited by Carl Ellis Nelson, 95–114. New York: Newman Press, 1973.

Sandner, Donald. *Navaho Symbols of Healing.* New York: Harcourt Brace Jovanovich, 1979.

Schmidt, Gilya G. "Martin Buber's Conception of the Relative and Absolute Life." *Shofar* 18, no. 2, 18 (Winter 2000).

Scholem, Gershom. *The Messianic Idea in Judaism.* New York: Schocken Books, 1995.

Shah-Kazemi, Reza. *Paths to Transcendence According to Shankara, Ibn Arabi, and Meister Eckhart.* Bloomington, IN: World Wisdom, 2006.

Shürmann, Reiner. O.P. *Meister Eckhart, Mystic and Philosopher.* Bloomington: Indiana University Press, 1978.

————. *Wandering Joy: Meister Eckhart's Mystical Philosophy.* Great Barrington, MA: Lindisfarne Books, 2001.

Stein, Murray. *Collected Works.* Vol. 6, *Analytical Psychology and Religion.* Ashville, NC: Chiron Publications, 2022.

Stephens, B. "The Martin Buber-Carl Jung Disputations: Protecting the Sacred in the Battle for the Boundaries of Analytical Psychology." *Journal of Analytical Psychology,* 46, no. 3 (2001): 455–491.

Taylor, Katherine W. "The Grail Quest and Its Meaning for Our Time." *Inward Light* XLIII, no. 95 (Fall/Winter, 1980).

Vivekananda, Swami. *The Complete Works of Swami Vivekananda.* 9 vols. Kolkata: Advaita Ashrama, 2004–2009.

Von Franz, Marie-Louise. *Aurora Consurgens.* Ashville, NC: Chiron Publications, 1974.

————. *Number and Time. Reflections Leading towards a Unification of Depth Psychology and Physics.* Evanston, IL: Northwestern University Press, 1974.

————. *Projection and Re-collection in Jungian Psychology.* La Salle, IL: Open Court, 1980.

Walsche, Maurice O'C, trans. *The Complete Mystical Works of Meister Eckhart.* New York: Herder & Herder, 2009.

White, Victor. *God and the Unconscious.* Dallas, TX: Spring Publications, 1952/1982.

————. *Soul and Psyche: An Inquiry into the Relationship of Psychotherapy and Religion.* New York: Harper & Brothers, 1960.

ENDNOTES

1   Lammers, *In God's Shadow*, 301.

2   Jung, *C.G. Jung Letters*, Vol. 2: page 138. Hereafter the *C. G. Jung Letters* will be referenced as *Letters*, volume number, and page number.

3   By *Eckhart archetype* I mean an historical deposit in the collective psyche of Germany. There are seven dimensions, or seven structural layers, that can be accessed through an historical regression back in time to this archetype, which can be activated by anyone who reads him deeply enough: preacher, counselor, confessor, teacher, theologian, mystic, and shaman.

4   Eckhart was highly influenced by the Beguine movement, a relatively large group of lay women, not Dominican or Franciscan nuns, but laity who flourished in Holland and Bavaria and who Eckhart encountered while preaching along the Rheine, especially in Strasbourg and Cologne. In *Psychology of the Unconscious* (*CW* 7), Jung quoted a passage from the Beguine Mechtild von Magdeburg (1212–1277). It seems right to me that in his earliest psychological attempts to formulate a hypothesis about the phenomenon of a *regressive reanimation of the father-and-mother imago* into an organized system of theological imagery through which the libido could be *introverted* and spiritualized he would choose a Beguine writer to illustrate his case study (*CW* 7, ¶¶132–135) before he would later turn to Eckhart, who learned a great deal from them while counseling them (Fox, *Breakthrough: Meister Eckhart's Creation Spirituality in New Translation*, 35). Hereafter references to *Breakthrough* will be referenced as *B*. References to Jung, *The Collected Works of C. G. Jung* will be given by volume and paragraph number.

5   McGinn, and Tobin, *Meister Eckhart: Teacher and Preacher*, 269. Hereafter references to *Meister Eckhart: Teacher and Preacher* will be referenced as *TP*.

6   Ibid.

7   Harrington, *Dangerous Mystic: Meister Eckhart's Path to God Within*, 71, 72. Hereafter references to Harrington's *Dangerous Mystic* will be referenced as *DM*, and page number.

8   When I was in the *Predigerkirsche* in Erfurt on the evening before the Summer Solstice in 2019, I got an opportunity to ascend the spiral staircase into the attic and it came to me later, while I was journaling by myself in my room that architecturally speaking the place is sanctified by the hand of God, as a sacred temenos for what Jung called the *transcendent function* in his 1921 essay on Eckhart: a "function, which is characterized by its absolute ascendancy over the will of the subject" (Jung, *Psychological Types*, CW 6: ¶412). Ascendency means the occupation of a position of dominant power or influence over something lower, such as the *ascendency of good over evil*. This is the meaning of the biblical word *ascend* in Eckhart's works: "The good is always on high—the higher, the better. What is Most High is the best. On the contrary, evil is always below, and the deeper, the lower, more inferior, and more subject, or subject to many things it is, the worse it is. This is evident from the treatise 'On the nature of the Superior,' and the argument is briefly thus. What is superior is always prior and consequently 'rich in itself'" (*TP*, 124).

9   Walsche, *The Complete Mystical Works of Meister Eckhart*, 589. Hereafter references to Walsche's *Complete Mystical Works of Meister Eckhart* will be referenced as *W* and page number.

10   *TP*, 249.

11   *Ein*, the One, or Oneness in Middle High German. Hereafter Middle High German will be referenced as MHG.

12   *W*, 310.

13   *TP*, 249.

14   *W*, 62.

15   *TP*, 248.

16   Eckhart wrote: "Justice in its perfection is Wisdom itself, or Wisdom's mother," *TP*, 161.

17   *TP*, 288.

18   *W*, 115.

19   *TP*, 237.

20   *W*, 298.

21   *W*, 400. Walsche defines this as the "ground" of God in footnote 9 right after this quote. But we must distinguish theologically and psychologically between the ground that can be known, and Ground that is without ground and forever unknowable.

22   *W*, 521–522.

23   *TP*, 252, 253.

24   Boethius taught in his *Arithmetic* that "all inequality may be reduced to equality." *TP*, 154.

25   As I see it the nuclear image of God in Eckhart's vernacular works is the archetype of the Messiah, the "Prince of Peace" (Isaiah 9:6).

26   Herrmann, "Donald Sandner: The Shamanic Archetype."

27   Dourley, *A Strategy for a Loss of Faith*, 101.

28   In Eckhart's vernacular sermons "'Jerusalem' denotes a 'vision of peace'... Let us pray to our Lord that we may be... established in this peace, which is himself" (*W*, 146, 147). Our Lord may be referred to cross-culturally as God, Christ, the Holy Spirit, or Allah. It is all One God. May this unitary peace be with us.

29   *Abegescheidenheit, gelâzenheit,* "detachment, or letting go" in Middle High German. I define *detachment* in this book in two ways: 1) as the right state of mind that is free from negative affect and emotion in a *relative* sense, yet is 2) awake to positive emotions, such as joy, happiness, bliss, and peace as states of being in an *Absolute* or transpersonal sense. Absolute detachment is above perfect humility and poverty as a matter of relative self-abnegation, but *ultimate detachment* so "narrowly approximates to naught" in Eckhart's view that "no room remains for aught betwixt zero and absolute detachment" (Jung, *PYM*, 239. Hereafter Jung's *Psychology of Yoga and Meditation* will be referenced as *PYM* and page number). Thus, whereas relative detachment is the state of humility and poverty in the soul, absolute detachment is above the will and the intellect and is equivalent to Zero, or Nothingness, which is the highest state the soul can arise to in her transcendence into God-consciousness, or *superconsciousness*. As we will see, the

Relative and the Absolute exist side by side and cannot be separated from one another in Eckhart's unitary theology of the soul in her states of transfiguration into Divinity, where: "God himself is blissful in the soul" (*CW* 6: ¶148).

30   *W*, 405, 406.

31   Nevertheless, Eckhart quoted Avicenna having said that God is "necessary existence" (*TP*, 48). It was perhaps from his Latin treatises that Eckhart formulated his notion in the vernacular sermons that our continuous birthing out of the groundless Godhead is *necessary* for God to exist in the soul in our own human incarnations.

32   W, 405, 406.

33   Ibid.

34   When Jung was asked during an interview in 1959 if he believed in God, he answered: "Difficult to answer. I *know*. I don't need to believe. I know" (*C. G. Jung Speaking*, 428). This is what Jungian analysts call empirical knowledge or the *relativity of the God*. Like his predecessor William James, Jung drew a limit on what can be known by focusing his researches into the phenomenology of the Self on the scientific study of the archetypes of the collective unconscious, for which he is famous. What Eckhart's theology of God, the Godhead, and the Ground actually was, as we will see, will always be shrouded in a *mystery* that will never be known because a number of his most important treatises have not survived the passage of time, for instance, such lost manuscripts as "On the Nature of the Superior" (*TP*, 124), and "Treatise on the Good" (*TP*, 165), both of which, from an analytical psychological standpoint are necessary in our attempts to fully comprehend his views on the Self and Nothingness, the relative and the Absolute, the knowable and the Unknowable. Nevertheless, as we shall see, one thing is clear and it is this: Eckhart argued, along with his most important source, "Rabbi Moses" or Moses Maimonides (1135–1204) that "the sages agree that the sciences cannot grasp the Creator, and only he himself understands himself" (*TP*, 101). After quoting the axiom of Socrates, "I know that I don't know," Eckhart wrote further, "which is like saying: 'The one thing I know about God is that I do not know him'" (*TP*, 101–102).

35   The Infinite in Eckhart's works is a highly abstract concept, for there are two aspects of infinity: an infinite that can be counted by Wisdom,

such as with the multitude of the stars, the Many, and an Infinite that extends beyond God into a bottomless Ground beyond all numbers, the One. Oneness and Nothing, or One and Zero, form a pair of supreme opposites in Eckhart's thought and leave us with an unsolved mystery in his theology of the Self and no-Self. I will distinguish, therefore, between the i = infinite, and I = Infinite in this book.

36   For instance, Jung's analysis in *Answer to Job* focused on the divine names YHWH, Sophia or Wisdom, and Christ, whereas Eckhart examined many Hebrew names of God in the Old Testament based most intensively on his reading of Maimonides, such as the four-letter name or Tetragrammaton, the twelve-letter name, forty-two letter name, and the Jewish names *Adonai*, and also *Shaddai*: "the name 'Shaddai, which is derived from 'dai,' or 'self-sufficiency," signifies that the 'divine essence is self-sufficient' in itself and in other things … Consequently, the name 'Shaddai' signifies that God is Existence Itself and that his essence is Existence Itself… Sufficiency Itself is everything that is" (*TP*, 93, 94). Moreover, Eckhart asserted that "Therefore the 'Name that is above every name' is not unnamable but 'omninameable.'" The word *omninameable* came from a Hermetic text known as the *Asclepius* 6:20, a text that was widely used by Eckhart (*TP*, 54; 133, f. 94).

37   *Gotheit* in Middle High German means "Godhead, or Divinity." Sometimes the terms *Grunt* and Godhead are used synonymously. This is because sometimes ground is simply the ground of the soul, sometimes it is the bottomless, groundless ground, an infinite Abyss, or *Abgrund*.

38   Eckhart's treatise "On the Divine Names" (*TP*, 21) is central to his whole theology of the birth of the Holy Spirit in the soul and one cannot understand his distinctions between God and the Godhead, heaven and earth, begotten Justice and Unbegotten Justice without it.

39   Evans, *Meister Eckhart by Franz Pfeiffer*, 2: 46. Hereafter references to Evans's *Meister Eckhart by Franz Pfeiffer* will be referenced by *EFP*, volume, and page number.

40   Herrmann, *Spiritual Democracy*.

41   *Nakedness* is one of the central metaphors in Eckhart's works for God. The origins of the word are biblical and probably derived from his study of the Old Testament and Moses Maimonides (1135–1204), who

treated the passage "I am who am" as the four-letter name (YHWH) or "Tetragrammaton" as "sacred and separated, written, and not pronounced, and alone signifies the naked and pure substance of the creator" (*TP*, 47). The name "Adonai" is used as a substitute for the four-letter name due to its sacredness and it was rarely spoken by Jews.

42   *Pantheist belief* can be found in the earliest records of shamanism, animism, and tribal societies throughout the entire world. It is not the human deity that is worshiped as God, so much as Star People, Sun and Moon and Planet Gods; Reptile People, Snake and Lizard; Winged People; Raven, Condor, and Eagle; Mammal People, Bison, Elephant, and Whale; Fish People, Salmon and Abalone; Stone People and great River and Mountain Gods or Goddesses (Ganga). All over the earth, the first nations celebrated the divinity in Nature and the Universe; "Nature's God"—the only reference to God in our Declaration of Independence, penned by Thomas Jefferson—is the way American democracy protected the first principle of our Constitution: the Freedom of Religion. Pantheistic elements can be found in Hinduism, Buddhism, Advaita-Vedanta, and the unitary theology of Eckhart, whose ideas about a transcendent and infinite God were viewed as *heresy* by the Catholic Church, although he was exonerated for his humility and obedience to his order, whereas the more unfortunate Italian friar, Giordano Bruno, was burned at the stake in 1600 for his heretical evangelizing of Nature's God by the Roman Inquisition. Today, Giordano is celebrated as a *pantheist* and a martyr of modern science, before the birth of Spinoza (1632–1367 CE).

43   *Panentheism* asserts its *belief* that God and the world are interconnected, with God being in the world and the world existing in God and asserts further a faith in transcendence and imminence at the same time. Theisms of many varieties disbelieve the influence of the world upon God; whereas panentheism (there are a plethora of proponents) believe the world's influence upon God is transcendent Absolute Truth. The main arguments in the philosophical and theological debates have to do with the *relationship between God and the world*. The primary problem as I see it is that the panentheistic Gods (in a "pluralistic Universe") tend to limit themselves to their specific God-images, names, or forms of God. Yet, if one studies all of the arguments from a *trans-dualistic*

378

reference point in Eckhart's highest understandings, theism and pantheism are present in the Higher Self in a transcendent realization of Unity. Pantheism and panentheism are present in Eckhart's works in equal measure, and his thoughts are contained in a Oneness and *equality* of all existence.

44 Fox, "Meister Eckhart's Spiritual Journey," *Western Spirituality,* 217–218.

45 John Dourley viewed Jung as *pantheist* when he wrote: "Jung's pervasive and expansive pantheism ... The pantheism endemic to Jung's understanding of the psyche's role in the creation of such Gods [religious and political] would undermine them all" (Dourley, *On Behalf of the Mystical Fool,* 177, 230). In contrast I see in Jung's writings both pantheism and panentheism in *equal* proportion to the One from which both perspectives emanate. Jung's scientific objectivity is the very reverse of dualism, which is *non-dualism.* The difference will be made clearer in what follows regarding my views on *trans-dualism.*

46 We do know that Eckhart died in Avignon. His body was probably buried by the brothers in his order, yet we cannot be certain of it, because he was being held in the French city where the pope resided by the Roman Catholic curia. I do think it is curious that historians and Eckhart scholars do not typically mention this sad fact very much, if they do at all; yet I want to stress it here because there is a mystery in it, and I am trying to draw our attention in the book to the historical tragedy that we have no place to honor him, as we do, for instance, with canonized saints, bishops, and popes, some of whom were corrupt and evil men, as Dante pointed out in the *Divine Comedy* when he put a few of them in the pits of Hell in the *Inferno.* This realization came to me in Erfurt, when I realized that there was no place to worship him, as we might the tomb of Jesus at the Church of the Holy Sepulcher. Yet, it was Eckhart, more than Christ, who drew our attention to the fact that the birth must take place in us, as did Jung.

47 Quint, *Deutsche Predigten und Traktate,* 355. Hereafter Quint's *Deutsche Predigten und Traktate* will be referenced as *Q* and page number.

48 "God's seed is within us. If it had a good, skilled, and industrious gardener to tend it, it would thrive all the better and grow up to God,

379

whose seed it is, and the fruit would be God's nature" (*W*, 558). *God's nature* sounds to me more panentheistic than pantheistic, so here in one of his finest treatises (*Traktate*), "The Nobleman," we can see the balancing of the two theories of God. This is a treatise Jung did not read because Pfeiffer did not include the *Nobleman*. One has to be able to hold these two views of nature's God and God's nature equally in consciousness at a higher level of seeing and divining to understand the paradox and rise above them unto a more unitary and spacious theology, where either hypothesis can be proven to be valid, depending upon one's religious or scientific calling from the vocational archetype.

49 *W*, 414.

50 *Wikipedia*, "Panentheism."

51 *W*, 293, 294.

52 *W*, 424.

53 Bernard McGinn wrote in his excellent introduction that Eckhart makes frequent references that "look like a species of pantheism, but such is not the case" (Colledge and McGinn, *Meister Eckhart: The Essential Sermons*, 75, 76. Hereafter *The Essential Sermons* will be referenced as *ES* and page number). On the other hand, I do not see Eckhart as a *panentheistic* preacher either, since he always somehow seems to arise or ascend above such subtle theoretical distinctions into transcendence through direct *empirical experience* of Absolute Existence, "eternal virtual existence in the archetype" or "Absolute Unity" (*ES*, 41), where both hypotheses may be seen as true in a *mystery* beyond all names of God, "when viewed in the Principle" (*ES*, 40), or "archetypal Idea, that is, the Word or Logos" (*ES*, 323, endnote 16). In other words, pantheistic and panentheistic visions of God are both *equal* in the principle, in the Ground of the Godhead. They are both archetypes, or Words of God, and as such they are *equivalent* hypotheses; for why should Spinoza's God, or Einstein's God, be lesser than the God of St. Thomas Aquinas? To create such a dualism is a false hypothesis, as One equals One in the "Word as Exemplar," which is "really real" (*ES*, 304, endnote 96).

54 Clark, *Meister Eckhart*, 1957.

55 *Isticheit* in Middle High German.

56 *Niht* in MHG.

57 Clark, 177.

58 *W*, 415.

59 Jung, "Transformation Symbolism in the Mass," *CW* 11: ¶446.

60 Spiritual Democracy in the total Universe reduces all inequality into equality. Spiritual Democracy is the whole Universe from which our individual and finite existence is conferred from the Infinite. We receive our existence (*esse*) in the soul from the totality of the Universe and only through the whole can our being be born in God's Wisdom, through the grace of the Holy Spirit.

61 In the eighth principle of his "Defense" during his heresy trial in Cologne, Eckhart stated that "the godlike man can perform God's works" in accordance with the teachings of Christ and the Evangelist. Quoting Jesus he said: "He who believes in me, the works I do he shall also do, and greater than these" (Jn. 14:12)" (*ES*, 75, 76). By this he meant the works of the Paraclete *after* Christ. It was this eighth article in his "Defense" that was the most problematic to the conventional theology of the Catholic Church during his times. I will return to this point later.

62 Jung, *CW* 11: ¶448.

63 The groundless Ground or *Grunt* of the Godhead was one of Eckhart's most original contributions to Dominican theology and to the Roman Catholic Church of his times, although it had heretical implications. The theoretical distinction was nevertheless at the center of Jung's attempts to champion the concept of the *relativity* of the God-images in the human psyche, which he attributed to Eckhart. Whereas there are a multitude of God-images in the human psyche, the Ground is groundless at its innermost depths. In it there are only negative qualities, too many to name. I will therefore limit the following list to *14*: the Ground is 1) Unfathomable, 2) Ineffable, 3) Nothing, 4) Abyss, 5) Non-existence, 6) Non-being, 7) Unspoken, 8) Privation, 9) Negation, 10) Unnumbered, 11) Unnamable, 12) Beyond God-Wisdom and the Trinity, 13) Endless Hidden Darkness, 14) Stillness.

64 Jung, *C.G. Jung Speaking*, 202–204.

65 Jung, "Christ, A Symbol of the Self," *CW* 9ii: ¶76.

66 As Jungian analyst, Lionel Corbett wrote: "Eckhart prefers a radically non-dual position, like that of Advaita Vedanta, which is that I and God

are actually one" (Corbett, *The Religious Function of the Psyche*, 35). The connection between Eckhart and Advaita Vedanta is a good one, although in my work on Advaita I used the term *trans-dual* because it is really a view from a vista above, and Eckhart shared this vision that we find in Sankara and Vivekananda as I've shown (Herrmann, *Swami Vivekananda and C.G. Jung*). Eckhart's elevation of the soul into Wisdom is in a Sky-Self from which his whole theology of the Word is preached, from very high up.

67 When Wisdom numbered the "Who numbers the multitude of stars" (Ps. 146:4), she saw in her mind of God that they were infinite in their series for they were all multiples of One. This is "the apex of goodness," the Good from the "one total cause," or the "moral integrity not to be counted" (*TP*, 163).

68 Jung, *Psychology of Yoga and Meditation*, 244.

69 *PYM*, 249.

70 *TP*, 272.

71 For my Jewish readers it is important to read this as a meditation on Isaiah 7:14: "Therefore the Lord himself shall give you a sign; Behold, a virgin shall conceive, and bear a son, and shall call his name Immanuel."

72 *W*, 39.

73 *ES*, 78.

74 Eckhart's knowledge and understanding of the Jewish philosopher and religious thinker Moses Maimonides (1135–1204) surpassed that of all Christian authors in the Middle Ages. He held Rabbi Moses in the highest esteem, quoted him profusely in his Latin works, and used him to critique Islamic philosophers, such as Avicenna and Averroes, as well as St. Thomas Aquinas.

75 *TP*, 111, 112.

76 As you'll see in the chapters ahead, Eckhart was a main influence on the evolution of Jewish thought about the coming of the Messiah through the works of the Israeli philosopher and promoter of world peace, Martin Buber, who wrote: "all mankind is accorded the co-working power, all time is directly redemptive, all action for the sake of God may be Messianic action" (Scholem, *The Messianic Idea in Judaism*, 179). On the other hand, Jung wrote in *Aion* about the "weakness of

the Messianic element in Judaism and the dangers attending it" due to the fact that in the Cabalistic tradition there were "two Messiahs, the Messiah ben Joseph (or ben Ephraim) and the Messiah ben David"; therefore, Jung detected "a split which in the end becomes a complete polarity," arising from "an inner disquiet with regard to the character of Yahweh" (Jung, *Aion, CW* 9ii: ¶¶168, 169).

77 Jung, "The Symbolic Life," *CW* 18: ¶638.

78 The state of equality is the golden mean of Spiritual Democracy.

79 When the Light of the Absolute ceases to illuminate the soul, she can fall again from goodness into relative evil, multiplicity, and sin, which is nothing in the sight of God-consciousness while she was in the presence of the illuminating Body of the Lord. No one is in this sense ever finally free of evil.

80 *W*, 41.

81 *TP*, 272.

82 "In his sight the evil one is brought to nothing" (Ps. 14:4). The final cause of creation is the whole Universe, which, of course, includes God's Creation of the opposites of good and evil, but from the point of view of God-consciousness, which is Light in infinite darkness, the human shadow is an infinitesimal part of the totality of the *Not-God* in Eckhart's theology; so small in fact is privation that it cannot be counted in relation to the hundreds of billions of galaxies that all add up to One when human negation is subtracted: $0 + 1 = 1$, or Zero + the simple One = the groundless Ground.

83 *Weib* in German means wife. I say *wife of Wisdom* here because she is the highest of the *four levels of the soul* in Eckhart's Latin treatises and vernacular sermons. The reference comes from Sermon 8 in Walsche, where Luke (10:38) said in the opening quote: "Our Lord Jesus Christ went up into a citadel and was received by a virgin who was a wife" (*W*, 77). The citadel is the *Wipfel,* top (of a tree, summit, or *treetop* in German) in the highest and noblest part of the soul (*Q*, 280, 288). This *Wipfel-Weib* apex is the place of Wisdom from which Eckhart delivered his vernacular sermons. In sermon 9, Eckhart told his followers that she was called "Martha" whose name Christ called out twice (*W*, 83). I'll be speaking about the Wisdom-*Wipfel-Weib*-Martha parallel throughout my text. In short, "wife" is, psychologically and theologically speaking,

a person who is fecund with the Word of God and fruitful with *Gewerbe*, a calling, work, or vocation in God's Light.

84   *Vünkelîn*, the divine little "spark," the highest, noblest, most intimate, and *infinite* part of the soul in its imminence.

85   Jung, "The Psychology of the Transference," *CW* 16: ¶361.

86   *CW* 6: ¶428.

87   Jung, "On the Relation of Analytical Psychology to Poetry," *CW* 15: ¶148.

88   Eckhart's metaphor here may indeed have come from his reading of Maimonides, probably at the University of Paris. In Jewish Kabbalism, the Tree of Life consists of ten *sefirot*, divine luminaries or emanations from *Ein Sof* (the Infinite). The sefirot at the treetop is called *Keter* (Crown). It is considered to be the place of the Superconscious Will beyond the conscious Intellect that extends into Nothingness. The ninth sefirot on the Tree of Life is called *Chokmah*-Wisdom. And the eighth is *Binah*-Understanding.

89   *W*, 429.

90   Von Franz, *Aurora Consurgens,* 153. Hereafter references to Von Franz's *Aurora Consurgens* will be referenced as *AC*, and page number.

91   Von Franz, *Number and Time.* 59.

92   *Number and Time,* 59.

93   *Number and Time,* 63.

94   *Number and Time,* 67.

95   *Number and Time,* 75.

96   *Number and Time,* 76.

97   An archetype has a spreading influence that is not always seen or known through acquired knowledge but can be experienced supernaturally through the highest forms of meditation or prayer; they exist in waves, fields, or thought-patterns that are transmissive in their virtual Exemplar. Not only was Eckhart highly influenced by Moses Maimonides, but he was also a contemporary with Rabbi Abraham Abulafia (1240–1295), who was an authority on the pronunciation of the Hebrew divine names, and developed a systematic method and some specific techniques of Jewish meditation practices. Abulafia believed the Trinity and Incarnation were false, and he went on a mission to attempt to convert Pope Nicholas III to Judaism in 1280. This was

happening while Eckhart was in Cologne, sitting at the feet of Albert the Great. Abulafia was about to be burned at the stake under the orders of the Pope, but when he entered the gate where the wood pile was assembled, he suddenly heard that the Pope had died of an apoplectic stroke the preceding night. He thanked God and returned to Rome and was then thrown into prison by the Order of the Friars Minor (Franciscans), but he was fortunately liberated four weeks later and headed for Sicily. He wrote works on the Divine Names, especially the four-letter name, on Maimonides's *Guide to the Perplexed* and the "Ten Sefirot of Nothingness" (Kaplan, *Meditation and Kabbalah*, 81). Although I have not been able to prove my hunch through direct literary sources, it is highly possible that Eckhart could have come upon his works at the University of Paris or have been influenced by him through osmosis in the highly charged spiritual atmosphere of medieval Europe, as the prior of Erfurt, or perhaps later as Meister. I say this because of the accent Eckhart placed upon Nothing, which is unmistakably Jewish, for it is referred to in Kabbalism as *Ayin* or "Nothingness." This was the highest spiritual level of consciousness attainable in classical Kabbalah, bringing "Something from Nothing." The term was used to connote the tenth stage of the Keter-Crown, or the highest Sefirot in the universe of Atzilut, above the second highest Sefirah, "Chokhmah-Wisdom." Nothingness was equivalent with *Ain Sof*, "The Endless One," "Infinite Being," or simply "The Infinite." *Ain Sof* also connotes "The Ultimate Nothingness," or "Nothingness End," to which a meditator ascends empirically and absolutely while praying on the divine Names (Kaplan, 299). All of this theology on Nothingness sounds remarkably like Eckhart! To me the intuition is verified by following Eckhart's sermons in the vernacular, which suggests that the later Parisian adventures is where he probably read Abulafia, or at least heard about his work and story about his trip to convert the Pope in Rome.

98 Jung, "The Philosphical Tree," *CW* 12: ¶433.

99 *CW* 16: ¶419.

100 *CW* 6: ¶429.

101 *TP*, 46. Although I like Bernard McGinn's translations of the terms *bullitio* and *ebullitio* as "boiling" and "boiling over" the accent Eckhart

placed in the vernacular on the Ground as the place of the *primal eruption* is more powerful and explosive and true to the cosmic energy of the Word.

102 *ES*, 109.

103 *AC*, 415.

104 *AC*, 411.

105 Jung, *MDR*, 69. Hereafter Jung's *Memories, Dreams, Reflections* will be referenced as *MDR*, and page number.

106 Eckhart's reassignment by his Order to Strasbourg from the University of Paris led him to become increasingly spiritually democratic in his maturity of age; equality with nuns and Beguines gave him the key that opened the door to his new theology of birthing God, or what Jung called spiritual motherhood.

107 Eckhart was essentially creating metaphors, parables that can be read as Jewish or Christian synonyms: Rachael being the mother of the Jews after Sarah, and Martha as a follower and emissary of Christ. He was preaching Spiritual Democracy to a Catholic audience in an effort to unite Judaism and Christianity long before Jung spoke of the reconciliation of the Western God-image. For Eckhart the union of God and Wisdom was the ultimate union between the Father and the Mother Goddess.

108 In a number of places in his Latin works Eckhart also identified Sarah with the rational faculty in man and Hagar with the sensitive (*ES*, 323, note 152.)

109 *ES*, 113.

110 *CW* 6: ¶428.

111 In Joaquim of Flora's (c. 1135–1202) writings, the Spiritual Church was supposed to arise in the *seventh age,* when sun and the moon would be united or conjoined. Joaquim's teachings announced the everlasting Gospel of continuing incarnation as a future fulfillment of the messages of the angel that appeared to John in Revelations 14:6. This eternal Gospel was later identified with the teachings of the Franciscan Order. Yet not all Dominicans agreed. For instance, Joaquim's ideas were disputed by Thomas Aquinas in his *Summa Theologica.* Whereas Eckhart did not comment on Joaquim, Jung liked to cite him and frequently did because of Jung's sense of urgency about

the need to celebrate the elevation of the Virgin Mother into the Trinity, in prediction for the *mysterium coniunctionis,* or conjoining of God and Goddess into a more all-encompassing experience of Divinity, which we also see in Vedic India.

112 *ES,* 113.

113 *ES,* 117.

114 *W,* 78.

115 *ES,* 109.

116 *ES,* 113.

117 *AC,* 421.

118 *AC,* 327.

119 *AC,* 386.

120 *CW* 16: ¶444.

121 *CW* 9ii: ¶115.

122 *CW* 9ii: ¶115, footnote 75.

123 Jung, "Answer to Job," *CW* 11: ¶758.

124 *CW* 6: ¶457.

125 *TP,* 213.

126 *TP,* 187.

127 *TP,* 148.

128 *TP,* 344.

129 *W,* 394.

130 *W,* 394–395.

131 *W,* 32.

132 *W,* 358.

133 *TP,* 258.

134 *TP,* 258.

135 *W,* 83, 84.

136 *W,* 84.

137 *Q,* 283. Some translations write "activity," but I agree with Miss Evans that *work (Wirken), vocation,* and *calling* are better.

138 *W,* 77.

139 *W,* 78.

140 See Frank Tobin's excellent translation in *TP,* 345, note 3.

141 *W,* 80.

142 *CW* 6: ¶77,

143 *CW* 14: ¶¶102, 103.

144 *TP*, 341.

145 "This agrees with the text 'Seek the things that are above' (Col. 3:2). It seems to coincide with the members of religious orders in the New Dispensation" (*TP*, 120).

146 *ES*, 82, 83. A new dispensation is a new teaching; it also means a text of some kind, like Eckhart's sermons, which contain a Dharma or teaching, like the sermons of the Buddha in the Dhammapada.

147 Eckhart's fourth major transition occurred in Cologne when he not only preached Wisdom but also *became* Wisdom speaking in dynamic action as the inspired and infused preacher of God's Word.

148 *W*, 140.

149 *W*, 142, footnote 7.

150 *W*, 140.

151 *W*, 46.

152 *W*, 226.

153 *W*, 230.

154 *W*, 358.

155 *W*, 360.

156 *W*, 298.

157 Jung, *C.G. Jung Speaking*, 361.

158 *W*, 378.

159 *TP*, 219.

160 *TP*, 263.

161 *TP*, 152.

162 *TP*, 168.

163 *TP*, 170.

164 *TP*, 129.

165 *TP*, 163.

166 *TP*, 162.

167 *TP*, 165.

168 *W*, 553.

169 *TP*, 221.

170 *ES*, 78.

171 *ES*, 90.

172 *ES*, 106.

173 *ES*, 111.

174 *ES*, 109.

175 *TP*, 321.

176 *ES*, 117.

177 *ES*, 93.

178 *ES*, 92.

179 *ES*, 168.

180 *ES*, 193.

181 *W*, 146, 147.

182 *W*, 280.

183 The lance was alleged to have been found by Crusaders during the siege of Antioch in 1098 CE, a battle that took place in the Syrian mountain range, with 20,000 to 40,000 men battling violently over two years.

184 In the *Votum Theologicum* of the Avignon Commission it was reported that "Eckhart defends the point that God is above every name and superior to all discourse and higher than everything we understand" (*TP*, 29). The main objection in Avignon was Eckhart's exclusion of *bonum* from the list of God's divine names, although *malum* was never equal to the Supreme Good or moral integrity in any way and was seen as a privation. "Names ought not to be denied to God" (*TP*, 29) they argued, while failing to comprehend Eckhart's meanings.

185 Rudin, "A Catholic View of Conscience," 153.

186 Stein, *Analytical Psychology and Religion,* 189.

187 Stein, *Analytical Psychology and Religion,* 187.

188 In the Grail myth the lance of Longinus was referred to as the spear of destiny. In the Perceval story, the bleeding Lance drew out the poison from the Fisher King's wounds. Thus, there was a psychic antibody in the Lance: its power to *heal*. This antitoxin protected the Fisher King from dying before he could crown Perceval as the new King, and the Grail that caught the blood of Christ could then be celebrated in the castle and the cure was administered for the common good of the people.

189 The Crusades were a series of religious wars, military expeditions that included kings, civilians, and knights enroute to the Holy Land, primarily between 1095–1291, intending to conquer Jerusalem and its surrounding areas from Muslim rule. The Last Crusade ended a year prior to Eckhart's study at the University of Paris in 1292. This

is highly significant since the theology of the Roman Catholic Church had defined its theory of holy war based upon the historical pattern of the Old Testament Israelite wars that were believed to have been initiated by God in alignment with Christocentric views taken from the from the teachings of the New Testament. The Crusades were based on Hebrew mythology of the so-called just war. Augustine of Hippo, one of Eckhart's champions, had Christianized this archaic notion, and it became a paradigm for Christian holy wars. Catholic theologians during the crusading period widely promulgated this archaic idea, even in the name of Mother Mary for Christianity. Augustine had argued that God has given the sword for governance for "good" reason, based on Romans 13:4. Protecting peace with the sword became a metaphor for salvation of the soul in the name of God's justice. This evil theory was taken further by St. Thomas Aquinas, who argued in his *Summa Theologica* that "just wars" (Augustine's term), violence, killing, and destructive attacks were to promote good and avoid evil. Aquinas's doctrine was used to support the Eighth Crusade in 1270, when Eckhart was a boy of ten. Augustine, Bernard, and Aquinas were all used as pawns by the Church to give support to the Crusades, almost all of which failed.

190 The nuclear core of the dualism as I see it was not good and evil, but peace and war, which the Crusades represented. As he said: "I never pray so well as when I pray for nothing and for nobody, not for Heinrich or Konrad. Those who pray truly pray to God in truth and in spirit, that is to say, in the Holy Ghost." (*W*, 358). Heinrich VI was the Hohenstaufen emperor of the German Crusade (*Deutscher Kreuzzug*) of 1197, a crusade launched by the Henry VI in response to the aborted attempt of his father, Emperor Frederick I, during the Third Crusade in 1189–1190. Konrad III of Germany joined forces with King Louis VII of France during the Second Crusade of 1147–1154. So, Eckhart was saying that he did not pray to any pope, king, or emperor, but only in the Self, or Holy Ghost, the living Word of God within him. He prayed best when he prayed for nothing.

191 *ES*, 149. This could easily be misinterpreted to mean that he shared a belief with the Catholic Church of his day that the Crusades had been "just." Eckhart's views on justice were far more innovative and

spiritualized than his predecessors. As I argue in this book, Eckhart's vocation, his calling as a theologian and preacher of God's Word, was to transform the Church's evil theology on the goodness or justice in killing, warfare, and external violence against "enemies" into a higher dispensation of justice, based on peace in the Old and New Testaments. Never once did Eckhart teach a theory of Augustine's or Aquinas's "just war," or preach in the name of Christ external slaughter in any way. The shadow and evil were always to be integrated and made conscious within.

192 *W*, 208.

193 *"Vielmehr soll die Seele im ersten Ausbruch, wo die (reine, volle) Warheit ausbricht und entspringt, in der 'Pforte des Gotteshauses' stehen und soll das Wort aussprechen und vorbringen"* (Q, 238).

194 *Durchbruch, durchbrechen,* in MHG.

195 *W*, 188.

196 Fox, *Creation,* "William Everson: Nature Mystic and Poet Prophet," Vol. 5: 3, 11.

197 As you'll see in the chapters ahead, the Crusades were a series of bloody campaigns to protect the most sacred religious site in Christianity: *The Church of the Holy Sepulcher.* After seeing a vision of a cross in the sky in 312 CE, Constantine the Great sent his mother, Helena, to Jerusalem to search for Christ's tomb. Three crosses were found in an archeological dig, one that had allegedly *cured people of death,* and this became known as the most sacred *Cross of Healing,* believed by Helena to be the actual cross Jesus had been crucified upon. The tomb had originally been sanctified as a temple to the gods Jupiter and Venus, after the first Jewish-Roman War by the emperor Hadrian. In 326 CE it was replaced by a Church, and upon excavation of the ground beneath, Helena and Macarius, Bishop of Jerusalem, believed they found the burial site of Jesus. This sacred burial site was named *Anastasis* ("Resurrection"). The site was consecrated in 335 CE Church of the Holy Sepulcher, where Jesus is said to have been crucified, buried, and rose from the dead. During the Crusades, all crusaders to the Holy Land, to protect this most sacred place in Jerusalem, wore a cross to symbolize God's Kingdom in Christ. The cross became an emblem of war, violence, and bloodshed in the name of Christendom by popes, bishops, and emperors of the Holy Roman Empire.

198 Stein, *Analytical Psychology and Religion: Volume 6 of the Collected Writings*, 178.

199 Jung, *Analytical Psychology*, 26.

200 *ES*, 5, 6.

201 Like St. Augustine, St. Bernard, and St. Aquinas, Albertus Magnus promoted the theory of the "just war" during the Eighth Crusade under the orders of pope Urban IV, who relieved Albert of his duties as bishop so he could preach the Christian mission to protect the holiest of religious sites in the Holy Land. He was sent to preach to German-speaking countries in 1263, when Eckhart was a toddler of three. Urban IV was the bishop of Rome, head of the Catholic Church, and ruler of the Papal States from 1261–1264. He was a member of the Latin patriarchate in Jerusalem seated at the Church of the Holy Sepulture, established in 1099 with the Kingdom of Jerusalem. In 1270, the Crusading armies were redirected to Tunis, where Louis IX of France died. When Jung was in Tunis, he said he could smell blood in the soil. Jung's theory of the Self provides an answer to the problem of splitting in Western, Near Eastern, and Middle Eastern religions. Religious splitting within Islam is a *reality* Jung wrestled with in an important dream during his travels to the Muslim city of Tunis, on the northern tip of Africa in 1920. He continued to grapple with the problem of religious dualism in Persian Zoroastrianism, Mithraicism, Manichaeism, and Islam between 1934 and 1939. By the time his seminars on Nietzsche's *Zarathustra* ended on the eve of WWII, he had zeroed in on the pivotal role that the figure of Khidr plays in Islamic mysticism. Jung cites the "colloquy with the friend of the soul," Allah, or the Self, as a paradigm for a dialogical method of active imagination, which, if used with right feeling and in an *embodied* way, can be employed as a technique for transcending splits within the historical God-image. (Herrmann, "Colloquy with the Inner Friend: Jung's Religious Feeling for Islam," 2009).

202 *TP*, 332.

203 *TP*, 333–334.

204 *PYM*, 249.

205 *W*, 117.

206 *AC*, 165, Footnote 44.

207 *AC*, 166.

208 *AC,* 167.

209 *TP,* 272.

210 Jung, *Dream Seminars,* 484.

211 Scholem, 182.

212 Scholem, 182.

213 *W,* 74.

214 Scholem, 231.

215 *W,* 213.

216 *AC,* 421. The Beghards were the masculine counterpart of the Beguines.

217 *AC,* 175, 176.

218 *AC,* 178.

219 The concept of a New Dispensation is a proposition that was first advanced in the field of analytical psychology by Los Angeles Jungian analyst, Edward F. Edinger, who wrote: *"The new psychological dispensation finds man's relation to God in the individual's relation to the unconscious.* This is the new context, the new vessel with which humanity can be the carrier of divine meaning" (Edinger, *The Creation of Consciousness: Jung's Myth for Modern Man,* 90). While I am an avid reader of Edinger's books and recommend them to people who want a practical understanding of Jung the question of what our relationship to God and the unconscious actually is happens to be something that I must part ways with him on, with regards to Jung's understandings and mine. One of the problems of separating the Jewish, Christian, and Jungian dispensations into three distinct evolutions of the historical God-image across time is that Edinger and those who follow him tend to leave Islam out, which Jung did not, as I have made clear in my previous writings. Both Eckhart and Jung included Islamic thought in their works.

220 Progoff, *Jung, Synchronicity, and Human Destiny,* 125.

221 Progoff, 126.

222 Progoff, 107.

223 *DM,* 172.

224 *W,* 293.

225 *AC,* 211.

226 *AC,* 215.

227 *AC,* 238.

228 *AC,* 280, 281.

229   *AC*, 281.

230   WC, 588, 589.

231   Progoff, *Jung, Synchronicity, and Human Destiny,* 104.

232   Progoff, 105.

233   *W*, 117.

234   *ES*, 80.

235   Jung, *Development of Personality, CW* 17: ¶296.

236   Rudin, "A Catholic View of Conscience," 153.

237   *TP*, 232.

238   *TP*, 233.

239   *TP*, 173.

240   *TP*, 103.

241   *ES*, 78.

242   *EFP*, 1: 436, 366, 284.

243   *EFP*, 1: 86, 143.

244   Hick, *Evil and the God of Love,* 220. Hereafter references to Hick's *Evil and the God of Love* will be referenced by *EGL* and page number.

245   *W*, 204–205.

246   *EFP*, 1: 212.

247   *TP*, 51.

248   *TP*, 95.

249   *W*, 378.

250   *W*, 79, 202.

251   *W*, 202.

252   *W*, 307.

253   *W*, 81.

254   *W*, 80.

255   *EFP*, 1: 5.

256   Jung, "Commentary on the Secret of the Golden Flower," *CW* 13: ¶73.

257   *CW* 13: ¶74.

258   *CW* 13: ¶75.

259   *CW* 6: ¶411.

260   *CW* 6: ¶415.

261   *CW* 6: ¶421.

262   *CW* 6: ¶414.

263   *CW* 6: ¶415.

264 *CW* 6: ¶417.

265 *CW* 6: ¶421.

266 *CW* 6: ¶421.

267 *W*, 110.

268 *CW* 17: ¶320.

269 *ES*, 140.

270 *TP*, 95.

271 *ES*, 263.

272 *CW* 9ii: ¶112, footnote 74.

273 *CW* 9ii: ¶143.

274 *TP*, 89.

275 *TP*, 125.

276 *TP*, 152.

277 *TP*, 163.

278 *EGL*, 42.

279 Ibid.

280 *ES*, 90.

281 *EGL*, 149.

282 *EGL*, 55.

283 *CW* 17: ¶302.

284 Lammers, *In God's Shadow*, 226.

285 *B*, 304.

286 Deciphering one's destiny is both a science and an art, often expressed most purely and spontaneously by poets in the theologies of the world, such as in the Rig-Veda by the Rishis. *Calling archetypes* are emergent principles that point us to the track that we are meant to run upon, on our own autochthonous Ground of being, pursuing our own right courses in life. *Destiny archetypes* are subjective revelations from the primordial Ground of the Godhead that signal our arrival at our true destinations in the Metaphysical Self. The feeling of having arrived, in Eckhart's vernacular sermons, at our destiny archetypes is confirmed by the experience of fulfillment in knowing that the calling from the Self was patterned by the outbreak from the Godhead, the primordial Word that summoned us to some high and noble undertaking. For Eckhart this apotheosis was channeled through his nuclear symbol of the Preacher, which brought him great joy and bittersweet suffering

and peace. The calling archetypes of the theologian and teacher were secondary to the central archetype of his destiny, as a speaker of God's Word: the ultimate destination that he lived and died for, whether in Erfurt or in Avignon after having given birth to many children of the Holy Spirit.

287 *EGL*, 83.

288 *EGL*, 84.

289 *EGL*, 88.

290 *ES*, 262.

291 *EGL*, 84.

292 *EGL*, 131.

293 *ES*, 128.

294 *W*, 39.

295 *EGL*, 194.

296 *ES*, 72.

297 *W*, 277.

298 *W*, 558.

299 *ES*, 114.

300 *W*, 557, 558.

301 *W*, 378.

302 *B*, 5.

303 *W*, 557.

304 *B*, 535.

305 *B*, 127.

306 Clark and Skinner, 200.

307 *W*, 146, 147. Here Eckhart makes it very clear in his preaching of a new theology of the Word that *Jerusalem* is a metaphor for *peace*, not *war*, in the Old and New Testaments, and his theory of justice is equally translucent: "Let us pray to our Lord" that "*we* may be 'man' in this sense and established in *this peace*, which is *himself (or herself)*." Justice for Eckhart did not mean a "just war" or Crusade in Jerusalem, which St. Bernard, St. Albert, and St. Aquinas were all hoodwinked by the popes of Rome to believe in since the time of Augustine, who coined the term. Eckhart was always a preacher of *Ultimate Peace*, and the *cross he carried was a true symbol of healing* between Jews, Christians, and Muslims in the Holy Land and Europe.

308 *W*, 280.

309 *W*, 169.

310 *CW* 11: ¶733.

311 *W*, 39.

312 *B*, 461.

313 *W*, 75.

314 Eckhart used Leah and Rachael synonymously with Martha in various sermons and Latin texts.

315 *ES*, 52.

316 *W*, 75.

317 *W*, 104, 105.

318 *W*, 109.

319 *W*, 237.

320 *W*, 281.

321 *W*, 344.

322 *W*, 344.

323 *W*, 445.

324 *W*, 588, 589.

325 *W*, 426, note 20. *"Da empfange ich einen Aufschwung,"* *Q*, 308.

326 *EFP*, 1: 74-75.

327 *EFP*, 1: 175.

328 *EFP*, 1: 180-181.

329 *CW* 6: ¶816, 817.

330 *Dream Seminars*, 180, 182.

331 Clark and Skinner, *Meister Eckhart*, 17.

332 *CW* 18: ¶1553.

333 *Dream Seminars*, 181.

334 *Dream Seminars*, 183.

335 *ES*, 112.

336 *Breakthrough*, 442.

337 Jung, *Mysterium Coniunctionis*, *CW* 14: ¶760.

338 Ibid., ¶768.

339 *CW* 6: ¶427.

340 *CW* 6: ¶422.

341 *CW* 6: ¶412.

342 *CW* 6: ¶418, Note 157.

343 *CW* 6: ¶422.

344 *CW* 6: ¶417.

345 *CW* 6: ¶422.

346 *W*, 318.

347 *W*, 486.

348 *W*, 140.

349 *ES*, 158.

350 *W*, 510.

351 *DM*, 71, 72.

352 Clark and Skinner, 200.

353 *W*, 517, 518.

354 *ES*, 192.

355 *W*, 500.

356 *W*, 501.

357 *DM*, 74.

358 *W*, 493.

359 *W*, 492.

360 *W*, 487.

361 *W*, 574.

362 *W*, 472.

363 Ibid.

364 *W*, 64.

365 *ES*, 188.

366 *ES*, 168.

367 *W*, 108.

368 *ES*, 139.

369 *ES*, 187.

370 *TP*, 227.

371 *TP*, 232.

372 *TP*, 227, 228.

373 *ES*, 99.

374 "To arms!" did not mean to Eckhart putting on the armor of a Crusader in quest of revenge and destruction and killing in the Holy Land since the Last Crusade had fortunately by this time ended in defeat for Christendom. This gave Christianity a chance to forge a new theology based, not on Augustinian and Thomistic "just war" theory, but on peace. Eckhart

knew well enough that to John Damascene and Ambrose, "the cross is the weapon of Christians" (*TP*, 230). But by *arms!* and *weapon,* he meant spiritual armory and weaponry. He meant the Cross as a symbol, not as a sign of war, like Constantine's vision, which the Crusades had all been based upon as an implement of external incipient violence, rather than violence turned within toward one's own pride and ego inflation. *Four things were needed Eckhart postulated* "for someone who is attacked: fortitude, circumspection, armor, and good trust ... Avicenna claims and proves by cases that trust is more important for a cure than the doctor and his instruments" (*TP*, 232). He quoted Avicenna here on trust as needed in cases for a cure, for he knew with Christ that the only *cure* for war is *trust* in peace and being a peacemaker. Ibn Sina, commonly known in the West as Avicenna, was the preeminent philosopher and physician of the Muslim world, flourishing during the Islamic Golden Age. Trust in Eckhart by the Catholic Church and the Holy See could have led to a much better theology and greater faith in the *healing power of the cross* as a symbol for Ultimate Peace and Absolute Goodness, not War, bloodshed, and evil. Instead, the Catholic Church sent Conquistadores to conquer indigenous tribes in the Americas, Africa, and the Pacific Islands, with such ferocity, violence, and evil that still today historians cannot tell us exactly how many indigenous peoples have been killed since the time of Columbus, and how many slave ships were sent to US ports. We in the United States live with the blood *guilt* that was shed on our soil by our European ancestors.

375 I learned this the hard way when I was a cook at the Refectory restaurant in Walnut Creek during high school. It was challenging work, but I loved it. I learned the true meaning of labor in a democracy. Moreover, the fact that it was called the "Refectory" seems almost implausible when I think about it today.

376 *TP*, 228.

377 *TP*, 229.

378 *TP*, 231–233.

379 *TP*, 233.

380 *ES*, 29.

381 *ES*, 87.

382 *ES*, 93.

383 *ES*, 94.

384 *ES*, 94.

385 *ES*, 95.

386 *ES*, 110.

387 *TP*, 329.

388 *TP*, 329.

389 *W*, 280.

390 *TP*, 330.

391 *TP*, 330.

392 *TP*, 330.

393 *ES*, 122.

394 *ES*, 124.

395 *ES*, 124.

396 *ES*, 127.

397 *ES*, 222.

398 *ES*, 230.

399 Jung, *Visions Seminars, Book One*: 136.

400 *ES*, 263.

401 *ES*, 77.

402 *ES*, 166.

403 *ES*, 71, 72.

404 *ES*, 72.

405 *ES*, 71, 72.

406 *ES*, 72.

407 *ES*, 75.

408 *ES*, 72.

409 *ES*, 75, 76.

410 *ES*, 44.

411 *ES*, 44.

412 *ES*, 72.

413 *ES*, 77.

414 *ES*, 77.

415 *ES*, 80, 81.

416 *ES*, 78.

417 *ES*, 203.

418 *ES*, 146, 147.

419 *ES*, 264.

420 *ES*, 147, 148.

421 *ES*, 152.

422 *ES*, 149.

423 *ES*, 18.

424 By nuclear symbol, I mean the most central image of the personality as a whole. It is the primary blueprint out of which the Self emerges into time, as a destiny-imprint on the soul.

425 *PYM*, 245.

426 In Latin sermon XLIX, Eckhart wrote: "the Son, as the perfect likeness, breathes forth love, the Holy Spirit" (*TP*, 237).

427 The first Parliament was held in Chicago on September 11, 1893, where the most illustrious and charismatic speaker was the Hindu monk Swami Vivekananda, who I wrote about previously in 2022. Eckhart, as I see it, was the link between East and West, Hindu and Buddhist, Christian and Islamic and Jewish spiritualities.

428 *CW* 16: ¶420.

429 *PYM*, 243.

430 Jung wrote in a letter in 1953: "It was Einstein who first started me off thinking about a possible relativity of time as well as space, and their psychic conditionality." See *Letters 2*: 109.

431 Dourley, *A Strategy for a Loss of Faith*, 115.

432 Wisdom and Sophia are two names for the Sky Goddess, as Eve was the Earth Mother who gave birth to the human race. Wisdom or Sophia was the Divine Mother of Eve and Mary, one might say, since she was in the beginning with God, in his eternal Godhead, or the Maternal Ground of the Goddess.

433 Jung, *Zarathustra Seminars*, 2: 1486.

434 *Letters 2*: 453–454.

435 A correction: Eckhart was not on his way to Rome when he died; he died in Avignon, where the Roman papacy was at the time of his condemnation.

436 *Zarathustra Seminars*, 2: 1487–1488.

437 *Zarathustra Seminars*, 2: 1533.

438 Jung, "A Psychological Approach to the Dogma of the Trinity," *CW* 11: ¶205.

439 *CW* 11: ¶235.

440 *CW* 11: ¶236.

441 I was an archer in my youth.

442 *CW* 11: ¶267.

443 Jung, "Letter to Pére Lachat," *CW* 18: ¶1553.

444 *CW* 11: ¶276.

445 Jung, "Answer to Job," *CW* 11: ¶¶693–696.

446 *CW* 11: ¶741.

447 *CW* 11: ¶742.

448 Herrmann, *William James and C.G. Jung*, see Chapter 6, "A Violent God," 41–68.

449 Jung, *Analytical Psychology*, 39.

450 *DM*, 35.

451 *DM*, 25, 32.

452 *W*, 553

453 Jung, *The Red Book*, 284. Hereafter references to *The Red Book* will be given as *RB* and page number.

454 *RB*, 286.

455 *RB*, 284.

456 *RB*, 287.

457 *RB*, 287.

458 *RB* 289.

459 Jung, "The Relativity of the God-Concept in Meister Eckhart," *CW* 6: ¶427, footnote 166; *EFP*, 1: 389.

460 *RB*, 289.

461 The idea of a new Christian dispensation within the Holy Roman religious orders was something Eckhart was well familiar with. The Holy Orders of the Church were led by the pontiff in Avignon, Pope John XXII, who had sanctified the seven sacraments in Catholic theology in the Second Council of Lyon in 1274, a year before Eckhart joined the Dominicans in Erfurt. The seven Catholic sacraments are 1) Baptism, 2) Confirmation, 3) Eucharist (Communion), 4) Penance (Confession), 5) Matrimony (Marriage), 6) Holy Orders (priesthood), and 7) Anointing the Sick.

462 *W*, 429.

463 Eckhart's wording was precise, and we must be careful not to change the meanings of his metaphors to fit in with contemporary movements in psychology and theology toward a return to the theologies of the Great Mother. To call it a *maternity bed* or a *paternity bed* would not be true to Eckhart's parabolical understandings, which were always ahead of his times and are still in advance of where we are today. A *childbed* is neutral because it is the soul that gives birth, with God *and* the Virgin Mother in a union of wifely fruitfulness and activity that can happen at any of the four levels of the soul, in a man or woman, since the fourth level, Sophia, can drop, and the first level, Eve, can rise. I will expand on this paradox in Chapter 25 on Eckhart's four soul types. It is also significant that he says a *childbed* because the divine birth is of a *child* in early latency, not an infant.

464 *RB*, 284, 287.

465 *RB*, 346, 347.

466 *RB*, 347, footnote 82.

467 *RB*, 350.

468 Jung, *Visions Seminars, Book Two*: 301, 302.

469 *RB* 289.

470 At the end of his treatise on *The Divine Names* Eckhart wrote out his main thesis in his fourth argument: "That which is above every name excludes no name, but universally includes all names in an equally indistinct way. None of these names will consequently be proper to it save that which is above every name and is common to all names. But existence is common to all beings and names, and hence existence is the proper name of God alone" (*TP*, 96). This is the ultimate meaning of Spiritual Democracy across the globe: that all names are *equal* in God and His Godhead in all human beings across the planet as Absolute Existence.

471 Jung, *Zarathustra Seminars*, 1: 183–184.

472 *Zarathustra*, 1: 175.

473 *Q*, 167.

474 *CW* 16: ¶367.

475 *CW* 16: ¶442.

476 *TP*, 404.

477 *CW* 16: ¶378.

478 *TP*, 300.

479 *TP*, 245.

480 *TP*, 330.

481 *TP*, 321.

482 *CW* 16: ¶448.

483 *CW* 16: ¶462.

484 *CW* 16: ¶463.

485 *TP*, 301, 302.

486 *CW* 16: ¶469.

487 *CW* 16: ¶533.

488 *MDR*, 68, 69.

489 *MDR*, 69.

490 *CW* 18: ¶371.

491 *CW* 6: ¶417.

492 Scholem, *The Messianic Idea in Judaism*, 1.

493 Scholem, 3.

494 Scholem, 6.

495 Scholem, 7.

496 Scholem, 8.

497 Scholem. 9.

498 Scholem, 25.

499 Scholem, 31.

500 Scholem, 342–343, Endnote, 25.

501 *Letters*, 2: 359.

502 *CW* 14: ¶¶443–444.

503 *W*, 293.

504 *CW* 9ii: ¶303.

505 *CW* 9ii: ¶304.

506 *TP*, 223–224.

507 *TP*, 224–225.

508 *W*, 74.

509 *L* 2: 134.

510 *L* 2: 135.

511 *PYM*, 237, 239.

512 Jung, *Dream Seminars*, 329.

513 Jung, *Visions Seminars, Book One*: 136.

514 *Zarathustra*, 1: 567

515 *Zarathustra*, 1: 723.

516 *Zarathustra*, 2: 842

517 *Zarathustra*, 2: 1487, 1488

518 Jung, *Children's Dreams*, 2008, 355.

519 Jung, "The Development of Personality," *CW* 17: ¶320.

520 Jung, "After the Catastrophe," *CW* 10: ¶441.

521 Jung, *CW* 11: ¶742.

522 Jung, *CW* 12: ¶10.

523 Rudin, "A Catholic View of Conscience," 137.

524 *CW* 10: ¶¶825-857.

525 Jung, "Good and Evil in Analytical Psychology," *CW* 10: ¶839.

526 *CW* 10: ¶853.

527 *CW* 10: ¶869.

528 *CW* 10: ¶866.

529 Jung, "Foreword to Neumann: *Depth Psychology and a New Ethic*," *CW* 18: ¶1408.

530 *CW* 6: ¶77.

531 *CW* 6: ¶457.

532 *W*, 463.

533 *CW* 6: ¶417.

534 *W*, 140.

535 Jung, "Jung and Religious Belief," *CW* 18: ¶1657.

536 Quint, *Deutsche Predigten und Traktate,* 355.

537 *Q*, 342.

538 *ES*, 47.

539 *W*, 49.

540 *PYM*, 239.

541 *W*, 267.

542 *ES*, 188.

543 *ES*, 203.

544 Jung, "Introduction to the Religious and Psychological Problems of Alchemy," *CW* 12: ¶15.

545 *CW* 12: ¶20.

546 "The philosophy of the Upanishads corresponds to a psychology that long ago recognized the relativity of the gods." Jung, "Psychology and Religion (The Terry Lectures)," *CW* 11: ¶140.

547 *CW* 12: ¶21.

548 "Take for instance, the word 'God.' The theologian will naturally assume that the metaphysical *Ens Absolutum* is meant. The empiricist, on the contrary, does not dream of making such a far-reaching assumption ... For him 'God' can just as well mean Yahweh, Allah, Zeus, Shiva, or Huitzilopochtli... He grants the divine image numinosity—that is, a deeply stirring emotional effect ... As a psychiatrist he is sufficiently hardboiled to be profoundly convinced of the relativity of all such statements ... His *religio* consists in establishing facts which can be observed and proved" (Jung, "Foreword to White's "God and the Unconscious," *CW* 11: ¶454). Clearly, any New Dispensation in the Jungian tradition would be based not on three myths alone, but on a plurality of religious experiences, which are common to the whole of collective humanity. For such reasons, I've adopted the term Spiritual Democracy to give better definition to what the relativity of the world's God-images really connotes and why Eckhart is at the center of this transformation process in psychology and Christian theology.

549 Here again, I turn to the paradoxical co-existence of pantheism and panentheism expressed in equal measure in Eckhart's works: "The seed of a pear-tree grows into a pear tree, that of a nut tree into a nut tree, God's seed into God. But if the good seed has a foolish or bad gardener, then weeds will grow and cover up and drive out the good seed so that it cannot reach the light and grow" (*W*, 558). The paradox of the opposites between a good and bad gardener is resolved by the healing of the split between *God's nature* and *Nature's God*. The reason I have been so hard on Catholic theologians, on this issue, and I hope not excessively so, is that we are at a turning point in the world, where Nature has the upper hand over the traditional Christian God-images. As a young man at UCSC I took instruction from a poet who I still consider to be the greatest Dominican that has lived since Eckhart, and that was Brother Antoninus. For Bill, as I knew him for fifteen years, *pantheism* was the ultimate reality. He believed this fervently and devoutly, because he was a disciple of the Carmel poet, Robinson Jeffers, as well as a being a practicing Catholic. Being a good gardener requires a natural gift for *gardening*, regardless of one's creed, school of religion, or faith. Eckhart wrote: "Means are twofold. One, without

406

which I cannot get into God, is work, vocation or calling in time, which interferes not one whit with eternal salvation" (*EFP*, 2: 93). Thus, if one is a Dominican monk tending pear trees in the Green Heart of Germany, or John Muir working on his wife's pear orchard in Martinez, California, the gardening is productive of the same fruit, from the same seed of *Nature's God* or *God's nature*, however one is called by the Self to look at Creation. The seed, in other words, is the calling from the vocational archetype. God's seed is the good seed of our destiny regardless of where one follows Jesus, or Alexander von Humboldt in his five-volume set *Cosmos*. I was born in Jeffers country, Carmel-by-the-Sea. How could I not help but claim my identity as a pantheist upon reading Jeffers? On the other hand, across the Monterey Bay, at UCSC, I encountered Everson and became a panentheistic writer after I read his catholic poetry. I straddled the opposites and jumped above them into the higher principle of seeing psychological and theological phenomena from a more unitary point of view outside Church. Eckhart was the best gardener the Church has produced, in my view, because he freed us of the problem of literalism through his parabolical wisdom as a *preacher-shaman of the Word*.

550 Jung, "Commentary on 'The Secret of the Golden Flower," *CW* 13: ¶¶74, 75.

551 *CW* 9ii: ¶296; footnote 13; *EFP*, 1: 274.

552 *TP*, 153.

553 *TP*, 152-156.

554 *CW* 9ii: ¶301.

555 *CW* 9ii: ¶302.

556 *CW* 9ii: ¶304.

557 *CW* 11: ¶882.

558 *CW* 11: ¶893.

559 *CW* 11: ¶887.

560 *Letters* 2: 586, 587.

561 Keeping with the metaphor of the *good, skilled, and industrious gardener* in Eckhart's treatise *The Nobleman* here, it is important to add that he had been meditating on the words: "'A nobleman went away to a distant country to gain a kingdom for himself.' That is the good tree of which our Lord says that it always brings forth good fruits and never

evil (Matt. 7:18)" (*W*, 558). This was in fact the section of the New Testament from which the prideful and evilly infected pope in Avignon charged Eckhart with having sown "thorns" and "thistles" from a "corrupt tree" (Matt. 7:16-18). God knows we need good gardeners today, to plant more trees to save the human race from self-extinction, during a time of rapid climate change. The pope's attempt to hew down and throw Eckhart's masterpieces into the "fire" (Matt. 7:19) reveals the problem we face today, from a vocational standpoint: we need good scientists, arborists, and planters and better theologians too to restore the integrity of our global environment and our atmosphere. A *good gardener* knows how to select the right seeds of redwood trees, for instance, whether she has faith in Jesus Christ, or Gaia. That is why I think the pantheist/panentheistic debate is nonsense, not only psychologically, but from a theological point of view. A person of faith and an atheist can work side by side, to save Mother Nature. And our time running out as many Bibles have been burning up in California's wild fires! I bow to my master, Antoninus/Everson for having given me a precious key to open up a wider doorway to the Self than the key of the Roman Catholic Church, before Eckhart.

562 *ES*, 128.
563 *W*, 292.
564 Jaffé, *Reflections on the Life and Dreams of C. G. Jung,* 190–191.
565 Jung, "The Transcendent Function," *CW* 8: ¶131.
566 *CW* 6: ¶413.
567 *TP*, 213.
568 *CW* 16: ¶353.
569 "Ye shall know them by their fruits. Do men gather grapes of thorns, or figs of thistles?" (Matt. 7: 16).
570 *CW* 6: ¶411.
571 *CW* 6: ¶426.
572 It can also happen in consultation, something I learned from my close two-decade relationship with my mentor, John Beebe. The problem of types that I discussed at length in previous chapters using the metaphor of the good gardener is psychologically relative. For not infrequently a person who is called to gardening listens not only to her inner woman but her *outer woman* too, an extroverted sensation function that is

central to her spiritual makeup. The spine of her personality exits on a vertical axis between extroverted sensation and introverted intuition as her inferior function. They are joined together in the middle, by her rational functions of feeling and thinking while she is tending her garden. I have had such types of patients in my practice who have taught me much about the vocation of the Self. But mostly, I learned how to be a good gardener myself from my reading of Emily Dickinson, whose garden in Amherst is now being restored to its original beauty.

573   *TP*, 336, 337.

574   *TP*, 335.

575   *W*, 493.

576   Eckhart called rest the highest stage of being "de-formed and transformed" (*überbildet*) "into a divine image, having become the child of God. Beyond this there is no higher stage, and *there* there is eternal rest and bliss" (*W*, 559). I like the word *überbildet* because it connotes over, or above. *There* in the superconscious we attain eternal life.

577   *W*, 406, footnote 19.

578   James, *Writings 1878–1899*, 191.

579   Ibid., 208.

580   James, *Writings 1902–1910*, 1281, 1283, 1289.

581   The postmodern reader may hear an echo of process theology in some of these lines and that is because of the fact that Charles Asher was influenced by this tradition as a theologian and Jungian analyst who I was in conversation with when I wrote these principles out. However, what is novel in process theology owes an unacknowledged debt of thanks to Eckhart's thinking that had been at the forefront of the best theological minds of Jung's age and ours.

582   *TP*, 287.

583   *CW* 18: ¶630.

584   *The Future of Man*, 157, 160.

585   Bartlett, *William Everson: The Life of Brother Antoninus*, 153.

586   Everson not incidentally was an Eckhartian long before we met. In a late poem called CANTO VI of *Dust Shall be the Serpent's Food*, Everson wrote in 1990: "The year [1958]. On a cot in my cell. / Absorbed in the writings / Of the medieval sage, Meister Eckhart, / Searching for mystical clues. I hear a knocking at my door. / It proves a student priest,

one of the newly ordained friars, / Completing their studies here at the House of Studies. / Before assignment to the apostolate. / Father Martin Gianini, dressed in clerical garb, / Black suit and clerical collar. "Brother Antoninus," / He began before I could greet him, / I have something to show you!" / He held out a sheaf of paper, / "Amazing stuff!" / "What is it?" I ask (*The Integral Years*, 315).

587 *W*, 293.

588 *W*, 292.

589 *W*, 152.

590 *W*, 152–153.

591 *W*, 589.

592 By this term I mean an archetype of transformation and transfiguration in the human soul or collective psyche of humanity that is still alive as a living symbol, a speaker of the Word that cuts through obstacles to Self-consciousness and can lead us to see what it means to be a humble human being born from the *humas*, the soil of our Mother Earth and what it means to be a teacher of truth.

593 *W*, 493.

594 *W*, 512.

595 *W*, 518.

596 *W*, 521.

597 *W*, 146–147.

598 *W*, 567.

599 *W*, 572.

600 *W*, 574.

601 *W*, 142.

602 *W*, 538.

603 *W*, 547.

604 *W*, 547.

605 *W*, 547.

606 *W*, 547.

607 *W*, 549.

608 *W*, 549.

609 *W*, 574.

610 *CW* 6: ¶416; *EFP*, 2: 8.

611 *CW* 6: ¶417.

612 *CW* 6 ¶417, footnote 155.

613 *W*, 491.

614 *W*, 518

615 *W*, 574.

616 *W*, 566.

617 *W*, 142.

618 *W*, 487.

619 *W*, 424.

620 *W*, 213.

621 *CW* 6 ¶417.

622 Jung, "The Psychology of the Child Archetype," *CW* 9i: ¶291.

623 *W*, 201, 202.

624 *W*, 255, see footnote 3.

625 *W*, 117.

626 *W*, 204, 205.

627 *W*, 200.

628 Fox, *Meister Eckhart: A Mystic-Warrior for our Times*, 201–220.

629 *DM*, 92.

630 *DM*, 94.

631 *Q*, 72.

632 *ES*, 92.

633 *DM*, 138.

634 *W*, 159.

635 *ES*, 230.

636 *DM*, 142.

637 *TP*, 90.

638 *TP*, 64.

639 *DM*, 152.

640 *DM*, 195.

641 *DM*, 209.

642 *DM*, 214, 215.

643 *DM*, 217, 218.

644 *DM*, 224.

645 *DM*, 231.

646 *DM*, 232.

647 *ES*, 321, footnote 80.

648 *W*, 58.

649 *W*, 553.

650 Jung, *Nietzsche Seminars*, 2: 941.

651 *EFP*, 2: 93.

652 *W*, 110.

653 *EFP*, 1: 399.

654 *CW* 12: ¶15.

655 *W*, 424, 425.

656 *TP*, 153.

657 *W*, 306, 307.

658 *TP*, 155.

659 *W*, 347.

660 *CW* 18: ¶1553.

661 *W*, 367.

662 *W*, 420.

663 *CW* 14: ¶781.

664 *CW* 14: ¶760.

665 *CW* 14: ¶768.

666 *Q*, 308.

667 *EFP*, 2: 34

668 *W*, 429.

669 *ES*, 25.

670 *ES*, 42.

671 *W*, 49.

672 *W*, 108.

673 *W*, 463.

674 *PYM*, 243, 244.

675 *ES*, 71.

676 Jung, "Foreword to a Catalogue on Alchemy," *CW* 18: ¶1661.

677 *DM*, 27.

678 *TP*, 321.

679 *Mercy:* An endnote on my use of the word *mercy* is called for here. Eckhart's belief was that the *highest work of God is mercy* (*TP*, 252). Eckhart scholars and postmodern translators, such as my colleague Matthew Fox, whose book *Breakthrough* I relied upon heavily to finish my thesis at UCSC, have translated the German word *Barmhertizkeit*

as *compassion* in the place of mercy, since it is more in line with his contemporary theology of "creation spirituality." As a native German speaker, I've used the old Middle High German usage of the word, translating it as mercy over compassion, along with more traditional translators in modernity. Yet compassion may be the better word choice in postmodernity and Matt may be right about this. Nevertheless, if this had been the end of Eckhart's thinking about mercy or compassion as the highest of God's works, his statement above would've been sufficient to satisfy our questioning concerning the highest works of humankind. As a teacher and preacher of parables, about what can be known and what can't be known about the Divine, Eckhart the *shaman-preacher of God's Word* went a step further, while speaking to a crowd of followers in the Cologne Cathedral: "you should not chatter about God. And do not try and understand God, for God is beyond all understanding" (*EE*, 207). There is deep wisdom in this, because it is only when we shut off the mind, when the mind-chatter ceases, that something new can be born in the soul, and a better understanding can emerge that presses us onwards to inquire further into the *trans-dual mystery of God's being* and non-being. Eckhart did not chatter about God's works; he did not chatter about the calling from the Word, nor should we chatter about the birth of the Self in us, but rather, be silent. Since it is only in complete quiet and detachment that we can enter the Ground of hearing, where the Word issues forth and from which we can say what is truly our own calling. Mercy or compassion form a complementarity of two distinct and interconnected linguistic metaphors that are both valid, psychologically and theologically. We must learn to see God irrationally, as Sophia sees God, naked in his or her Godhead. We have to have a beginner's mind and take God at her/his Word. Eckhart was a *Word-shaman*, a dispenser of sacred medicine for whomsoever is called to imbibe the truth of his wisdom from the wellsprings of his teachings. He was called by the Holy Spirit to comfort us and his aim was always directed to healing. His vocation as a *preacher-shaman* was to relieve us from our suffering by freeing us of pain, anguish, and woe through the prayer of quiet. He wrote: "That is what the physician is there for, to make the sick healthy" (*EE*, 239). Eckhart the physician, the medicine-person, the *shaman-teacher*,

413

even prayed to "our loving and merciful God, who is Truth" to grant him and all of us who read his blessed *Book of Divine Consolation* that "we may find the truth within ourselves and come to know it" (EE, 239). Finding truth and knowing it requires letting go of whatever it is that ails us and keeps us from speaking God's Word from our own subjective and transsubjective Ground. What, then, can be higher than God's mercy, or her merciful works? As I've been saying at length in this book about the vocation of the Self, the calling, if our entire life were devoted to being merciful (*hesed* in Hebrew), or compassionate (*rachem* in Hebrew), and engaged continuously in vocational activities that are sacred, we would eventually wind up with *compassion fatigue*. Above God's works, therefore, is complete detachment: "I also praise detachment above all mercifulness, because mercifulness is nothing else than man's going out of himself to the shortcomings of his fellow men, and through this his heart becomes troubled. But detachment remains free of this, for nothing can ever trouble a man unless things are not well with him" (*EE*, 287, 288). When our patients are not well, we are not well; we suffer with them, as God suffers with us. It is for this reason that Eckhart liked to quote Luke 5: 31: "They that are whole need not a physician; but they that are sick." Here is the beauty about the paradox of mercy and detachment, sickness and health, compassion and disinterest; for in the highest state of the soul, as Wisdom (*Chokhmah* in Hebrew), Sophia needs no medicine, because she is the remedy for our suffering and for God's suffering. She infuses us with immunity from evil and this leads us to run into final peace. That is why we would all be wise to rise up, into the fourth level of the soul, anima or animus, to embrace wisdom as our *mothering and birth function* and soul-wife. When we are in our right professions as God's physicians, practicing our true vocations, in whatever career our visions have led us to vocalize, it is always good to take time to allow our souls rise higher up to the tree-top where Wisdom dwells. Impartiality and rest can help us become rejuvenated from overwork, and detoxify the infections that contaminate us with their poisons, so that in our attempts to be of service to God and humanity our works will be *compassionate and just*.

680 Matthew Fox and I have been meeting for lunch regularly at Sailor Jacks. We also visited Bill Everson's grave together twice at St. Dominic's Dominican cemetery.

681 *TP*, 230–233.

682 *CW* 8: ¶948.

683 *ES*, 122.

684 *Q*, 437.

685 Jung, "The Undiscovered Self," *CW* 9i: ¶534.

686 *Letters* 2: 57.

687 *CW* 11: ¶233.

688 *CW* 18: ¶1552.

689 *CW* 11: ¶236.

690 *CW* 11: ¶235.

691 *CW* 11: ¶240.

692 *Q*, 186.

693 It is also important to acknowledge here that I had read Matthew Fox's excellent Introduction to his book *Breakthrough*, yet we have our own understandings of Meister Eckhart, who I believed to be a shaman in my thesis.

694 *W*, 79, 202.

695 *W*, 367.

696 *W*, 44.

697 *CW* 8: ¶870.

698 *ES*, 109.

699 I learned through some research recently (although I did not know this at the time of my dream) that some old German theological books were, in fact, bound in pigskin, which suggests symbolically the archaic nature of the book containing old (Dominican) and new (Jungian) wisdom combined in this seventh volume.

700 *W*, 553.

701 *Letters*, 1: 377.

702 *W*, 541, 542.

703 *CW* 14: ¶780.

704 *CW* 14: ¶391.

705 *W*, 400.

MEISTER ECKHART AND CG JUNG INDEX

A

Abyss 21, 22, 45, 56, 93, 108, 119,
  140, 141, 182, 202, 258, 283,
  313, 326, 351, 352, 353, 354,
  355, 377, 381
after Christ xiii, xiv, 79, 193, 206,
  330, 331, 334, 381
Age of Aquarius 240, 241, 248,
  257, 303
agnostic 21, 40, 41, 139, 280
antidote 88, 96, 128, 131, 186,
  287, 295, 303

B

bare mind 166, 171, 290, 313
Beguine 9, 88, 112, 123, 191, 300,
  373, 386, 393
belief 21, 31, 34, 36, 37, 41, 72, 98,
  126, 140, 142, 149, 174, 188,
  228, 229, 238, 276, 289, 315,
  325, 378, 390, 405, 412
blissful 164, 165, 171, 181,
  236, 376

bottomless 21, 48, 127, 254, 283,
  353, 377
breakthrough 38, 39, 114, 254,
  308, 309, 363, 367, 373, 397,
  412, 415
breath 15, 19, 38, 49, 56, 79, 147,
  201, 208, 210, 221, 229, 230,
  246, 258, 294, 335, 401

C

calling archetype 114, 335,
  395, 396
climate change 18, 51, 54, 258,
  288, 324, 408
colloquy 69, 74, 117, 158, 159,
  204, 217, 218, 226, 367, 392
Comforter 57, 131, 189, 206,
  208, 301
compassion 10, 19, 23, 29, 139,
  213, 311, 413, 414
Cosmos xiii, 15, 28, 29, 36, 41, 48,
  93, 115, 116, 120, 129, 132,
  146, 147, 154, 221, 240, 252,
  265, 280, 354, 407

crucifixion 93, 109, 178, 195, 255, 299, 324, 325

D

defense 4, 9, 21, 53, 87, 103, 119, 140, 150, 184, 186, 187, 189, 190, 251, 260, 315, 363, 366, 381
democratic xiv, 19, 36, 45, 50, 51, 106, 107, 136, 171, 176, 195, 228, 276, 277, 284, 298, 300, 303, 309, 328, 361, 386
destiny archetype 395
destiny dream 147
duality xiv, 248, 314

E

empirical psychology ix, x, 32, 90, 134, 320
emptiness 15, 39, 133, 181, 240, 298, 313, 360
empty 35, 46, 51, 57, 65, 84, 93, 133, 178, 202, 220, 259, 263, 362
equality 10, 13, 14, 15, 17, 18, 20, 27, 31, 39, 50, 53, 71, 85, 108, 116, 129, 131, 147, 150, 151, 152, 154, 155, 171, 172, 176, 181, 195, 201, 221, 240, 252, 283, 284, 285, 286, 288, 294, 298, 299, 300, 313, 375, 379, 381, 383, 386
eruption 113, 120, 124, 127, 158, 181, 265, 293, 295, 358, 386
eternal now 15, 78, 133, 295, 306, 313, 343, 358, 359

ethical 54, 152, 178, 187, 227, 244, 302, 318

F

feminine xiv, xv, 65, 66, 67, 73, 74, 75, 88, 91, 121, 124, 149, 153, 159, 217, 218, 219, 230, 275, 297, 300, 313, 334, 346, 347
freedom xiv, 2, 3, 22, 25, 42, 56, 140, 149, 175, 208, 225, 237, 241, 277, 280, 294, 378

G

gateway 113, 146, 294, 345, 361
gender xiv, xv, 193, 259, 357
gifts 6, 17, 18, 84, 109, 114, 125, 130, 208, 234, 311, 338, 406
giving birth 62, 87, 180, 218, 219, 226, 240, 264, 271, 290, 306, 313
grace of God 185
Grail 51, 55, 56, 58, 112, 201, 217, 372, 389
groundless 21, 35, 263, 283, 353, 376, 377, 381, 383
Grund 14, 15, 17, 22, 124, 130, 247, 248, 294, 296, 302, 314, 353

H

healer 28, 97, 99, 102, 108, 112, 138, 167, 201, 282, 288, 295, 301, 302
healing x, 2, 4, 28, 43, 51, 52, 54, 58, 59, 96, 99, 101, 103, 109,

111, 112, 123, 137, 150, 163,
169, 196, 229, 232, 243, 258,
271, 277, 278, 289, 292, 295,
297, 302, 305, 310, 344, 349,
350, 357, 371, 391, 396, 399,
406, 413
heresy xiv, 1, 7, 9, 12, 42, 51, 78,
87, 102, 103, 115, 125, 188,
189, 190, 191, 192, 283, 315,
378, 381
heretic 8, 187, 190, 211
highest power 77, 121, 137, 158,
165, 251, 252, 344
highest virtue 42, 108, 290, 302
Holy See xiv, 42, 94, 104, 105,
108, 116, 130, 186, 190, 191,
192, 193, 399

I

Immanuel 27, 106, 152, 158, 283,
349, 382
Imprinter xiii, xiv, 77, 158, 207,
250, 251, 252, 305
incarnation 5, 48, 50, 52, 92, 106,
109, 120, 130, 151, 154, 188,
193, 201, 211, 220, 221, 233,
236, 238, 251, 260, 262,
263, 306, 331, 334, 335, 346,
358, 359, 360, 361, 362, 376,
384, 386
inferior function 69, 117, 162,
223, 409
infinity 21, 220, 235, 252, 376
in peace 26, 27, 28, 177, 277, 278,
313, 399

Inquisition xiv, 34, 109, 111, 123,
307, 378
intuition 15, 35, 69, 70, 79, 90,
93, 94, 96, 97, 99, 109, 111,
117, 142, 158, 162, 163, 168,
178, 238, 252, 311, 334, 346,
385, 409
irrational 13, 15, 16, 73

J

Jerusalem 106, 121, 122, 152, 179,
187, 231, 263, 375, 389, 391,
392, 396
Journaling 6, 289, 309, 374
Justice 19, 107, 108, 136, 145, 152,
166, 178, 181, 186, 187, 189,
192, 195, 234, 252, 284,
299, 311, 314, 374, 377, 390,
391, 396

K

key 112, 115, 141, 146, 158, 160,
161, 187, 204, 225, 226, 237,
240, 248, 264, 270, 290,
386, 408
King of the Jews 50, 105, 106, 153,
158, 231, 233, 239

M

mercy 27, 29, 151, 177, 187, 235,
252, 265, 277, 284, 287, 310,
311, 328, 412, 413, 414
Messiah 3, 50, 53, 54, 55, 106,
121, 122, 153, 231, 232, 233,
234, 236, 239, 265, 375,
382, 383

Metaphysical ix, xiii, xiv, 31, 47, 48, 53, 93, 94, 96, 134, 137, 141, 143, 146, 147, 235, 246, 259, 262, 274, 282, 334, 395

Methods 50, 73, 91, 134, 157, 160, 163, 164, 166, 169, 177, 229, 248, 250, 264, 299, 312, 344, 361, 362, 384, 392

mother of God 74, 88, 91, 120, 219, 222, 230, 248, 251, 264, 335

N

nakedness 124, 165, 167, 377

natural science 104, 116, 254, 265, 274, 293, 296

Nature's God 17, 18, 35, 295, 343, 345, 346, 378, 380, 406, 407

New Dispensation 126, 151, 179, 388, 393, 406

new religion 125, 220, 221, 359, 361

non-dual 381

nothingness 15, 39, 91, 108, 115, 127, 143, 149, 150, 166, 172, 177, 181, 205, 220, 233, 237, 246, 248, 249, 252, 254, 255, 258, 263, 265, 280, 285, 290, 298, 313, 314, 353, 359, 375, 376, 384, 385

nuclear symbol 52, 53, 54, 202, 203, 328, 352, 354, 395, 401

numinous 3, 6, 22, 24, 43, 51, 52, 99, 114, 126, 225, 247, 316, 329, 331, 332, 334, 343, 348, 349, 351, 352, 354

O

Oneness 17, 19, 30, 31, 32, 39, 40, 48, 66, 67, 72, 93, 98, 99, 103, 104, 105, 115, 117, 131, 132, 133, 142, 149, 153, 163, 169, 184, 185, 224, 261, 263, 300, 306, 374, 377, 379

P

Panentheism 14, 34, 35, 36, 37, 38, 41, 77, 129, 149, 342, 378, 379, 380, 406

Pantheism 34, 35, 36, 37, 38, 41, 77, 129, 149, 342, 379, 380, 406

peacemaker 27, 59, 106, 260, 265, 272, 273, 276, 278, 367, 399

prayer of quiet 74, 298, 302, 332, 413

Preacher's Church 5, 12, 108, 164, 166, 168, 197, 343

Preaching 9, 11, 12, 15, 52, 71, 79, 110, 112, 122, 123, 126, 140, 161, 165, 175, 185, 191, 249, 265, 284, 295, 300, 302, 314, 373, 386, 396

primal eruption 113, 120, 124, 127, 158, 181, 293, 295, 358, 386

Prince of Peace 107, 179, 232, 260, 276, 375

privatio boni 76, 110, 140, 141, 142, 146, 193, 278

privation 98, 99, 110, 140, 142, 143, 144, 152, 184, 196, 252, 381, 383, 389 projection xiv, 64, 70, 71, 72, 74, 75, 103, 104, 106, 116, 120, 154, 184, 185, 202, 205, 221, 225, 227, 228, 229, 269, 270, 282, 320, 372

psychic antibodies 144, 368

psychic infection 44, 102, 104, 108, 109, 144, 185, 192, 289

psychoid ix, 163, 354

psychological theology 48, 116, 135

Q

quiet 21, 30, 39, 46, 74, 133, 240, 294, 298, 299, 301, 302, 323, 330, 332, 344, 413

R

Red Book 5, 134, 204, 215, 217, 219, 220, 271, 364, 370, 402

redwoods 5, 18, 56, 195, 280, 288, 308, 309, 310, 311, 319, 408

relativity 32, 68, 75, 110, 114, 116, 121, 122, 134, 135, 192, 204, 209, 218, 229, 237, 238, 244, 245, 250, 264, 289, 305, 331, 376, 381, 401, 402, 405, 406

repentance 140, 141, 168, 169, 182, 270

resurrection 175, 284, 325, 359, 367, 391

right state 171, 248, 285, 287, 296, 375

running xvii, 4, 11, 26, 27, 28, 29, 30, 41, 60, 93, 146, 177, 233, 243, 263, 276, 347, 408

S

Satan 69, 76, 102, 154, 185, 236

seeing 16, 30, 39, 45, 71, 86, 95, 97, 104, 129, 134, 150, 155, 179, 236, 251, 263, 298, 304, 380, 391, 407

Self-figure 67, 119, 202, 204, 212, 217, 256, 257, 258, 269, 270, 332, 338

seven virtues 108, 294, 300, 302

shamanic archetype 28, 105, 293, 302, 368, 375

shaman-preacher 113, 301, 303, 339, 413

silence 18, 20, 25, 78, 114, 172, 233, 243, 248, 277, 280, 310, 313, 332, 337

sky 10, 19, 29, 152, 167, 280, 295, 341, 382, 391, 401

snake 67, 79, 96, 101, 102, 103, 104, 105, 292, 293, 294, 378

space 12, 18, 22, 37, 92, 154, 284, 306, 332, 344, 401

spaciousness 16, 151, 152, 155, 163, 171, 208

spiritual democracy 4, 19, 39, 42, 43, 95, 116, 150, 173, 208, 309, 343, 367, 368, 369, 377, 381, 383, 386, 403, 406

spiritual motherhood 4, 62, 75, 87, 90, 102, 103, 219, 224, 225, 255, 386

stillness 29, 39, 277, 313, 381

striding 26, 272, 273, 276, 277

superconscious 16, 42, 51, 77, 92, 94, 113, 119, 120, 122, 150, 155, 274, 277, 342, 384, 409

superior function 117, 162

supernatural knowledge 42, 157, 163, 339

synchronicity 95, 111, 115, 116, 124, 159, 228, 284, 311, 318, 319, 330, 340, 342, 346, 371, 393, 394

T

techniques 124, 160, 163, 170, 171, 249, 261, 283, 291, 312, 313, 339, 361, 362, 384, 392

Third Person xiii, 39, 49, 230, 342

transcendence 30, 31, 34, 35, 42, 51, 55, 77, 93, 170, 171, 180, 249, 361, 372, 375, 378, 380

transcendental x, 38, 49, 70, 94, 143, 163, 228, 250, 260, 274, 276, 306, 312, 313, 332, 334

transcendent function 73, 93, 117, 158, 164, 262, 264, 374, 408

trans-dual xiv, 10, 15, 16, 31, 38, 45, 48, 105, 135, 138, 148, 187, 274, 276, 277, 295, 296, 314, 318, 334, 342, 354, 382, 413

translation 1, 91, 113, 242, 310, 311, 327, 342, 363, 365, 367, 373, 385, 387

transpersonal 46, 85, 121, 124, 126, 146, 151, 194, 202, 228, 234, 248, 316, 347, 368, 375

treetop 16, 64, 77, 122, 383, 384

Trinity ix, xiii, 19, 21, 22, 38, 39, 49, 65, 66, 67, 68, 70, 73, 91, 94, 115, 116, 125, 129, 130, 136, 149, 158, 204, 209, 221, 230, 275, 308, 313, 314, 334, 335, 342, 381, 384, 387, 401

trust xiv, 127, 128, 150, 351, 361, 399

two crosses 128, 175, 177, 180, 183, 195, 282, 325

typology 4, 62, 70, 85, 93, 94, 96, 154

U

unfathomable 21, 79, 119, 125, 313, 353, 381

V

Vedanta 108, 126, 290, 378, 381, 382

vision of peace 106, 152, 290, 375

vocational archetype 159, 225, 279, 280, 318, 335, 380, 407

vocational dream 2, 110, 113, 164, 280, 331, 332, 334, 338, 343, 344, 355, 368

Vocation of the Self iii, 84, 93, 106, 107, 112, 143, 150, 153, 209, 238, 251, 282, 284, 301, 339, 409, 414

void 45, 55, 84, 108, 119, 314, 352, 354, 359

W

Way to God 6, 28, 95, 283, 361, 362

Wisdom's mother 299, 374

witness 229, 329

World Soul 6, 153, 217, 250, 293,
339, 369

Z

Zen 14, 95, 162, 222, 254,
285, 308

Zero 54, 90, 133, 192, 235, 236,
240, 249, 263, 294, 375,
377, 383

Zion 122, 179, 232, 236

Printed in the United States
by Baker & Taylor Publisher Services